# LITERARY PRACTICE AND SOCIAL CHANGE IN BRITAIN, 1380–1530

The New Historicism: Studies in Cultural Poetics

STEPHEN GREENBLATT, GENERAL EDITOR

# LITERARY PRACTICE AND SOCIAL CHANGE IN BRITAIN, 1380–1530

EDITED BY LEE PATTERSON

University of California Press
*Berkeley · Los Angeles · Oxford*

University of California Press
Berkeley and Los Angeles, California

University of California Press, Ltd.
Oxford, England

© 1990 by
The Regents of the University of California

**Library of Congress Cataloging-in-Publication Data**

Literary practice and social change in Britain, 1380–1530 /
edited by Lee Patterson.
    p.   cm.—(The New historicism; 8)
    Bibliography: p.
    Includes index.
    ISBN 0-520-06486-0 (alk. paper)
    1. English literature—Middle English, 1100–1500—
History and criticism.    2. Social history in literature.
3. English literature—Early modern, 1500–1700—History
and criticism.    4. Scottish literature—To 1700—History
and criticism.    5. Literature and society—Great Britain—
History.    6. England—Social conditions—Medieval
period, 1066–1485.    7. England—Social conditions—16th
century.    8. Scotland—Social conditions.    I. Patterson,
Lee.    II. Series.
PR275.S63L5 1989
820.9′002—dc20                                        89–32023
                                                          CIP

Printed in the United States of America
1   2   3   4   5   6   7   8   9

# Contents

# Introduction

## Critical Historicism and Medieval Studies

### Lee Patterson

"Always historicize!" The motto that Fredric Jameson announced at the beginning of the decade as Marxism's only "transhistorical imperative" has now, at its end, been inscribed on the banner under which literary studies as a whole seems to be marching.[1] This is perhaps most visibly the case in Renaissance studies, where the so-called New Historicism has generated both innovative work and widespread discussions of historicist methodology. But analogous and heated debates are also taking place among Romanticists, Americanists, and intellectual historians; indeed, no area of literary study has been immune from the impulse to traverse the terrain between literary texts and a material world that constitutes the not-literature of history. These reflections have inevitably revealed different assumptions and interests, and clearly no single label can be usefully applied to the historicist enterprise as a whole, least of all the already assigned, hotly contested, and irredeemably vague "New Historicism."

To replace "New Historicism," a term with which even those who coined it are now evidently uncomfortable, Howard Horwitz has recently proposed the more broadly based term "critical historicism," on the model of Nietzsche's attack upon the uncritical objectivism of academic history.[2] The term also recalls Horkheimer's classic essay on "Traditional and Critical Theory," which contrasts the critical thinking that attempts to grasp the historical contingencies of its own activity to a technocratic practice that protects itself from self-reflection by appeals to scientific objectivity.[3] And since it is both capacious and as yet un-

---

1. *The Political Unconscious* (Ithaca: Cornell University Press, 1981), 9.

2. "'I Can't Remember': Skepticism, Sympathetic Histories, Critical Action," *South Atlantic Quarterly* 87 (1988): 790.

3. First published in 1937, the essay is included in Max Horkheimer, *Critical Theory: Selected Essays*, trans. Matthew J. O'Donnell and others (New York: Continuum, 1972), 188–243.

appropriated by any single group, "critical historicism" is able to refer to a wide range of historicist initiatives while still asserting the crucial fact of initiation itself, of work that conceives of itself as something other than business as usual.

This sense of innovation is, despite the risk of presumption, worth stressing. The reemergence of historicism in literary studies will be experienced by many medievalists as a vindication, the recovery of a practice that medieval studies was wise enough never to have left behind. But it is a return with a difference, a difference that the medieval studies of the future—and it is by no means inevitable that medieval studies will have a future—must inscribe within its practice if it is to recapture general scholarly attention. The marginalization of medieval studies within the academy is a phenomenon worthy of the reflection not only of beleaguered medievalists but of their often surprisingly ill-informed colleagues as well. The fact is that the Middle Ages has from the beginning served the postmedieval Western historical consciousness as one of the primary sites of otherness by which it has constituted itself. According to the universally accepted scheme, our world begins with what historians now call the early modern period, what cultural historians have always called the Renaissance. This is a modernity that is defined above all by its difference from the premodern Middle Ages: humanism, nationalism, the proliferation of competing value systems, the secure grasp of a historical consciousness, the idea of the individual, aesthetic production as an end in itself, the conception of the natural world as a site of colonial exploitation and scientific investigation, the secularization of politics and the idea of the state—all of these characteristics and many others are thought both to set the Renaissance apart from the Middle Ages and to align it definitively with the modern world. On the other hand, as the name given it by the Renaissance declares, the Middle Ages is a millennium of middleness, a space that serves to hold apart the first beginning of Antiquity and the Renaissance rebeginning. And ever since the Renaissance, medieval premodernity has with few exceptions been experienced by modernity as "Gothic"—exotic and romantic, to be sure, but also esoteric and obscure. In a word, as alien. Roget's *College Thesaurus* provides the following synonyms for the word *medieval:* feudal, knightly, courtly, antiquated, old-fashioned, outdated, quaint.

Despite the obviously prejudicial effect that follows from this definition, it has been not merely accepted but on the whole embraced by the institution of medieval studies. The reason is not far to seek. The sense of the Middle Ages as other confers upon the medievalist an unquestionably professional self-definition, no small endowment in a social world in which the utility of humanistic study is always in question. Since the object of study is so unfamiliar, so radically different, the medievalist must acquire appropriately difficult scholarly abilities: a knowledge of obscure languages, mastery of a wide range of historical techniques (paleography, philology, codicology, diplomatics), a capacity to sustain interest in texts most readers dismiss as obvious or tedious, and an ability to attend to large stretches of writing that are, by any standard, otiose (few medieval texts are too short). A tolerance for boredom and a capacity for *Sitzfleisch* are prime requisites for the aspiring medievalist. Not surprisingly, the medievalist is professionally prepared not by being educated but by being "trained," and the professional structure of medieval studies remains, as a consequence, remarkably hierarchical. Medieval studies is a clerisy, and the more difficult of access are its central mysteries the more authority is invested in the high priests.

What also follows from the designation of the Middle Ages as definitively other is the entrenchment of a positivist methodology. If the activity of understanding is defined as the observation of otherness, then the self that does the observing need hardly be taken into account; since the object of study is, by definition, an *object,* then the subjectivity of the observer is irrelevant. The relationship is entirely technical: medieval culture is an enigma to be solved rather than a living past with claims upon the present. Indeed, a lack of contemporary relevance stands as one of the prime indicators that an account of a medieval text is sufficiently historical—sufficiently objective—to be taken as reliable. To be sure, such a project is necessarily embarrassed both by the transhistoricity of literature—the *Canterbury Tales* is present to us in a way that the Rising of 1381 is not—and by the way in which textual interpretation confronts the critic with acts of judgment that require continual recourse to his or her own values. But the positivist response to this embarrassment is to reduce literature to an epiphenomenon: literary meaning is seen as the effect of a determinative historical context, a context that is itself reduced to homogeneity in order to provide a sufficiently straightforward interpretive grid. In medieval studies this homogenization has been particularly intense, as is evident in the concern—amounting at times to an obsession—with anachronism. For if texts can be shown to bear meanings that do not accord with what has always been taken to be authentically medieval, then the notion of a homogeneous, monolithic Middle Ages that has always provided interpretive stability to the entire project (and, not coincidentally, has answered to larger cultural and political needs) is called into question.

The otherness by which the Middle Ages was stigmatized by the Renaissance thus remains in force, supported on the one hand by a humanist master narrative that defines modernity as postmedieval and on the other by a professionalized medieval studies in quest, like all professions, of legitimacy and devoted to an objectivist methodology that privileges a knowledge of "historical facts" over the negotiations of interpretation. In a very powerful sense, the Middle Ages is and always has been taken to be the realm of the past, of the historical. One effect of this has been to force the medievalist opposition into ahistoricity: young scholars interested in renovating medieval studies by integrating it into literary studies as a whole have tended to insist on the modernity of the Middle Ages. Arguing that medieval interests prefigure modern preoccupations, this project typically takes the form of using one of the various recent forms of theory as the agency by which to relocate medieval texts in contemporary contexts. While the results are occasionally stunning (Howard Bloch's *Etymologies and Genealogies* is an exemplary instance), the essentialist and idealist character of much recent theorizing can render this work vulnerable to the charge that Caroline Bynum has called "presentism."[4] As the essays in this collection demonstrate, in different ways and to different degrees, there is no desire here to stigmatize any form of theoretical thinking as, by definition, historically irrelevant. But for those who believe in a social determination of cultural production, writing must be understood as above all a social practice and therefore in need of as detailed a historical contextualization as possible. What this means for critical practice is that the insights generated by theoretical formations such as psychoanalysis, structuralism, and deconstruction need to be located within and subordinated to a social analysis (Louise Fradenburg's essay here provides a particularly fine example of the incorporation of psychoanalysis within a historicist reading).

4. R. Howard Bloch, *Etymologies and Genealogies: A Literary Anthropology of the French Middle Ages* (Chicago: University of Chicago Press, 1983); Caroline Walker Bynum, *Holy Feast and Holy Fast: The Religious Significance of Food to Medieval Women* (Berkeley and Los Angeles: University of California Press, 1987).

In a larger sense, the renovation of medieval studies requires not simply the importation of theory but a sustained critique of the assumptions that underwrite the prior alienation of the Middle Ages as a whole. For these assumptions derive from the modernist effort to escape from history by absorbing it: Jürgen Habermas has explained how modernism "discloses a longing for an undefiled, immaculate, and stable present," and Paul de Man has shown that the other by which modernity defines itself is not a particular past but the very fact of historicity itself.[5] The goal of a self-assertive medievalism must be not the denial of the historicity of the past it seeks to recover but the affirmation of the historicity of the present in which it practices: the Middle Ages is indeed the realm of the historical, but so is every other period, including our own. And since what connects the medieval past and the modern present is their historicity, it is historically focused methods of analysis that are best able both to respect historical particularity and to reveal such socially determined continuities as class and gender.

The current return to history in literary studies is widely understood as a reaction against the privileging of the autonomous text that, first as New Criticism and then as deconstruction, has dominated literary studies in the postwar period. Yet to read this historicism as simply reactive—as the triumphant return of a maligned past—is to misread recent critical history in a way that fatally obscures its lessons. This is especially the case for medieval studies, which particularly needs a genuinely critical historicism, one familiar with its own past and alert to the meaning of its assumptions and procedures. The textuality that has been displaced should not be seen as simply a negative to be rejected, for it has itself generated both the need and the possibility of a newly defined historicism, and it has done so not through the excesses of which its opponents have accused it but by the internal dynamic of its own logic. The development of a critical historicism can be described in terms of two phases, albeit such a distinction is more analytical than chronolog-

5. Habermas, "Modernity—An Incomplete Project," *New German Critique* 22 (1981); reprinted in Paul Rabinow and William M. Sullivan, eds., *Interpretive Social Science: A Second Look* (Berkeley and Los Angeles: University of California Press, 1987), 142–44; de Man, "Literary History and Literary Modernity," in *Blindness and Insight: Essays in the Rhetoric of Contemporary Criticism* 2d ed. (Minneapolis: University of Minnesota Press, 1983), 142–65.

ical; and a narrative of the process can indicate the differences that the detour through textuality has made.

The first phase began in the 1960s and 1970s with the deconstructive revision of the New Criticism of the postwar period. The privileged category of New Criticism was that of the literary, whether as instantiated in canonical texts that were the objects of New Critical interpretive attention or as a general literariness that was the subject of New Critical theorizing. The defining mark of the literary was self-referentiality, the characteristic by which textual elements are referred primarily to other elements within the text rather than to the world at large: Wimsatt's "iconicity," Jakobson's "poetic function." This formalist insistence upon the specifiability of the literary was in large part motivated by a desire to protect humanistic study from invidious comparisons with an increasingly dominant scientific establishment. Far from being simply an ornamental luxury concerned with matters of taste, literary study was to be endowed with its own subject, a *Fach* that was not just a series of texts but literariness itself. Moreover, if this definition of the literary privileged the object of study, it also defined the method of critical analysis as objective and rational, as being as nonliterary as anything the scientist could boast. If the literary text was autonomous, self-referential, and capable of bearing a special value, then the critical language that sought to unlock its mysteries was discursive, communicative, and rational.

The opposition between literature and criticism was, among many other founding acts of discrimination, dismantled by deconstruction. The claim to stand apart from and, in some sense, above the poetic object was for deconstruction a typical example of philosophical hubris. Such a practice assumed that there was a form of discourse that was somehow metalinguistic and nonliterary, capable of presenting the truth of a verbally intricate object without itself becoming entangled in the intricacies of its own verbalization. The point for deconstruction was not that there was no such thing as the literary but that there was, in fact, nothing else. Far from impeaching the privileged category of the literary, deconstruction extended it to cover writing as a whole; and it both raised New Criticism's delicate techniques of verbal analysis to further levels of subtlety and applied them to texts that had previously been thought to reside entirely outside the borders of literature—borders that were now revealed to have been an illusion in the first place.

For New Criticism, works of literature were to be distinguished from historical documents because they represented a special use of language, were uncontrolled by specific, pragmatic intentions, and referred not to the transitory world of events but to transhistorical meanings, truths about the human condition. For deconstruction, in contrast, not only were these truths open to radical question but intention was always absorbed by the self-motivated structures of language regardless of the type of document, and the incapacity of writing to represent reality was similarly extended across the field of discourse as a whole. In other words, the New Critical critique of *literary* reference was solidified by deconstruction into a philosophical position: not only literary texts but all forms of writing stood at an unbridgeable distance from that which they sought to represent. And in appropriating the nonliterary to the literary, deconstruction sequestered the world of events into a realm of presence closed to the irreparably deficient activity of writing. "The bases for historical knowledge are not empirical facts but written texts," said de Man, "even if these texts masquerade in the guise of wars or revolutions."[6] In describing wars and revolutions as texts in disguise, de Man was not just dramatizing what Gadamer had called "the linguisticality of being," the claim that reality, including the world of past events, comes to us only as clothed—and masked—by language. He was also insisting that not only do the texts that witness to history require interpretation but interpretation reveals them to be irremediably different from, and endlessly deferring, the immediacy and presence they take to be their subject.

Any form of historicism must begin by bracketing (if not simply rejecting) the deconstructive insistence that textuality entails what Derrida has called "the horizontality of a pure surface, which represents itself from detour to detour."[7] In fact, American criticism seems on the whole to have taken this problem too seriously. That no historical agency has access to the Real does not mean that historical investigation is per se preempted, nor does the fact that we cannot reproduce the past *wie es eigentlich gewesen,* in the notorious phrase, mean that we can say nothing about it that is both illuminating and useful. As Paul Rabinow and William Sullivan have wisely said: "Pointing up repeated failures to discover any but historically contingent foundations for

6. "Literary History and Literary Modernity," 165.
7. *Writing and Difference,* trans. Alan Bass (Chicago: University of Chicago Press, 1978), 298.

thought does not in itself have to provoke a crisis of inquiry and under-standing. The failure to provide such foundations has not hindered the conduct of successful inquiry."[8] But to recognize that the problematic of representation need not paralyze the literary historian is not to imply that it can be ignored. Textuality is inescapable: the literary historian can neither read history off literary texts nor use a determinate or "ob-jective" historical context to stabilize the "subjective" meaning of in-determinate literary texts. And, on the positive side, if "history" is itself a text, if the founding distinction between history and literature can no longer be maintained, then the barrier that formalism erected between them can be taken down, and the way is opened to a kind of historicism that can range freely across the discursive field as a whole and is no longer blind to its own historicity.

The first phase of the reemergence of historicism in American criti-cism developed, therefore, from an antifoundationalist poststructural-ism that both mounted a hermeneutical critique of positivism and re-directed critical attention to "historical" texts that had previously been thought to lie beyond the literary critic's ken. This first phase was above all preparatory and enabling. Engaging in the kind of polemic that Clif-ford Geertz has termed "intellectual weed control," it cleared the ground of inhibiting presuppositions and marked out the terrain for future cultivation. It also spurred an effort to locate American histori-cism within the far more fully developed European tradition of philo-sophical or hermeneutical historicism, a tradition that had never previ-ously made much of an impression upon the pragmatic liberalism of American criticism. The second phase, now vigorously under way, is defined by a more mature attempt to come to grips with another, even more persistently excluded European tradition of historicism—that which derives from Marx. This phase represents a salutary confronta-tion between American literary critics, largely educated in the modern-ist traditions of an impersonalizing formalism, and a set of experiential values previously hidden from professional view. Critical practices have come to be recognized as life choices.

The issues currently under debate within critical historicism engage and often dispute the central terms of the Marxist tradition. They can be usefully mapped in terms of three axes of opposition. The first has as one of its elements the traditional Marxist model that insists upon

8. "The Interpretive Turn," in *Interpretive Social Science*, 23–24.

the distinction between the production of material goods and the re-production of cultural relations. Although now rarely maintained in terms of the largely discredited opposition between base and super-structure, this position nonetheless requires a truly materialist analysis to specify the material if not economic causes of cultural phenomena. Against this is set a symbolic approach that seeks to maintain the unity of the social whole by applying an anthropological conception of cul-ture as driven by semiotic rather than material needs. Here the task of historical understanding is defined as interpreting signs rather than ana-lyzing forces—as, in short, cultural poetics.

A second, rather different axis can be formed on the question of agency. On the one hand are those who insist on the priority of agency over impersonal processes in the making of history, who maintain the efficacy of subjective meanings, intentions, and beliefs, and who see the literary work as bespeaking but also simultaneously criticizing the ide-ology of its time. On the other are those who hold to a darker, Fou-cauldian conception of an inescapable metaphysics of power, for whom social life as lived is different from but ultimately controlled by the social as hegemonically thought, and for whom the unities of a culture finally override its differences.

Finally, the third axis draws a distinction at the level of practice: at one end are literary historians who believe in the power of the exem-plary instance and for whom every moment is, in a return to the ex-pressive unity of *Geistesgeschichte,* synecdochic; at the other are those for whom historical understanding requires empirical completeness, for whom the writing of literary history is a systematic technique as well as a craft, and for whom the illustrative instance can never do more than illustrate the presence of forces whose efficacy requires other forms of demonstration.

None of these beliefs and procedures is necessarily independent of any of the rest, although some obviously sit more comfortably together than do others. Nor is there, in my view, any way of determining which of these attitudes is either theoretically more correct or practically more productive. Not only is the proof of the pudding, as always, in the eating, but correctness is a standard no more applicable to questions of theory than to other interpretive activities: since theorizing is as histor-ically contingent as any other form of intellectual practice, there is no norm of rectitude by which correctness can be adjudicated. In the final analysis, the conflicting imperatives of historicism can be resolved only

through a process of negotiation, a process that certainly requires theoretical self-reflection but that can never be settled by appeals to theory.
For the resolution at which these negotiations will arrive can lay claim
not to theoretical but to *political* efficacy, even if that claim may in many
if not most instances never be articulated. In Simon Clarke's words,
"The way we understand history cannot be dissociated from the way in
which we try to make it": the choices we make as literary historians are
consistent with the choices we make as citizens.[9] Or at least we would
want them to be. Continuity among the various parts of our lives is, to
be sure, a goal to be achieved rather than a given fact, but one way it
can be secured is by understanding the full meaning of the professional
practice in which we are engaged.

While the essays collected here are all written in the context of a broadly
conceived critical historicism, each defines its relation to that practice
differently. Paul Strohm's essay on Chaucer and Usk begins as an investigation of political biography and reminds us that an accurate sense of
social and political value depends upon an investigation of the primary
materials that literary critics have too often left to historians with quite
different agendas. But while it valuably recuperates the tradition of J. R.
Hulbert and Edith Rickert, two of Chaucer's best early biographers,
the essay then uses the concept of refraction to consider how politics
relates to aesthetics, how these two men's different styles of political
action are embodied in different styles of writing. Similarly, David Wallace's essay operates at the level of an intentionalist analysis, explaining
Chaucer's relation to Italian humanism both materially and politically
and showing how the *Clerk's Tale* rather irresolutely negotiates among
the humanists' political differences. A similar irresolution is also ascribed to Chaucer in my essay on the *Miller's Tale,* which uses recent
economic historiography to ground political values in the material conditions of late fourteenth-century society. All three of these essays assume the priority of agency at the same time as they see the poet as
articulating an ideology by eschewing, in any direct and explicit form,

9. "Socialist Humanism and the Critique of Economism," *History Workshop* 8 (1979):
139. This point has been illustrated above all by feminist critics: see the important article
by Judith Newton, "History as Usual? Feminism and the 'New Historicism,'" *Cultural
Critique* 9 (Spring 1988), 87–121.

ideological statement. In a sense, they refuse to install the poet as the sovereign master of the meaning of his texts, which they see as expressing values (negotiation, subjectivity) that go beyond any narrowly partisan agenda: Chaucerian politics are disingenuously and uncertainly apolitical.

Of the four remaining essays, that of Theresa Coletti is most clearly aligned with the New Historicist concern with literature as cultural practice. She shows how the massive Records of Early English Drama project constructs a narrowly conceived model of history—misrepresented as history *tout court*—that obscures the plays' functioning as forms of social action. Similarly, by exploring the complex negotiations by which Hoccleve's *Regement of Princes* consolidated a wide range of disparate interests into a single, monarchically legitimizing voice, Larry Scanlon's essay shows how monarchical power relations are reproduced within the social structure. The remaining two essays relocate their literary texts within fields of discourse that reveal the arbitrariness of the very designation "literary." Anne Middleton shows how Langland's self-naming in *Piers Plowman,* which serves to identify work and life, establishes as the central unit of spiritual significance a biographical exemplarity that finds analogues in a wide variety of contemporary social practices. And Louise Fradenburg applies the psychoanalytic notion of the primal scene—by which she means less the illicit sight of parental sexuality than the confrontation with the contingency of personal origins and hence with mortality—to texts articulating the self-definition of Edinburgh as a city in the late fifteenth and early sixteenth centuries. What these two essays provide explicitly, and what is implied in the rest, is a liberating transgression of the usual boundaries that divide the literary from the historical, a challenge to the way in which the topography of literary studies has traditionally been drawn. And while each essay defines its project in distinct terms, all share an interest in reconceptualizing literary historicism.

The return of historicism to literary studies is usually understood as a function of the widespread politicization of the human sciences, indeed of the academy as a whole, that has marked the decades of the 1970s and 1980s. This process has been driven primarily by the entrance into literary studies of a wide variety of socially based interests: various forms of ethnic studies (African-American, Chicano, Asian-American), of gay and lesbian studies, and, above all, of feminism. The mechanism of transformation has derived not simply from the fact that changes in society and in the demography of academic institutions entail changes in the way literature is understood. For what these socially based projects have revealed is the priority of the social itself in the constitution of culture: what had previously been taken as natural—given, universal, normal—has been unmasked as socially determined. What has followed from this is the challenge not only to the canon as it is currently constituted but to the processes of canonicity themselves, and above all to the category "literature" that has always been taken by literary studies as its foundational assumption. And from here it is a very short step to a full-scale historicization of all value and the accompanying legitimization of explicitly political modes of analysis.

But this narrative of development fully accounts neither for the virtual universality of the turn to historicism nor for the swiftness of its triumph. That the academic community is as vulnerable to fads and fashions as other elements in society goes without saying, and the attraction of the new is as seductive here as elsewhere. But the speed and completeness of the ascendancy of historicism seem remarkable: it is a rare journal or conference that is not preoccupied by debates over "new historicism," "cultural materialism," "neo-Marxism," "cultural criticism," "the politics of literature," and so forth. Clearly the topic answers to more profound needs than those generated exclusively within the academic profession itself.

Although it is perhaps too soon to historicize this latest wave of historicism, some comments are nonetheless in order. In *The Philosophy of History,* Hegel argued that historiography is coterminous with the state, that making histories presupposes the making of history:

> We must suppose historical narration to have appeared contemporaneously with historical deeds and events. . . . It is only the state which first presents subject-matter that is not only *adapted* to the prose of History, but involves the production of such history in the very progress of its own being.[10]

Historiography not only records but, as a cultural form, bespeaks the workings of the state, of the established system of law by which power

---

10. Cited by Hayden White, *The Content of the Form* (Baltimore: Johns Hopkins University Press, 1987), 12. For a case history of the emergence of the idea of history in a society in which it was previously lacking, that of the Hawaiians, see Marshall Sahlins, *Islands of History* (Chicago: University of Chicago Press, 1985).

is most immediately and visibly exercised. Where does that locate the historian? For Michel de Certeau, since historians "do not make history, they can only engage in the making of histories. . . . They reflect on the power that they lack."[11] It is tempting to ascribe the current ascendancy of historicism to such a compensation. As intellectuals come increasingly to be confined within the academy, as the academy continues to be isolated from the centers of economic and political power, and as postmodern aesthetic production becomes fully appropriated by capitalist commodity production as a whole, literary studies seeks to recover a sense of cultural wholeness by establishing the idea of social totality as a privileged instrument of analysis. Similarly, as the latest stage of capitalism all the more effectively occludes the social as an idea and erodes it as a fact, replacing it with what Robert Bellah and his colleagues have called "the radically individualistic ideology" of "the improvisational self," literary studies recuperate earlier forms of social action and reinstall the social as the crucial agency of cultural production.[12]

But what is striking about the return to historicism is that while it may well have been ignited by a compensatory reaction, by a desire to enact in the closed world of the university a social engagement foreclosed in the world at large, its effects have made vividly clear that there is in fact no closed world of intellectual practice, that the social really is, as every form of historicism has always claimed, inescapable. What may have begun as compensation has been fulfilled as reality. For the public reaction to the rehistoricization of literature has served to remind the academy that, like it or not, it does play a central role in the world of political action. The responses of William Bennett, the former secretary of education, of Lynne Cheney, the current chairman of the National Endowment for the Humanities, of Allen Bloom, the author of *The Closing of the American Mind,* and of various journalists and columnists all bear witness to the fact that the development of a critical historicism within literary studies is felt as a profound challenge. What it challenges is precisely the ahistoricity of value that the Bennett-Cheney-Bloom reaction wishes to support, a reaction that, ironically, by its very existence reveals that ahistoricity to be an illusion. The at-

11. *The Writing of History,* trans. Tom Conley (New York: Columbia University Press, 1988), 8.
12. Robert N. Bellah et al., *Habits of the Heart: Individualism and Commitment in American Life* (Berkeley and Los Angeles: University of California Press, 1985).

tempt to protect the eternal verities of the humanistic tradition from politicization is an effort to efface the material conditions of life as irrelevant to cultural production.

This is a program entirely consistent with the larger Reagan-Bush strategy of effacing the particularities of social and economic reality by vague if coded talk of "values," a word that indicates for many Americans, as Bellah put it, "the incomprehensible, rationally indefensible thing that the individual chooses when he or she has thrown off the last vestige of external influence and reached pure contentless freedom." [13] It is also consistent with the sequestering of the liberal arts within an academy that is itself cut off from society as a whole, a university defined as a place where, in Bloom's shameful words, the "theoretical life" can be lived apart from the "primal slime" of society. [14] To insist that these two realms cannot be separated, that value is always historically contingent (that is, political), that the university is itself a function of social interests and has a responsibility to debate and determine social facts and social values, that the material conditions of life are inescapable—all of this is to contravene a very specific political program and to place oneself, willy-nilly, in a posture of opposition. Literary historians would do well to follow the example of Bennett, Cheney, Bloom, et al. by recognizing that matters of real political significance are at stake. The question is not whether we are going to engage in a politically charged critical activity or not. It is, rather, to recognize that since all forms of criticism are evidently and by definition political, which form we choose to practice is an act with consequences.

This book had its beginnings in a special session of the Modern Language Association meetings in December 1984 organized by Louise Fradenburg and chaired by myself. She, Larry Scanlon, and Paul Strohm gave papers in that session, early versions of the essays that appear here. An earlier version of my own essay has been published in *South Atlantic Quarterly* 86 (1987): 457–95.

13. "The Quest for the Self: Individualism, Morality, Politics," in *Interpretive Social Science,* 372.
14. *The Closing of the American Mind* (New York: Pantheon Books, 1987), 245.

# William Langland's "Kynde Name"

## *Authorial Signature and Social Identity in Late Fourteenth-Century England*

### *Anne Middleton*

A good poem, even if it is signed with a full and well-known name, intends as a work of art to lose the identity of the author; that is, it means to represent him not actualized, like an eye-witness testifying in court and held strictly by zealous counsel to the point at issue, but freed from his juridical or prose self and taking an ideal or fictitious personality; otherwise his evidence amounts the less to poetry.

> John Crowe Ransom,
> "A Poem Nearly Anonymous," in
> *The World's Body*

At certain moments in the history of literature . . . producing a text—as an ideal goal for the writer—is extremely problematical. . . . The difficulty for such writers, as for such times, is in being able to distinguish adequately between the author as a human being (whatever his self-characterization), the author as a producing writer, and his production. Those moments and those writers ought to become a more prevalent theme of literary study, for their exemplary uncertainty, which to them appears abnormal, brings into question otherwise reified, "normal" notions held about texts.

> Edward Said, *Beginnings*

## A POET NEARLY ANONYMOUS

Why is the author of *Piers Plowman* a poet nearly anonymous? William Langland, an older contemporary of Chaucer, spent at least two decades making and revising the first English poem to attain a national readership and influence while its author lived. Its survival to the present century in over fifty manuscripts, none clearly a direct copy of any of the others, implies that copies of the poem must have numbered in the hundreds by 1400.[1] The poem was immediately and widely imi-

---

1. A. I. Doyle, "Remarks on Surviving Manuscripts of *Piers Plowman*," in *Medieval English Religious and Ethical Literature: Essays in Honour of G. H. Russell,* ed. Gregory

tated, but those who adopted its distinctive idiom did not credit Langland with its invention. Rather, the poem's fictive hero Piers Plowman, who is rarely present in the narrative and seldom speaks, was widely taken to be the center and source of authority for the poet's powerful innovation, and in contemporary imagination Piers effectively supplanted the author as a putatively actual historical being, the origin of a mode of speech and action that abruptly found in his name a condensed rationale for its own continued articulation.[2]

While Langland lived, Piers Plowman figured significantly in current discourses of religious and political dissent. He was named as an exemplary, if hypothetical, person by the rebel forces in the Rising of 1381, and as one of the actual leaders of the rebellion by some chroniclers of these events. For over two hundred years it is Piers's example, not Langland's, that is repeatedly adduced to authorize an enduring vernacular literary tradition of cultural criticism broadly underwritten by Langland's stylistic example.[3] In this same period, however, Langland himself, in a near-vacuum of external biographical documentation, virtually vanished from public notice as a known English author, diminished by the sixteenth century to "that nameless malcontent" to whom the conservative Puttenham attributed the poem.[4] Yet Langland evi-

---

Kratzmann and James Simpson (Cambridge, Eng.: D. S. Brewer, 1986), 35–48; John A. Burrow, "The Audience of *Piers Plowman*," *Anglia* 75 (1957): 373–84, reprinted with corrections and a new postscript in Burrow, *Essays on Medieval Literature* (Oxford: Clarendon Press, 1984), 102–16; Anne Middleton, "The Audience and Public of *Piers Plowman*," in *Middle English Poetry and Its Literary Background,* ed. David Lawton (Cambridge, Eng.: D. S. Brewer, 1982), 101–23, 147–54.

2. Anne Hudson, "Epilogue: The Legacy of *Piers Plowman*," in *A Companion to Piers Plowman,* ed. John A. Alford (Berkeley and Los Angeles: University of California Press, 1988), 251–66, provides a succinct account and bibliography of the influence and afterlife of the poem. Elizabeth Kirk, "Langland's Plowman and the Recreation of Fourteenth-Century Religious Metaphor," *Yearbook of Langland Studies* 2 (1988): 1–21, explains the social circumstances and literary traditions within which Langland's invention of the plowman took on a volatile new signifying power in this period. On the appropriation of Piers's name, see Pamela Gradon, "Langland and the Ideology of Dissent," *Proceedings of the British Academy* 66 (1980): 179–205; John N. King, "Robert Crowley's Editions of *Piers Plowman:* A Tudor Apocalypse," *Modern Philology* 73 (1976): 342–53; and Barbara A. Johnson, "From *Piers Plowman* to *Pilgrim's Progress:* The Generic and Exegetical Contexts of Bunyan's 'Similitude of a Dream'", Ph.D. diss., Brown University, 1983.

3. See, in addition to the above, David Lawton, "Lollardy and the 'Piers Plowman' Tradition," *Modern Language Review* 76 (1981): 780–93.

4. The ideological significance of Puttenham's attribution should not be overlooked. As David Norbrook points out, the *Arte of English Poesie* (1589) spoke for a courtly definition of the function of literature in society (*Poetry and Politics in the English Renaissance* [London: Routledge and Kegan Paul, 1984], chap. 2). Puttenham's view of the poem as

dently intended to associate his name irrevocably with his work, for he signs it in all three of its surviving versions (the A, B, and C texts, representing three successive states of composition), inscribing these signatures more fully, deeply, and indelibly in the fabric of the narrative with each revision. While there is no evidence to suggest that either Langland or his scribes ever attempted to efface these signatures, they apparently never functioned culturally as ascriptions. As far as his contemporaries, and those who for two hundred years continued to appropriate his invention, were concerned, the only name William Langland ever made for himself in writing was that of his elusive hero Piers Plowman.

The question that begins this essay is in effect the founding question of all modern study of this poem.[5] If the riddle of authorial identity that occupied scholars at the turn of this century has since been reframed by more recent interpreters, its central importance to historical understanding of both the writer and his cultural moment has not diminished. In this essay I shall argue that Langland's elusive identity defines, both for the earliest readers and imitators of his poem and for modern literary scholars of late medieval literature and culture, a locus of what Edward Said calls "exemplary uncertainty" that requires both Langland's interpretive community and our own to revise their traditional notions of what constitutes the integrity of a text and the ground

---

fundamentally a satire, and its author's literary role and lineage as comparable to those of "Lucilius, Iuuenall and Persius among the Latines," contrasts sharply with the Protestant "prophetic" views of it articulated in the age of Edward VI, particularly by John Bale and Robert Crowley. Both had taken an exceptional interest in *Piers Plowman* and the name and historical situation of its author, and became for later generations the major sources of information (and misinformation) about these matters. Bale, seeking for internal clues to the author's name, hit upon *"Robert* Langland," probably deriving the given name from a scribal error in the first line of a new passus and a new vision: "Thus *yrobed* [y robert] in russet y romed aboute" (B 8.1); Crowley, the first printer of the poem, apparently owed his information to Bale. See George Kane, *Piers Plowman: The Evidence for Authorship* (London: Athlone Press, 1965), 37–45; and King, "Tudor Apocalypse." In his introductory summary of the poem, however, Crowley nevertheless refers to the poetic speaker in much of the Vita as Piers rather than Will, the name Langland gives to his dreamer-persona.

5. For a brief discussion and full bibliography of the "authorship question," see Anne Middleton, *"Piers Plowman,"* Chapter XVIII of *A Manual of Writings in Middle English 1050–1500,* gen. ed. Albert E. Hartung (New Haven: Connecticut Academy of Arts and Sciences, 1986), 7:2224–27, 2429–31. The two complementary studies that survey the issues and documents and the literary significance of late medieval authorial self-disclosure are George Kane, *Evidence for Authorship,* and *The Autobiographical Fallacy in Chaucer and Langland Studies* (London: H. K. Lewis, 1965).

and limits of its representative claims. In particular, Langland's authorial evanescence, to his contemporaries and to us, invites a reconsideration of relations between the projected design of the author's work and the immanent form of the authorial life, and the ways in which a published authorial name attempts to regulate and mediate these problematic connections and distinctions. Text and context, "external" and "internal" information, narrative progression and digression, the generic and the specific, the common and the proper, blur and fail to sustain themselves as useful heuristic distinctions in stabilizing either Langland's "authorship question" or ours. In every one of its many versions from Langland's lifetime to our own, the "authorship question" is *au fond* a question about boundaries, about what is inside and outside the field of interpretation—what is "proper" to the authorial enterprise as such, and what it has in common with other cultural work—and what kind of interpretive attention this indeterminacy invites.

As we shall see in detail below, Langland explicitly poses such questions within the work itself, and it is in precisely those moments when he brings them sharply into the foreground that he signs his name in the text. For the fourteenth century, the authorship question posed by Langland's work opens to view not only the ambiguous status of vernacular literary authority in this period, but the moral and political claims of vernacular cultural productivity in general to embody "truth." During the poet's lifetime, and for the two following centuries of his work's greatest influence, these are volatile and contested questions, which Langland represents in their most culturally encompassing and historically concrete forms. To specifically literary-historical hindsight, the precarious fortunes of Langland's name as author illustrate some of the uncertainties latent in the enterprise of large-scale vernacular fiction-making in the latter fourteenth century, the period of its first decisive articulation in England. This literary era has been seen as one of unsteady transition from conventions of authorial anonymity to those of authorial individuation and self-advertisement; yet these changing literary procedures for the representation of authorship, and the rich formal heterogeneity of the vernacular literary works in which they appear, are not isolated or culturally insulated phenomena. Instabilities in the literary presentation and reception of identity may, I suggest, be understood more productively as part of a still more pervasive late fourteenth-century "crisis of the proper" concerning representation itself, a crisis more fundamentally political than literary. It is within this broader discursive field that Langland presents the status of his authorship as a matter of paradigmatic importance: the making of this poem, the nature of its representative claims, and the elusive social identity of its author, acquire—with more specificity in each of its revisions—the aspect of urgent contemporary political concerns. In the terms offered by John Crowe Ransom's formulation of represented authorial identity (the terms that have for most of this century implicitly defined the "literary" or "internal" approach to the authorship question), it is his "juridical" self that Langland increasingly brings to the foreground by his disposition of his name in his work. He calls into question the very possibility of sustaining as an author an "ideal and fictitious personality" that can remain exempt from answerability to a larger contemporary "point at issue" in the depiction of his authorial enterprise as cultural work.

For twentieth-century interpreters of Langland's poem, the apparently idiosyncratic qualities of the text as a literary production—its heterogeneous literary form, the affinities of its style—have with remarkable consistency seemed explicable only by reference to the identity of the author: the course of inquiry has repeatedly enacted a kind of scholarly ascesis, an ascent from the unknown to the unknown. Indeed, to the early twentieth-century scholars who first posed and debated the "authorship question," the very boundaries of the literary text were (as for different reasons they still are) at issue: in its initial version, the questions under most intense dispute were whether the same writer composed all three surviving versions of the poem, and what circumstances conditioned the course of its production as a sequence of revisions. Since these indeterminacies arose from ambiguous "internal evidence," they seemed capable of resolution only by appeal to information that lay outside the text. Scholars sought decisive "external" documentation, either in the form of extraliterary biographical records that might corroborate or supply a name for this elusive writer, or through comparative investigation of analogous examples of authorial self-presentation in other medieval poems that might establish the norms within which Langland's authorial self-disclosures within the poem might be understood. Both kinds of "external" inquiry were conceived as factual constraints upon interpretation, "historically" grounded controls of the almost limitless interpretive inferences that are everywhere tantalizingly invited by the poem itself concerning the

actual social identity and life-circumstances of the author. Biography—
a text or tissue of data woven by inference into knowledge but conceived as distinct in character and truth-value from a literary record—
would in this view stabilize the range of legitimate inferences that the
poetic text can not in itself contain or disclose.

The chief "external" record of authorship cited in these debates
seems to offer all the documentary solidity that turn-of-the-century
scholars sought. It is a Latin note written about 1400 in the Trinity
College Dublin manuscript of the C version of the poem. The earliest
surviving manuscript of any version of the poem, it originated and for
some time remained (as did most of the surviving C texts) in the south-
west Midland region of the poet's own origin, as determined by dialect
evidence. The memoranda among which this Latin note appears show
considerable local knowledge of South Wales border events and families: there is, in other words, good reason to trust its report as informed
about the matters it records.[6] It declares "willielmus . . . de Langlond"
to be the maker of the poem, names Langland's father as a member of
the gentry who held land of the Despensers in Oxfordshire, and reveals
that Langland, at least as a writer, did not use his father's surname.[7]
One early inference from this note—that William was illegitimate—is
certainly itself illegitimate: individuals in the fourteenth century might

---

6. This note appears in full in Appendix I. On this and other external attributions of
authorship, see Kane, *Evidence for Authorship,* 26–51. For the most recent argument about
the dialect evidence on the poet's native place, see M. R. Samuels, "Langland's Dialect,"
*Medium Aevum* 54 (1985): 232–47. Malcolm Parkes has recently determined that the Trinity
College Dublin manuscript "must have been made in the first half of the 1380s" and is
thus the earliest surviving manuscript of any version of the poem (cited in George Kane,
"The 'Z Version' of *Piers Plowman,*" *Speculum* 60 [1985]: 912).

7. The fortunes of the Despenser family—their spectacular rise and as spectacular fall
in royal favor and power—roughly brackets the poet's lifetime. The chief magnate adherents of Edward II in the 1320s, they had consolidated their standing during the Welsh
border wars and continued to prosper under the reign of Edward III. The family's already
declining political fortunes went into ultimate eclipse with the accession of their long-
standing opponents, the house of Lancaster, in 1399, and with the lack of male heirs after
that date; see *Dictionary of National Biography* (Oxford: Oxford University Press, 1917–)
5:860–67, s.v. Henry le Despenser (d. 1406), Hugh le Despenser (d. 1265), Hugh le Despenser the elder, Earl of Winchester (1262–1326), Hugh le Despenser the younger (d.
1326), and Thomas le Despenser, Earl of Gloucester (1373–1400). As Paul Strohm has
argued for the post-1400 alteration of the "Chaucer tradition," it may be that the death
or decline from social power of Langland's immediate circle of readers and kindred intel-
lects—and possibly patrons—by the mid-1380s has as much to do with the pattern of
transmission and reception of the poem as changing literary fashions per se ("Chaucer's
Fifteenth-Century Audience and the Narrowing of the 'Chaucer Tradition'", *Studies in
the Age of Chaucer* 4 [1982]: 3–32).

be known by more than one surname, a practice I shall have occasion to examine more closely. Yet both in content and placement, this note is hardly fully "external" to the poetic text: it is appended to a copy of the poem and serves as an implicit commentary upon it, at least to the extent that it acknowledges that there is an indeterminacy to be re-solved about the author's existence. It is, in other words, at best further testimony to a fourteenth-century question of authorial identity, rather than a decisive contemporary answer to it. Moreover, it shows the kind of information that, for this witness, counts as an answer: the note places the author, not with respect to his literary productions, place of residence, profession, or institutional situation, but in relation to fam-ily, lineage, and property-holding—relations conspicuously absent from the poem's "internal" account of the author's identity. This strangely precise, as well as rare, "external" record takes on an overde-termined quality as a comment upon Langland's authorial self-representation. Derrida's formulation of the divided and duplicitous motives surrounding the inscription of the proper name—that it in-volves on the one hand the "narcissistic desire to make one's own 'proper' name 'common,' to make it enter and be at one with the body of the mother-tongue; and at the same time the oedipal desire to pre-serve one's proper name, to see it as an analogon of the name of the father"—could scarcely be more apposite.[8]

If the turn-of-the-century formulation of the "authorship question" has receded from scholarly and critical agendas, the initial terms for dividing the labors of inquiry have remained largely undisturbed. "His-torical" knowledge comes from that which is seen as "external" to the poem, "literary" understanding is derived "internally"—and they offer two virtually incommensurable orders of truth. That which went with-out saying for the writer, the knowledge internal to his practice, must be reconstructed externally by the modern scholar of medieval texts, and the secure externality or otherness of the latter's knowledge re-mains his distinctive property and armature, constraining and legiti-mating rather than enabling his access to the internality of writerly knowledge, and guarding his interpretive labors against the cardinal sin of medieval literary scholarship, "anachronism." It will be part of my purpose to reframe the classic form of the "authorship question" by

8. *Of Grammatology,* trans. Gayatri Chakravorty Spivak (Baltimore: Johns Hopkins University Press, 1976), lxxxiv.

collapsing the division between its "internal" and "external" aspects, by considering within one field of vision the documentary designs of the literary text and the literary strategies of many contemporary documents adduced as "external" records.

In some respects, much recent criticism of the poem has anticipated this move: the old pursuit of the actual historical identity of the author beyond or behind the poem has for nearly two generations been regarded as something of an embarrassment, a largely irrelevant distraction from the more fundamental business of interpreting the work "itself," and its *persona,* as the authorial presence is called when conceived as a function of literary design.[9] Yet in some of the best recent study of the poem, Langland as the producer of the text rather than its product has enacted a return of the repressed. Even though interpreters no longer seek to define what turn-of-the-century scholars usually termed the "character and opinions" of the writer, his education, social location, antecedent textual materials, and working methods are often substantial, if largely submerged, hypotheses that underwrite detailed readings of the poem: a posited actual historical individual now lurks in what is commonly described as his "context," which is now seen as revealed in certain of the internal procedures of the poem.

9. These two conceptions of the limits of the text tend to correlate closely with two opposed views of textual criticism, a long-standing debate in medieval literary studies but articulated anew in this generation chiefly in disputes over Kane and Donaldson's landmark editions of *Piers Plowman* (see Appendix II). The latter position, in which meaning is a matter of authorial design and reception is a distinct and separable phenomenon, is associated with Kane and Donaldson's radically Lachmannian enterprise of reconstructing the authorial text; the former, loosely Bedierist, argues both the quixotic nature of this project given medieval circumstances of textual reproduction, and its errors of principle in the face of medieval attitudes to authorial "propriety" in the work. See Anne Hudson, "Middle English," in *Editing Medieval Texts,* ed. A. G. Rigg (New York: Garland, 1977), 42, 44; and Barry Windeatt, "The Scribes as Chaucer's Early Critics," *Studies in the Age of Chaucer* 1 (1979): 119–42. While Kane and Donaldson would probably not dispute the claim that meaning is in part a social construction, they differ from their critics about how this construction is to be represented in the edited text and what reconstruction of the text recovers.

This debate has supplanted the "authorship controversy" as the locus of the most fundamental recent discussion of what counts as historical interpretation of this poem, or of medieval poems generally. Critics on all sides of this editorial controversy have lately begun to acknowledge that what is at stake in their disagreement is ultimately nothing less than the privileging of the subject, as well as of the "literary," a central issue of postmodern literary theory; see Lee W. Patterson, "The Logic of Textual Criticism and the Way of Genius: The Kane-Donaldson *Piers Plowman* in Historical Perspective," in *Textual Criticism and Literary Interpretation,* ed. Jerome J. McGann (Chicago: University of Chicago Press, 1985), 55–91; and Kane, "The Text," in *Companion to Piers Plowman,* ed. Alford, 175–200.

Yet if the fourteenth-century writer William Langland reemerges in these accounts as a kind of back-formation of the intertextualities of his work, his reappearance has thus far tended to silence rather than invite further questions about the historical forces that cast enigmatic emphasis upon the identity and social location of the author, rendering them at once urgently important and elusive to the meaning of the poem. What seems at first a salutary critical decentering of that authorial subject that it had been the goal of earlier scholarship to discern "in" or "behind" the poem has in practice been a less than fully enabling interpretive move, because the kinds of discourses that are thought to constitute and determine both the content and "author-function" of the work have not thus far differed greatly from those disclosed by old-fashioned source study. The Langland that emerges from some of the most learned and thorough recent analyses of his work is, to be sure, no longer the sublimely impatient and impassioned enthusiast, scornful of formal niceties and deliberate art, that emerged from earlier criticism. On the contrary, he is crabbedly learned, a writer steeped in others' writings, and deriving directly from them, rather than from his worldly position or experiences, the armature of his individuation. His authorial design and character is seen as determined "from the outside" by antecedent texts, but this "external" environment, manifested in a poetic subject who has incorporated and assimilated its discipline, is defined almost exclusively by one kind of writing in particular: the canonical regimen of medieval Biblical interpretation. What drives William Langland's twenty-year labor of composition and revision is, in this view, no more and no less than what drives his reading of the texts he incessantly cites: "*Piers Plowman* is a poem being controlled from the outside. . . . Langland read to discover a description of himself; as he found it, he wrote it down." He could locate this discourse, and intervene in it, only in books: "the picture that emerges is that of a man eking out his poem slowly, even tediously, while poring over a variety of commentaries and preachers' aids."[10] Yet both the initial impetus and the end of these labors of authorship remain obscure. If what Langland was composing through this process of voracious textual appropriation was himself, how might such a remarkable authorial intent arise from

10. Judson Allen, "Langland's Reading and Writing: *Detractor* and the Pardon Passus," *Speculum* 59 (1984): 359; John A. Alford, "The Role of the Quotations in *Piers Plowman*," *Speculum* 52 (1977): 99.

its alleged immediate sources? How, in other words, might such a relentlessly "external" regimen be assimilated and given back as the "internal," as the apparent constituents of a subject located in space and time? And even more puzzling, why? What would prompt a writer steeped in such materials to give them back to his contemporaries in this expository form as a "description of himself"? And what kind of reception might he find for such a project?

By aligning the literary forms and social motives for the representation of individual identity, and the formation and recording of names, in the later fourteenth century, I propose to set forth the terms within which naming acquired the standing of a necessary, encompassing, and contested "point at issue" for Langland and his culture. If the age of Shakespeare discloses, as it does to Stephen Greenblatt, an essentially theatrical imagination at work in various ordinary discursive practices, then I suggest that several kinds of social records not confined to the "literary" in the age of Chaucer and Langland show people appearing to each other narratively, and improvising individual and communal identities, not in the unitary rhetorical category of the role but in the temporal span and generic model of the life.[11] To be intelligible is to have a comprehensively revelatory story, and to signify historically or literarily—to make a name for oneself—in this age of heraldic cognizances as well as of literary signatures is, in Huizinga's happy formulation, to "choose the text for the sermon of one's life."[12]

## THE FUNCTION OF LATE MEDIEVAL LITERARY SIGNATURE

R. W. Chambers and George Kane have demonstrated that Langland's internal signatures resemble in form and techniques those widely used by other late medieval writers. This comparative literary context, it is suggested, "explains" Langland's practice by rendering it "normal": internal signature was indeed more pervasive, formally sophisticated, and diverse in vernacular writings of the thirteenth through the fifteenth centuries than at any other time in European literature before or since.[13] Yet two problems attend this demonstration if, as most scholars

11. Stephen Greenblatt, *Renaissance Self-Fashioning from More to Shakespeare* (Chicago: University of Chicago Press, 1980).

12. Johan Huizinga, *The Waning of the Middle Ages* (New York: Doubleday, 1954), 231.

13. R. W. Chambers, "Robert or William Langland?," *London Medieval Studies* 1 (1948,

have done, we stop rather than start our inquiry here. The one, peculiar to Langland, we have noted: if these self-inscriptions—because widely used at the time and therefore presumably legible as such—were to be understood as communications and records of authorship, they were in this instance a conspicuous failure. The other reframes the first in a more general form: if this practice was "normal" and widespread in late medieval writing—and indeed confined almost entirely to this period—what then was its function? What are the norms of literary practice and social action and understanding within which it is "normal"? The question has rarely been posed, because it is widely assumed that we already know the answer. The strange case of William Langland, however, suggests that we know less about the literary and social meaning of this practice than we thought.

A good deal of recent discussion of medieval authorial self-representation has regarded this pervasive internal self-naming as but one aspect of the broader late medieval "discovery of the individual," and has considered literary manifestations of "poetic individuality" as among several kinds of evidence of new interest in the representative and signifying power of the self. But as the ensuing account will suggest, the pervasive practice of complex literary signature in this period is not an *illustration* of this cultural phenomenon but an important grammatical operator in bringing about a broader cultural transformation; as such, it is a rearguard action, a gesture fraught with ambivalence and nostalgia, not a sense of discovery or progress. As a means of deobjectifying the written artifact and restoring to it the authenticating presence that has been drained from it by the documentary and administrative culture whose gestures it borrows, it uses the letter to discredit the consequences of a culture of letters, of "writing and hiding myself." [14]

---

for 1939): 430–62; Kane, *Evidence for Authorship* and *Autobiographical Fallacy.* On the genre-specificity of this practice in medieval vernacular writing—its association with romance, as distinct from *chanson de geste, lai,* and *fabliau*—see David F. Hult, *Self-Fulfilling Prophecies: Readership and Authority in the First "Roman de la Rose"* (Cambridge, Eng.: Cambridge University Press, 1986), 30–33.

14. Rousseau; see Derrida, *Of Grammatology,* 142. On the pervasive cultural practice of reappropriating authoritative discourses so as to shift their significance, see Michel de Certeau, *The Practice of Everyday Life* (Berkeley and Los Angeles: University of California Press, 1984), esp. 24–28. This practice, which I have here (somewhat unsatisfactorily) called borrowing, Certeau calls "wigging" (*la perruque*), and he emphasizes that this "art of diversion" does not permanently alienate anything of value from the ordinary authoritative use of the discourse but creates—on official time, so to speak—proliferating un-

It is an almost universal (though almost universally unstated) presupposition that the purpose of late medieval literary signature is the same as that of more modern and direct forms of declaration of authorship: it is simply *attributive*. Because the signatures in *Piers Plowman* have been examined chiefly under the impetus of the "authorship controversy," this assumption is even stronger in Langland scholarship than in studies of other late medieval writers. As attribution, internal signature in general is thought to be an authorial intervention in the economic functioning of the work in a system of circulation and reproduction. In this view, the signature is there to satisfy some "natural" wish of readers to be satisfied about who made this poem, and it serves as a kind of proprietary declaration of the author's craft or "hand" in the work—information that contributes to its cultural worth by specifying the value added to language by a particular fabricator. In other words, it is often discussed as if it were a primitive attempt at copyright. By naming himself, the author is in effect naming his price and attempting to control in his absence from the means of reproduction transactions in what he has made—though his audience may of course pay his price in the form of patronage or prayers for his soul, familiar medieval modes of literary exchange, rather than in the more modern ones of posthumous fame, canonical position, or royalties.

Since attribution, by whatever methods, is assumed to be an inextricable part of our appreciation of the work (a term that is itself at root economic), it becomes self-evident and unproblematic that an author should wish his name circulated with his work; how he puts it in circulation is thought to be a secondary consideration of technique or vocabulary rather than meaning. The various formal techniques of signature characteristic of late medieval writing then become simply synonymous means, adapted to manuscript culture, toward the essentially economic end familiar in the age of print. The internality of a signature—the difference between anagrammatic wordplay in the poem and a colophon at the end, for example—does not alter its function but merely adjusts its tone and placement to the author's material and social circumstances: it makes a witty game out of the transaction between

---

official meanings. It is Certeau's general sense of this appropriation as an "art of diversion" that informs my understanding of Langland's signature practices. For an extended fourteenth-century example that offers a broad analogy to Langland's "diversion" of the proper, see below, 70–73.

author and public, while securing the "maker's mark" against casual effacement. By making his name inextricable from the poetic fabric rather than placing it in a colophon where it may more easily be omitted in transmission, the poet defends his reputation against the deepest ravages of Adam Scriveyn, while he considerately anticipates the interest of later readers in attribution.

Internal signatures in medieval texts, then, are commonly read as having the same cultural meaning as both a textually separable declaration of authorship such as a colophon or a title page in a printed book and the internal "maker's mark" in other artistic media such as sculpture, metalwork, or painting. Yet both modern analogies from the age of print and those drawn from medieval nonverbal arts (which do not in the same way lend themselves to copying) are in this case misleading. It is only the social and material arrangements for mechanical reproduction of the written text that make it possible to form the ideas of literary property that underwrite this assumption about medieval motives for internal authorial self-naming.[15] In late medieval literary texts, internal signature regulates, I shall argue, proprieties that are in the first instance grammatical and ontological rather than economic: it proclaims and governs the representative claims of the work rather than the circulation or exchange value of the maker's "hand."

The most widely used forms of internal signature in late medieval literature, however—those that we will find Langland using with developing complexity and skill as he revises the poem—demand certain ways of reading and using the text in order to be legible as names at all, and the form and terms of that legibility alter their meaning. Their

---

15. See Hult, *Self-Fulfilling Prophecies*, 25–64. Perhaps the most complete and helpful formal classification of techniques of medieval literary signature to date, comparing methods used in the verbal and visual arts, nevertheless implies that each of these devices has the same attributive purpose; see Erik S. Kooper, "Art and Signature and the Art of the Signature," in *Court and Poet: Selected Proceedings of the Third Congress of the International Courtly Literature Society,* ed. Glyn S. Burgess (Liverpool: Cairns, 1981), 223–32. Evidence from the visual and plastic arts in late medieval and early modern Europe, however, suggests that signatures in these media have at most a publicizing rather than authenticating function. Contracts for specific commissions by painters or sculptors—for example, of alterpieces—often specified which parts of the work the master must execute himself in order to fulfill the terms of payment; see Michael Baxandall, *Painting and Experience in Fifteenth Century Italy* (Oxford: Oxford University Press, 1972), 3–14, and his *The Limewood Sculptors of Renaissance Germany* (New Haven: Yale University Press, 1980), 102–6. Where they were considered significant in the plastic arts, guarantees of the "maker's hand" were included in the terms of production, not merely declared after the fact by the object.

function, I propose, is not attribution but, to use Daniel Poirion's term for an analogous contemporary practice, *autodefinition;* their referent is not the absent maker but his confected presence, a living "entente" animated and reproduced in the act of reading. What the name inscribed in the poetic text proclaims is not the author's verbal fabrication, but an ethical fabulation of which he makes himself the center; the value signified is not that of his craft but that of his life. Although both modern textual culture and the visual and plastic arts contemporary with the poem provide, as we have suggested, misleading analogies to this practice, late medieval culture does furnish at least one closer and more provocative parallel: the personal badge or cognizance. It is the social function of these devices that Poirion calls "autodefinition," and their vogue happens to coincide closely in time with that of complex internal literary signature.[16] While neither practice appears to be the immediate inspiration for the other, the use of this individual heraldry in fields of meaning traditionally commanded by the familial coat of arms helps to define succinctly the cultural ambivalences we will also find registered in the literary signature.

In chivalric warfare, "banners and pennons bore hereditary coats of arms, [while] standards and ensigns displayed personal badges, *devises* and mottoes," and during the later middle ages there was an increasing tendency to substitute the latter for the former in battle.[17] Several practical circumstances of military technology and organization may be cited to account for this change: the redundancy of the shield that bore the coat of arms after the advent of plate armor; the clarity and ease of identifying in the heat of action a simple badge, such as the cockleshell or barbican, in contrast to the increasing difficulty of making recognizable and accurate representations by the complicated—and difficult to document—quarterings of the noble family; the increase in the use of professional soldiers and standing armies along with hereditary nobility and shorter-term occasional warfare; and perhaps a concomitant wish by the crown to signify that its military enterprises rewarded talent and personal loyalty.[18] The devices chosen, originally the personal "arms of

16. Daniel Poirion, *Le Poète et le Prince* (Paris: Presses Universitaires de France, 1965), 59–67.

17. Malcolm Vale, *War and Chivalry: Warfare and Aristocratic Culture in England, France and Burgundy at the End of the Middle Ages* (London: Duckworth, 1981), 97.

18. On these developments, see Vale, *War and Chivalry*, 95–99, 105, 110, 114, and 147–151; Philippe Contamine, *Guerre, Etat et Société à la fin du Moyen Age: Etudes sur les Armées des Rois de France, 1337–1494* (Paris and The Hague: Mouton, 1972), 675–76.

peace" used in the tournament, manifest, as Vale and many others have noted, "the contemporary taste for allegory"—or, as I should prefer to call it, self-personification.[19] To adopt such an autodefinition was "to choose a text for the sermon of one's life." As an elective sign of the self, the device "rassemble les actions éparses dans la continuité d'une intention première": one's presence on the field of action is proclaimed by such a symbol to be a life with a unitary design, a story for which one has chosen the theme and the genre, and which as an exemplary paradigm serves to unite others around it.[20] These "devices" were brought into currency in England during Langland's lifetime under the very highest sponsorship: the Garter, badge of the order founded by Edward III, and later the White Hart of Richard II both illustrate the implicit and compacted ideal narrations around which these symbols organized allegiance—stories of the transformation of private or occulted referents into public totems of presence and intention.[21]

19. Vale, p. 97. As both Vale and Poirion observe, the device chosen, as illustrated in the Italian *impresa,* which derives from this personal chivalric badge, frequently involved nominal wordplay, whether visual, as in a rebus, or the verbal duplicity of a pun or a common noun enclosed within the proper name; frequently these compacted devices alluded cryptically to a renowned incident or theme in its bearer's life—an event or sentiment as often amatory as martial. The badge thus devised made an event known to familiars the sign of the knight's public identity, while its cryptic form continued to differentiate the knight's "friends," who would know the story of the badge, from those to whom it was simply the sign of the knight and those of his livery. The device thus simultaneously proclaimed and occulted identity, evoking in effect two different levels or arts of reading: one peculiar to the bearer's adherents, the other defining the common beholder as outside the circle of privileged interpretation.

The distinction between the arms of war and the arms of peace is set out with particular clarity in the will of the Black Prince; see F. H. Cripps-Day, *A History of the Tournament in England and France* (London, B. Quaritch 1918), 63; Vale, *War and Chivalry,* 90, 97.

20. This formulation is Poirion's (63). As Vale notes, "when badges of the kind worn in the tournament were adopted in warfare, the distinction between 'arms of peace' and 'arms of war' lapsed" (98). In other words, when the "affective theme" compacted in the personal badge adopted for purposes of exercise and ceremonial differentiation also supplants the familial coat of arms as the "published text" of the knight's identity in battle, an idealized life-story, cryptically encoded in the device, replaces lineage as the primary referent of the knight's self-identification at war, and his followers are now implicitly defined not necessarily as hereditary adherents of his family, but as those who know and adopt as their own what the device represents. They are the fit readers of the published story of his identity.

21. The familiar story of the foundation of the Order of the Garter, explicating its motto *honi soit qui mal y pense* (may the shame be his who thinks evil of it), explains how this intimate object came to be elevated by royal fiat from a token suggesting private duplicity and compromised sexual honor to a publishable collective symbol of loyalty and honor. Although this explanatory anecdote is first related in the sixteenth century by Polydore Vergil, scholars have recently argued for its authenticity; see A. G. Rigg, "John

It is not as a possible source of the practice but for their similar mode of signifying that the personal devices of late medieval heraldry offer a suggestive parallel to the methods and contextual meaning of late medieval literary signature. Like these, the anatomized and inwoven name of the author becomes, within the literary situation in which it is displayed, the title or rubric of a life-as-designed, the sign under which the "menyng" (intent) of the work is declared and made coextensive with the "intente" of the author realized in the purposive and exemplary patterns of a compactly represented life. It is under this modal sign that those who see it are asked in turn to represent themselves— to interpret their actions, and to offer them for interpretation. The "given" name of the author is within the work reinvented as if *chosen* (or perhaps as if it had chosen him), and his civil or public identity— what Langland will call his "kynde name"—is made to function as a sort of diacritical marker of the narrative of which he is the subject, an artificial memory device operating systematically rather than discretely in "pointing" the text and anchoring its ethical legibility and its social designs upon those who read it.[22] As the signature techniques Langland uses undergo development in revision from relatively open to more indirect forms, they also acquire systematic relations with each other in disclosing the narrative principles of the work. In this development the surname—foregrounded as a subject of wordplay in A but given realized signatory status in B—is pivotal, permitting the civil circumstances of the authorial project as well as the poetic subject's spiritual identity to be assimilated to literary form, to become narratable;

---

of Bridlington's *Prophecy: a New Look*," *Speculum* 63 (1988): 601; and Margaret Galway, "Joan of Kent and the Order of the Garter," *University of Birmingham Historical Journal* 1–2 (1947–50): 13–50. Implicit in this story is a radically "nominalistic" notion of the power of such an adopted symbol: the badge is *by design* unintelligible to anyone who does not already know the anecdote of its establishment. The emblematic object has been shifted from its socially customary legibility and transplanted, "raised," into another sphere of meaning by a process that does not so much presuppose as confect a new bond of social knowledge and intimacy. Authorial signatures likewise play with this confection of intimacy with the poet, and likewise underscore the interpreter's share, as an initiated reader, in completing their meaning.

22. For the term "pointing," see J. A. Burrow, *Ricardian Poetry* (New Haven: Yale University Press, 1971), 69–78. Possibly adopted from the vocabulary of the physical presentation and ornamentation of a manuscript text, and denoting as well the rhetorical elaboration of a discourse, the verb "point" in fourteenth-century English seems to have meant, as Burrow analyzes its use, not only "to describe in detail" but to indicate thereby a virtual *scale* of narration, the proprieties of ornamentation and amplitude.

and it is to this move, intimately tied to the formal choices that enabled the B-C continuation, that I now turn.

## FORMS AND METHODS OF
## LITERARY SIGNATURE

Langland's internal self-naming takes two main forms, both widely used in contemporary French and English writings. The first, the "open" or referential method, requires little discussion—and causes little interpretive controversy; it is familiar in the writings of Chaucer and Gower as well as Langland. By this device, especially frequent in dream-visions, persons in the fiction simply address or refer to the first-person narrator or dreamer by name, or the subject introduces himself (examples from the poem are A-3, C-1, and C-3; see the appendix). Generally this open referential form is used by Langland to display the baptismal name of Will alone, but it also aids in the recognition of more indirect forms of signature, such as the famous anagram of the surname in Will's speech to Anima, the creature of many names, retrospectively summarizing his quest thus far: "I have lyued in londe . . . my name is longe wille" (B.15.152, B-3 in the appendix).

While open referential self-naming may be accompanied by further deictic marking, more indirect forms virtually require it, and for this purpose there are several kinds of local signals that an authorial name is to be read in the discourse. Among the more patent devices, illustrated in the example cited, are the depiction in the narrated events of social or ceremonial occasions (the formal introduction of a new character on the scene to other persons present, formal confession, or juridical testimony) or textual forms (such as the last will and testament) that require explicit self-naming for their execution as gestures. In these performative moments the subject's intent is rendered "for the record," and the representation of these acts in narrative thus calls attention to the constitutive and stabilizing power socially attributed to written documents as such. A more subtle and mobile device, exploited by Chaucer as well as more exhaustively by Langland, is locally intensified allusion to the first-person's physical characteristics or social circumstances. Jokes about bodily stature and habit (Chaucer's doll-like "shap" or "noyous" weight, Langland's tall leanness and "long clothes") are not simply descriptive specifications, for verisimilitude or "authentication," but invariably in both poets' work coincide with—and, in effect, announce—complex and very often "signed" accounts of the poetics of the work. The presence of self-references to physical characteristics, like that of the signatures to which they usually point, calls redoubled attention to the author's modal contract with the user of the text, and evokes as part of that contract both reader's and writer's embodiment in a specific sociohistorical situation. We shall find Langland using such moments of bodily self-awareness and occulted signature to translate writerly into readerly self-consciousness.

At the opposite end of the spectrum from these explicit, and explicitly pointed, open forms of signature are the wittier and more occulted devices based on anagrammatic methods, in which wordplay upon the name is made by an anatomy of its parts.[23] It is the "occulted" technique of anagram, Langland's second main signature method and the basis for his system of cross-referencing signature mnemonics in the B and C versions of the poem, that will require our closer attention—as indeed the device itself demands a peculiar kind of self-conscious attention to be legible, as well as a sustaining repertory of accompanying

23. I borrow the term "occultation" from a highly self-conscious and mannered textual interpreter, almost an exact contemporary of Langland, John Ergome or Erghome, who wrote, some time between 1364 and 1373, an extensive Latin commentary on the so-called Bridlington Prophecies—and may have written the prophecies themselves as well; see Michael J. Curley, "The Cloak of Anonymity and the *Prophecy of John of Bridlington*," *Modern Philology* 77 (1980): 361–69, who presents the arguments for and against Ergome's authorship of the prophecies; and Rigg, "John of Bridlington's *Prophecy*," 596–613, who argues against the attribution. Ergome introduces his work with a commendation of his endeavors to Duke Humphrey de Bohun, in which he encodes "against envious detraction" his own name in an elaborate riddle, one of the most complicated signatures I have found in this period: "si super consequentiae notam caput miserationis vellitis adjungere, nomen obscurum et obsequium salutare"; it was M. R. James who unlocked the syllables of Ergome's name in it: "The Catalogue of the Library of the Augustinian Friars at York, now first edited . . . ," in *Fasciculus J. W. Clark dicatus* (Cambridge, Eng.: Cambridge University Press, 1909), 11.

Following this introduction, Ergome provides three prologues to the commentary, each in a different mode. The first is a highly ramified example of the "four-cause" scholastic prologue, the third a summary of its *forma tractatus;* see A. J. Minnis, *Medieval Theory of Authorship* (London: Scholar Press, 1984), 161, 168. The second, however, expounds, with examples from the text, the ten "methods of occultation" used in the prophecies to represent names, dates, and historical events. Among these are the representation of noble persons by their cognomens or heraldic badges, bilingual anagrams of the syllables of names, and the representation of numbers in the letters of Latin words used as common nouns (e.g., cuculi = ccli, 251). It therefore seems appropriate to collect under the term "occulted" all those signature methods that involve some rearrangement or reconstruction of the discourse in order to yield a name. It is also worth noting that for Ergome, anagrams, number codes and heraldic cognomens were classified together as forms of secret or initiate's language.

conventions, some of them requiring social as well as textual skills for recognition.

Anagrammatic naming, whether or not it functions as signature, bases not only its wit but its very legibility on the reader's consciousness of using partly extratextual knowledge to decode it. Here Chaucer offers an efficient example of how the device works, though not in a signatory function. In the tragedy of King Peter of Cyprus in the *Monk's Tale*, we learn that "the *wikked nest* was werker of this nede"; we could only recognize the name of Oliver de Mauny (OF *"mau ni"*)—to say nothing of the agency of Bertrand du Guesclin, referred to only by his coat of arms as "the feeld of snow, with th'egle of blak therinne"—if we already knew, as those in John of Gaunt's circle would have known, the names of the key players in this recent example of Fortune's treachery.[24] This example also illustrates the self-referential, almost self-congratulatory, air that accompanies an act of anagrammatic understanding. An anagrammatic signature turns the reader's attention back upon itself, so that he is forced not only to acknowledge the dimension of social presence and extratextual competence involved in his recognition of the name but also to delight in the several simultaneous kinds of specifically "readerly" mental acrobatics it demands.

Unlike open referential signatures, those made by occultation require the reader to reassemble the proper name dispersed among the common terms of the poem ("I have lyued in londe . . . my name is longe wille" [B.15.152]). Their power to disclose a name not only resides in but calls attention to the beholder's share, as they displace his attention momentarily from the referential to the formal aspect of words. Occulted signatures induce in the reader a momentary high awareness of his operative arts of reading, a perception that is the counterpart of the bodily self-consciousness that both heralds authorial self-reference and supports its use in indicating an operative poetics. By foregrounding for an instant the textual medium itself, forcing one to notice not only the arts of making and reading such disclosures but also the shared social space and physical circumstances within which that art is exer-

---

24. *Canterbury Tales* VII, 2386 and 2383, in *The Works of Geoffrey Chaucer*, ed. F. N. Robinson, 2nd. ed. (Boston: Houghton Mifflin, 1957). See Vale on the armorial display and chivalric rituals observed at the memorial requiem for Bertrand du Guesclin in the abbey church of St. Denis on 7 May 1389, several years after his death (92).

cised, they insist on the embodied social dimension of literary processes.

Syllabic anagram, Langland's second main signature device, shares with his first, simple vocative naming, the property of audibility: we can hear as well as see on the page the name, distributed into separate monosyllabic words rather than as a whole. In this respect anagrammatic naming differs from that other occulted form of signature widely used in the late Middle Ages, the acrostic, which anatomizes and redistributes the name by letters rather than by syllables. Though made on the same dispersive principles, the two signature forms are differently legible, and define and regulate quite different interpretive premises, as they also presume different social means of perpetuation—differences that are crucial for understanding Langland's choice of signature techniques and their social significance.

The acrostic signature, depending for its legibility largely on the physical layout of the page and book, rules the order of the parts in which it appears, and it can only be seen, not heard.[25] It implies, therefore, not only an authorial commitment to spatial and architectonic form, but access to and confidence in stable scribal institutions for its transmission. It foregrounds and celebrates the "writtenness" of writing: in the acrostic the author becomes entirely and literally a man *of letters*. But if the acrostic is an efficient little Derridean postulate, unambivalently proclaiming the absence of the author, the anagrammatic signature pointedly raises and repeatedly worries the possibility of authorial presence in the work. It implicitly argues the nonautonomy and non-self-evident character of texts, and proclaims the perpetual inseparability of the author's life from that which he makes, and from which in some sense he does not—and can not—ever wholly withdraw his sustaining voice. Anagrammatic naming implies that "menyng" is al-

25. The order of parts in Thomas Usk's *Testament of Love,* which survives only in a somewhat garbled early printing, could be reconstructed when it was discovered that the head letters of its sections spelled out an acrostic, *margaret of vertw haue mercy on thin usk;* see the edition of this work in *The Complete Works of Chaucer,* ed. W. W. Skeat, vol. 7 (Oxford: Clarendon Press, 1897). Robert of Basevorn's *Forma Praedicandi* is likewise articulated by sections whose head letters spell his name; see Th.-M. Charland, *Artes Praedicandi: Contribution a l'Histoire de la Rhétorique au Moyen Age* (Paris: J. Vrin, 1936), 81. Nicholas Trivet, in his *Annales,* distributes an anagrammatic signature over fifty-six quarto leaves in the section head letters; see Nicholai Triveti, *Annales,* ed. Thomas Hog (London: English Historical Society, 1845), xvii. (I owe this reference to Michael J. Curley.)

ways's *someone's* meaning; it resides in, and represents, persons and their "intentes."[26]

Here Erik Kooper's typology of signatures, making a systematic analogy between the forms used in painting and literature, is useful. Though he does not make this specific argument for his analogy, he sees the acrostic as the literary equivalent of the included self-portrait of the painter: each foregrounds and celebrates as such the dominant and basic representative unit of its respective medium—the alphabet, the painted image—the artifice that represents the hand of the artificer. The anagrammatic signature, however, is the literary equivalent of the rebus, or visual pun, and like it, doubles and foregrounds the number and complexity of the acts required for its decoding. The rebus represents a thing, a physical object, whose common name is the same as, or sounds like, the proper name of the painter: Kooper gives the example of Lorenzo Lotto's signature, in the form of an object called a *lotto* held by one of the represented persons in the painting. The anagrammatic signature likewise demands that we notice the several acts of translation between representative modes that are required to read the "proper" name in common objects.

The wit of the anagrammatic signature thus derives from the perpetual double life of the text, its claim to represent the spoken and audible voice of someone's "menyng" as well as visible signs representing the meaning of things. In this way—whether or not the text is in practice ever actually voiced—it tends to problematize rather than celebrate the written as a means of stabilizing communicative authority. Broken into syllables that are also intelligible as words in themselves, the anagrammatized name acquired a double reference, becoming both common and proper at once. Yet its second reference—its signatory aspect—must be called into play either by deictic markers drawing attention to its status as a name (as in the third signature of the B version, " 'I have lyued in londe,' quod I, 'my name is longe wille' ") or by *some-*

26. If, as I have argued elsewhere, the ultimate ground of signification is conceived by Langland to be transcendent—divine "menyng"—it is nevertheless imagined as sustained by a deity understood in terms of magnified personhood and intentionality, a God from whom emanates not merely the mathematical harmony of the cosmos, but the chief language of mediation between the divine and human, that of historical process, through which intentionality as well as abstract design may most reliably be grasped as "read" and "heard." See "Two Infinites: Grammatical Metaphor in *Piers Plowman*," *ELH* 39 (1972): 169–88.

*thing already known* and brought into play extratextually. For example, in order to understand the Lond of Longyng as an anagrammatic signature (as I shall argue it is), we must already know by other means that the author's surname is Langland, although in this case, as we shall see, the means have been made available to us more openly elsewhere in the text.

Both forms of audible signature used by Langland—his open vocative naming and the anagram of his surname—are made so as to seem to complement and interact with what the interpreter presumably knows of the author by social means, whether direct acquaintance or reputation: his stature, his apparently clerical habit, and his habits of delay and evasion. In this respect their effect is much like the open self-naming and comic self-reference of Chaucer to his rotund "shap" and bookishness. If the solitary reader happens to lack social intimacy with the writer, these devices nevertheless confect it as one of the operative fictions of the work. Because unlike acrostics, anagrammatic signatures *appear* to derive their legibility from a stable *social* rather than scribal medium, one normally expects to find them in writers who in fact have a fairly secure and enduring institutional base of operations and are known by name and literary reputation over a considerable period of time to their primary audience—particularly court or coterie poets. Though this is widely assumed to have been Chaucer's actual situation, it suggests that the question of Langland's immediate circle and his following may require considerable reexamination.

Whatever their implications about his relation to an actual primary audience, however, Langland's signature methods also have fundamental consequences for literary mode. They encourage the reader's sense that the author's social, vocal, and even physical presence is also somehow "in" the text, that the words on the page represent a person as well as his product, and that it is his coherence as intelligible actor and the paradigmatic and exemplary form of his life, rather than the formal properties of the work as artifact, that secure its value to the user. They define a problematic of bodily presence and biographical integrity into the act of reading and specify the boundaries of meaning within which signatures are articulated as the literary career, the life-in-writing, not the single work.

It is this larger, if largely implicit, poetic argument that supports the use of reference to the "maker's" bodily shape, a device heavily exploited by Langland and one of the commonest "pointing" conventions to highlight either kind of audible signature. Signalling the presence of the anagrammatized name, it invites the reader to reconstruct the proper, to reassemble the dispersed body of the author, like Osiris, from its syllabically distributed common parts, exactly as the red and blue letters used by the scribe help the reader pick out visually the alphabetically distributed acrostic signature. Stout "Geffrey" as well as "longe wille" uses this pointer repeatedly. The author "points to" his person—as Chaucer literally does in the famous Harvard portrait panel—as an image of "myn intente," using the same gesture with which in the Ellesmere marginal portrait he points to his text, and thereby makes a functional equivalence between them.[27] The ultimate referent of the written text, these gestures imply, is the life lived, and the specific finite body becomes the guarantor of the general truth of the discourse. Langland's work declares its own integrity of form through the systematic interrelations of its several signatures that punctuate the text, marking out milestones in a trajectory of reading as well as living, rendering the name and person of the author as a periodically recurring *common place* for reflection on what lies "before and behind." "Pointing" his work with his own name and presence—his social and legal and physical as well as his spiritual history—Langland's signatures function as an artificial memory device, giving his life-work the usable form of a life remembered.

## FROM SIGNATURE TO SIGNATURE-SYSTEM: THE A VERSION

As the poem stood in the A version, probably at the end of the 1360s, Langland's signature practices were much like those of Chaucer in the *Hous of Fame:* openly referential, and largely discrete, using the baptismal name alone in close proximity to "pointing" remarks about the dreamer-author's distinctive physical characteristics and social habits. Yet even the A text displays some of the elements of cumulative and

27. See Donald Howard, *The Idea of the Canterbury Tales* (Berkeley and Los Angeles: University of California Press, 1976), 13–15, on the Ellesmere and "Hoccleve" portraits of Chaucer; for the "Harvard" portrait, see the frontispiece to *The Works of Geoffrey Chaucer,* ed. Robinson. David F. Hult reproduces a similar portrait of the author of the *Roman de la Rose* gesturing toward himself with one hand, like Chaucer in the "Harvard" portrait, while with the other he points to the book that lies before him on his writing desk; see *Self-Fulfilling Prophecies,* fig. 5, p. 83.

cross-referential use of signature that will mark out the main narrative movements of the two longer versions. As Langland begins to develop his signature-system at this first surviving stage of composition, signatures that would be immediately apparent as such to readers with social access to the living author—such as the simple ones of A-1 and A-2 naming Will in the third person—are unlocked in retrospect for readers who lack such supplementary knowledge. Signatures such as the third instance in the A version (A-3) not only seal the identification of Will with the author but force the reader to reintegrate the merely iterative and episodic into a new composite picture.

The sequence of three signatures in the A version illustrates this cumulative process and serves as a base for the development of the more complex identifications of B and C. Will, who is named initially in A as the first penitent to weep at Repentaunce's sermon (A-1) and then as a writer (copyist) rewarded by merchants for "copying their clause" in the pardon (A-2), is finally identified as the dreamer, "I," who narrates the poem, as he adds to his roles that of a philosophical seeker (A-3). This cumulative identification process will be repeated and expanded in the B and C signature-systems, making more and more of the extratextual knowledge needed to identify a signature in A explicit in the text in B and accessible as operative knowledge at an even earlier point in the narrative sequence in C. The third of the three signatures in the A version (A-3 in the appendix) signals the presence and mode of utility of the name in several ways at once, and the passage therefore provides a little anthology of Langland's basic signature techniques and the "pointers" he uses to indicate them. The details and methods of self-identification in this passage will provide the basic repertory of signatory devices and notations of Will's "character" upon which the signature-system of the two long versions is built. The scene also illustrates the way moments of signature become moments of poetic reflexivity, disclosures of the literary mode and claims to "truth" that the poet proposes for his work.

In this passage, Langland uses multiple "pointers" to draw attention to the presence of the authorial name. Thought is said to address the dreamer by his "kynde name," and as if to underscore the point, the dreamer notes his surprise that this new figure knows his name (A.9.62–63). But that name is not actually given in the text until fifty lines later, when Thought finally and formally introduces Will to his next instructor, Wit (A.9.118). This entire encounter with Thought is, however, permeated with further insistence upon the individuating physical and social characteristics that are to remain constant features of authorial signature and self-presentation in the two later versions. To the dreamer's first glimpse, Thought appears "a muchel man . . . lik to myselue"; Wit, who succeeds him—despite Will's remark that he looks nothing like anybody we know ("lyk to non oþer," [A.9.110])—is also conspicuously "long and lene." What might at first appear to be figurative attributes of these instructors are turned as well to a witty notation of relationship and resemblance: whatever Thought's and Wit's intrinsic capacities as faculties, the reader may at this signal justifiably begin to suspect that they resemble Will too much to do him any good. The specific condition of the subject of this pedagogical progress—inscribed in a characteristic bodily form that hereafter becomes a ground of both recognition and apology—thus becomes a constant point of reference for narrative logic, and a measure of instructive adequacy.

This third signature of A, however, also uses the rarefied and elaborate wit of some of its more recondite "pointers" to indicate the register in which further signatures are to be recognized, and how they are to be used, in subsequent versions of the poem. The implicit academic setting of this formal introduction and "dispute" binds Will's identity, and his artful techniques of self-disclosure, to precisely those aspirations to privileged clerical discourse that are to be contested throughout the subsequent narrative development of all versions. This scene exacts from the reader, and from the narrative subject Will, the capacity to pursue elaborate wordplay, and rewards those who have an eye for the apposite wit of cited scriptural texts. The third signature of A thereby acquires some of the diacritical force that the signatures in concert will have in the long versions: it indicates the kind of reading the work will demand, and signals that such reading is a particular kind of cultural work, with specific—and contested—claims to authority.

The wordplay that interweaves the activities as well as the names of Will and Wit, that traditional alliterating pair in moral discourse (A.9.117–18), and the fact that this formal handing-over follows three days of disputation (A.9.107–8), momentarily places this figurative event within a social scene identifiable at the literal level as one of the solemn rituals of a public university occasion. It recalls the *commendatio,* the formal speech of introduction by which the regent master presented the *inceptor,* the candidate in theology who had already engaged in the three days of disputation that culminated his proof of himself as beginner or *incipiens,* to the chancellor. This customary interlude of academic wit often involved puns on the candidate's name or identifying characteristics, and also might take as its theme a scriptural text that was used as a topic in the disputation.[28] In this instance the nearest antecedent scriptural text is the one just cited by Thought, at the beginning of his three-day "disputation" with Will. There he had defined Dobet as one willing not only to practice virtue but to teach it, and cited in support of this moral imperative—apparently without irony— St. Paul's ironic remonstrance with the wisdom-loving Corinthians: "libenter suffertis insipientes cum sitis sapientes" (willingly you suffer fools, since you yourselves are wise, 2 Cor. 11:19). Its appropriateness here is enhanced by the latent wordplay provisionally linking fools (*insipientes*) with beginners or those possessing only elementary mastery in a discipline (*incipientes*). By the B stage of composition, precisely this wordplay has already been marked as pivotal in an earlier episode: it occurs in B's Pardon scene, which like this one turns on the issue of whether the seeker in question is an earnest and obedient apprentice to the authoritative *magisterium* or a presumptuous fool.[29] The lines surrounding Thought's introduction thus not only foreground Will's name as signature, but compactly establish the represented maker of this poem as an aspirant to a specifically clerical and learned legitimacy. This atmosphere of erudite contention permeates narrative development for several subsequent passus, and culminates in the learned riddles at the Banquet of Clergy.[30] The identity of the author and the character of his literary project are thus at once both disclosed and oc-

---

28. Amid the long and arduous trial of wit and learning that was the formal university examination, this one moment was traditionally devoted to the ritual display of intellectual play; see James Weisheipl, "The Curriculum of the Faculty of Arts at Oxford in the Early Fourteenth Century," *Mediæval Studies* 26 (1964): 164; A. G. Little and F. Pelster, *Oxford Theology and Theologians, ca. 1282–1302* (Oxford: Clarendon Press, 1934), 45–47.

29. The priest who challenges Piers over the Pardon in the B version invokes a similar play on these two words, insultingly suggesting that the plowman, who to his surprise is "lettrid a litel," having learned his ABCs from "Abstynence þe Abbesse," might well "preche . . . as diuinour in diuinite, wiþ *dixit insipiens* to þi teme" (Ps. 13:1; B.7.140–41); the text he suggests at the corresponding point in the A version is "Quoniam literaturam non cognoui" (Ps. 70:15). As Judson Allen has shown, Langland would have found both texts discussed together in Hugh of St. Cher's Psalter commentary: "Langland's Reading and Writing," 356.

30. See my essays, "Two Infinites," and "The Passion of Seint Averoys [B.13.91]: 'Deuynyng' and Divinity in the Banquet Scene," *Yearbook of Langland Studies* 1 (1987): 31–40.

culted: hereafter Will's name and his poetic enterprise claim the privileged company of texts whose intricacies of verbal art both provoke and reward the reader's full powers of reflection and interpretation. At this last signatory moment of the A text, Langland attaches his vernacular enterprise firmly to the culture and company of high-literate speculation and indicates the arts of reading that will be required to use it well.

It is already evident in the A version, then, that acts of authorial self-naming have more than an occasional function as momentary evocations of actual or fictive social intimacy with an audience. Their self-reflexive and diacritical importance in the narrative is intensified in the B and C revisions, while their dependence for legibility as signatures on extratextual knowledge of the poet's person is gradually diminished. If in the A-text scene we have just examined these notations of Will's bodily "shap" functioned for their primary audience as no more than throwaway moments of self-reference, designed initially for the amusement of those of Langland's contemporary readers who knew him by sight—much like the Eagle's disparagement of "Geffrey's" unsuitable weight for visionary air travel in the *Hous of Fame*—such lines would nevertheless not have been lost on a reader of the C text who lacked direct or indirect social familiarity with the author. By this point in the C narrative the reader would not only identify Will as the name of the dreamer and maker (he is named both at C.1.5 and earlier in the C version of the present episode; see C.10.71, replacing A.9.64), but recognize in Wit Will's own distinctive stature, already specified as "longe" (C.5.23–24). A reader of C would also have been taught by the form of these signature events to associate something else with moments of self-naming and self-reference: in the revised and expanded versions of the poem, they are staged with increasing fullness both to evoke excuses and *apologiae* of the subject's insufficiency, and to exact from him a broad reexamination of his position—in his quest, in his allotted time on earth, and in the trajectory of the work that is the poem.

As moments of signature are in revision linked by these additional common features as events, and begin to refer to each other, they declare their diacritical force with increasing clarity in each of the two long versions. The effect of these changes, from moments of signature to a signature-system, is to convert the increasingly expendable fiction of social intimacy with the author into a broader kind of enabling knowledge and textual competence as the ground of the "truth" of the work. The signatures of the B and C versions are disposed through the work not only (as in A-3) sporadically to foreground the poetic and intellectual aspirations of Langland's project, but systematically to mark and display the critical points of genesis and transformation of that project, realized as a succession of critical turning points in the author's life. The moments of signature become narratively pivotal events that render biographical and poetic self-awareness synonymous.

Access to the "truth" of the poem (that is, its binding formal principle as well as its objective) is thus realized narratively, not as vertical ascent in an epistemological or eschatological order but in the literary form of a chronicle of a life remembered, disclosing its immanent design in moments of subjective crisis, each of which is marked by signature. For the reader, the activity of recognizing the author's name is thus gradually set in parallel with the endeavor of following a sustained narration; to those who apprehend the applied ethical and subjective importance of the difficult and abstract questions broached by the poem's discursive wanderings—and to them alone—will Langland disclose and explain himself. That is, *only to someone capable of reading the poem as a narrative with an immanent design*—and not simply, as Robert Crowley evidently considered it, a collection of "goodly allegories" or local figurative amplifications of scriptural themes—*will the signatures be systematically legible as such at all.*[31] It is a critical commonplace that the poem represents the mode of access to truth as applied, ethical, and grounded in subjective experience. What the disposition of the authorial name in his poem discloses, however, is Langland's progressively deeper understanding and more fully conscious acceptance—comparable to that of Augustine—of both the literary and social consequences of developing a philosophic and spiritual quest in the narrative form of an apparently historically specific life-story.

## THE SIGNATURE SYSTEM OF THE
## B AND C VERSIONS

### NAMING AND NARRATIVE CRISIS

It is only with the B version that the surname is introduced into the signature system, and only at this stage, therefore, that Langland begins

---

31. For an argument that it is this kind of reading that was largely lost soon after 1400, see my essay "The Audience and Public of *Piers Plowman*," 119–20.

to exploit anagrammatic methods: a syllabic anagram requires more than the monosyllable Will to exist. An extreme skeptic might even wish to argue that only here do signatures as such first appear at all: that all occurrences of the baptismal name Will alone denote only the common noun, the faculty, personified in the dreamer, and not a proper name, and hence need not be regarded as references to the author. Such a view offers, as I believe the foregoing analysis of A shows, a less thrifty account of such passages as A-3 than one that acknowledges the additional presence of signatory force. This objection, however, will always have slightly more plausibility than those against the anagrammatized full name of the third B signature (appendix B-3). The case for Langland's signature-system as a whole has traditionally rested heavily on this line.

In B, as in A, three signatures have been identified, two of them survivals from A: the first and last of A's three are retained, while A's second, in which Will as a copyist is rewarded by the merchants, is rewritten so that the merchants' gratitude is now directed to Piers, "þat purchaced þis bulle." The keystone for all demonstration that the poem contains an authorial signature in any form is therefore the third instance in B, the anagram of Will Langland in "'I haue lyued in londe,' quod I, 'my name is longe wille.'" Despite Manly's dissent, and what appears to be skepticism in John Norton-Smith's recent observation that the line "hints at an English equivalent for the Latin noun *longanimitas, longanima*, 'long-sufferance'", there has been no convincing account of this line that succeeds in explaining away its signatory function—although as we have already seen, that function need not exclude (and in this poem often conspicuously and efficiently includes) other figurative significances.[32] Like the third signature of A (now the second in B), this one collects and secures those that precede it: Will's long leanness, twice evoked in the A passage we have examined, is now elevated from a visible to a verbal distinction, no longer a bodily trait but a cognomen.

The identification of full-name signature in the two long versions of the poem does not, however, depend on this line alone. The keystone of the signature system lies earlier in the narrative, so securely embedded in the sequence of events that it is beyond removal by the alteration

---

32. John Norton-Smith, *William Langland* (Leiden: E. J. Brill, 1983), 89. See also note 5 above.

of any single line in C. Langland's first explicit anagrammatic signature in the B expansion of the poem is in fact the Lond of Longyng—the name of the site of the first episode of the B continuation. Just as it is from this vantage point of suddenly unmasked desire that Will is forced to look both "before and behind" at the course of his quest, it is the name of this visionary place—a semantic field already present but lying dormant in A—that anchors both antecedent and subsequent instances of authorial self-naming.

It has never to my knowledge been noticed that the Lond of Longyng is an authorial signature, and on its face the suggestion may seem far-fetched, although we have already met several far more arcane contemporary instances of occulted naming, and more could be adduced. The proof of such a claim, however—to the extent that matters of interpretation lend themselves to proof—lies not in the citation of other poets' similar practices, but in the quality of the readings of this poem that such a hypothesis enables. Regarding the Lond of Longyng as a pivotal signature, the most deeply inscribed in a system of signatures first fully articulated in the B version, renders visible large principles of narrative structure and authorial "foreconceit" that are among the most rarely glimpsed features of Langland's sprawling poetic production. As a signature, the Lond of Longyng invites us to take our bearings in the allegorical narrative from Will's position, a position that is realized as historically concrete as well as figurative: such mnemonic narrative marking is, I shall argue, precisely the purpose of the signature-system. In order to demonstrate both the genesis and the literary function of the Lond of Longyng as signature, a place of absolute authorial as well as spiritual self-confrontation and self-revelation, we too must scan the narrative path leading toward and away from it from "before and behind."

We may take our first sighting from the uncontested later anagrammatic signature in B, "I haue lyued in londe . . . my name is longe wille." At the moment when the dreamer identifies himself as "longe wille" who has "lyued in londe" he is speaking to a new instructor. Ordinarily called Anima in the B text, and transformed into Liberum Arbitrium in C, this creature has introduced himself by explaining that he has many names, depending on his several functions in the soul. The topic of discussion thus momentarily foregrounds the proprieties of naming, and sets up an occasion for Will to offer his own in return as a sign of his "menyng," just as his instructor has explained his capacities by glossing his name. Before introducing himself with this conspicuous, and conspicuously pointed, anagram, however, Will becomes diverted by the sheer rhetorical intricacy of Anima's gloss, eagerly seeking to know "the cause of all hire names." For this characteristic deflection of his desire for self-knowledge into curiosity for "science" he draws Anima's swift rebuke as "oon of prides knyʒtes." This deferral of Will's answering self-presentation gives an added function to that disclosure: when Will finally introduces himself, he is not merely declaring but defending his enterprise. The moment thus takes its place in a succession of such humiliations and new beginnings that are regularly "pointed" with his signature.

The texts of St. Bernard that Anima adduces to support his rebuke designate the thematic terms and the kind of narrative incident within which Will's identity is disclosed to himself as well as the reader repeatedly throughout the poem. *Beatus est qui scripturas legit et verba vertit in opera* (blessed is he who reads the scriptures and turns their words to works) and *Sciencie appetitus hominem inmortalitatis gloriam spoliavit* (the appetite for knowledge has robbed man of the glory of immortality) recall the contraposition of words and works that anchor Will's pivotal formal function in the narrative and embed them in its verse language.[33] They also call up in the reader's memory several earlier occasions of reversal, framed in like terms: Will's ambitious ransacking of the world for intricate answers to increasingly subdivided questions is repeatedly disrupted and transformed by encounters that humiliate this ambition. On such occasions, Will's illusory progress through the world of knowledge is deflected inward, toward a strenuous confrontation of the self and its motives. By this point in the poem this recurrent oscillation between ambition and shame has become the governing pattern of narrative development: each humiliation of Will's striving

---

33. The sources of these two texts are, respectively, Bernard's *Tractatus de Ordine Vitae* (*Patrologia Latina* 184:566), based on Matt. 7:24, and *Sermo IV in Ascensione Domini* (*Patrologia Latina* 183.311); the latter is incorporated by Hugh of St. Cher in his commentary on Ephesians 4:9–10 (*Post. in Univ. Bbl.* vol. 7, fol. 174ᵛ): see John Alford, "Some Unidentified Quotations in *Piers Plowman*," *Modern Philology* 72 (1975): 396, 397. On the importance of this alliterating triad of terms in linking thematic and self-referential authorial disclosures, see John A. Burrow, "Words, Works, and Will: Theme and Structure in *Piers Plowman*," in *Piers Plowman: Critical Approaches,* ed. S. S. Hussey (London: Methuen, 1969), 111–24.

shatters the preceding line of narrative figuration and in turn becomes the site of a new one.[34] It is these restorative ruptures that are the locus of authorial signatures. We have examined one such moment of self-reflexivity in Will's A encounter with Thought and Wit. Anima's rebuke in B—the one that evokes Will's anagram of his name—most vividly recalls, however, an earlier one by Dame Scripture, *multi multa sciunt et seipsos nesciunt* (many know many things, but know not themselves, B.11.3), the humiliation that had sent him in despair into the Lond of Longyng. By looking forward in the poem from this moment, we also begin to apprehend what is at stake in looking backward, and to grasp the terms of their equivalence.

Conceding to Anima that what he really seeks is not many things (the nice distinctions of the soul's many names) but only one, charity, Will's contrite return to a project of self-understanding marks the penultimate turning point in the poem. It initiates the long and sublime narrative sequence, the most sustained of the entire poem, that culminates in the narrator's vision of Christ's victory at the Crucifixion. With a fine and characteristic irony, that scene of redemption is realized in precisely the two dramatized forms that Will here indicates to Anima that he least expects: as both "champions fight" and "chaffare" (exchange, B.15.164). That one whom he looks forward to knowing "sooþly," he concedes, is neither knight nor merchant and embodies the antithesis of that pride of which Will himself has just been accused—*non inflatur, non est ambiciosa, non querit que sua sunt* (he is not boastful, nor overweening; he asks not after his own goods, 1 Cor. 13:4–5). Though he has been told that this Christ, the goal of all his longing, "is in all places," Will admits that thus far he has not found him "bifore ne bihynde," having glimpsed him only "figuratyfly" (C.16.294), "as myself in a mirour" (B.15.162); *hic in aenigmate, tunc facie ad faciem*, 1 Cor. 13:12).

Emphasizing, like A's major signature, the subject's insufficiencies and his renewed commitment to his project, Will's anagrammatic introduction of himself in B likewise becomes a moment of long perspectives for the reader. From here forward to Will's Good Friday sleep lies an unbroken thematic path toward his one "face to face" vision of char-

---

34. See my essay, "Narration and the Invention of Experience: Episodic Form in *Piers Plowman*," in *The Wisdom of Poetry: Essays in Early English Literature in Honor of Morton W. Bloomfield*, ed. Larry D. Benson and Siegfried Wenzel (Kalamazoo, Mich.: Medieval Institute Publications, 1982), 91–122.

ity, the thing itself, acting in human form "in Piers armes." And just as
it is a brief reflection on Will's name and on the proprieties of naming
in general that begins this long motion, it is the true identity and
proper name of the champion himself, not at first fully blazoned as he
approaches the ground of trial, that as in chivalric romance becomes a
focus of interest at the end of this long arc of development, both before
and after the redeemer's battle (B.18.10–25; 19.10–29). Christ's blazoned
name is thus made to designate the central, unique, unrepeatable event
in history that measures and renders intelligible what goes before and
after, while Will's reiterated signature becomes the sign of historical
recursiveness and narrative repetition as the condition of the subject in
temporal life.[35] Yet while Will's anagrammatic signature-speech to Anima offers a conspectus of what lies "bifore" Will, it also makes present
to memory as "in a mirour" what lies "bihynde" him: an earlier signed
moment of humiliation and self-confrontation in the Lond of Longyng, an event that in turn recalls and reframes the starting point of his
quest.

On that antecedent occasion, in the opening lines of the B continuation, when Will looked at "myself in a mirour," his gaze met only
mortality as far as the eye could see. "Scorned" by Scripture for his
inability to find himself and his place amid the speculative intricacies
that are all he sees when he gazes at the sacred page—*multi multa sciunt
et seipsos nesciunt*—he falls into Fortune's tutelage and finds his place in
the world. In "a Mirour þat hiȝte middelerþe" she shows Will his land
of heart's desire, promising all the "wonders" he has sought since the
opening lines of the poem. The place where Fortune rules is called by
his "kynde" name: the Lond of Longyng. This "avanture" into Fortune's realm, occurring at about the midpoint of the poem in its two
long versions, proclaims a new beginning, a re-vision of the nature of
his project, enabled by yet another act of retrospection. Will's fall into
the Lond of Longyng restages the first adventure of the poem, his first
inquiry into the ownership and end of all worldly provisions, paradoxically instigated by the tutelage of Holichurche.

From the moment in the first dream when Will asks Holichurche
about the disposition of the "money of this molde" as if the fate of the

---

35. See my essay, "Making a Good End: John But as a Reader of *Piers Plowman*," in
*Medieval Studies Presented to George Kane,* ed. Edward Donald Kennedy, Ronald Waldron,
and Joseph S. Wittig (Cambridge, Eng.: D. S. Brewer, 1988), 243–66; esp. 248–50.

world's treasure were inextricably parallel to that of his soul, the mixed
motives of the subject's inquiry and interests are thrown into high relief, and they set the terms for the oscillating order of narrative development. For the duration of his life—made coextensive with that of
the poem—he seems determined to approach truth by a kind of peripheral vision, along a circuitous route lying always "on þi left half,"
through the perpetually "ravishing" distractions of the false. In such
terrain, significance can reveal itself only in opposition, in a series of
unrelenting exposures of Will's apparent progress as merely thriftless
repetition. Will's fall into the Lond of Longyng, a few lines into the B
continuation, underscores this pattern of narrative reversal with a chilling economy, for it repeats, motif for motif, his first exploratory "avanture" out into the visionary terrain called up by his first dream of the
poem. Just as in his first dream he had looked on his "left half" to be
"rauysshed" at the sight of Lady Meed, Will is again "ravished" by the
"wondres" Lady Fortune presents, and the similarity of their blandish-
ments suggests that they are sisters under the skin: riches, array, carnal
favors, a retinue compliant to her followers' pleasures, and the highly
visible aura of public respectability that attends lofty kinship.

The deepest ravages of both temptations, however, lie in their effects
on history itself as discourse: they consist in the construction of glam-
orous but false and ultimately ruinous master narratives. Lady Meed
despoils the kingdom by rendering both its account of its past and its
imagination of its future in purely acquisitive and self-serving terms:
she explains her pivotal role in the king's successes and failures at war,
and draws a lesson from this past that countenances future conquest.
The realm ravaged by Fortune is no less discursive, and its mode is
likewise historical narrative. Although her handmaidens the Three
Temptations offer Will all the outward trappings of worldly importance, for Lady Fortune herself, as for Lady Meed, revisionist history
is the ultimate temptation: she proposes to reconstruct the story of
Will's own life as a romance of adventures, an endless unfolding of
opportunities for glory, to be seized or forever lost. Offering a molli-
fying alternative to Scripture's sudden radical exposure of Will's quest
as flight—as a spasmodic pattern of repeated avoidances rather than a
continuous approach—Fortune provides alluring hopes for his future,
and easy and convenient terms for arranging his end. His life-story is
seductively displayed for him in the narrative form of secular romance,
in which "middel elde" represents the mean between the extremes of

youthful giddiness and the miserliness of old age, a time for the fulfillment of all one's earthly powers and designs.[36]

The Lond of Longyng is thus patently and schematically a place of
temptation for Will-as-common-noun, as the power of ethical volition:
Fortune's two "damsels" are *concupiscencia carnis* and "Coueitise of
eiʒes," and "Pride of parfit lyuynge pursued hem boþe" (B.11.13–15).[37]
But it is also a place for Will as author to disclose the massively revised
terms of his art in the long versions. It is "Elde" who offers, in contraposition to Fortune's, a version of Will's life-history that throws narrative emphasis on making a good end rather than on the mediate en-
chantments and negotiations of the prime of life. With the approach of
old age Will comes to regret the "forward" (agreement or contract) he
made with the friars, while Fortune was his friend, to be buried by
them instead of in his parish churchyard. Under Elde's tutelage he now
desires to dispose his life within the integrity of a biographical circle
rather than the open and episodic form of adventure-tale: "At kirke þere
a man were cristned by kynde he sholde be buryed" (B.11.67). But it is
within the terms of his revised desire to represent himself "kyndely"
that Langland inscribes his name in the scene.

As Will vehemently castigates the friars' mercenary trade in such
spiritual "forwards" as the one he had made at Fortune's behest and
now wishes to rewrite, Lewte intervenes to ask Will to explain and
justify his anger (B.11.84–85); from this point the scene begins explicitly
to bring the terms of its own literary "forward" into the foreground of

---

36. See John Burrow, "Chaucer's Knight's Tale and the Three Ages of Man," in *Essays
on Medieval Literature,* 30. It is the superimposition of two three-age schemata in the
conceptual organization of this scene—one civil and worldly, the other a diagram of
spiritual progress—that gives complexity and depth to the representation of Will's aging
over the course of the poem. As Burrow notes (29), according to Giles of Rome, whose
discussion of the ages of man in *De Regimine Principum* derives from Aristotle's *Rhetoric*
and was also used by Dante in the *Convivio,* middle age is the ideal prime of life, a mean
between the extremes of unstable youth and pusillanimous age, the *"colmo de la nostra
vita"* (*Conv.* 4.24.3). Moral poems and homiletic writings, however, found these middle
years, precisely because they encompass the fruitfulness of one's worldly powers, a time
of extreme moral peril, when heedlessness of the soul's good is even more dangerous than
it is in youth because more likely to have become a settled practice. As Burrow has shown
elsewhere, Will's confrontation with Ymaginatif, which comes to him at the age of "fyue
and fourty wynter," marks the boundary between middle and old age, when according to
homiletic moralists thoughts of one's worldly projects and ambitions should yield to
thoughts of "thin ende" ("Langland *Nel Mezzo del Cammin,*" in *Medieval Studies for
J. A. W. Bennett,* ed. P. L. Heyworth [Oxford: Oxford University Press, 1981], 21–41).
37. See Donald Howard, *The Three Temptations: Medieval Man in Search of the World*
(Princeton: Princeton University Press, 1966), 161–214.

attention. Lewte's challenge, Priscilla Martin has suggested, raises the question of the morality and limits of satire, particularly the danger to the subject in taking immoderate pleasure in exposing the faults in others while, as a condition of its rhetorical posture, it appears to allow the criticizing subject to remove his own condition, and the limits of his ethical charter, from the field of scrutiny. "It is only on the question of satire," she argues, "that Langland can formulate the problem latent in the entire poem: . . . that the 'personality' of a literary work may color its 'doctrine' ".[38] This formulation is, however, not an incidental effect in this scene, but defines the terms of its structural centrality and the memorial role of the signature in the poem.

In the Lond of Longyng, as in the later anagrammatic signature that points backward to it, the author's name accompanies a disclosure and renegotiation of the literary terms of the work. Will, who was in the early visions situated at the periphery of the community of the folk as it turns toward its collective penitential enterprise, an engaged observer who forecasts and mimes in his own weeping and seeking the canonical motions by which journeying becomes a penitential labor, here fully introjects this massive social project as his own—indeed, as *himself*: he does not so much abandon the field full of folk as *become* it, his wanderings now a prophetically significant mimesis of the story of his people. He marks this development, which enables the B–C continuation, by making his name signify not only the person but the place in which this labor is undertaken: a *longe launde* is, among other things, the strip of land a plowman plows.[39] As a place-name, his authorial surname has the surface form of many that were to become fixed and heritable in this century: it seems to specify the landholding, dwelling, or birthplace that could serve to distinguish him in written record from a neighbor or relative with the same baptismal name. Yet the addition that in contemporary usage serves to mark a socially significant difference here serves to redouble the force of the given name alone, underscoring its generic power: though formally a proper name or surname, the "long land" designates what he possesses in common with all mortals, his unsatisfied desire or will. At once disclosing and occulting his identity, Will's enigmatic authorial name is paradoxically both proper

38. Priscilla Martin, *Piers Plowman: The Field and the Tower* (London: Macmillan; New York: Harper and Row, 1979), 70.
39. *OED*, s.v. "land," sb., I.7.

and common, a condensed confession and a device that enables him to go on "writing and hiding himself." As inhabitant and heir of the Lond of Longyng that has so far defined the space of his life, he has, in Augustine's words, "become a problem to himself"—a project of social reclamation and cultivation in the first person—and his literary signature, with its accompanying moments of intensive self-reference, has become a narrative and critical, not an attributive, mnemonic.

The ground of this fully signatory moment at the midpoint of the two long versions is not wholly a new invention at the second stage of composition, however: it already lay dormant, awaiting cultivation, as early as the A version. In A the Lond of Longyng, not yet developed as a place of absolute self-confrontation, appears only as it were in peripheral vision: it lies on the road not taken in the allegorical landscape Will traverses on his way to the episode that launches the B continuation. In the third dream of the A version, Dame Study rudely interrupts her husband Wit's instruction to pronounce Will unworthy of such pearls of wisdom: he seeks knowledge, she claims, only so that he can retail it elsewhere to general applause for his own cleverness (A.II.5–16). Her accusation is precisely echoed by the "scorn" of her successor Dame Scripture that precipitates Will's fall into the Lond of Longyng; on this earlier occasion, however, Will succeeds in turning aside his accuser's wrath. Placated by his protestations of humble devotion to her discipline, Study at last gives Will the road-directions that will bring him to the house of Clergy and his wife Scripture—at which happy turn of events he professes himself, in a compromising simile, "gladdere þanne þe gleman þat gold haþ to ȝifte" (A.II.III).

This "heiȝe wey" to Scripture traverses a figurative landscape much like the one Piers had delineated for the folk who asked his guidance to truth, but where Piers's way led through the social discipline of the commandments and sacraments, Study's lies through the marked and unmarked hazards of individual temptations:

> And rid forþ bi ricchesse, ac reste þou not þerinne,
> For ȝif þou couple þe wiþ hym to clergie comist þou neuere;
> And ek þe longe launde þat leccherie hatte,
> Leue hym on þi left half a large myle or more,
> Til þou come to a court, kepe wel þi tunge
> Fro lesinges & liþer speche & likerous drinkes.
> Þanne shalt þou se sobirte, & simplite of speche,
> Þat iche wiȝt be in wille his wyt þe to shewen.
>
> (A.II.II6–23)

It is this "longe launde þat leccherie hatte"—lying, like the domain of Lady Meed, "on þi left half"—that is developed and populated in the opening moments of the B–C continuation to produce a more extended trial of Will's motives, not only as pilgrim but as maker. The Lond of Longyng, built up on a slender strip of terrain merely glimpsed by the way in the first version, is in the long versions resituated *in medias res,* in several senses: Fortune addresses her gratifications to the desires and powers characteristic of the middle of life, and her appeal presents itself both about midway in the poem and midway in Will's life's journey. As the name of the place, and the surname of the person, from which the long versions begin, it reframes the fundamental narrative premise of the poem by an act of superimposition: Will's satiric critique of his world is now subsumed in a massive historical reclamation of the subject's life in the light of salvation history. It is by proclaiming at this point his full name that the poetic subject assumes the prophet's mantle, and his representative status. He becomes, to adopt a phrase whose contemporary legal usage will prove resonant in understanding the social significance of this move, a "son of the people."

## LANGLAND'S "KYNDE NAME" AND NARRATIVE "KYNDE"

If the anagram of Will's name in his meeting with Anima initiates the final progression of the poem—a penultimate turning point much like that experienced by Dante when for the first time in the poem the poet hears his own name in the first syllables Beatrice addresses to him— then the Lond of Longyng, to which that later signature alludes narratively, may be understood as Will's *selva oscura,* encountered, like Dante's, *nel mezzo del cammin de nostra vita* (midway in our life's journey). While Dante's self-confrontation initiates his poem, however, Langland's merely alludes by echo to the beginning of his, proclaiming a second "coming to himself" halfway through its and his life's duration. Overlaying a second narrative order on his first, he not only associates his poetic enterprise with contemporary civil and religious discourses of social instruction (a chief preoccupation of A's three visions), but, like Dante, now proposes to understand through cosmic vision his own position in time, developing the deep correspondences between biography and redemptive history. In both cases self-discovery is revealed as a profound and self-conscious transformation of literary genre; Will here rediscovers the resources of "kynde" in his own "kynde name."

John Burrow has recently invoked just this analogy to Dante in his analysis of the episode immediately following the fall into the Lond of Longyng, namely Will's encounter in passus 11–12 with Ymaginatif.[40] The latter figure not only integrates into a single vision what had appeared to be the conflicting testimony of nature and scripture, but also pointedly commands Will-as-maker to justify his apparently dilatory and distracting way of spending his earthly time and wits: it, too, is a moment of literary as well as eschatological and moral self-justification. Like Dante's thirty-three years on the Good Friday of the Jubilee Year 1300 on which the poem begins, Will's age at this critical and extended self-confrontation halfway through his poem is specified explicitly— twice, in fact—in the B-text. It is forty-five years: the duration of Fortune's favor in the Lond of Longyng (B.11.47), it also measures the time during which Ymaginatif has followed Will, ceaselessly but unavailingly urging him to "mynne on þyn ende" (B.12.4). These ages are in both poems resonantly significant numbers: Dante's is the age of Christ at the crucifixion, and therefore, in Augustine's belief, the age of the resurrected perfect body reunited to its soul; Will's forty-five, however, as the traditional boundary between *juventus,* the middle term of life's three ages, and *senectus,* marks what ought to be a turning point from limitless projects to a vision of their end.[41] Ymaginatif rebukes Will for spending these years "medling" with "makynges" instead of with prayers and his psalter. Burrow asks whether this admonitory vision is meant to be understood as "fact or fiction," and favors—as I do—a factual reading in which, however, there is little functional difference between them. By the process that Judson Allen calls *assimilatio,* the truth and integrity of an individual life-history is wholly absorbed into the functions of a massively figurative exemplary narrative.[42] But Bur-

---

40. "Langland *Nel Mezzo del Cammin.*"

41. On the age of thirty-three as the "perfect stature" of the resurrected body, see Augustine *Civ. Dei* 22.15, in *The City of God,* trans. Henry Bettenson (Harmondsworth, Middlesex: Penguin Books, 1972), 1065–66.

42. *The Ethical Poetic of the Later Middle Ages* (Toronto: University of Toronto Press, 1982), 248–87.

row does not consider the possibility I propose here, that the Lond of Longyng is itself an act of still more pointed authorial self-reference. Such a view tends, however, to confirm both Burrow's reading of the episode and his understanding of the general compositional technique it involves as broadly comparable to Dante's way of yoking together the literary uses of biographical and cosmic time to order and articulate narrative time. As Allen says of this method, in his last published essay, it is the multiple figurative determinants of his story that "leave [Langland] free to be self-absorbed as he writes."[43] It is, of course, the same kind of self-absorption that sustains Augustine's twin projects of confession and universal history, and for both, the common language of *inventio* and *dispositio*, the terms of composition of both self and world, is Scripture.

There could be no more decisive mark of this absorption than a signature that transforms the author's name into the place-name of his own *selva oscura*, the Lond of Longyng. As a signatory device, it is not unparalleled in the later medieval vernaculars: Antoine de la Sale, too, makes his surname into a place of exemplary self-discovery, a room or chamber (*salle*) of reflection and speculation in an allegorical castle. But in Langland's poem this place is transformed by retrospection: years later, as he has faced all but his final humiliation, he recalls it to Anima/ Liberum Arbitrium, the Creature of Many Names, in a new light. The "mirour" that once gave back to his "rauysshed" gaze an image only of his boundless desires is remembered at last in Anima's/Liberum Arbitrium's presence—and thereby rendered for a reader—as the place where Will first glimpsed Charity "as myself in a mirour": in retrospect his humiliation becomes a *felix culpa*. Ymaginatyf provides Will with the texts that authorize and render intelligible such a narrative development: *quem diligo, castigo* (whom I love I chastise, Apoc. 3:19; Prov. 3:12), and *virga tua et baculus tuus, ipsa me consolata sunt* (thy rod and thy staff, they have comforted me, Ps. 22.4; B.12.10–15). It is, however, to the extent that this *assimilatio* in the final revision adduces contemporary social texts as well as scripture in authorial self-disclosure that Langland raises troubling questions about the kind of cultural authority he claims, as well as the narrative genre he asserts, by the disposition of his "kynde name."

---

43. "Langland's Reading and Writing," 357.

## "KYNDE NAME" AS COMMON PLACE AND PROPER PLACE

In the C version, Langland engraves his name and identity in the text still more emphatically than in the B text, while at the same time he makes the referential significance of this act of self-disclosure newly problematic. On the one hand, in C the primary loci of signature occur much earlier in the narrative sequence and are conspicuously pointed as such. As we have noted, minor revisions in C move forward the first unambiguous use of the authorial given name to the opening moments of this version of the poem: in her first speech to the dreamer, Holichurche addresses him at once by name ("Wille, slepestou?" C.1.5). Throughout the C version, the sequence of self-disclosures that echo and elaborate each other to form what we have described as a mnemonic signature-system is marked more firmly, not only by such revisions as these, and other minor adjustments in already existing signatures, but by their realigned reference to an entirely new episode of extended authorial self-justification, introduced into the C text between the first and second vision. Here, in a waking encounter with Reason and Conscience in London "in a hote heruest" (C.5.1–108), Will is now forced to account for more than the integrity and form of his project as spiritual history: he must now attempt to justify it as social production.

The C version of Will's introduction of himself to the Creature of Many Names is revised to point retrospectively to this new locus of authorial self-justification. We have noted that the anagram of the full name in B points back to the Lond of Longyng as the referential center for the B signature-system, at the midpoint of both the poem and Will's life. At the same point in C, Will introduces himself to Anima (in C renamed Liberum Arbitrium) by his local habitation alone—and that habitation has changed: "Ich haue yleued in Londone manye longe ʒeres." Yet if the anagrammatic character of the latter version of this line is less obvious in isolation, it serves just as economically as its B counterpart to point to the new referential center for C's signatures, and to suggest a revised relation between the author's professed worldly habitation and the character of his enterprise.

By changing the locus of Will's identity and the ground of his work from a fictive rural place to an actual urban one, Langland in the C version opens the authorial project to a newly strenuous and circumstantial interrogation, in which the "point at issue" in justifying the authorial form of living is its conformity not only to scriptural master narratives but to contemporary social discourses concerning the grounds of civil identity, particularly as expressed in recent statutes distinguishing legitimate work, "leel labor," from idleness.[44] In his fullest portrait to date of "myself in a mirour," Langland projects the question concerning authorial identity in C into decisively "juridical" as well as existential terrain, and his authorial "confession" on this occasion has two distinct dimensions. It is only after his confession to, and release by, his inquisitors as civil authorities that Will, knocking his breast, enacts a confession of sinfulness as part of penitential rectification. By dividing Will's enacted self-assimilation to the discourses of authority between dreaming and waking, civil and spiritual jurisdictions, Langland raises a troubling larger question about the inevitably apologetic dimension of his culturally powerful discourse of equivalence between the world and the book.

In its circumstantial fulness, the new episode in C rehearses the entire repertory of signals that enable the "pointing" of subsequent signatures: it is here that the reader first hears of Will's characteristic bodily "shap" ("I am to long, lef me, lowe to stoupe"), mentioned less directly later in his quest in his encounter with Thought and Wit, and confronts with more sustained attention the pretensions to clerical status implicitly proclaimed by Will's anomalous hermit's habit mentioned in the opening lines of the poem. The "truth" of these signals, however, which in B furnish forth the materials for a resonantly enigmatic association of Will with the figure of the prophet-penitent, becomes in C the topic of rigorous cross-examination. Will's recurrent claims to the elective poverty, *otium,* and learning of the cleric—and hence the very method of his poetic enterprise, grounded as it is in the assimilation of the authorial self to scriptural discourse—are exposed by this encounter as face-saving social rationalizations, apologetic reconstructions of his anomalous outward poverty and perpetually unsatisfied desire that allow him to claim exemplary power for the form of his life and work, while evading the regulation and status definition that could warrant such a defense. His poetic ambitions for his work—specifically, its as-

---

44. The major points of both Reason's and Conscience's inquiry, and the form of Will's replies, follow closely the provisions of the Second Statute of Laborers of 1388; see *Statutes of the Realm* (London, 1810), 2:56–59. The details of this resemblance warrant separate treatment, which I expect to provide in the near future.

pirations to the company, readership, and expository methods of the learned and powerful—are now unmistakably and compromisingly associated with a London dominated by the pursuit of Lady Meed.

As an event, the "autobiographical" interlude in the C text has the characteristic form of the other signatory episodes we have examined: a challenge that suddenly interrupts and deflects the course of Will's designs, producing in succession first a rationalization then an access of shame and confession, and issues in a contrite resolution to embark upon a new course of both life and work, in a narrative of penitential retrospection that reimagines the world under the dispensation of salvation history. Under the dual pressures of its placement in the poem and the historical specificity of its realization, however, this episode of authorial self-disclosure reevaluates the delicate equilibrium between self and world marked out by the signatures of B. In this chief poetic self-disclosure of the C version, Langland exposes the instability of his poetic project of biblical *imitatio*—of rendering narrated or lived action intelligible by scriptural citation, by reference of the lived to the already written—by emphasizing, through Will's wily, detailed, and desperate application of it to his own case, its inevitably interested character.

By placing this moment of primary authorial self-disclosure, and the reference point for the authorial name, early in the poem, and by staging it as an unsought encounter that befell Will during his youth rather than midway in his life's journey, Langland now portrays the access of poetic self-awareness as the condition for beginning his grand project rather than the occasion of a massive revision and introjection of a narrative of visionary "avanture" initially conceived in other terms. Moreover, where the transformed *ars poetica* of B is extracted from Will as the price of his second seduction in the poem, in C it becomes a moral—and now also legal—consequence of his first, the Vision of Lady Meed. Reason and Conscience, who advise the king regarding Meed's marriage, are in C promoted for their good counsel to "cheef chancellor" and "kynges iustice" at the end of the first dream, and it is in this capacity, as powers who invoke at the literal level civil rather than spiritual sanctions, that they accost Will in London.

Still young and able-bodied, oblivious not only to the threat of old age but even to the attractions of power that belong to the middle years, Will at the beginning of this encounter is largely unconscious of life-designs of any kind; unreflectively he indulges his bodily appetites and spends his time and wit on "makings" (compositions) about the "lollares of Londone and lewed ermytes" among whom he lives. For these productions (made, he insists, under Reason's tutelage) he is unpopular with his fellow denizens of Cornhill, but to the view of his interrogators Will's life is indistinguishable from theirs. The challenge to Will proposed by this inquest is to establish the terms of his difference from these contemporaries, while at the same time validating his capacity to represent them. The enterprise he resolves to begin must be licensed by Reason and Conscience as "leel labor," in which the rest of his life's work becomes a kind of palinode to the "makings" of his idle youth. Yet it is the civil suspicions attached to Will's idleness rather than the dangers to his salvation in his further deferral of penitential reflection that in C invokes the corrective attention of the authorities. If at the end of the episode Will once again manages to pass the test to which he is subjected by refiguring his identity in the terms offered by his challengers, the social significance of his reprieve is deeply ambiguous, and the "kynde" with which Will's "kynde name" associates him remains suspect, transgressive.

Even more striking than C's temporal resituating of the primary authorial self-disclosure early in the narrative sequence and early in Will's life is its changed geographical locus, which exacerbates rather than resolves the "question of authorship." The surname—which in B was derived anagrammatically from *longe launde,* a rural holding transformed into the figurative Lond of Longyng, the "kynde" place of unsatisfied desire that is the author's sole birthright—is rederived in C as an anagram that embodies as part of his name his urban habitation, London, a locus of impropriety that he is here accused of having chosen in order to evade the bond between man and his "kynde" rural place. In the C version of his duplicitous identity, Will is a man "of" "London and opelond bothe," enigmatically at once urban and rural. His laboring "lymes" are both verbal and corporeal, and his inheritance and his reward both are, and are not, of this world (C.5.43–62).

London now becomes the primary and definitive ground of his identity as author; if not his own native place, it is nevertheless the birthplace of Will's authorial enterprise. As the adopted basis for his name, London is at the literal or historical level the functional equivalent of the figurative rural Lond of Longyng: the metropolis is the place in the "real world" that is constituted by, and draws to itself, the boundless desires of Will and his "kynde" for reward and legitimacy. Because it appears to be an elective rather than ancestral ground of identity, Will's prolonged residence in London attracts the suspicions of Reason and

Conscience concerning his "liflode." Fundamental to this encounter is the assumption, which Will apparently shares with his interrogators, that London is virtually no one's "proper" place; whatever aspects of his identity Will derives from this habitation must be pretensions or disguises, since the commune's proper work, its collective "liflode," is based in rural production.

This urban encounter is superimposed on, and represented by his inquisitors as, a time urgently requiring participation in the rural harvest in the face of a shortage of laborers. Dense as it is with overtones of the Gospel parables of the harvest and with apocalyptic urgency, it is, in view of the subsequent resonance of this scene, its literal historical terms that are particularly arresting—and it is these that send us into contemporary practices of naming and pseudonymy for further understanding.[45] At the historical level, Will is here taken by Reason and Conscience for a fugitive rural laborer, indistinguishable from the suspect class of ill-defined idlers and poseurs among whom he dwells. His precariously asserted (and ultimately redefined) sense of worth derives, it seems, from the satirist's righteous indignation, yet, like Lewte later in the Lond of Longyng, Reason and Conscience here reveal that under the circumstances it is an insufficiently clear distinction to sustain either Will's life or his work. To the eye of the civil authorities, Will's "mak-

---

45. The present argument does not deny the structural importance assigned to the scene by its rich scriptural figuration. The "hote heruest" in which it takes place glances back at the tillers of the field in the initial vision of the Prologue, and forward to both the agrarian labors of Piers's transformed and domesticated pilgrimage and the final vision of a world of agrarian production, again under Piers's governance, under the apocalyptic threat of Antichrist's ultimate assault. The plowman's role as the ideal center of this spiritual enterprise, as Elizabeth Kirk has recently shown, is, however, by no means a traditional representation (see "Langland's Plowman"), and Will's pretensions to a place within this rich metaphoric rural economy are similarly ambiguous.

The anomalies of Will's position are most trenchantly figured in scriptural parables, not only those that implicitly govern the figurative structure of the scene, such as the parable of the vineyard (Matt. 20:1–16), and those Will invokes explicitly in his own defense (Matt. 13:44 and Luke 15:10; cf. C.5.94–100), but those he seems unwittingly to reenact. The most telling of these, the parable of the dishonest steward (Luke 16:1–13), traditionally one of the most difficult of the parables to render as ethical or eschatological example, profoundly complicates Will's self-representation. Commanded to specify by what craft he means to "betere . . . þat bylyue the fynden" (improve the lot of those that provide you with the means to sustain life), Will's swift disavowal of the option of manual labor (C.5.23–25) echoes the desperate—and morally problematic—resourcefulness of the dishonest steward discovered squandering his lord's property and facing dismissal: to dig I am unable, to beg I am ashamed; "I am resolved what to do, that when I am put out of the stewardship, they may receive me into their houses" (Luke 16:3–4; cf. C.5.22–29). The sense of his own social status that forecloses agrarian labor simultaneously opens the route of creative bookkeeping as a means of rectification, transforming continued chicanery into the higher prudence.

ings" make no significant difference in the good order of the world, and his professed identity is suspiciously fictive. And just as it is under Lewte's later scrutiny, the legitimacy of Will's clerical self-identification is also brought under question. Despite these crushing liabilities in his self-defense, however, his accusers release him—surprisingly under his own recognizance ("For in my conscience y knowe what Crist wolde y wrouhte"). Exhorted to lead hereafter "the lyif þat is lowable and leele to thy soule," and fervently resolving to "bigynne a tyme / That alle tymes of my tyme to profit shal turne," Will goes to church to undertake the penitence that all parties seem to understand is enjoined upon him by this exchange. Knocking his breast, he falls asleep, only to dream the next vision of the several that comprise the rest of the poem. The visionary duration of Will's life, the making of the poem that records it, and a life of penitential self-knowledge through confession are thereby, as in B, rendered synonymous. Yet the literal and outward mode of this revised life involves no removal of either habitation or habit. To the eye, he is, and remains, a hermit *manqué,* living a rule of one, still to all appearances a fugitive from honest toil, and still subject to all the suspicions attached to this class: the London layabout slides imperceptibly into the prophet without honor in his own country, and for the remainder of the poem Will is both deserving and undeserving of the scorn he increasingly attracts. He has chosen the texts of which his life is a sermon, and while they are as inescapable as his "kynde name," they are no less duplicitous in their range of implication.

The scriptural texts that underwrite Will's determination of his identity as habitual penitent, and the prophetic status this confers on his insufficiency and unlikeliness to represent God's word, have recently been well studied; these accounts also tend to focus chiefly on the representative force of the given name.[46] But this author has also acquired

46. See Richard K. Emmerson, "The Prophetic, The Apocalyptic, and the Study of Medieval Literature," in *Poetic Prophecy in Western Literature,* ed. Jan Wojcik and Raymond-Jean Frontain (Rutherford, N.J.: Fairleigh Dickinson University Press; London and Toronto: Associated University Presses, 1984), 40–54; Robert Adams, "Some Versions of Apocalypse: Learned and Popular Eschatology in *Piers Plowman,*" in *The Popular Literature of Medieval England,* Tennessee Studies in Literature 28 (Knoxville: University of Tennessee Press, 1985), 194–236. John M. Bowers, in *The Crisis of Will in "Piers Plowman"* (Washington, D.C.: Catholic University of America Press, 1985), gives an extensive and useful account of the intersection of the biographical and didactic designs of the narrative, but he devotes his attention to the given name Will as the locus of enigmatic identity and does not examine the intertextualities of the authorial surname.

for narrative purposes a complicatedly typifying surname—or as Derrida would insist, *that which functions as* a surname—and as a "proper" name it both differs from that of the poet's father and associates the represented author with a place teeming with "improper" labors and identities. What is the significance of this move? What social texts authorize it, and how do they illuminate the form of the "kynde name" and its deployment as a memory device? How in fact does a surname function in late fourteenth-century England?

## NAMES PROPER AND IMPROPER: IDENTITIES FOR THE RECORD

It is hardly incidental to our story that it is in precisely this period that most historians of personal names place the final general stabilization of the English surname in its modern form: that is to say as the heritable and conventional paternal addition. We may begin to understand the cultural determinants of this practice by letting Langland's own Virgil—Conscience—explain it to us. In the C version of his long speech refuting Meed's claim that what she stands for, limitless reward, is what keeps the kingdom running, Conscience invokes the complex grammatical analogy that Skeat labeled "barely intelligible and very dull." Because it is complex and learned (even the king notes that "Englisch was it neuere"), it in turn requires analogies to support its applicability.[47] Mercede is to Meed—exchange on terms specified is to the open-ended seduction of unspecified promised favor—as "rect" is to "indirect" grammatical relation. "Rect" relations, Conscience explains, are those marked by the addition of correct case endings that declare the relation of modifier to modified and specify the function of the expression in the statement; the "indirect" or unmarked term seeks to grasp to itself all cases, genders, and numbers, while evading all regulated connection (C.3.360–69). These additions, he says, may be thought of as working like surnames: if I wish to claim my father's "ryhte" as my inheritance, "þat is nat resonable ne rect to refuse my syre

---

47. See Lavinia Griffiths, *Personification in Piers Plowman* (Cambridge, Eng.: D. S. Brewer, 1985), 36; Margaret Amassian and James Sadowsky, "*Mede* and *Mercede*: A Study of the Grammatical Metaphor in *Piers Plowman* C IV.335–409," *Neuphilologische Mitteilungen* 72 (1971): 457–76. Skeat's remark is part of his note to C 4.292 ff. (C 3.332 ff. in Pearsall's edition): *The Vision of William Concerning Piers the Plowman, in Three Parallel Texts*, ed. Walter W. Skeat (London: Oxford University Press, 1886), 2:49.

name." The surname, like the case ending, regulates proprietary relations; to disavow the paternal surname is to sever one's connection to a "kynde" ancestral place; it violates the very grammar of "proper" relations.

This comparison succinctly declares the chief function of the surname in common law, and explains why in England by the fourteenth century, well before this occurred anywhere else in Europe, anybody who had occasion to appear in or make a written record of any kind—and by this time that included peasants, many of whom possessed their own personal seals for the purpose—already had a name that followed the common modern form: a given or baptismal name plus a heritable surname that matched that of the father, whether or not it any longer actually declared either the father's own given name (as, say, the name Robertson does) or his occupation (consider, for example, Chaucer, whose father was not a shoemaker but a winemerchant).[48] It was by this sustained continuity of heritable surname across generations as a regulatory convention, rather than by its real reference to paternal given name or occupation, that rights, tenant as well as free, were claimed and maintained through time: to be a copyholder was to hold one's rights by "copy of the court roll" in the manorial court, and it was in this practical sense that the functional name of the father, as the name of one's paternal ancestors, was powerful.

The two names, first and last, virtually divide between them one's spiritual and civil identity.[49] For virtually all matters before God's tri-

---

48. See C. M. Matthews, *English Surnames* (London: Weidenfeld and Nicolson, 1966), 43–44; P. H. Reaney, *The Origin of English Surnames* (London: Routledge and Kegan Paul, 1967), 300–316.

49. Here and throughout this exposition, I use the term "civil" for those temporal and publicly accountable activities that fall outside the specific concern of spiritual authority and ecclesiastical jurisdiction and are governed by common and statutory law—in other words, those that in a later age might be said to occupy "public" space and identity and come to be the concern of the "state." The term should not be understood to imply the jurisdiction of the civil, as against common, law.

Like "public," "civil" is a term that must be applied with caution, and with alertness to its specific local utility in marking distinctions of heuristic and expository use in interpretation. I do not contend that these were the terms in which medieval writers and thinkers conceived the terms of their worldly relations. The special and limited senses in which a nascent "public" sphere was available as an imaginative ground for distinctive forms of late medieval thought and action is a topic beyond the scope of this essay. I would contend, however, that such a space—in Habermas's sense of an arena in which participants tacitly agree to relinquish for purposes of discursive exchange their class status and identifications—exists as at least a literary idea, or ideal, in this period, and that it is a distinctive notion of this cultural moment. See my essay, "The Idea of Public Poetry

bunal one acted under the given or baptismal name, the name that proclaimed the individual's beginning in this world as a moral agent and
marked all his new beginnings of spiritually significant relations. Examples include the custom of the confession and the practice that still
survives in the marriage service: both are sacramental performative occasions in which the parties avow their intentions and constitute their
own spiritual "estate" by given name only ("I William take thee Catherine . . ."). This notion of the individual as capable of making provi-
sion for the benefit of his soul extended to the making of wills for the
disposition of personal property, even by peasants holding in villein
tenure, a practice no longer unusual by the latter fourteenth century.
These wills, which were proved in the ecclesiastical court, had become
customary with the active encouragement of the Church—and not only
because such pious benefactions brought to the Church what might
otherwise by default have been claimed by the lord; they reflected what
a person was in the eyes of Church belief and authority.[50] But as the
given name regulated all one's acts of beginning and became the sign
of one's elective relations—imposed at birth, it was one's own with
baptism, and marked every successive sacramental initiative—the surname governed one's endings, the effective sign of the network of one's
involuntary relations with the world; naming one's progenitor, it also
specified and disposed the real property that would remain for one's
blood kin at death.

For all matters that could come before the king's courts or the manorial court concerning rights in real property, what functioned as the
*proper* name was the conventional surname, which in later usage came
to stand alone for the person in such actions ("Wragg is in custody").
And since it was its distributive and regulatory force that mattered—
the surname functionally transmitted paternal right, not the father's
given name or personal occupation—the place-name of a paternal hold-

---

in the Reign of Richard II," *Speculum* 53 (1978): 94–114; for an opposing view, see Paul
A. Olson, *The Canterbury Tales and the Good Society* (Princeton: Princeton University
Press, 1986), 7 and passim. What makes the discourses of both dissenters and their opponents in the later fourteenth century so remarkable is their explicit contention for the
high ground in defining such a space; some of this contest is evident in the documents of
the 1381 rebellion cited below.

50. M. T. Clanchy, *From Memory to Written Record* (Cambridge, Mass.: Harvard University Press, 1979), 184; Michael M. Sheehan, *The Will in Medieval England* (Toronto:
Pontifical Institute of Mediaeval Studies, 1963).

ing could have for freeholders virtually the same force locally in differentiating the several properties of the same extended family, marking various seats and holdings within it, as the conventional surname has generally for matters of real property inheritance against claimants outside the kin group. Instances recorded within Langland scholarship demonstrate the utility of this convention. A family in which the same two or three male given names recur in two or more adjacent generations may distinguish the holdings of a son from those of a nephew of about the same age by referring to one by the name of the holding that was or would be his, rather than by the sire's surname: William Langlond, for example, rather than William de Rokayle.[51] Which surname William used, and under what circumstances, would depend on the claims and distinctions he and his family wished it to make for him, and therefore to some degree on where he lived and worked in relation to this proprietary identity—just as a boy tends to lose the appellation Junior to the extent that he moves as an adult outside the territorial and social range of its utility in marking a difference. Whatever we may infer about Langland's practice in this regard, then, we are not entitled to assume that the difference of his sire's surname from his own meant that he was a bastard, as a few early critics argued. Yet precisely this identification of the functional person through lineality and land rights, represented in the common form of naming in English, became a focus of considerable new social anxiety in the 1370s and 1380s—the years in which Langland composed the two long versions of his poem that he invested with his surname.

If in this period the modern English name form more or less stabilized because it functioned to distribute certain rights, within Langland's lifetime it also began for the first time to suggest on several fronts various practical functional liabilities and to be exploited in social fictions that had a paradoxical capacity for destabilizing or disrupting proprietary claims. The common law of inheritance of real property rights by now slept so securely that it began to dream monsters, formed out of its own relentless logic. There could be no clearer example of such a

---

51. Oscar Cargill, in "The Langland Myth," *PMLA* 50 (1935): 36–56—a largely tendentious argument against the evidential solidity of opposition to Manly's view of the authorship of the poem—nevertheless contains some valuable if incomplete information from various fourteenth-century records of the Rokayle and But family names, including just the circumstance we have described occurring within three adjacent generations of the Rokayle family (48).

demonic consequence than the "exception of bastardy" as it came to be applied in the fourteenth century. Since in the parlance of the common law the bastard was *nullius filius,* "son of no man"—or alternatively, in a suggestive phrase to which which I have adverted before, "son of the people"—by this logic no one could determine that he was by hereditary status a villein, and he was therefore by default defined as free.[52] The unseemly numbers of small inheritance claims to property that now begin to appear in judicial records, countered by the defendant's assertion that the claimant was a bastard, suggest that the social benefits of this supposedly shameful state did not pass unnoticed: by making such a claim one might obtain a final determination, valid against all subsequent common-law actions, of one's status as free, in the very act of having one's claim to the piece of property in question (not surprisingly often studiously trivial and minute) rejected. The right to the property, it turned out, was the instrument, not the objective, in such actions. Structurally considered, one obtained a civil advantage here through an act of *dissociation* from traceable paternity, gaining a determination of freedom from a decision against one's paternal "right."

A second way in which it might be perceived as disadvantageous to have one's traceable and stable familial or household name a matter of record became immediately apparent with the first Poll Tax, and dramatically more so with its second and third collections not long afterward, when a nationwide investigation into massive tax evasion was met with what quickly became the Peasants' Revolt of 1381. The Poll Tax was the first tax to be levied by the "head" (poll), or individual person, instead of, for example, by the household or the village, the units of taxation drawn upon by the Lay Subsidies, that fiscal innovation which had immediately preceded the invention of the Poll Tax and remained in place after the disastrous civil consequences of the latter measure had become all too obvious.[53] The Poll Tax was imposed at the rate of 4d. per person on all lay men and women over fourteen years of age; only those who regularly begged for a living were exempt.

---

52. Norma Adams, *"Nullius Filius:* A Study of the Exception of Bastardy in the Law Courts of Medieval England," *University of Toronto Law Journal* 6:2 (1946): 361–84, esp. 361, 370, 377; Paul R. Hyams, *Kings, Lords and Peasants in Medieval England: The Common Law of Villeinage in the Twelfth and Thirteenth Centuries* (Oxford: Clarendon Press, 1980), dates the widespread use of this "absurd, if humane, conclusion" no earlier than the second quarter of the fourteenth century (181). (The phrase is that of Pollock and Maitland.)

53. M. W. Beresford, *Lay Subsidies and Poll Taxes* (Canterbury: Phillimore, 1963).

The secular clergy were also liable: the beneficed were to pay a shilling and the unbeneficed a groat; like the lay beggars, the mendicants were exempt. While it was in principle a radically more equitable way of raising revenue than the Lay Subsidies, from the perspective of the great mass of those on whom it was levied it cut across the unit of production and obligation in which their names had meant something, the family holding. The aged grandmother or disabled uncle or unmarried daughter in one's own household was liable for the same tax as its primary producers, the man and woman of the house, which is why people in the former categories (women in particular), were suspiciously underrepresented in the returns from the first collection in 1377. The second and third levies, in 1379 and 1381, introduced a slight gradation for personal wealth, yet they were met with still more widespread and conspicuous evasion, on a scale that the Exchequer could scarcely overlook. While the Poll Tax returns are the most massive documentation of English personal names and occupations before the Parish Registers were introduced in 1538, their silences—the unnamed and unaccounted for who raised by their absence the suspicion of the authorities—also speak eloquently about the perceived limits to the advantages inherent in being named and recorded as a being with an individual civil identity.[54]

Still more dramatic instances of this perception are shown in the suspicion, growing throughout the 1370s and 1380s, that the social signifying power of the conventional naming pattern could be turned to the construction of civil fictions. Throughout the 1370s several Commons petitions begin to speak of "rumor" (in the sense of uproar or tumult), and of "illicit conventicles," "gatherings against the peace," and "false and traitorous allegiances" about in the land; bands of would-be malefactors capable of concerted subversion, and amassing money for some threatened action, are now seen in what had formerly been perceived chiefly as a major public nuisance and a mounting burden on public charity, the "sturdy beggars" and "stafstrikers" of no fixed abode wandering about the country in great numbers. Alan Harding has noted that many of these expressions mark a major transfer of vocabulary: oathbound conspiracies, which during the war scares in the first decade of the fourteenth century had described the activities of lords and knights suspected of fomenting quarrel and revolt as liveried

---

54. See Matthews, *English Surnames*, 44–46.

"maintainers," were now attributed to, projected upon, the laboring and servant classes.[55] What the petitioners fear from these amorphous groups is hard to determine—perhaps an English version of the Jacquerie (1358); the possibility of consorting with the French enemy is mentioned. But the common theme of their writings is a threatening indeterminacy of identity in "landless men": the focus of anxiety is the civil intelligibility of motive that derives from a stable place of work and residence, which in turn is a function of lineality and its "right" relationships. Landless men are those who have detached themselves from the basis for their names, and one scarcely knows what to call them, or what to expect of the communities they could form.

Such fears, and a variety of civil fictions to articulate them, are abundant in the literature of the 1381 Revolt. The representative status of the named actors in these events has proved to be very hard to interpret. Actual persons, craft typenames, nonce names, sectarian code names, obvious pseudonyms, and patent evasions mingle in the chronicles under the same naming conventions as purported actors in a newly defined arena of civil events. Persons of indeterminate status between the fictive and the actual become the "one head" under which the rebels, those previously unnamed in chronicles of significant public actions, enter the records and are comprehended by the chroniclers as an improvised, indeterminate, unnameable, and therefore threatening new social body; a "great society" made by common volition and bound together by oath—made, that is to say, chiefly of words and deeds, confected names and improvised identities. A rich collection of such indeterminate beings, suspended between the hypothetical and the actual, populate the so-called Letter of John Ball, recorded by Walsingham as having been addressed to the men of Essex. Identifying himself as Johan Schep "som tyme Seynte Marie prest of York and now of Colchestre," Ball in his cryptic message

> greteth wel Iohan Nameles, and Iohan the Mullere, and Iohon Cartere, and biddeth hem that thei bee war of gyle in borugh, and stondeth togidre in Godes name, and biddeth Peres Ploughman go to his werk, and chastise wel Hobbe the Robbere, and taketh with yow Iohan Trewman,

55. Alan Harding, "The Revolt Against the Justices," in *The English Rising of 1381,* ed. R. H. Hilton and T. H. Aston (Cambridge, Eng.: Cambridge University Press, 1984), 188–92.

and alle hiis felawes, and no mo, and loke schappe you to on heued, and no mo.[56]

The mix of kinds of signification in these names is dizzying. While a William Trueman is named in King's Bench records as having berated Nicholas Brembre for injuries suffered during his mayoralty as the latter rode with the king to meet the rebels at Mile End, John Treweman "and alle his felawes" looks to be a coinage allied to the generic typename Lollards gave themselves, distinguishing the correct beliefs of "trewe men" from the false opinions of all outside their sect.[57] Hobbe the Robbere may or may not be Langland's coinage, though Piers certainly is, and Ball's exhortation later in the letter to "do wel and bettre and fleth synne" seems to close the case for some knowledge on the part of the speaker or writer of these key terms of Langland's text. John Carter and John the Miller may be meant as typenames of the skilled rural and town craftsmen groups among which the revolt spread most deeply and quickly—though other chroniclers, such as Knighton, soberly list them along with Jack Straw (to whom he attributes the actions assigned by other chroniclers to Wat Tyler) as actual persons in the crowd that descended on London. (Knighton's version of this report makes Ball's letter several messages, spoken by Jakke Mylner, Jakke Carter, and Jakke Trewman). The Dieulacres Chronicler also attributes Wat Tyler's deeds to Jack Straw—and goes on to name Piers Plowman as one of his confederates.[58] And what are we to understand of John Nameless? Possibly that the surname Nameless in this context itself counts as an act of defiance and solidarity—that a parody of the common name-form calls into question the social function to which it is perceived to be attached, landed proprietorship.

The point to notice here is not simply that Piers's name appears in this company, or even that some took him for a living rather than fictive contemporary (though this speaks volumes we cannot open here about

56. Walsingham, *Historia Anglicana*, 2.33–34, as reprinted in *The Peasants' Revolt of 1381*, ed. R. B. Dobson, 2nd. ed. (London: Macmillan, 1983), 381. Knighton's account of these subversive utterances or writings makes this message into several by various persons; see Dobson, pp. 381–82.

57. For William Trueman, see Andrew Prescott, "London in the Peasants' Revolt: A Portrait Gallery," *The London Journal* 7 (1981): 133. On special Lollard terminology, see Anne Hudson, "A Lollard Sect Vocabulary?" in *So Meny Peple, Longages and Tonges: Philological Essays . . . presented to Angus McIntosh*, ed. Michael Benskin and M. L. Samuels (Edinburgh: M. Benskin and M. L. Samuels, 1981), 15–30.

58. See Rodney Hilton, *Bond Men Made Free* (London: Temple Smith, 1973), 177–78.

the social potency of Langland's invention), but something much more pervasive: the oddly fluid reality of all these named persons and the indeterminate referentiality of their gnomic utterances. Whether we attribute this effect to the perceivers' and recorders' beliefs about, or inability to fathom, these events or to the actors' designs scarcely matters beyond a certain point: at this historical moment they seem to share a conviction that individuals and groups were suddenly able to constitute and publish themselves at will as something new and credible, to coin and circulate social redefinitions of the self and the community—fictions, if you will—as operative fact. The Dieulacres chronicler who put Piers among the rebel leaders also avers that "Jack Straw"—to whom, recall, he attributed Wat Tyler's acts—was actually the pseudonym of a disgraced son of a Kentish gentry family by the name of Culpeper. To be sure, one may detect here a bit of the enduring and somewhat snobbish belief, evident in many romance plots, that social articulateness and an air of apparently natural authority in someone of mean social estate is always a sign of gentle birth going about in hiding, since the real lower orders do not possess such skills. But one can also reverse the emphasis of this notion, and put a less romantic and sanguine color on it: that articulate disaffection can issue in a radical reconstruction of oneself and an equally radical realignment of one's communal identity and functional "estate." The Evesham chronicler's dark suspicions along these lines are more explicit: he regarded all the rebel names I have considered as adopted pseudonyms, *nomina imponentes,* chosen by the rebel leaders for protection of their plans, and Hilton takes these manifestations as evidence that such names were indeed chosen rather than derisively imposed after the fact by confused or hostile observers.[59]

It may seem that describing rebel identities as inventions and improvisations slights these actors' own accounts of their intents as conservative rather than innovative: for both the 1381 rebels and Wycliffite dissidents, "newefangelnesse" was what they most abhorred in the religious and political culture they opposed, and they steadfastly asserted antique warrant for their claims. Yet in standing for the "trewe communes" or as "true men" they claimed the power to recognize and reinstate primal arrangements that had been obscured by various latter-day sophistries of interpretation; their claim of access to this original "truth" lay not in a distinctive method, but in their identity as members

59. *Bond Men Made Free,* 178.

of a continuous interpretive community that had never ceded the interpretive authority it asserted, and that insisted that its primary texts lend themselves to direct vernacular understanding. In their own view they are not appropriating or deforming the discourses of authority but restoring them to correct usage. Their names as dissenters, as recognizable calques on canonical proper-name forms, thus become their "true" names, and the "diversionary practice" of putting them in circulation becomes "an art of living in the other's field," thereby reclaiming it as always and again their own.[60]

A final instance from the records of 1381 illustrates, with an impacted pungency of meaning fully appreciated by its chronicler, the contemporary sense of the capacity of dissent to improvise new forms of self-definition by the recasting of traditional social discourses. As an extended narrative, this example illustrates, more precisely than the chroniclers' briefer efforts to name the agents of current upheavals, how the coining of identities using traditional forms and proprieties can be at once a conservative and transforming act. The incident appears in Walsingham's remarkably full account in the *Gesta Abbatum* of the uprising of the tenants on the estates of the Abbey of St. Albans.

Throughout his description of these events, which he offers as a sustained and stylistically ambitious interlude in a larger work governed largely by different rhetorical principles, Walsingham pays close attention to the constitutive power of ceremonious display in shaping events. Though Walsingham pronounces their objectives unreservedly abhorrent, he nevertheless represents the rebel leaders as eloquent, and their designs as coherent enough to constitute a profound threat to the discourses of power in which they skilfully intervene. They speak with an almost Roman resonance, as if conscious that their actions are watched by a larger world: William Gryndecobbe, local leader of the rebellion, declares himself a willing martyr for a greater cause. Walsingham represents the tenants themselves as self-consciously wielding a powerful rhetoric of allusion to founding texts and constitutive ritual, though their rhetoric of citation is radically different from the Abbot's. And he is above all pointedly aware that these events occupied Corpus Christi week, a period of explicit liturgical and popular commemoration of the community as, and as the recipients of, the sacramental body of Christ.[61]

---

60. De Certeau, *Practice of Everyday Life*, 24–25.
61. See John Bossy, "The Mass as a Social Institution 1200–1700," *Past and Present*

The incident that demonstrates the tenants' mastery of improvisatory self-definition occurred early in the revolt, and it assumes in Walsingham's self-consciously dramatic account the status of a virtual *leitmotif* of the tenants' prolonged resistance, a pivotal expression of their grievances and a condensed metaphor of the meaning of their outrages. It erupts into luminous narrative intelligibility against a background of long-standing dispute between the abbots and their tenants over the abbey's exclusive milling rights: decades before the revolt an earlier abbot had confiscated the tenants' household millstones and used them as the paving-stones of the floor of the monastery parlor, then under construction. In the first days of the 1381 revolt, the people of the town of St. Albans and the surrounding countryside had heard rumor of the events in London and sent a deputation there to learn more of its extent. Rather than defending the abbey precincts against the spread of these disruptions into the abbot's domain, as the monastery had evidently hoped, they had returned from London filled with Wat Tyler's cause. Besides invading the abbot's woods and fields in procession "with great pomp," releasing his prisoners from jail, and demanding of the abbot a new charter of their liberties, the rebellious tenants now break into the abbey parlor, pull up the millstones from the floor where they had been "set as a memorial of the ancient dispute between the abbey and the townsmen," and carry them outside and

> hand them over to the commons, breaking them into little pieces and giving a piece to each person, just as the consecrated bread is customarily broken and distributed in the parish churches on Sundays, so that the people, seeing these pieces, would know themselves to be avenged against the abbey in that cause.[62]

The gesture is dense with impacted meaning. An improvised lay transformation of the sacrament honored with special ceremony during Corpus Christi week, it both subsumes and alters its customary purpose. On the one hand it enacts the reformation of the community of the faithful as participants in the body of Christ, but on the other it does

---

100 (1983): 29–61, and his *Christianity in the West 1400–1700* (Oxford: Oxford University Press, 1985), 57–75, 91–97; Mervyn E. James, "Ritual, Drama, and Social Body in the Late Medieval English Town," *Past and Present* 98 (1983): 3–29.

62. *Gesta Abbatum Monasterii Sancti Albani*, ed. H. T. Riley, 3 vols., Rolls Series 28:4 (London: Public Record Office, 1867–69), 3:309. The translation is that of Rosamond Faith, in "The 'Great Rumour' of 1377 and Peasant Ideology," in *English Rising*, ed. Hilton and Aston, 66; her account of this and other actions of the period expressing "symbolic victories" is germane to the present discussion.

so defiantly without benefit of clergy, as the constitutive ceremony of a new definition of community.[63] The compacted metonymies implicit in the millstones' new symbolic function are no less daring: they are made by ceremonial imposition to stand for the commodity, bread, in whose production they are instrumental, while the parodic ritual of their consumption alludes to the traditional iconography of foolery and the social license allowed to its expression.[64] The fortunes of the millstones in this narrative—the rise and fall of their imposed meaning—parallel those of the charters demanded by the rebels and their supplantation by new ones that rewrite the tenants' liberties in accordance with their wishes (wishes that prominently include the right to household millstones henceforth). As at the end of the story the new charters are abrogated in favor of the abbey's customary privileges, the millstones are stripped of their new role in a constitutive civil sacrament to return to their formerly imposed function as mute "memorials" of the abbots' rather than the tenants' definition of community.

The overdetermined significance of this action was not lost on the chronicler—nor on the abbot and the king: first among the reparations exacted from the tenants, once their effective power of resistance is diminished by the collapse of the revolt in London and by the king's threatened visitation, is the abbot's insistence, as the price of his intercession on their behalf against the king's wrath, that they restore the stones to their place as flooring.[65] Walsingham focuses insistently on the instigator of this parodic ritual, one Johannes Barbitonsor, as a master of bad faith, a kind of Sinon who is particularly worthy of the execution meted out to him by Justice Tresilian.[66] The enactment of this reformed sacrament as a gesture of defiance, which appropriates the discourses of authority to dismantle and reform their constitutive power, becomes the centerpiece of a highly colored and rhetorically unified narrative of contest for command of the community's history. By this absolute and condensed representation of the issues at stake in the revolt, and its self-conscious stylistic distinction from the rest of the

63. Walsingham is sensitive to the rebels' conscious reimposition of meaning on the term "community"; see *Gesta Abbatum* 3:305.

64. I owe this perception to V. A. Kolve, who is working on the representation of the fool in medieval art and literature; this information appeared in a lecture by Professor Kolve to the Medieval Studies group at Berkeley in Fall 1984, and I cite it with his permission.

65. *Gesta Abbatum* 3:346–47.

66. *Gesta Abbatum* 3:339, 347, 350.

*Gesta Abbatum,* Walsingham's narrative fully warrants Marc Bloch's description of it as a "veritable milling epic."[67]

Though the St. Albans rebels do not republish their individual identities under new names, their improvised sacrament enacts a similar renegotiation of identity at the level of the community. With a power of interpretive insight that virtually outstrips his own express partisanship, Walsingham's story of the reciprocal manipulation of public symbols complements the chroniclers' briefer witness to the unsteadiness of the proper signification of the person, showing how the social space and register of a collective act of defiance as well as the identity of an individual dissenter may be dramatically shifted to the register of the proper, and thereby claim to reinstate rather than overturn primal "truth": new names become true names, and rebellion and dissent become reinstated tradition, a sacrament of a new "commune."

## AUTHORSHIP, IMPROVISATION, AND THE RHETORIC OF PRESENCE

The violence, perceived as well as actual, of 1381, together with considerable interpretive depth in representing a phenomenon that in their explicit moral pronouncements upon it both Commons and chroniclers profess to find an inexplicable and sinister breach in nature, testifies to a "crisis of the proper" in the latter decades of the fourteenth century. Proper names, like the proprietary rights they represented and regulated, go into a kind of liquefication in these documents. One's name, in effect, becomes one's own convention for an identity that coheres around one's voluntary acts and oath-bound confederates, rather than around stability of seisin and lineal status: as an instrument for claiming rights, its "propriety," the integrity it proclaims, is less paternal than personal; the unit it stabilizes and defends is not the holding but the life, and a community restored to self-presence by constitutively "memorial" acts and rituals. Like Langland's disposition of his "kynde" name in his poem, these powerful improvisations mark a profoundly revised account of the individual's powers to interpret, and to represent, the "commune."

The generation surrounding the two long versions of *Piers Plowman*

---

67. "The Advent and Triumph of the Watermill," in *Land and Work in Medieval Europe,* trans. J. E. Anderson (New York: Harper and Row, 1969), 157.

is filled with notable enactments of this proposition—that the operative unit of thought about identity was the life and community as made through the enacted reclamation of founding texts. It clearly underlies the efforts of Margery Kempe to form her life in the image of the holy woman; it is movingly audible in the testimony of the Lollard Thorpe, who analyzes and rejects the prospect of his recantation in terms of the social example it would give to, and the fragmented and illegible life it would compose for, those who trust him. To renounce the beliefs and practices he shares with the community of Lollard adherents that had formed him would be to "slay so many spiritually that I should never deserve to have grace of God to edify his church, neither myself nor any other life."[68] He would, in effect, be publishing a false and unedifying fictive self that would remain forever untrustworthy as an example to others. Those such as Philip Repingdon who have recanted have become radically and irreversibly unknowable, not only to either side but even to themselves, because they would not, in Thorpe's revealing phrase, "stretch forth their lives" to be fully known as representative of the texts that ground them. It is in terms like these, of "stretching forth a life," I believe, that we should understand Langland's internal self-naming as a sustained formal diacritic in his poem. His increasingly full depiction of his "making" as a life-consuming and life-defining activity, perpetually running counter to both ecclesiastical and civil dicta for the orderly disposition of one's time and effects, and his formation of his name as that of a kind of parodic landholding, a heritage of self-formation through desire—a Lond of Longyng in which there is no secure seisin—become a far less "literary" and conventional practice when set against the simultaneous imagination of the rebellion as made by "landless men," a confederation of John Namelesses.

The social significance of the identity Langland disposes with his signature also takes on a different look in the light of these contemporary developments. It becomes easier to see how a poem in nearly all respects theologically orthodox could seem ripe for appropriation by both civil and religious dissenters. These concurrent social texts not only illuminate certain patterns in the reception of the poem, however,

68. Thorpe's testimony in 1407 before Archbishop Arundel—a text known to More, Bale, and Foxe—is printed in part by Anne Hudson, *Selections from English Wycliffite Writings* (Cambridge, Eng.: Cambridge University Press, 1978), 29–33, and in full, in a fitfully modernized English from an early print (Short Title Catalogue 24045), by A. W. Pollard, *Fifteenth Century Prose and Verse* (London, 1903), 97–174.

but open new approaches to Langland's literary intentions, suggesting as they do his full awareness, and increasing assimilation, of the most destabilizing consequences of his own authorial self-representation. It would be mistaken to associate his complex gestures of self-naming, and the concept of the self-authorizing integrity of a life lived in the image of the total scriptural coherence that underwrites it, solely with dissent, even though our examples have been drawn chiefly from such texts; contemporary forms of lay piety that are unmistakably orthodox—indeed the outlook and practices of the *devotio moderna* generally—are likewise predicated upon such an idea. What Langland's self-reference seems rather to have in common with these late medieval discourses, both orthodox and dissenting, is a paradoxical skepticism and anxiety about the established agencies for textual distribution of authority. It is important to avoid attributing a necessarily "progressive" or revolutionary character to these phenomena: indeed, those who enacted them saw them rather as restorative of some simpler and more directly mediated form of exemplification and authority.

Orthodox or dissenting, the contemporary discourses to which Langland's practice of self-representation has its closest affinities are based on a rhetoric of presence, on resistance to the independent intelligibility of texts without reference to their authorship as actions. These late medieval forms of social and spiritual piety enact a powerfully nostalgic rearguard action on behalf of ideas of communal and personal integrity disposed locally and face-to-face rather than from above or outside. They envision individual and communal life as so permeated by lived scripture that its integrity is wholly transparent, as St. Francis had insisted, "without a gloss." Like Langland they speak on behalf of an ethic based on the lived rather than formalized deployment of authorizing texts, and propose a renegotiation of traditional relations between textual fixity and human action. If graven images were profoundly suspect, those that formed spontaneously in the individual memory and imagination steeped in direct assimilation of canonical texts of scripture and the lives of the saints—metonymies or images of equivalence that suggested themselves to Margery Kempe in daily domestic life—were fundamentally trustworthy, because their syntax of relation was implicit in a customary grammar of living. Inscribing in his poem a name and equivocal occupation that loosely allied his improvisatory activities with these, Langland claims for himself and those who undertake to define their own actions within this terrain an ex-

tremely risky social authority. That such a move was fully self-conscious
I do not doubt. That it assured that he would *as author* join the John
Namelesses of his age to the memory of posterity is one of the profound witticisms of historical process he shows every sign of having
accepted with equanimity.

## CONCLUSION: SELF AND WORLD AS "NOMINALIST TEXTS"

I am, finally, arguing here for a different syntax of relation than has
traditionally been proposed between Langland's formal practices as a
poet and the social actualities and discourses he is often said to reflect
or represent. Most attempts to account for the felt connection between
Langland's conceptually shifting and disturbing procedures of composition and the contemporary "world," whether of ideas or of social actions, represented by his poem go no further in characterizing this relation than a richly suggestive homology—at bottom a kind of fallacy
of imitative form. His techniques of composition, or his processes of
thought, are often said to mirror various discontents with, or break-
downs of, medieval didactic authority and the discursive modes characteristically used to promote it: chaotic times or discredited languages
seem to require the semblance of chaos in their representation.[69]

Langland's increasingly circumstantial self-personification through

69. Among the scholars and critics who have seen Langland's procedures as a mirror
of his discontents with the formal or social discourses that constitute his artistic means
are Morton W. Bloomfield, *Piers Plowman as a Fourteenth-Century Apocalypse* (New
Brunswick, N.J.: Rutgers University Press, 1961), 34; Charles Muscatine, *Poetry and Crisis
in the Age of Chaucer* (Notre Dame, Ind.: University of Notre Dame Press, 1972), 71–110;
Mary Carruthers, *The Search for St. Truth* (Evanston: Northwestern University Press,
1973), 11, 171–72; Martin, *The Field and the Tower*, 10–14.

David Aers, in *Chaucer, Langland, and the Creative Imagination* (London and Boston:
Routledge and Kegan Paul, 1980), proposes a more active and intentional relation than
these broad homologies between Langland's methods and contemporary dissent, but the
dynamics of the exchange he proposes are problematic. It is difficult to see from what
source the imagination in such instances, whether individual or collective, might derive
the penetrating freedom of vision that it counterposes to orthodox or established practices, to understand by what means it is sustained, from what sources it takes voice, or—
as in the case of Langland—why it is so often rewarded with social approval within the
very discourses to which it is in sentiment opposed. The possible middle term in such a
relation, namely oppositional practices which themselves have a substantial social history
and a richly allusive (and elusive) language of word and gesture that is everywhere parasitic upon, and renewed by, those that nominally support "official" ideology, requires
more examination.

the construction and mnemonic disposition of his name in his *histoire,* in its problematic relation to his growing absorption of a historically specific level of social referentiality into the *discours* of his poem, seems to require a more exacting understanding than the assertion of a resonant cultural simile.[70] Regarded as a highly self-conscious special case of what Lavinia Griffiths has called his "nominalist" approach to personification, Langland's self-naming contains an implicit argument about the constructive nature of the social improvisations he both depicts and fictively enacts. As she describes the capacities of Langland's technique: "The personification trope allows for some exploration of an abstraction—and of a person. It also allows for the exploration of the relationship between experience and the words used to make sense of it, and of the relationship between words and the fictions they compose."[71] Langland's practices in characterizing himself as a named actor draw extraordinary and somewhat unsettling speculative attention to the ways in which, in life as in art, making sense of one's world is a matter of publishing a powerful fiction, and self-discovery or self-revelation a process of aligning oneself in relation to the distributive narratives of authority. The border of legitimacy between "making," making known, making believe, and making up, is always open to question, and it is at these boundaries that Langland inscribes his authorial name.

In allowing the contemporary world of social fiction-making, exemplified by the disposition of the proper name and the evasion of status-determination, to penetrate the discourse of his poem and to dispose the development of its narrative action, Langland makes a powerful argument about the nature of such social practices—an argument substantially different from that of his contemporary Gower about the same phenomenon. Such improvisations of identity may be disruptive of stable grammatical referentiality (a point Langland makes repeatedly in his own application of grammatical analogy), but they are also for this very reason constitutive of all rhetorical discourse, including his own.

70. Griffiths, *Personification,* adapts this distinction between story and discourse from Benveniste as discussed by Todorov (8). She suggests that Langland's techniques of personification are distinguished by the intensity and diversity of the exchanges between these two levels of organization: his mercurial willingness to collapse a nascent event back into the discursive term from which it arose, and his quickness at the procedure more frequently associated with personification-allegory, the generation of expository distinctions from narrative events.

71. *Personification,* 63.

For Langland it is these transgressive interventions that renew rather than decompose cultural meaning. For Gower and Froissart, the contemporary arguments-in-action of the 1381 rebels were, in the original sense of the term, barbarous incursions: invasions of bestial nonsense into the world of intelligible action. For Langland, as for several of the more perceptive (if still unremittingly hostile) monastic chroniclers such as Walsingham, the threat posed by these acts was precisely that they *were* intelligible, all too powerfully so. These writers disapproved of the text being written before their eyes, but they could read it perfectly well—and therein lay its power. If Walsingham merely registers the forceful legibility of such improvisation, Langland foregrounds its consequences by incorporating this way of making sense of experience into the narrative order of the poem, and into his construction of authorial identity. Scriptural *assimilatio* is in their narratives a malleable activity, the language of discovery and disclosure of both self and world, and as a vernacular it is in principle available to all, and limitless. The contemporary circulation of *nomina imponentes* and the publication of new identities sanctioned by the traditional representational syntax and semantics of scriptural citation are constructive forms of social discourse, arguments in action. Langland identifies such practices as both the tools of his authorial trade and the means by which his society may "come to itself." The terms of his art become the nature of the community: as "commun craftes" they are as inescapable in sustaining life as breathing or speaking.

Langland's alignment with the new pieties of the later Middle Ages is discernible not merely in his aversion to fixed and stable images and methods of interpretive mediation, where it has usually been seen, but in a positive practice implicit in this negative tropism: his equally strong insistence on the first person as the necessary locus of such mediation—on enactment rather than image as the center of exemplification. Such principles underlie both Margery's project and that of William Thorpe, both the Lollard distrust of graven images in favor of individual and communal identities that were thought to recreate those of scripture directly, and the noble sponsorship of eremitical rather than cenobitic forms of regular observance.[72] The model invoked in every case is the reconstructed self in a reconstituted community.

72. See W. R. Jones, "Lollards and Images: The Defense of Religious Art in Later Medieval England," *Journal of the History of Ideas* 34 (1973): 27–50; J. Anthony Tuck,

It is in his acknowledgment of the full implications of the "nominal-ist text," and not in explicit doctrinal or political allegiance, that Lang-land declares his deepest affinity with what can only to historical ret-rospection appear as reformist or heterodox sentiments and practices, expressed in forms that had not yet fully precipitated their differences into dissenting and orthodox aspects. It is in his perpetually inadequate yet obsessively necessary "making" that he best represents the commun-ally as well as individually restorative project of salvation history as the confrontation, at once shameful and exhilarating, of "myself in a mirour."

### APPENDIX: SIGNATURES IN *PIERS PLOWMAN*

I. Note on verso of last leaf of copy of C version, Trinity College Dub-lin MS D.4.1 (c. 1400):

> Memorandum quod Stacy de Rokayle pater willielmi de Langlond qui stacius fuit generosus & morabatur in Schiptoun vnder whicwode tenens domini le Spenser in comitatu Oxoniensi qui predictus willielmus fecit librum qui vocatur Perys ploughman.

> To be remembered: that Stacy [that is, Eustace] de Rokayle [was] the father of William de Langlond; the which Stacy was born and dwelt in Shipton-under-Wychwood, holding [land] of the lord Despenser in Oxfordshire; the aforesaid William made the book that is called Piers Plowman.

George Kane, *Piers Plowman:*
*The Evidence for Authorship, 26.*

II. Internal signatures recognized by Kane (*Evidence*). Citations are from:

> *Piers Plowman: The A Version,* ed. George Kane (London: Athlone Press, 1960);
> *Piers Plowman: The B Version,* ed. George Kane and E. Talbot Donaldson (London: Athlone Press, 1975);
> *Piers Plowman: An Edition of the C-Text,* ed. Derek Pearsall (Berkeley and Los Angeles: University of California Press, 1979).

---

"Carthusian Monks and Lollard Knights: Religious Attitudes at the Court of Richard II," in *Reconstructing Chaucer: Studies in the Age of Chaucer, Proceedings, No. 1, 1984,* ed. Paul Strohm and Thomas J. Heffernan (Knoxville, Tenn.: The New Chaucer Society, 1985), 149–61.

A-1)        Þanne ran repentaunce and reherside his teme
            And made wil to wepe watir wiþ his eiȝen.
                                A.5.43–44; B.5.61–62; C.6.1–2

A-2)        Þanne were marchauntis merye; many wepe for ioye,
            And ȝaf wille for his writyng wollene cloþis;
            For he copiede þus here clause þei couden hym gret mede.
                                A.8.42–44; cf. B.7.38–39, C.9.41–42:

            Thanne were Marchauntȝ murie; manye wepten for ioye
            And preiseden Piers þe Plowman þat purchaced þis bulle.
                                                    B.7.38–39

A-3)        A muchel man, me þouhte, lik to myselue,
            Com & callide me be my kynde name.
            "What art þou," quaþ I þo, "þat my name knowist?"
            "Þat þou wost wel," quaþ he, "& no wiȝt betere."
            "Wot ich?" quaþ I; "who art þou?" "þouȝt," seide he þanne.
            ...........................................................

            Þouȝt & I þus þre dayes we ȝeden,
            Disputyng on dowel day aftir oþer,
            Ac er we ywar were wiþ wyt gonne we mete.
            He was long & lene, lyk to non oþer,
            Was no pride on his apparail ne no pouert noþer,
            Sad of his semblaunt & of a softe speche,
            I durste meue no mater to make hym to iangle,
            But as I bad þouȝt þo be mene betwene,
            To putte forþ som purpos to prouen hise wittes.
            Þanne þouȝt, in þat tyme, seide þis wordis:
            "Where þat dowel, & dobet, & dobest beþ in londe,
            Here is wil wolde wyte ȝif wit couþe hym teche."
                A.9.61–65, 107–18; B.8.70–74, 117–29; C.10.68–72, 112–24

Cf. C:
            "That wost þou, Wille," quod he, "and no wyht bettere."
                                                    C.10.71

B-1) = A-1

B-2) = A-3

B-3)        "What is charite?" quod I þo; "a childissh þyng," he seide:
            ...........................................................
            "Where sholde men fynde swich a frend wiþ so fre an herte?
            I haue lyued in londe," quod I, "my name is longe wille,
            And fond I neuere ful charite, bifore ne bihynde.
            ...........................................................
            I seiȝ neuere swich a man, so me god helpe,
            That he ne wolde aske after his, and ouþerwhile coueite
            Thyng þat neded hym noȝt and nyme it if he myȝte.
            Clerkes kenne me þat crist is in alle places

Ac I seiȝ hym neuere sooþly but as myself in a Mirour:
*Hic in enigmate, tunc facie ad faciem.*
And so I trowe trewely, by þat men telleþ of it,
Charite is noȝt chaumpions fight ne chaffare as I trowe."
B.15.148, 151–53, 158–64

Cf. C:

"Charite," quod y tho, "þat is a thyng forsothe
That maistres commenden moche; where may hit be yfounde?
Ich haue yleued in Londone monye longe ȝeres
And fonde y neuere, in faith, as freres hit precheth,
Charite, þat chargeth naught, ne chyt, thow me greue hym.
. . . . . . . . . . . . . . . . . . . . . . . . . . . . . . . . . . . . . . . . . . . . . . . . . . . . .

For thogh me souhte alle þe sektes of susturne and of brethurne,
And fynde hym, but figuratyfly, a ferly me thynketh;
*Hic in enigmate, tunc facie ad faciem.*"
C.16.284–88, 293–94

C-1)    What the montaigne bymeneth and þe merke dale
And þe feld ful of folk y shal ȝou fair shewe.
A louely lady of lere in lynnene yclothed
Cam doun fro þe castel and calde me by name
And sayde, "Wille, slepestou? seestow þis peple,
Hou bisy þei ben aboute þe mase?"
C.1.1–6

Cf. A, B:

Com doun fro þat clyf & callide me faire,
And seide "sone, slepist þou?"
A.1.4–5; B.1.4–5

C-2)  = A-1, B-1

C-3)   "That wost þou, Wille," quod he, "and no wyht bettere."
C.10.71; cf. A-3, B-2

## III. Anagrams and signatory cross-references:

1)    And ek þe longe launde þat leccherie hatte,
Leue hym on þi left half a large myle or more,
A.11.118–19

2)    For I was rauysshed riȝt þere; Fortune me fette
And into þe lond of longynge and loue she me brouȝte
And in a Mirour þat hiȝte middelerþe she made me biholde
. . . . . . . . . . . . . . . . . . . . . . . . . . . . . . . . . . . . . . . . . . . . . . . . . .

Couetise of eiȝes conforted me anoon after
And folwed me fourty wyunter and a fifte moore.
B.11.7–9, 46–47; cf. C.11.169–73, 194–95

3)    "I am ymaginatif," quod he; "ydel was I neuere
Thouȝ I sitte by myself in siknesse ne in helþe.

I haue folwed þee, in feiþ, þise fyue and fourty wynter,
And manye tymes haue meued þee to mynne on þyn ende,
And how fele fernyeres are faren and so fewe to come."

B.12.1–5

"Y haue folewed the, in fayth, mo then fourty wynter."

C.14.3

4)    Thus y awakede, woet god, whan y wonede in Cornehull,
Kytte and y in a cote, yclothed as a lollare,
And lytel ylet by, leueth me for sothe,
Amonges lollares of Londone and lewede ermytes,
For y made of tho men as resoun me tauhte.
. . . . . . . . . . . . . . . . . . . . . . . . . . . . . . . . . . . . . . . . . . . . . . . . . . . . . . . . .
"Y am to wayke to worche with sykel or with sythe,
And to long, lef me, lowe to stoupe,
To wurche as a werkeman eny while to duyren."
"Thenne hastow londes to lyue by," quod Resoun, "or lynage ryche
That fynde the thy fode? For an ydel man þow semest,"
. . . . . . . . . . . . . . . . . . . . . . . . . . . . . . . . . . . . . . . . . . . . . . . . . . . . . . . . .
"When y ȝong was, many ȝer hennes,
My fader and my frendes foende me to scole,
. . . . . . . . . . . . . . . . . . . . . . . . . . . . . . . . . . . . . . . . . . . . . . . . . . . . . . . . .
That laboure þat y lerned beste þerwith lyuen y sholde.
   *In eadem vocacione in qua vocati estis.*
And so y leue yn London and opelond bothe."

C.5.1–5, 23–27, 35–36, 43–44

# 2

# Politics and Poetics
## Usk and Chaucer in the 1380s
### Paul Strohm

London in the 1380s was, in the words of Thomas Usk, dominated by "confederacie, congregacion, & couyne."[1] Control of city government shifted, and shifted again, between Nicholas Brembre and the other merchant-oligarchs on the one hand, and John Northampton and the craftguildsmen on the other.[2] Beyond this immediate factional horizon lay other, shifting planes of alliance. Brembre and his fellows were linked with Richard II; Northampton received intermittent encouragement from John of Gaunt. These alliances, taking shape in the early years of the decade, adumbrated the eventual struggle of 1385–88 between Richard's court party and the Duke of Gloucester's aristocratic appellants. Not surprisingly, advancement and wealth were tokens in the game. Richard's opponents claimed during the treason trials of 1387–88 that the royal party had rewarded even relatively humble followers with "diversz Manoirs, Terres, Tenementz, Rentes, Offices, & Baillifs," and the charge is at least partially sustained by evidences of advancement for Richard's followers.[3] Both sides hurled themselves into recruitment with a mounting intensity that crested in the summer of 1387, when the king himself spent July and August traveling about the midlands and retaining in his personal service men of every county he passed through.[4]

In such a situation, factional involvement was a virtual inevitability

1. "The Appeal of Thomas Usk against John Northampton," *A Book of London English, 1384–1425*, ed. R. W. Chambers and M. Daunt (Oxford: Clarendon Press, 1931), 29. Further citations from the *Appeal* are included in the text.
2. The best account of this rivalry is Ruth Bird, *The Turbulent London of Richard II* (London: Longmans, Green, 1949). (Hereafter, Bird.)
3. *Rotuli Parliamentorum: The Rolls of Parliament*, vol. 3 (London, 1783), 230. (Hereafter, R.P.) Entries in the *Calendar of Patent Rolls, 1385–1389* (London: Stationer's Office, 1900) attest to that advancement. (Hereafter, CPR.) See note 17 below for citations.
4. *The Westminster Chronicle, 1381–1393*, ed. L. C. Hector and Barbara F. Harvey (Oxford: Clarendon Press, 1982), 186. (Hereafter, West.)

for the upwardly mobile lawyer or civil servant who sought a position in the royal household, in administrative or judicial service, or in city government. Tout has shown that an exceptional few were able to weather the period as members of a politically neutral "lay bureaucracy."[5] For most of their contemporaries, however, the politics of faction did not simply constitute an interesting additional possibility for advancement in the world but was itself the very means by which worldly success was to be sought, attained, and preserved.

Londoners like Thomas Usk and Geoffrey Chaucer were confronted constantly with the possibilities and perils of factional affiliation. Each, as a writer and member of a lay intelligentsia, was pressed toward additional decisions about the uses of art in the service of faction. Each probably also entertained some awareness of the other. Judging from his compliment to Chaucer in the *Testament of Love* and the way in which he sought to use that work in his courtship of Chaucer's own political faction, Usk would seem at least partially to have modeled his career on Chaucer's own, to have been a "reader" (as well as ultimate "misreader") of the older poet's career.[6] Chaucer's more secure position would have insulated him from the political demimonde in which Usk moved, but he must at least have noted the cautionary lesson of Usk's hectic career.[7] Although each was a factionalist, each ultimately dealt with matters of affiliation in his own way. Usk embraced the politics of faction completely, while Chaucer sought ways of containing and moderating the impact of its all-or-nothing approach. Moreover, each made artistic choices that were continuous with his personal choices. In his *Testament,* Usk sought to turn literary form to personal account, importing materials of personal and factional apology and complaint into an apparent *consolatio*. In his works, Chaucer mainly avoided direct personal and political commentary, finding a counterpart for his experience of faction on the literary plane of genre- and discourse-conflict. Comparison of the respective personal and artistic choices made by the two writers in the course of the 1380s can tell us much about the careers of artists under political pressure, and about the way in which that pres-

---

5. T. F. Tout, *Chapters in the Administrative History of Medieval England,* vol. 3 (Manchester: Manchester University Press, 1928), 447. (Hereafter, Tout.)

6. *The Testament of Love,* in *The Complete Works of Geoffrey Chaucer,* vol. 7, ed. W. W. Skeat (Oxford: Clarendon Press, 1897), 3.4.248–59.

7. As Tout, at any rate, believed; see "Literature and Learning in the English Civil Service in the Fourteenth Century," *Speculum* 4 (1929): 386.

sure can either overbear inherited genres or encourage their maintenance and use as a way of restating and exploring conflicts at the level
of literary form.

## USK'S CAREER

Probably born among London tradespeople and himself a scrivener,
Usk seems to have worked obscurely in his trade before his appointment with then-mayor Northampton in the spring or summer of 1383.[8]
The basis of his original appointment—as scrivener or clerk—is clear.
In his 1384 *Appeal* against John Northampton for treason, Usk tells us
in his own words that Northampton and his faction hired him "to write
thair billes" (23). The Latin Inquisition based on his *Appeal* agrees, adding the explicit expansion that he was employed as "*skriveyn* ad scriben-
dum billas suas."[9] Northampton was soon to request more than scribal
help, though, because he and his party of small masters were preparing
to face Nicholas Brembre and his royalist party of merchants, victualers,
and other capitalists in a mayoral election to be held in October 1383.
The *Appeal* describes an initial series of meetings at which Northampton and his associates developed a program of "four poyntz," with Usk
evidently transcribing them: that aldermen should be limited to one-
year terms, that the Common Council should be elected from the crafts
rather than the wards, that no victualer should hold judicial office, and
that victualers from outside London could sell freely within the city

8. Earlier but inconsequential mentions of Usk appear in *Calendar of Close Rolls, 1381–85* (London: Stationer's Office, 1920), 125 (hereafter, *CCR*), and in *Calendar of Letter-Books . . . of the City of London: Letter-Book H*, ed. Reginald R. Sharpe (London, 1907), 30. Further citations from the *Letter Books* are included in the text. His family evidently lived in the London area, for Knighton reports the grim detail that his head was set over Newgate in order to shame his relatives who lived in that area ("in illis partibus morabatur"); see *Chronicon*, ed. J. R. Lumby (London, 1889), 2:294. He is usually described in the Patent and Close Rolls as a "scryvein" (*CCR*, 1381–85, 476; *CPR*, 1381–85 [London: Stationer's Office, 1897], 467, 470, 500). In later documents, including the chronicle accounts of his trial and punishment, he is often called "clericus," but surely more in the sense of "clerk" or "secretary" than "cleric"; see Walsingham, *Historia Anglicana*, vol. 2, *Rerum Britannicarum Medii Aevi Scriptores*, ed. H. T. Riley (London, 1864), no. 28, part 1, p. 116. Favent, alluding to his ultimate appointment as Under-Sheriff of Middlesex, calls him "serviens regis ad arma" or sergeant-at-arms of the king, this being the high watermark of his career; see *Historia Mirabilis Parliamenti*, ed. May McKisack, in *Camden Miscellany* 14 (1926): 19. (Hereafter, Favent.)

9. "Extracts from Inquisitions Taken at the Trial of John Northampton," in Edgar Powell and G. M. Trevelyan, *The Peasants' Rising and the Lollards* (London: Longmans, Green, 1899), 28. Further citations from the Inquisition are included in the text.

(24). While evidently excluded from the inner circles that framed this program ("atte some tymes wer ther more pryuier than I"), Usk was shortly to move from scrivening to a wider range of activities. His first job as publicist and organizer was to spread word of Northampton's populist program among those likely to be favorably influenced: "the mair . . . made me, Thomas Vsk, go to the comunes to enforme hem of the ordinance a-yeins the Fisshmongers, & for to haue thair wil ther-of . . . that they sholde chese for the comunes to the parlement Richard Norbury and William Essex" (25). Much of Usk's canvassing was soon aimed at influencing the upcoming mayoral election. To this end, he tells us, he visited the Goldsmith's Hall to "speke to hem that I knewe," with the aim of persuading them to "helpe to the eleccion of John Northampton" (27). Some of the contemplated help may have strayed beyond the bounds of normal factional activity; Usk tells us, for example, that some of Northampton's supporters went armed to the Guildhall on election day (27).

The prospects of Northampton and his followers dimmed when Brembre won the disputed election on October 13. Rather than accept the result, Northampton entered into what Usk describes in the *Appeal* as a period of "fals informacion & excitacion, couyns, & gadrynges, & confederacies" designed to overturn the result by guile or by force (29). As a participant in the "couyn," Usk was one of a delegation that visited John of Gaunt on the very day of the election, seeking his support for the issue of a royal writ ordering a new election (28). Rebuffed by Gaunt, the party fell back on a series of civil agitations, in which Usk admits himself "ful helpere & promotour" (29–30). On 7 February 1384, invited to a dinner "cum suis," Northampton showed up with some four hundred persons representing different trades and provoked a disturbance that led to his arrest (*West.*, 62). Charges were brought to the king that Northampton's efforts to create various disturbances were a threat to the city, and the king ordered that he be held in custody in Corfe Castle until he should clear himself of the charges against him (*West.*, 62–64). Usk remained at least briefly active on Northampton's behalf. Soon after the arrest, Usk went again to the duke in the company of others, "to enfourme hym that John Northampton was the beste mair that euer was" (30). Usk's circumstances were, however, about to change.

According to the official sources, Usk himself was arrested between July 20 and 6 August 1384 (*West.*, 90; *CPR*, 1381–85, 500), and imprisoned in London at the will of Mayor Brembre. According to the rather jaundiced view of the Westminster chronicler, Usk realized during his imprisonment that no other way of escape was available to him except that of turning against his former allies. Yielding to those who now prevailed, he is said to have busied himself with shrewdness and artfulness ("astu et arte") to win the friendship of those whom earlier he had known to be his chief enemies (*West.*, 90). Embellishing the official record that placed Usk in the custody of the mayor, the chronicler goes on to suggest that a consequence of his collaboration was his release from prison and lodging at the mayor's own house ("in domo majoris manebat"). There he is said to have composed the *Appeal* he launched against Northampton and certain followers while throwing himself on the mercy of the king. A trial rich in incident culminated in Northampton's condemnation to death, a sentence later modified at the intercession of the queen (*West.*, 92). Usk was subsequently conveyed to London by an order of August 20, to be held by the mayor in safe custody until further notice (*CCR*, 1381–85, 476). Following hearings at the Tower that resulted in further convictions, Usk was fully pardoned of all treasons, felonies, and other offenses by signet letter entered on September 24 (*CPR*, 1381–85, 467). Yet Usk's betrayal of his former associates and his subsequent pardon were to ruin his reputation for good. Four years later, under new accusation with his new allies, he would still be remembered and labeled as "faux & malveise" (*RP*, 234).

For a period of three years dating from his pardon, Usk disappears from official records. As I will discuss below, this is undoubtedly the period in which the *Testament of Love* was composed. More relevant to the present consideration is an adjustment of attitude signaled in the *Testament:* from the simple concern with self-preservation that no doubt motivated his betrayal of Northampton before king and council at Reading to a more positive expectation of a fresh and profitable tie to the royal faction of Walworth, Philipot, Brembre, and the other leading capitalists of London.

Events surrounding and subsequent to the Wonderful Parliament of 1386 conspired to advance his progress toward this goal. The climactic event of the Wonderful Parliament was the successful imposition by Gloucester and his followers of a Continual Council upon Richard to supervise the governance of the realm. Wholly unreconciled to this curtailment of his authority, Richard devoted himself throughout 1387 to a series of maneuvers intended to overthrow the authority of Gloucester and his fellow aristocrats. Among such royal actions the Westminster chronicler notes an elaborate judicial challenge to the actions of the preceding parliament mounted at Nottingham in August 1387 (186), a personal tour of the northern counties in which Richard recruited many men to his service (186), and an attempt in October 1387 to secure the loyalty of the city of London by oath (206). Throughout those crucial months in mid-1387, Richard seems to have entertained and rejected a number of schemes of harrassment, judicial indictment, and even assassination of the opposing Lords. The Westminster chronicler reports a conspiracy to murder Gloucester in April, 1387 (184), an ominous command on November 11 that Gloucester and Arundel attend the king (208), and an exchange between the king and Suffolk about the possibility of murdering Warwick (208–10). Needing persons for his service, Richard throughout this period liberally distributed badges or *signi* and employed other stratagems to recruit able followers to his cause (186).

Usk was recruited at this time. A letter of Privy Seal dated 7 October 1387, from the king to the mayor, alderman, and Commons of London expresses gratitude for their positive action on his request to appoint Thomas Usk under-sheriff of Middlesex, promising that he will not construe the appointment as precedental, in prejudice to the city's franchise (*Letter-Book H,* 317). In the eyes of the appellants, as revealed in the twenty-sixth article of Appeal that they would bring forward on 3 February 1388, there was no doubt of the intent underlying this action: The royal party had conspired to appoint Usk, a false and maliciously disposed member of their faction ("une faux & malveise person' de lour covyne, Thomas Huske") to be under-sheriff of Middlesex, in order to draw false indictments against Gloucester and other adversaries of the king (*RP,* 234).

In October of 1387, Usk's appointment as under-sheriff and embrace by the royal faction must have seemed charged with limitless possibility. Now styled Sergeant-at-Arms of the king (Favent, 19), richly rewarded (at least in the undoubtedly inflated account of the appellants [*RP,* 230]), associating with Brembre and others of his caliber, Usk must have believed that his long-awaited harvest of preferment was at hand. Events, however, rapidly reversed themselves. On 13 November 1387, the Lords and their followers joined together in arms; on November 14 they informed the king of their intention of appealing treason against his principal followers (including Alexander Nevill, Archbishop of

York; Robert de Vere, Earl of Oxford; Michael de la Pole, Earl of Suffolk; Justice Tresilian; and Nicholas Brembre); on November 17 they gained from the king a promise that the Appeal would be considered by Parliament in February 1388 (*West.*, 210–14). With the advantage of hindsight, we can see that the king's feeble challenge to the appellants was doomed by the events of mid-November, and the fate of his adherents effectively settled at that time. (The five principals seem to have sensed as much, since all but Brembre promptly fled or went into hiding.) An entry on the close rolls for 28 December 1387 orders Usk—already in the custody of the mayor and sheriffs of London—to be brought forward to give information (*CCR*, 393). How many days prior to December 28 Usk was arrested is not certain, but from mid-November onward he must have understood that his new allegiance was not to bring him the joy he had imagined.

The Articles of Appeal were first read to the Merciless Parliament on 3 February 1388. Brembre, as one of the five principals, was sentenced and hanged on February 20. Usk was one of the smaller fish to be taken up later in the same net. Sharing his fate was his fellow intellectual and co-conspirator John Blake, who had assisted Justice Tresilian in framing the questions favorable to the king's prerogative at Nottingham. Arraigned together on March 3 for high treasons and linked in a conspiracy to procure false indictments against the Lords, each pursued a line of defense unlikely to sway the now-triumphant appellants—that of loyalty to the king. Usk's statement, an echo of Blake's, was that he had done all at the command of the king (*RP*, 240). In the supercharged factional atmosphere of the trial, admission of having served the king was equivalent to confession of guilt, and the statements of Usk and Blake were simply treated as confessions (*RP*, 240). Blake was to be drawn and hanged, and Usk was to suffer a more extreme fate—drawing, hanging, beheading, and display of his head on the portal of Newgate (*RP*, 240). Archcontroversialist that he was, Usk died defending his final position. According to the Westminster chronicler, he went resolutely to his death, reciting penitential psalms "valde devote," refusing to admit that he had wronged John Northampton and insisting that the accusations against Northampton that he had spoken in council before the king "erant omnia vera" (*West*, 314–16). His emphasis on his appeal against Northampton suggests his recognition that the severity of the sentence was based upon his earlier shift of allegiance to the royal party as well as upon his more recent career of factional service to the king. But it may also suggest that he had grown sick of his reputation for falsity and wished finally to be known as a person able to stand by a final choice, however barren that choice might be.

Usk (together with his fellow sufferers of 1388 and, ultimately, their principal accusers as well) experienced both the immediate possibilities and eventual perils of factional activity. Jerked from obscurity by Northampton, singled out for the menacing courtship of mayor Brembre, elevated abruptly to the king's sergeancy-at-arms, rewarded with lands and rents, he then abruptly lost position, lands, and life during the appellants' brief sway. Perhaps the relatively humble position of London scrivener from which he set out left him little choice in the matter. But his was a notably single-minded pursuit of the rewards of political faction, in which concerns of advancement tended in their immediacy and urgency to override a balanced assessment of his personal prospects.

## CHAUCER'S CAREER

As the son of a prosperous London merchant and sometime servant of the Crown, Chaucer was born with assured access to the very ranks of gentry in court service to which Usk so fervently aspired.[10] In any comparison of the two careers we should note that Usk, with more ground to cover, could not necessarily afford Chaucer's more becoming kind of restraint. Whatever his initial advantages, though, Chaucer marshalled them effectively, presenting a model of circumspection in pursuit of factional reward that might have served poor Usk well.[11]

The briefest account of Chaucer's early progress must take note of his post as *valettus* in the household of the Countess of Ulster, dating from 1357; his marriage by 1366 to Philippa Roet, herself the daughter of a knight and sister to the mistress and eventual wife of John of Gaunt; and his switch to the royal household as *valettus* by 1367 and as *esquier/armiger* in 1368.

By 1374 Chaucer had laid the foundation for a life of security in royal service. This foundation consisted of a series of clearly interrelated steps

---

10. *Chaucer Life-Records,* ed. M. M. Crow and C. C. Olson (Oxford: Clarendon Press, 1966), 4. (Hereafter, Crow.)

11. The ensuing discussion of Chaucer's political circumspection in the mid-1380s has received significant independent corroboration in S. Sanderlin's recently published "Chaucer and Ricardian Politics," *Chaucer Review* 22 (1988): 171–84.

that enabled him to move to London and away from the immediate physical environs of the court, while remaining on call to his court sponsors for a variety of special assignments and duties. First of these steps was his rent-free lease for a house "supra portam de Aldgate," entered 10 May 1374 during the mayoralty of Adam de Bury, himself an active member of the London court party along with John Philipot, Nicholas Brembre, and others (Crow, 144–46; Bird, 18–19). Closely associated was his royal appointment, enrolled on 8 June 1374, as Controller in the Port of London for wool and petty customs, under the already formidable Brembre (Crow, 148; Bird, 2–7). In addition, he and Philippa received a life annuity from John of Gaunt, and he was granted an uninterrupted continuation of the life exchequer annuity from Edward III that he had been receiving since 1367 (Crow, 271, 151). The close association of these gestures provides an early and impressive glimpse into Chaucer's ability to manage his own affairs. While no single component of his move to London could have been accomplished without the active cooperation of one or more superiors, only personal activity on his own behalf could have assured simultaneous action on all these fronts.

Thus established in London, Chaucer was able to continue his service to the court (the period 1376–81 was, for example, that of his most active employment abroad), but also to temper that service by a slight and eventually important degree of personal latitude. Fostered by the geographical removal from Westminster to London, by the continuation of his "Lancastrian connection," and by his own keen sense of the dangers of factional activity, Chaucer's independence was to serve him well in the difficult years between the first stirrings of parliamentary discontent in 1385 and their aftermath in the Wonderful Parliament of 1386 and the Merciless Parliament of 1388.[12] For in those very years, when Usk was seeking so unreservedly to enter into the service of the royal faction, Chaucer was wisely and systematically curtailing the extent of his factional visibility.

Chaucer probably realized as early as 1384–85 that the wind was

---

12. I certainly do not mean to revive the idea that John of Gaunt was Chaucer's "patron," a theory dispatched when J. R. Hulbert pointed out that Chaucer's marital connections through Philippa were probably the basis for the Lancastrian annuity (*Chaucer's Official Life* [Menasha, Wis., 1912; reprint, New York: Phaeton, 1970], 79–84). Still, the Lancastrian interest remained a center of influence partially detached from the Ricardian court, and one to which Chaucer enjoyed at least a degree of personal connection.

blowing against the royal party. Richard was the object of open attack from Arundel in the Salisbury Parliament of 1384, and the same year saw probably bogus charges that Gaunt was plotting against the life of the king (*West.,* 66–80). Parliamentary evidence of mounting militancy can be seen as early as 1385, in a bill of particulars indicating dissatisfaction with royal patronage and household extravagance, and suggesting a series of measures by which revenue could be increased. One of the measures that Chaucer might have taken to heart requested appointment of customs officials only upon the advice of the king's council (rather than "par . . . desir singuler"), their remuneration according to desert and their service without deputies.[13] The bill containing this request was adopted by the Parliament of 1385, and the implementation of its advice was entrusted to a select committee of lords but was apparently neglected (Palmer, 97). Nevertheless, a "reading" of this and other currents—especially when their effects were likely to be enhanced by the withdrawal of John of Gaunt from English affairs between 1386 and 1389—seems to have lain well within Chaucer's often-demonstrated powers of political analysis.

A possible harbinger of Chaucer's withdrawal to Kent in 1386 is his October 1385 appointment as Justice with the Commission of the Peace for Kent. The appointment itself may be interpreted as a sign of royal favor, and the fact that Chaucer's fellow justices included such archroyalists as Simon Burley and Robert Tresilian might also argue that it represented a strengthening of royal ties (Crow, 348, 363). Further, Chaucer may have accepted the appointment without actually becoming a resident of Kent; as Crow points out, most of his fellow justices (excepting certain men of law) were residents of the county, but "statutory sanction for the principle of residence" did not come until 1388–89 (363). Even so, this appointment may signal a determination on Chaucer's part, formed as early as 1385, to withdraw to Kent. It anticipates the apparent indication of changed residence in Chaucer's election as Knight of the Shire for Kent in or about August 1386, and the certain indication of his move in the grant of his house over Aldgate to another tenant on 5 October 1386 (Crow, 364–69).

If Chaucer sought relief from factional strife in his withdrawal to Kent, then he made a mistake in accepting election as Shire-Knight to

---

13. "The Impeachment of Michael de la Pole in 1386," ed. J. J. N. Palmer, *Bulletin of the Institute of Historical Research* 42 (1969): 97–101. (Hereafter, Palmer.)

what became the Wonderful Parliament of 1386. There he found himself in the extremely awkward situation of a Ricardian representative at a session strongly bent on limiting the royal prerogative. He witnessed the passage of legislation deeply hostile to Richard, including the appointment of Gloucester and others as a "graunt & continuel Conseil" charged to amend blemishes on the crown (*RP,* 221), the impeachment of de la Pole, and also the presentation of a petition of Commons that deeply embarrassed his own situation by asking that all controllers appointed by the king for life be removed because of their "grauntz oppressions & extorcions" (*RP,* 223).

Chaucer appears not to have been directly touched by the 1386 petition. His controllership was not a life appointment in the first place, and he might have been shielded in any event by Richard's temporizing reply that these persons would be examined before his council, with the good to be continued and the bad removed. Nevertheless, the chronology of events suggests that this petition precipitated a precautionary action on Chaucer's part. On November 19, Letters Patent gave effective control of the kingdom to the antiroyal Continual Council (*West.,* 166–74). On November 28, Parliament itself ended (*West.,* 176–77). On December 4 and 14, successors were appointed to Chaucer's controllerships of the wool and petty customs (Crow, 268–70). No particular pressure seems to have been brought upon Chaucer to resign his posts. Crow reports that "There is . . . no evidence that a general inquiry was made as a result of which Chaucer might have been removed from office nor that any of the controllers appointed for life were discharged as a result of the council's investigation" (269). Brembre, a more ardent factionalist than Chaucer might ever have been, continued beyond 1386 in his collectorship, so no wholesale purge of Richard's adherents could have taken place. Chaucer's action, in other words, seems to have been voluntary, based on his independent decision to scale down his visibility as a member of the royal faction.

Chaucer's readiness to curtail his royal commitments is also suggested by an apparently voluntary step taken in response to an action of the Merciless Parliament of 1388. The Merciless Parliament is remembered mainly for condemning a number of the king's intimates for treason. The Parliament also sought, however, to circumscribe Richard's authority by issuing a series of petitions that called for, among other things, a purge of the royal household (23) and a wholesale voiding of royal annuities (30). The petition for a purge of the household evidently never came to much. A good deal nearer to Chaucer's case was a petition calling for nullification of all those annuities granted by Richard, his grandfather, or his father that included the clause "Quousque pro Statu suo aliter duxerimus ordinand' " in all cases where the persons had accepted subsequent grants from the king (*RP,* 247). Chaucer's annuity might have fallen into the affected category. Crow points out that it contains the indicated wording and that conversion of his wine grant into an exchequer annuity might have applied the enactment to his case (123, 338). In any event, Chaucer granted his Exchequer annuities to John Scalby on 1 May 1388—a date that probably fell between the first promulgation of the petition and the adjournment of Parliament on June 4.

As an old court hand, Chaucer probably knew that he stood a good chance of weathering the petition with his annuity intact; despite Richard's agreement to the petition, no general nullification of annuities or any large-scale transfer of annuities seems to have occurred (Crow, 339). Nevertheless, Chaucer would have had several good motives for acting when he did. (1) He might have sold his annuity to Scalby, in order to raise ready cash.[14] (2) He might have sold the annuity as a hedge against possible loss in the event of vigorous prosecution of the Commons' petition (Crow, 339). (3) He might have intended a further scaling down of his connection with the court. No one of these motives excludes the others. Very possibly he acted on some combination of all three, since any or all would have furthered his apparent objective of leading a modestly restricted life in Kent until circumstances would permit a safe reentry into national affairs.

Did Chaucer really need to be so cautious? A further look at those adherents of Richard who suffered in 1388 would certainly suggest so. In addition to a much larger number of people arrested or forced to abjure the court, eleven persons were condemned for treason by the Merciless Parliament: the five principals (Alexander Nevill, Robert de Vere, Michael de la Pole, Tresilian, and Brembre); four chamber knights (Simon Burley, John Beauchamp, John Salisbury, and James Berners); and the strategists Usk and Blake—the first three dying in exile and the remaining eight through capital punishment. Chaucer had

14. As argued by Samuel Moore, "Studies in the Life-Records of Chaucer," *Anglia* 37 (1913): 19–25.

at least some documented contact, and in some cases intimate contact, with eight of the eleven.

Robert de Vere, Duke of Ireland, served as the king's chamberlain (and hence Chaucer's superior in the household) and in that category endorsed and possibly personally signed Chaucer's 1385 petition for a permanent deputy in the office of controller (Crow, 168).[15] Michael de la Pole, as chancellor between 1383 and his impeachment in 1386, signed documents related to the 1383 appointment of a deputy controller (Crow, 165), opened the Parliament at which Chaucer served, and would in other ways have been a conspicuous figure in Chaucer's eyes. Robert Tresilian had served as Chaucer's fellow justice of the peace for Kent between 1386 and his death and must have been well known to him (Crow, 361). Nicholas Brembre served as collector of wool customs and hence as Chaucer's immediate superior throughout most of the latter's term as controller (Crow, 172).

Chaucer was even more closely linked with those chamber knights who were to meet their deaths in the weeks immediately following his resignation of his annuities. The venerable and powerful subchamberlain Simon Burley, whose office under Robert de Vere placed him in effective control of the household (Tout, 331), held the concurrent position of Constable of Dover Castle, which made him the supervisor of Chaucer's activities as justice of the peace for Kent (Crow, 360). He was brother of John Burley, with whom Chaucer went on a royal mission in 1376 (Crow, 43). Chaucer must certainly have had frequent contact with Burley in his official life, and may possibly have had literary contact as well. Burley appears to have been devoted to secular as well as devotional and instructional literature: his forfeited goods included nine French romances and the unidentified English "book of the forester and the wild boar."[16] Among the three additional chamber knights who were to die on May 12, John Beauchamp is listed with Chaucer as an esquire of the household in 1368 (Crow, 95), and John Salisbury is listed with Chaucer in the same capacity in 1372 (Crow, 100); the third,

15. Hulbert argues that this signature was merely a piece of the chamberlain's "official business" and indicates no close connection ("Chaucer and the Earl of Oxford," *Modern Philology* 10 [1912–13]: 433). Whatever conclusions we draw about the closeness of the connection, however, we may assume that Chaucer knew de Vere as a major official of the household in which he served.

16. M. V. Clarke, "Forfeitures and Treason in 1388," in *Fourteenth Century Studies* (Oxford: Clarendon Press, 1937), 122.

James Berners, was presumably no less in Chaucer's orbit. Usk and Blake served Richard in specialized capacities, and were not really of the court. Chaucer might, however, have encountered them in London in the 1380s, and Usk's early acquaintance with several of Chaucer's literary works may well argue for personal contact. Both men died just three days after Chaucer's resignation of his annuities.

In late April 1388, then, Chaucer saw the Archbishop of York, the Duke of Ireland, and the former chancellor of the realm in flight; Tresilian and Brembre dead; the chamber knights likely to die; and many more in peril. At that moment, any reasonable way of minimizing his royal ties must have seemed worth a second look. Of course, so modest a step as the reassignment of royal annuities for probable cash payment, taken barely a month before the adjournment of the Merciless Parliament, would hardly have saved Chaucer had the appellants and their supporters singled him out as an active participant in the royal strategies of 1387. No single step saved Chaucer from indictment, but rather a whole series of prudent adjustments of his relations with the court party, possibly beginning as early as his removal to London in 1374 and certainly beginning with his removal to Kent, probably in 1385 and certainly by October 1386. These modest disassociations did not constitute a denial of his factional ties—Brembre had certainly shown that one could be a factionalist from a London base, and Chaucer's identity in Kent was that of a king's man—but they nevertheless represent a careful calibration of their extent.[17]

Few could have predicted the rapidity with which Richard would successfully reassert his authority in 1389. The Westminster chronicler,

17. An instructive contrast to Chaucer's prudence is provided by the cases of the doomed Chamber knights, who—along with Thomas Usk and John Blake—conspicuously sought royal preferment in the crucial period 1385–87. The earlier career of John Beauchamp of Holt is somewhat difficult to disentangle from that of at least one namesake who might have served in the royal household, but 1385–87 may be identified with certainty as his own period of greatest advancement. On 12 August 1385 he is mentioned as King's Knight, and he receives five major grants in 1385–87; on 5 June 1386 he is mentioned as keeper of the king's jewels; on 8 June 1387 as steward of the household; on 10 October 1387 he is named Lord of Beauchamp and Baron of Kydermyster—the first barony to be conferred by royal patent (*CPR,* 1385–89, 16, 179, 306, 363). On 6 October 1385 James Berners received a substantial grant "by word of mouth" of the king, and yet another on 6 November 1387, even as the appellants were gathering in arms (*CPR,* 1385–89, 27, 371). John Salisbury received a grant on 29 August 1385 as "usher of the chamber," and a superior grant on 31 October 1385 (*CPR,* 1385–89, 15, 41). In the opinion of the appellants, both Usk and Blake were well rewarded (*RP,* 230), though the lavish bestowals of which the appellants complain are unrecorded in the *CPR.*

for example, wryly notes that the king spent the remainder of the summer and the next autumn after the end of the Merciless Parliament indulging himself in the chase: "Rex vero deinceps per totum autumpnum venacioni indulsit" (342). On 8 May 1389, however, Richard asserted his majority and successfully claimed sole governance of the kingdom ("solum regni gubernaculum" [*West.*, 390]). As Tout points out, Chaucer was one of the two "old courtiers" soon thereafter "cautiously given preferment" (457). On 12 July 1389 Chaucer was appointed Clerk of Works, with other appointments to follow (Crow, 402). Such preferment may have come none too soon; in the period 1388–89 Chaucer was the object of several actions for debt (Crow, 384, 388, 391). Yet the positive consequences of 1389, no less than the shocking deaths in 1388, confirm the practicality of his conduct of affairs.

## WRITING FOR A PURPOSE

At different crucial moments in his life, Usk sought to mobilize his literacy on his own behalf. His first position with Northampton was as secretary, "to write thair billes" (*Appeal*, 23). Then, having decided to give evidence against Northampton, Usk used his period of confinement with Brembre during the summer to 1384 to write with his "owne honde" the *Appeal* against Northampton, which would purchase his pardon from the king and council. Finally, pardoned but underemployed in 1385–86, he composed his *Testament of Love* in order to persuade the members of the royal faction that he was in full control of his actions and choices and ready for significant service.[18] Henry Bradley

---

18. The narrator of the *Testament* writes from confinement in a "derk prison, caitived from frendshippe and acquaintaunce, and forsaken of al that any word dare speke" (1.1). Since Usk endured at least two actual prison terms—from July to September 1384 and from November or December 1387 until his death—commentators have been at some pains to attach the composition of the *Testament* to one or the other, or to establish a third (see Ramona Bressie, "The Date of Thomas Usk's *Testament of Love*," *Modern Philology* 26 [1928–29]: 17–29). Certainly, though, the example of Boethius (which Usk heavily used in Chaucer's translation) offered a literary rather than historical precedent for Usk's representation of imprisonment. A number of internal indications suggest that Usk is using the state of imprisonment figuratively rather than literally: "Depe in this pyninge pitte with wo I ligge y-stocked," he says, "with chaynes linked of care and tene" (1.1). Assuming that Usk need not have been literally imprisoned except by his own "care and tene" when he wrote, we can turn to a combination of internal and external evidence to establish the likely dates of composition. Since the *Testament* includes references to his early allegiance to Northampton, his confrontation of Northampton at the trial, and his failure to gain preferment in the aftermath of the trial, we would not want to date the

was on solid ground in finding evidence of "special purpose" in Usk's writings.[19] Whatever might be thought of the ethics of the *Appeal* or the florid art-prose of the *Testament,* each is designed for a purpose and each compels admiration as a piece admirably bent to the objectives for which it is written.

The goal of Usk's *Appeal* is not really exoneration from the charges immediately at hand; he freely indicts himself as a helper and promoter of Northampton's "euel menyng" in every possible way (29). Rather, Usk is aiming at a longer-term objective by providing detailed and persuasive information that will be helpful in obtaining the convictions of Northampton and his friends. In this respect, Usk appears to have been a very "good" witness—much better, in fact, than the Westminster chronicler implies. The chronicler characterizes the recitation of the written *Appeal* as containing a great number of enormities and crimes ("multa enormia et sinistra" [90]) and says that at the trial itself Usk unblushingly recited articles detailing numerous and odious misdeeds ("mala non pauca et odiosa" [92]). Yet Usk would claim with some apparent justice in the *Testament* that his *Appeal* adhered closely to "the sothe . . . of these things in acte" and that its goal is to record "true meninge" (1.6). Usk's account was persuasive enough to serve as the principal basis of Northampton's conviction and to be carried nearly sentence-by-sentence into the Latin Inquisition that joined the records of the trial.[20]

Usk probably realized that, considering the climate into which he was launching his *Appeal,* his point would be sufficiently made if he simply identified Northampton as a factionalist who had chosen the wrong side—just as Usk's own statement three years later that he had acted on behalf of the king would be taken by the appellants as prima

---

commencement of the work much before 1385. Since Usk's employment in the king's service by late summer or early fall of 1387 presumably alleviated the disappointment of which he complains, we must imagine the work completed by mid-1387. For simplicity, we might simply think of the work as having been composed in 1385–86.

19. "Thomas Usk," *Dictionary of National Biography* (London: Oxford University Press, 1949–50), 20:60–62.

20. The *Appeal,* couched in simple and idiomatic English, is obviously designed for high accessibility. When the author of the usually parallel Latin "Inquisition" differs from Usk, the motive is more often than not to elevate and obscure his phrasing. Usk's fear that after the election "eueri man sholde haue be in others top" (28) becomes a generalized report of the spread of "rumor et insurrectio" in the Latin of the Inquisition (31). Omitted altogether is his prediction that, had Northampton been reelected, he would have "sette al the town in a rore" (27).

facie evidence of guilt. Certainly it is toward placing Northampton's actions in a context of factional activity that most of the rhetoric of the *Appeal* is bent. "Confederacie, congregacion, & couyne" (29) are Northampton's modes, Usk tells us again and again. His is not the only faction, to be sure, but it is the least worthy of the two. Strong distinctions are drawn between Northampton's constituency of "comun people . . . pore people . . . [and] smale people" and the substantial group of the "worthy & wysest . . . grete men . . . [and] worthy persons" whom they opposed. Because of Northampton's factional activities, Usk tells us, "dissension ys arrise betwene the worthy persones & the smale people of the town" (25). A case in point is Northampton's active support of a statute against usurers, according to which "many of the worthiest of the town sholde haue be ther-by enpesched" (26).[21]

Usk's purpose in writing the *Appeal* comes to the fore at the conclusion, when he emphasizes his suit for the "grace & mercy" of the king and his intention of being as "repentant" as he is able (31). Such professions, omitted from the Latin Inquisition as irrelevant to the case at hand, were nevertheless very relevant to Usk's controlling motive of saving himself from harm. The end of the manuscript has been greatly damaged, yet among the scattered phrases with which it concludes are several that may prefigure a new trend of thought: ". . . but euer stonde be the town & be the worthy . . . ght may do next my lige lorde wol . . . be redy at al tymes where I shal to a vowe. . . ." These incomplete references to his continuing loyalty to the worthy, his preparedness to do the king's bidding, and his readiness to serve suggest that in the summer of 1384 Usk was already thinking that his service to the Brembre faction might be continuous rather than short-term, and that he might hope for future advancement from his new allies. If so, he seems to have been disappointed in the months immediately following his pardon. Yet once again he took his pen in his "owne honde," this time to write *Testament of Love* as an outcry against his present difficulties and an expression of his future hopes.

The *Testament* has been dogged by largely unwarranted imputations

---

21. Usk's depiction of a struggle between the rich and the poor of the city is certainly heightened; the actual contestants in this factional struggle were the major capitalists of the city, including a number of masters of the powerful victualing guilds, on the one hand, and a number of the lesser masters, especially of the nonvictualing guilds, on the other (Bird, 63–85). In short, the struggle was between an emerging upper-middle-class patriciate and a somewhat more broadly based segment of middle-class citizens, with the poor as usual unheard.

of plagiarism, and even when admired it has often been misapprehended as an "erotic allegory" or a philosophical treatise.[22] Yet it remains a considerable and impressive work, a work mistaken for 300 years as having been written by Chaucer himself, and a tour-de-force in its own right: completed in a period of eighteen months or less, in a language still rarely employed for literary purposes, by an autodidact who learned penmanship as a member of the scriveners' guild and who rather touchingly represents himself plying his own trade, earnestly scribbling like Shamela to record Love's words (3.4). The source of this energy and enterprise resides, I believe, in the communicative situation of the work—a situation in which Usk, having deserted one faction and not yet won the confidence of the other, composed a work designed to bridge the gap between himself and his hoped-for associates by persuading them of his essential trustworthiness.

Of course, no literary work can be regarded strictly as a "communication."[23] The social content of a literary work, including particular motives of communication between author and intended audience as well as other social motives more broadly conceived, must be understood not as directly "reflected" but as "refracted" through the range of possible generic and discursive choices made available to the author.[24] Usk's communication with his intended associates is itself refracted through the available form of a *consolatio* or allegory of consolation. This is, as we shall see, an expressive condition that Usk partially accepts and partially chafes against, producing a work crisscrossed with heterogeneous and often inconsistent generic and discursive materials.

Usk reminds us in his prologue that he is a frequent borrower from

---

22. Usk's own modern editor, Skeat, refers to Usk's work as resulting from "the most barefaced and deliberate plagiarism" (xxv). C. S. Lewis treats the *Testament* as a flawed but interesting example of an "erotic allegory" that leads the reader "from profane to sacred love" (*The Allegory of Love* [1936; reprint, New York: Galaxy Books, 1958], 231). Insisting on the philosophical emphasis of the work, and especially of its third book, is George Sanderlin, "Usk's *Testament of Love* and St. Anselm," *Speculum* 17 (1942): 69–73. The work has been viewed in its full political context only by Ramona Bressie, "The Date of Thomas Usk's *Testament of Love*"; see also an abstract of Bressie's dissertation in *Abstracts of Theses,* humanistic series, vol. 7 (Chicago: University of Chicago Press, 1928–29), 517–20.

23. On the senses in which a literary work is and is not a "communication," see, respectively, V. N. Volosinov, *Marxism and the Philosophy of Language,* trans. Ladislav Matejka and I. R. Titunik (New York: Seminar Press, 1973), 86, and Jonathan Culler, *Structuralist Poetics* (Ithaca: Cornell University Press, 1975), 131–32.

24. M. M. Bakhtin/P. M. Medvedev, *The Formal Method in Literary Scholarship* (Cambridge, Mass.: Harvard University Press, 1985), 18.

Boethius, and the general form and thrust of his work are derived from the *Consolation*. The intent of Boethius's work is, of course, to instill fortitude; despite early dissatisfaction with his fate, he comes to understand that God has ordained all for profit if not delight, and that even within his constrained circumstances he can exercise his free will by choosing virtue and eschewing vice. This is a framework that Usk means to emulate, and he does so to a considerable degree. His work involves a protagonist confined in a figurative prison of despair over his troubled worldly circumstances (book 1) who is encouraged by Love to reject such worldly measures of happiness as dignity, riches, renown, or power (book 2), and who achieves a recognition of his own freedom of choice (book 3), further amplified in Christian terms by the introduction of Anselm's idea of grace as a necessary incentive and aid to restoration of his "inner mannes helth" (3.9).

So seen in its largest outline, Usk's work would appear to possess its own kind of Boethian restraint; but Usk was not a restrained person, and the *consolatio,* with its encouragement of resignation, proves in other ways to be a less-than-adequate form within which to express his worldly disappointments and expectations. The text of the *Testament* consequently turns out to be a good deal less orderly and predictable than a broad summary of its contents would suggest, as Usk seizes upon a succession of textual strategies in an attempt to embody his persistent non-Boethian desires.

"In this boke," Usk tells us, "be many privy thinges wimpled and folde" (3.9), and one recurring subject for allegorization within the work is his factional situation, including his earlier mistaken allegiances and his present hope for acceptance by the Brembre faction. In 1.3, for example, he introduces an allegory in which, wandering to see "the wynding of the erthe in . . . winter," he is affrighted by "grete beestes . . . and heerdes gonne to wilde." He boards a ship, assisted by several persons: "Sight was the first, Lust was another, Thought was the thirde; and Wil eke was there a mayster; these broughten me within-borde of this shippe of Traveyle." The seas are rough: "The wawes semeden as they kiste togider; but often under colur of kissinge is mokel old hate prively closed and kept." He is finally driven to an isle, "where utterly I wende first to have be rescowed." On that isle he finds "a Margaryte-perle, the moste precious and best that ever to-form cam in my sight." He lingers on the isle, pledging service to the Marguerite but evidently fated to "desyre that thing, of which I never have blisse." By the domestic beasts gone wild (and the later treacherous waves), we may understand his former associates; by the ship of travail, the judicial process of his *Appeal* against Northampton; by the island of seeming refuge on which he lingers in hope and despair, the new alliance into which he has been provisionally but not wholeheartedly received. Possession of the Marguerite has shifting meanings throughout the work, some spiritual; yet here it seems to suggest devoted service to his new associates, devoutly given and fully rewarded.

Allegorical discourse will not, however, contain all the material that Usk wishes to introduce. In 1.6, for example, he provides his protagonist with his own life-history, with proper names suppressed and with a few elevating touches (aldermen, for example, become senators), but essentially in the direct style of the *Appeal*. In his youth, he tells us, he was drawn into certain "conjuracions" or conspiracies, touching on "grete maters of ruling of citizens." Early on he was moved by advantage to himself and friends and by mistaken notions of "commen profit." Soon, however, he came on his own to see that "firste painted thinges" actually purposed "malice and yvel." Subsequently imprisoned by "tho persones that suche thinges have cast to redresse," he was to confess as a way of ending rancor and promoting peace. Seeing an opportunity to help the "comune wele to ben saved," he determined to help "al shulde I therthrough enpeche myn owne fere." He then summarizes his written *Appeal*, concluding with his reiteration that the "governour" of the conspiracy "shoop to have letted thilke eleccion, and have made a newe, himselfe to have ben chosen; and under that, mokil rore to have arered." He states that in framing the *Appeal*, he served only "trouthe of my sacrament in my ligeaunce, by whiche I was charged on my kinges behalfe." What he cannot understand is the "janglinge of these shepy people . . . [who] oughten to maken joye that a sothe may be knowe."

A strategy underlying all of Usk's references to his own career is to increase his acceptability to the Brembre faction by portraying his choices as the result not of opportunism but of free will. The earlier allegory of Usk tossed at sea emphasizes, for example, that he was not impressed or dragooned onto the storm-tossed ship that bore him away from his former associates and toward a new factional resting place. His was a conscious choice supported by first-hand appraisal, personal inclination, and rational reflection; his will, as he reminds us, was master of the decision-making process. His new associates, who are the implied audience of this allegory as well as of the work as a whole, are to understand that free choice rather than expedience has brought him to their camp. Similarly, in the more literal account of his actions in 1.6, Usk mentions but deemphasizes the fact that his confession and appeal against Northampton were arranged during his imprisonment by the Brembre faction as the price of "lyfe and frenesse of that prison." Emphasized instead are his independent conclusion, prior to his arrest, of the maliciousness of his first associates and his eagerness that his confession serve the truth (not to mention the "comune wele," "the citee of London," "pees," "our god," and "my kinge"). His clear wish is that his new associates see him not as a constrained or halfhearted follower, but as a free and wholehearted convert to their cause.

Free will is the basis on which Usk stakes his claim: "If I by my good wil deserve this Margarit-perle . . . and have free choice to do what me lyketh; she is than holden, as me thinketh, to reward th'entent of my good wil" (3.3). In this sense, Usk's emphasis on his own free inclination toward the Brembre faction is consistent with the larger frame of his argument, in which free will supported by grace will enable his protagonist to reject unstable earthly attachments in favor of inner harmony. The only problem is that Usk's assertion of free will in his factional choices seems to have a different and more worldly object than the more elevated choices urged upon him by Love at the end of book 3; here and often in the work, the reward he envisions seems to be of precisely that sort which his larger argument urges him to scorn.

Staged within the consolatory form of the *Testament* is therefore a subversive counterargument for precisely the kinds of limited approval and short-term reward against which Love will so forceably argue. In the course of this counterargument, many of the familiar devices of the consolatory allegory are invaded or bent to new use. The voice of Love, which addresses the protagonist in familiar terms of correction and reproof, is suddenly and unpredictably bent toward purposes of factional vindication. She is capable of great heat, for example, over the fact that Usk's associates in the Northampton camp were slow and inconsistent in reimbursing his travel expenses: "Who yave thee ever ought for any rydinge thou madest?" (1.7). Of course he deserted such a pack of knaves; he would have been a fool to do otherwise: "What might thou more have don than thou diddest, but-if thou woldest in a fals quarel have been a stinkinge martyr?" (1.7). Love, we find, is a factionalist herself. When informed of Usk's appeal against Northampton, she comments with satisfaction, "Ever thou were redy for my sake" (2.4). Abandoning her detachment, she vies with the protagonist in creating self-aggrandizing images that promise his ultimate glorification, likening him to the lost sheep of Israel (1.8), to Adam and others whose transgressions have opened the way to spiritual progress for mankind (1.8), to those Christian martyrs whose passion is yet to be written (2.9), to David who has been found true in service and will "with holy oyle of pees and of rest . . . be anoynted" (3.1), and to Paulinas, Perdicas, and other noted turncoats who ultimately enjoyed rich reward (3.2).

The nature of the reward that Usk contemplates is finally left open to question in the work as a whole. While the heavenly reward of grace is celebrated in the work's conclusion, a much more mundane version of grace is constantly propounded through covert channels. The actual purveyor of grace in the world, we have already learned, is the king, who rewarded Usk with pardon at the time of his appeal against Northampton: "To the gracious king art thou mikel holden, of whos grace and goodnesse somtyme hereafter I thinke thee enforme" (2.4). As a result of the king's status as head of the very political faction Usk seeks to join and as potential source of patronage, many of the promises of reward within the *Testament* come to seem double-sided, referring not only to heavenly but to worldly matters as well. The king, Love reminds Usk, rewarded you once before: "What goodnesse, what bountee, with mokel folowing pitè founde thou in that tyme? Were thou not goodly accepted in-to grace?" (2.14). And, when she promises him double of all that he lost ("yeven thee comfort in hope of weldoing, and of getting agayn the double of thy lesing" [2.10]), we cannot but wonder in what coin the payment is to be made.

These crosscurrents ultimately manifest themselves as unresolved problems at the level of literary form. The *Testament* remains, to be sure, a *consolatio,* its central theme the transcendence of worldly attachments through the exercise of will assisted by grace. That this dialogue leading to spiritual comfort is interrupted by intermittent visions of exaltation and stretches of unmediated apology is not in itself unusual, since the *consolatio* as shaped by Boethius and others has always been mixed, in its dialogic content and even in elaborate formal variation (as in Boethius's alternation of prose and verse passages). Usk, however, pours into his visions and apologies so much impulse toward self-exoneration, so much desire for remediation of his worldly circumstances, that he virtually creates a counterutterance within the external form of his work. In this counterutterance he remains a petitioner, still unconsoled and awaiting reward, like the disappointed lover of a secular vision who waits outside the garden wall for the fulfillment of his disappointed desires. Seen in this sense, the *Testament* becomes not only a *consolatio* but simultaneously a political *planctus* or complaint, bewailing woes the redress of which remains in the worldly, rather than heavenly, realm.

Penning the *Testament* in a state of undoubted isolation, Usk seems never to have permitted himself the fantasy of presenting his work aloud to an admiring circle. It is aimed rather at "good reders" and "inseers" who will examine his manuscript in private and, he hopes, penetrate his allegory to understand and act upon what he has said. Whether the *Testament* actually reached such readers is open to question. Usk's own holograph may have been the only manuscript ever to exist; the manuscript upon which Thynne based his edition of 1532 may have been Usk's own, and in any event neither it nor any others have been found. Secular "grace" in the form of the king's preferment did come to Usk in 1387, but it doubtless came less from his literary exertions than from the king's urgent need to mount a counterstratagem against the appellants and from Usk's reputation as one ready to bend to the task at hand. Whatever its bearing on Usk's worldly fortunes and ultimate misfortunes, however, the *Testament* remains a fascinating literary complement to some of the tendencies evident in his public life. The public record reveals him as a person of profoundly divided impulse. Some appearance of division is an inevitable consequence of the differing regard in which he was held—as an object of scorn by the Northampton partisans against whom he turned and by the appellants against whom he unsuccessfully schemed, and as a serviceable if not admirable person by the faction of Brembre and the king. But division may also be found between his own self-interested conduct on the one hand and his idealized self-portrayals on the other. He could turn against Northampton for mixed reasons of pressure and temptation, even as he pleaded concern for "al maner of felicite to the cite" (*Appeal*, 31). He could accept complicity in a shady scheme against the appellants as a fair price for royal preferment, yet, the tables turned, could go to his death exhibiting fortitude in his new factional choice and piety as he recited penitential psalms and other devotional texts (*West.*, 314). So too does the *Testament* represent a refraction of some of these same divisions into available but heterogeneous literary forms, uneasily fusing the *consolatio* of a man who finds in grace its own reward with the complaints and laments of an unsatisfied and self-justifying spirit that has not abandoned hope of worldly vindication and reward.

## CHAUCER'S CAREER AND CHAUCER'S ART

The only one of Usk's intended readers whom we know with certainty is Geoffrey Chaucer, praised in the *Testament* as "the noble philosophical poete in Englissh" who has "assoyled" the question of necessity in his "tretis" of *Troilus* (3.4). Usk's reference to Chaucer is probably something other than that of a novice writer to an established literary figure. Excepting only Deschamps's salute to Chaucer as "grand translateur," Usk's is the first *literary* reference to Chaucer, and he may actually know somewhat less about Chaucer's works than is commonly supposed.[25] Writing in 1385–86, he might only have heard about *Troilus* as a nearly or recently completed work; certainly his confidence that Chaucer had cleared up the question of necessity reveals some misunderstanding of Troilus's actual doctrinal confusion (*Troilus* 4.958–1078). While his reference to Chaucer seems literary rather than political, it probably carries a political charge. For he would have known Chaucer as a successful adherent of the very faction to which he wished to belong, and his mention of Chaucer within a work so calculated to advance factional aspiration cannot be thought politically innocent. A speculative, but I believe wholly reasonable, conclusion is that Chaucer's career embodied for Usk a source of inspiration and precedent in two respects: he was a literary artist, and also an artist who had thrived in the service of faction. But if Usk sought to use Chaucer as a model of what he wished to become, he would seem to have misunderstood the significance of Chaucer's example. While Chaucer's poetry may decidedly be linked to his political and social experience, the interchange between Chaucer's life and work occurred at a deeper level than Usk appears to have imagined.

The reader of Chaucer must be struck by how infrequently he at-

---

25. For Deschamps's salute, see Derek Brewer, *Chaucer: The Critical Heritage* (London: Routledge & Kegan Paul, 1978) 1:39–42. For a persuasive argument that Usk did not know Chaucer's *Boece* at all, but used a French version, see Virginia Bording Jellech, "*The Testament of Love:* A New Edition," (Ph.D. diss., Washington University, 1970).

tempted to advance his worldly career through literary exertions. J. R. Hulbert argued convincingly as long ago as 1912 that Chaucer's career was "typical" for that of an esquire of the king's household and that he "received no exceptional favours."[26] The ultimate implication of Hulbert's point is that Chaucer's advancement occurred independent of his writings, in the usual, worldly ways: through his early positioning in the household of the Earl and Countess of Ulster, through his good marriage, through his service to Edward III, and the like. As Chaucer himself tells us plainly in the *House of Fame,* his reading (and presumably writing) were accomplished on his own time, after the completion of his "rekenynges" at the port of London (652–60). While some of his works may have reached philistines in the mold of the Eagle or the God of Love or the Man of Law, his completed poems and narratives were normally shared among a sympathetic circle of social equals like Scogan and Bukton and Vache rather than pressed upon his betters in a vain quest for patronage or advancement.[27]

Certainly exceptions and possible exceptions exist. The *Book of the Duchess* obviously bears on John of Gaunt's loss of his wife Blanche. We must note, however, that the form of the association is delicate and allusive, conveyed through the *tretable* dialogue of two speakers who— whatever the Black Knight's social superiority—are both gentlepersons, bound by ties of sympathy and civility that regulate their exchange. At the time the poem was written, John of Gaunt was already Duke of Lancaster by virtue of his marriage to Blanche and certainly in a position to offer Chaucer patronage. Yet the poem remains less a plea for support or advancement than an assertion of sympathy from one who, though a social inferior, nevertheless occupies a modest niche in a social edifice large enough to contain aristocracy and gentlepersons alike. In this connection, we recall that Chaucer's poem is without dedications, that no sumptuous presentation copies of any works date from his lifetime, and that all his major works are free from the impedimenta with which his French counterparts as well as such English contempo-

---

26. *Chaucer's Official Life,* 79.

27. For Chaucer's philistine readership, see Alfred David, *The Strumpet Muse* (Bloomington: Indiana University Press, 1976), 122–23. Recent arguments that Chaucer wrote for an audience composed largely of social equals and near-equals, including fellow gentlepersons and civil servants in and about the royal household, have been admirably surveyed and extended by V. J. Scattergood, "Literary Culture at the Court of Richard II," in *English Court Culture in the Later Middle Ages,* ed. V. J. Scattergood and J. W. Sherborne (London: Duckworth, 1983), 29–43.

raries as Gower and Lydgate sought either influence for their ideas or preferment for their accomplishments.

Chaucer not only rejects poetry as a major avenue to self-promotion but tends to avoid its use for immediately factional or even topical purposes. Naturally, some of his works tantalize us with possible applications. Perhaps, as Richard F. Green has pointed out, *Melibee* and *Boece* may be seen as advice to princes, with a possible (though very uncertain) relation to Chaucer's advancement. *Melibee* may be further associated with one or another of Richard's peace initiatives. A poem such as "Lak of Stedfastnesse," with an envoy possibly addressed to King Richard and enjoining him to "be honorable, / Cherish thy folk, and hate extorcioun," has been linked to occasions as diverse as Richard's opportunity to castigate the appellants in 1389 and his obligation to restrain his own allies near the end of his reign.[28] In all these cases, though, the political sentiments expressed are quite general in nature. "Lak of Stedfastnesse," for example, could as well be connected with the agitations of Commons against the *extorsiones* of lawless noblemen and their retinues that surfaced in 1384 and 1388 (*West.*, 354). One has great difficulty in establishing immediate tactical objectives for works so broad in their range of possible application.[29]

The poet who wished for his *Troilus* to follow in the steps of "Virgile, Ovide, Omer, Lucan, and Stace" (5.1792) cannot be thought a humble person, however delicately phrased his wish. Yet the ambition that his work be assimilated into a poetic tradition created and defined by persons of genius does not necessarily entail worldly advancement or even contemporary renown for himself as *auctor*. In this sense, we may suppose Geffrey, the narrator of the *House of Fame*, to be speaking for Chaucer when he disclaims any personal intent to be known:

28. Richard F. Green, *Poets and Princepleasers: Literature and the English Court in the Late Middle Ages* (Toronto: University of Toronto Press, 1980), 166; Gardiner Stillwell, "The Political Meaning of Chaucer's *Tale of Melibee*," *Speculum* 19 (1944): 433–44; George B. Pace and Alfred David, *The Minor Poems of Geoffrey Chaucer* (Norman: University of Oklahoma Press, 1982), 77–78.

29. We must remember, by way of contrast with his usual practice, that Chaucer was well able to make a point on his own behalf when he wished. He had no difficulty in giving an apparently self-interested nudge to his friend Henry Scogan, kneeling "at the stremes hed / Of grace" ("Envoy," 43–44). Even more explicit is his envoy to "Complaint to His Purse," in which he aims to bring his straitened financial situation to the attention of the new king. The opening lines of the envoy recapitulate the three bases of Henry's claim (conquest, lineage, and free election) and the conclusion of the envoy (with its plea that Henry, who has the wherewithal to amend harms, take notice) suggests that Chaucer knew how to move from banter to urgent supplication once he had made up his mind.

Sufficeth me, as I were ded,
That no wight have my name in honde.
(1876–77)

Throughout his writings, Chaucer shows a marked tendency to suppress the particular coordinates of his own worldly situation, and to connect his work with a tradition of "poesye" (*Troilus* 5.1790) that existed before him and will survive him.

For all its suppression of the topical and the personal, however, Chaucer's world of "poesye" bears no less a charge of historicity than the more obviously controversial and tendentious passages that periodically erupt within the writings of Usk. Its historicity is, however, to be sought on a different textual plane, less that of direct topical and personal reference and more that of aesthetic choice. Chaucer's experience of faction may, in other words, ultimately find its expression less in overt reference than in the seemingly aesthetic categories of form and style.

Much of the most provocative Chaucer criticism of the last three decades has revolved around the perception that Chaucer forges his poetry out of what one recent critic has called "many contrasting parts," and we may certainly notice his attraction throughout his career to those poetic forms that permit juxtaposition of relatively isolable units and the maintenance (rather than resolution) of contrast between them.[30] In this sense, the vision poem, with its possibilities for contrast between the matter of prologue and dream and its added possibilities for extension of conflicts within the dream itself, is a natural starting point for Chaucer, and a natural proving ground for formal principles that will be realized fully within the *Canterbury Tales*. While this essay affords no place for a satisfying formal analysis of the dream visions, we might simply note the possibilities afforded by a work like the *Parliament of Fowls* for exploring contrasting views of love in its social aspect,

---

30. The phrase "many contrasting parts" is C. David Benson's in *Chaucer's Drama of Style* (Chapel Hill: University of North Carolina Press, 1986), 23. See especially the discussion of Chaucer's contrastive use of style in Charles Muscatine, *Chaucer and the French Tradition* (Berkeley and Los Angeles: University of California Press, 1957), and the description of Chaucer's "inorganic" form in Robert M. Jordan, *Chaucer and the Shape of Creation* (Cambridge, Mass.: Harvard University Press, 1967). Recent studies emphasizing Chaucer's use of unresolved stylistic and formal contrast, in addition to Benson's, include: Larry Sklute, *Virtue of Necessity: Inconclusiveness and Narrative Form in Chaucer's Poetry* (Columbus, Ohio: Ohio State University Press, 1984), and Helen Cooper, *The Structure of the Canterbury Tales* (London: Duckworth, 1983).

both in the relation of the prologue (with its vision of "commune pro-fyt" as expounded in the Dream of Scipio) to the dream (with its spec-ification of the varieties of love) and within the dream itself (with its contrast of the garden of Venus and the bower of Nature, and with its further exploration of the socially based disagreements of the birds even within Nature's precincts).[31]

The *Canterbury Tales* extends and realizes this principle of variation more fully, as noticed by admirers as far back as Lydgate, who described the variety of the tales:

> Some of desport / some of moralite
> Some of knyghthode / love and gentillesse,
> And some also of parfit holynesse,
> And some also in soth / of Ribaudye.[32]

The full purposefulness of Chaucer's introduction of generic and dis-cursive variety into his collection may be glimpsed when his work is compared to other narrative collections of the Middle Ages. For, as Helen Cooper has recently and perceptively argued, Chaucer's is the first such collection to reject internal narrative consistency—whereby saint's lives, tragedies, *nouvelles,* or other similar kinds are associated within a common frame—in favor of a strong generic mix.[33] Chaucer's attitude toward genre should not, of course, be oversimplified. More often than not, he invokes generic terminology in a spirit of exuberant misuse, as when the Miller promises "a legende and a lyf / Bothe of a carpenter and of his wyf" (1.3141–42), and his tendencies toward par-ody (*Thopas,* the *Nun's Priest's Tale*) are pervasive. Even parody, though, represents a bemused recognition of the persistence and importance of generic features, and the relentless parody of genres and modes within the *Nun's Priest's Tale* represents a form of homage to a tendency that was already well established within the tradition of the beast epic.[34] Genre, as such, is less the object of Chaucer's allegiance than it is a

---

31. Unresolved contradictions within the *Parliament* are discussed by John P. McCall, "The Harmony of Chaucer's *Parliament of Fowls*," *Chaucer Review* 5 (1970): 22–31; Michael P. Kelley, "Antithesis as the Principle of Design in the *Parliament of Fowls*," *Chaucer Review* 14 (1979): 61–73; Larry M. Sklute, "The Inconclusive Form of the *Parliament of Fowls*," *Chaucer Review* 16 (1981): 119–28.

32. *Siege of Thebes,* ed. Axel Erdmann, EETS ES 108, part 1 (London, 1911), 22–25.

33. *The Structure of the Canterbury Tales,* 8–55.

34. See, for example, W. F. Bryan and Germaine Dempster, eds., *Sources and Ana-logues of Chaucer's Canterbury Tales* (1941; reprint, New York: Humanities Press, 1958), 646.

contrastive principle based upon narrative segmentation with emphasis upon differences in perspective, style, and voice between the different segments—effects that are carried forward by the generic multiplicity of the *Canterbury Tales.*

So considerable, in fact, is Chaucer's commitment to a formal principle of contrastive juxtaposition that many strategies of his poetry that have been explained in other terms may in fact be seen as devices to enable the perpetuation of contrast; the impatience of the lower fowl in the *Parliament,* the Miller's boozy interruption of the Knight in the *Tales,* and the vocational squabbles of the Canterbury Pilgrims may all be seen less as insights into personality than as ways of toppling the privileged status of some genres as opposed to others, of introducing new forms and their associated voices on an equal footing with more traditional content, of maintaining substantive and stylistic quarrels rather than resolving them.

Chaucer's poetic of high and unresolved generic and stylistic contrast may ultimately be seen as a literary restatement of his own varied social and political experience, and particularly of his experience of political faction. In this sense, I am arguing for a "reflection" of Chaucer's social experiences within his literary oeuvre, but a reflection manifested less in the overt content of the works than in the socially conditioned choices that Chaucer makes from among the world of generic and stylistic possibilities available to him. As with Usk, Chaucer's social concerns are thus less "reflected" than (in Bahktin's sense) "refracted" through a special and separate order of textual possibilities. Usk, however, seized on the genre of *consolatio* in a hectic, transformative, and ultimately destabilizing way. Not that consolatory allegory was ever as neatly resolvable into "literal" and "allegorical" orders of meaning as critics traditionally supposed; a certain instability of reference was one of its most vital properties.[35] But Usk's importation of large chunks of self-serving and relatively unmediated discourse leaves his intended consolation in some disarray, its surface strewn with false generic clues, incompatible levels of discourse, and other marks of mixed literary and personal impulse. Chaucer, on the other hand, works *through* available genres, refracting experience into literary forms in a way that both respects and renegotiates the meanings they traditionally bear. Chaucer's

35. As persuasively set forth by Carolynn Van Dyke, *The Fiction of Truth* (Ithaca: Cornell University Press, 1985).

imagined world is ultimately no less socially determined than that of Usk, but in working through literary traditions of generic and stylistic difference he assimilates his social vision into a textual model of unresolved and unresolvable conflict.

Each writer's career discloses a distinctive patterning, both of personal and literary choices. Usk's highly self-interested and precipitate personal choices seem consistent with his attempts to bend literary form to personal purposes of immediate advancement. Chaucer's balanced assessment of factional possibilities in his own life seems consistent with his broad and impartial use of literary form in ways that acknowledge and accept conflict within the realm of literary experience.

Neither Usk nor Chaucer nor any other intellectual in royal or aristocratic service could have escaped matters of faction—any more than could chamber knights like Burley, justices like Tresilian, merchants like Brembre, lawyers like Blake, clerics like Wycliff. Yet Chaucer managed throughout his life to exhibit a more balanced assessment of possibilities, a less headlong plunge toward factional affiliation. So too does his poetry sidestep the temptation to make a direct case, offering instead a mediation of faction that—while acknowledging the inevitability of unresolved conflict—still avoids many of the less productive contradictions of Usk's more personal program. To poor, erratic, overardent Usk, Chaucer must have remained an elusive and constantly frustrating example, with his calmer and broader-based and ultimately more successful attitude toward both the politics and the poetics of faction.

# 3

# "No Man His Reson Herde"

## Peasant Consciousness, Chaucer's Miller, and the Structure of the Canterbury Tales

### Lee Patterson

In 1906 Robert Root described Chaucer's appeal in the following terms:

> We turn to Chaucer not primarily for moral guidance and spiritual suste-
> nance, nor yet that our emotions may be deeply and powerfully moved;
> we turn to him rather for refreshment, that our eyes and ears may be
> opened anew to the varied interest and beauty of the world around us,
> that we may come again into healthy living contact with the smiling
> green earth and with the hearts of men, that we may shake off for a while
> "the burthen of the mystery of all this unintelligible world," and share in
> the kindly laughter of the gods, that we may breathe the pure, serene air
> of equanimity.[1]

This passage provides a remarkable synopsis of values that have always
been at the center of Chaucer criticism: that the poet is a keen and
genial observer of humankind who is himself emancipated from narrow
self-interests, that because he is (as Root elsewhere put it) "in the
world, but not of it," he is able to trace with forbearance what Blake
called "the Physiognomies or Lineaments of Universal Human Life."[2]
Hence some fifty years after Root's book, one of the greatest of the
next generation of Chaucerians, E. Talbot Donaldson, described Chaucer as possessed of "a mind almost godlike in the breadth and humility
of its ironic vision;" and in 1985 Derek Pearsall introduced his excellent
book by insisting that the Canterbury Tales neither "press for [n]or permit a systematic kind of moral or ideological interpretation," while de-

---

1. *The Poetry of Chaucer* (Boston: Houghton Mifflin, 1906), 44.
2. Root, *Poetry of Chaucer,* 32; Blake, "Prospectus of the Engraving of Chaucer's Canterbury Pilgrims," in *Poetry and Prose of William Blake,* ed. Geoffrey Keynes (London:
Nonesuch Press, 1943), 637.

scribing "the general moral purpose of the *Tales*" as being "always to give the advantage to a humane and generous understanding."[3]

But while this humanist tradition of criticism has, by and large, and with great success, established the terms by which Chaucer's poetry is interpreted, it has declined to subject its own central category—the poet's ideologically unconditioned, even transhistorical consciousness—to interpretation.[4] Yet surely Chaucer's uncanny ability to present himself as the historically undetermined poet of a correspondingly dehistoricized subjectivity is itself a historical event, just as we must similarly acknowledge that the unmasking of ideology is itself, inescapably, ideological (always understanding, of course, that by ideology we mean not simply a crude false consciousness but rather an organized system of beliefs, meanings, and values by which people endow their world with significance and thereby make it accessible to practical activity). If an ideologically free space cannot exist, where then does Chaucer stand when he describes "the varied interest and beauty of the world"? And if we agree that Chaucer's subject is subjectivity itself— "the Physiognomies or Lineaments of Universal Human Life"—what interests of his own led him to this topic?

I

The current and virtually universally accepted interpretation of Chaucer's social position is that he stood between—and hence to some extent apart from—the two great cultural formations of his time, the court and the city. A bourgeois within the court, he was a royal official in the city—a complexity of allegiance that, it is argued, freed him from any narrowly partisan commitments. According to Paul Strohm, who has developed this argument in greatest detail, both within the court and the city, and in the transit between the two, Chaucer found himself negotiating a highly factionalized world that taught him that "the process of understanding [was] less a matter of ranking alternatives on

---

3. E. Talbot Donaldson, ed., *Chaucer's Poetry,* 2d ed. (New York: Ronald Press, 1975 [1958]), 1100; Derek Pearsall, *The Canterbury Tales* (London: George Allen and Unwin, 1985), xiv.

4. The only real alternative that Chaucer criticism has provided to this tradition has been Exegetics, which I have discussed in this context in chapter 1 of *Negotiating the Past: The Historical Understanding of Medieval Literature* (Madison: University of Wisconsin Press, 1987).

some vertical scale of moral choice, than of adding alternatives on a horizontal and less judgmental plane in order to reveal the full range of possibilities inherent in a subject." Now Stephen Knight has translated this social mobility into economic terms, arguing that Chaucer stands between the natural economy of the feudal nobility and the exchange economy of his bourgeois origins.[5] To put a complex matter simply, Knight sees Chaucer as both condemning the rampant cash nexus of the mercantile ethos while simultaneously insisting upon the rights of a newly emergent, market-generated subjectivity, a paradox that is finally resolved only by his escape into the orthodox piety of the *Parson's Tale*.

But there are serious historical problems with this kind of analysis, regardless of the terms in which it is articulated. For by accepting as the central division of Chaucer's social world an opposition between the city and the court, this understanding omits and effectively erases the rural world that was, recent historians have argued, the most socially combative and historically progressive element of late medieval English society. What makes this erasure possible is the widespread acceptance by literary critics of the idea that medieval society can be understood in terms of an opposition between the *Naturalwirtschaft* of a country that is economically inert, socially repressive, and culturally backward, and, on the other hand, an economically innovative, socially mobile, and culturally avant-garde town that is the locus of a progressive *Geldwirtschaft*. It is important to realize that what underwrites this account is the assumption that the town—and the open market that is its raison d'être—is the solvent of the feudal mode of production: urban freedom from the reciprocal dependencies of feudalism allows for the creation of a free-floating individual, capable of entering into contractual relations; labor is divided into the specializations necessary for the eventual triumph of industrialization; and an emergent civic humanism provides the foundations for the development of parliamentary democracy.

What we have here, in other words, is the familiar and oddly inescapable Whig interpretation of history, with the heroic bourgeoisie, here instantiated in the form of the medieval merchant adventurer, as

---

5. Paul Strohm, "Form and Social Statement in *Confessio Amantis* and *The Canterbury Tales*," *Studies in the Age of Chaucer* 1 (1979): 33; Stephen Knight, *Geoffrey Chaucer* (Oxford: Blackwell, 1986).

history's prime mover.[6] For as R. J. Holton has recently pointed out, this reading of the transition from feudalism to capitalism depends upon the classic Enlightenment notion that history proceeds

> in terms of the progressive realisation of a system of "natural liberty" achieveable through free market relations. . . . The assumption is that given the removal of barriers economic freedom (or "capitalism") becomes established of itself. This position, as Talcott Parsons pointed out, implies that capitalism "needs no specific propelling force—if it consists merely in rational conduct why should it?" This he regards as the "orthodox Anglo-Saxon view of economic history."[7]

Indeed, even if one reads the changes brought about by the rise of a money economy negatively, the essential terms of the analysis do not change. Rather than arguing that individuals are now free to determine their own economic fates for themselves, with a consequent increase in innovative entrepreneurialism and technological development, we could instead, in a quasi-Marxist way, describe these changes in terms of the infection of personal relations with the cash nexus, the subjection of natural value to the relentless commodification of the market, and the process by which the worker, who under feudalism was either himself part of the means of production or, better yet, possessed them, becomes alienated from his own labor. But such a neo-Smithian Marxism, as it has been cogently termed, still sees the agency of economic and social transformation as the town-based market economy—and still stigmatizes the country as a regressive brake upon the productive forces.[8]

6. Herbert F. Butterfield, *The Whig Interpretation of History* (London: G. Bell, 1931).

7. R. J. Holton, *The Transition from Feudalism to Capitalism* (New York: St. Martin's Press, 1985), 35, 38–39. The citation by Parsons is from his *The Structure of Social Action*, 2 vols. (New York: Free Press, 1968 [1937]), 1:157. For a recent account of the transition from the orthodox point of view, see Carlo M. Cipolla, *Before the Industrial Revolution: European Society and Economy, 1000–1700*, 2d ed. (New York: Norton, 1980 [1976]), for whom "the urban movement of the eleventh to thirteenth centuries [was] the turning point of world history. . . . The urban revolution of the eleventh and twelfth centuries was the prelude to, and created the prerequisites for, the Industrial Revolution of the nineteenth century" (146–49).

8. Robert Brenner, "The Origins of Capitalist Development: A Critique of Neo-Smithian Marxism," *New Left Review* 104 (1977): 25–82. This is not to say that Marx himself does not provide the materials for such an analysis, as in his chapter on money in the *Grundrisse: Foundations of the Critique of Political Economy*, trans. Martin Nicolaus (1857–58; Harmondsworth: Penguin Books, 1973), especially 156–58. For Marx's by no means consistent views on the transition, see Holton, *Transition*, 64–102; R. S. Neale, "Introduction," in *Feudalism, Capitalism and Beyond*, ed. Eugene Kamenka and J. S. Neale (Canberra: Australian National University Press, 1975), 3–27; and—for an especially lucid account—Jon Elster, *Making Sense of Marx* (Cambridge, Eng.: Cambridge University Press, 1985), 301–17.

In fact, political interests quite apart, the idea that the dynamic of late medieval society can be understood in terms of the opposition between a feudal natural economy and a capitalist money economy has been for many years under attack by medieval historians.[9] Over forty years ago, M. M. Postan called the rise of the money economy "one of the residuary hypotheses of economic history: a *deus ex machina* to be called upon when no other explanation is available"—cautionary words that have had too little impact upon literary critics.[10] Similarly oversimple is the notion that the changes in late medieval English society can be understood as a struggle between progressive urban centers dominated by a mobile bourgeoisie and free citizenry and, ranged against them, a hierarchical and static rural feudalism dominated by a conservative nobility and Church. It is clear, for example, that the agrarian economy was thoroughly monetized and exchange-oriented throughout the Middle Ages, that peasant society had been for many centuries highly stratified and differentiated, and that there existed since at least the twelfth century a vigorous, monetized, and even credit-based peasant land market, a market for agricultural wage labor, and small-scale but essential rural industry and commodity production.[11] Similarly, both lay and ecclesiastical landlords were engaged in sophisticated techniques of estate management and in the calculative pursuit of profit maximization, many members of the seigneurial class were deeply involved in the world of international trade, and even the quintessential noble activity of warfare was pervaded with the values of the cash

9. The central figure in this effort is M. M. Postan, many of whose papers have been collected into two volumes, *Medieval Trade and Finance* (Cambridge, Eng.: Cambridge University Press, 1973), and *Essays on Medieval Agriculture and General Problems of the Medieval Economy* (Cambridge, Eng.: Cambridge University Press, 1973), and whose interpretation of the period as a whole is summarized in his *The Medieval Economy and Society* (1972; Harmondsworth: Penguin Books, 1975). Also important here is the Soviet historian Evgeny A. Kosminsky, *Studies in the Agrarian History of England in the Thirteenth Century*, trans. Ruth Kisch, ed. Rodney H. Hilton (Oxford: Blackwell, 1956)—a book that collects work done in the 1930s.

10. "The Rise of a Money Economy," *Economic History Review* 14 (1944); reprinted in *Essays on Medieval Agriculture*, 28. Another prominent Chaucerian (besides Knight) for whom the rise of the money economy is a central interpretive category is R. A. Shoaf, in both *Dante, Chaucer, and the Currency of the Word* (Norman: Pilgrim Books, 1983), and *The Poem as Green Girdle: Commercium in Sir Gawain and the Green Knight* (Gainesville: University Presses of Florida, 1984).

11. Rodney H. Hilton, *The English Peasantry in the Later Middle Ages* (Oxford: Clarendon Press, 1975), and *Class Conflict and the Crisis of Feudalism* (London: Hambledon Press, 1985), a collection of many of his essays; see also *The Peasant Land Market in Medieval England*, ed. P. D. A. Harvey (Oxford: Clarendon Press, 1984).

nexus.[12] Finally, the notion that medieval cities were "non-feudal is-lands in a feudal sea"—while pointing to an important truth—can too easily be exaggerated.[13] If in theory *Stadtluft machts frei,* in practice a city like London tightly restricted access to citizenship, while civic life as a whole was dominated by a conservative merchant patriciate that imposed upon the city much the same structure of dominance and sub-ordination as was in force across the feudal world as a whole.[14]

It has been argued that what this revisionary history demonstrates is that feudalism was really capitalism writ small, that the full-scale capi-talist development that took place from the sixteenth century forward was the realization of processes that were always present and that simply required technological developments and shifts in attitudes to bring about their triumph.[15] This is of course simply a variant on the Whig

12. For the role of monasticism in the development of the calculative pursuit of profit-maximization that, following Sombart and Weber, is usually regarded as the central char-acteristic of capitalism, see H. E. Hallam, "The Medieval Social Picture," in *Feudalism, Capitalism and Beyond,* ed. Kamenka and Neale, 29–49. On landlords' adaptation to changed circumstances, see Harry A. Miskimin, *The Economy of Early Renaissance Europe, 1300–1460* (Cambridge, Eng.: Cambridge University Press, 1975 [1969]), 32–47; and for the individual nobleman as a manager of his estates, see K. B. McFarlane, *The Nobility of Later Medieval England* (Oxford: Clarendon Press, 1973), 53.

On the aristocratic participation in trade, see Sylvia Thrupp, *The Merchant Class of Medieval London* (1948; Ann Arbor: University of Michigan Press, 1962), 243–44, 256–63. T. H. Lloyd, *The English Wool Trade in the Middle Ages* (Cambridge, Eng.: Cambridge University Press, 1977), entitles his fifth chapter, "Edward III—Woolmonger Extraordi-nary."

For a detailed argument that "an attitude towards war as a speculative, but at best hugely profitable trade . . . was shared by all who joined the mercenary armies of Edward III and Henry V," see McFarlane, *Nobility* 19–60; the citation is from 21. See also Philippe Contamine, *War in the Middle Ages,* trans. Michael Jones (Oxford: Blackwell, 1984), 90–101. As Contamine says, "Money was the almost obligatory link between authority and soldiers. According to contemporaries themselves, this phenomenon accelerated from the mid-twelfth century" (90).

13. Postan, *Medieval Economy and Society,* 239.

14. The repressive effect of the patriciate upon medieval London life has been well-described by Thrupp, *Merchant Class:* "The central psychological prop of the economic and political inequalities that developed was in the individual's inescapable respect for authority. . . . The bourgeois context did nothing to free the individual from this kind of pressure but seems rather to have intensified it. Since everyone knew that the preservation of the local civic liberties hung upon the continuance of orderly behavior, all emotional resources were drawn upon to secure this end" (16). "Among responsible citizens, . . . the necessity of public order was probably the dominating idea" (75) because of the "chronic fear of incurring the royal displeasure through failure to maintain high enough standards of law and order" (99).

15. This argument has been most vigorously advanced by Alan Macfarlane in his *The Origins of English Individualism* (Oxford: Blackwell, 1978) and his subsequent work. For

thesis that capitalism represents the natural condition of economic man. The only true alternative to this account is that offered by recent Marxist historians, for whom the key component of *all* nonsocialist economies is the governing classes' exploitation of the producers in order to extract surplus value.[16] These historians understand feudalism not simply as an inefficient means by which the individual seeks to fulfill his economic destiny but as a mode of production characterized by the direct rather than indirect exploitation of labor by the ruling classes. Similarly, markets—and the cities that developed around them—represent not an alternative to the feudal mode of production but, given the need of the exploiting class to extract surplus value in the form of money, an element necessary for the proper functioning of the feudal economy.[17] For Marx, medieval merchant capital was never itself progressive or transformative but remained parasitic upon the truly productive forces of society—forces that had always been and (until at least the eighteenth century) remained agricultural.[18] In sum, the prime mover in feudal society was thus not protocapitalist trade but the growing surplus value that the landowning class was able to extract from the agrarian economy. Thus it is that contemporary medieval historians have discovered, to cite the title of a recent, highly influential article,

a useful account, see K. D. M. Snell, "English Historical Continuity and the Culture of Capitalism: The Work of Alan Macfarlane," *History Workshop* 27 (1989): 154–63.

16. The crucial figures here are Rodney Hilton (see note 11), Maurice Dobb, and Robert Brenner; the central topic upon which their work has centered has been the nature of the transition from feudalism to capitalism. The issue is surveyed in *The Transition from Feudalism to Capitalism,* ed. Rodney Hilton (London: Verso, 1978)—a collection of essays, mostly from the 1950s, concerned with the seminal book by Dobb, *Studies in the Development of Capitalism* (New York: International Publishers, 1947), and including an important introduction by Hilton; see also John E. Martin, *Feudalism to Capitalism: Peasant and Landlord in English Agrarian Development* (Atlantic Highlands: Humanities Press, 1983); *Feudalism, Capitalism and Beyond,* ed. Kamenka and Neale, and Holton, *Transition.* For theoretical comments as well as empirical studies, see also Hilton, *Class Conflict,* and Guy Bois, *The Crisis of Feudalism: Economy and Society in Eastern Normandy c. 1300–1550* (Cambridge, Eng.: Cambridge University Press, 1984). The work of Dobb and Hilton is discussed by Harvey J. Kaye, *The British Marxist Historians* (London: Polity Press, 1984).

17. For a recent discussion, with extensive bibliography, see R. J. Holton, *Cities, Capitalism and Civilization* (London: Allen and Unwin, 1986); see also Rodney Hilton, "Towns in Societies—Medieval England," *Urban History Yearbook* (1982): 7–13, and "Medieval Market Towns and Simple Commodity Production," *Past and Present* 109 (1985): 3–23.

18. Marx's attack on merchant capital as not being what he calls in the first volume of *Capital* "the really revolutionizing path" of transformation can be found in chapters 20 and 47 of *Capital III.*

"The Agrarian Roots of European Capitalism"—a discovery that sees the agricultural sector as being the locus for Marx's "really revolutionizing path" of transition by which the producer becomes himself a capitalist.[19]

Understanding economic life in terms of class struggle, these historians have argued that what brought about the collapse of feudalism and the transition to capitalism was the growing ability of the late medieval peasant to withhold surplus value and turn it to his own, independent economic interests. Thus historians such as Maurice Dobb and, especially, Rodney Hilton have followed Marx's lead in describing the period 1350–1450 as the golden age of the English peasant. As Hilton has pointed out, "Medieval peasants were quite capable, in economic terms, of providing for themselves without the intervention of any ruling class. In this they differed from ancient slaves, and from modern wage workers who have to work on the means of production in order to gain their living."[20] Since it always possessed (even if it did not yet own) the means of production, when the medieval peasantry developed sufficient strength to resist the grossest forms of seigneurial exaction it was able to retain the surplus value of the agrarian economy, which had up to this time been appropriated by the ruling classes. Hilton describes the results in the following terms:

> Between 1350 and 1450 . . . we find that relative land abundance was combined, for various reasons, with a relaxation of seigneurial domination and a notable lightening of the economic burden on the peasant economy. Peasant society, in spite of still existing within (in broad terms) a feudal framework, developed according to laws of motion internal to itself. The village community was dominated by the richer peasant families, who ran the manorial court in its jurisdictional, punitive and land-registration functions. The limits on rents and services were firmly fixed well below what the lords wanted.

Hence, concludes Hilton, "it is possible that the century after the Black Death was the golden age of the middle rather than of the rich peasantry (the yeoman)."[21] But it is also the case that this rural economy is

---

19. Brenner's article appeared first in *Past and Present* 97 (1982): 16–113, and is now reprinted in *The Brenner Debate: Agrarian Class Structure and Economic Development in Pre-Industrial Europe*, ed. T. H. Aston and C. H. E. Philipin (Cambridge, Eng.: Cambridge University Press, 1985), 213–327.

20. Rodney Hilton, *Bond Men Made Free* (1973; London: Methuen, 1977), 41.

21. "Reasons for Inequality Among Medieval Peasants," *Journal of Peasant Studies* 5 (1978): 271–83; reprinted in *Class Conflict*, 149. Hilton's *The English Peasantry* provides a description of this golden age.

the seedbed for later capitalist development. As Dobb pointed out, and as Hilton and Brenner have shown in detail, "It is then from the petty mode of production (in the degree to which it secures independence of action, and social differentiation in turn develops within it) that capitalism is born."[22]

The effect of these arguments is to present a very different picture of late medieval English society than we are used to seeing. Rather than the merchant class and the city functioning as the agents for change, they are instead to be understood as dependent upon an ever more profligate and financially insecure seigneurial class.[23] Conversely, however, the agricultural economy remains strong, but always at a local level: while the increased agricultural productivity of the postplague years does not, because of the decline in demand, lead to a substantial increase in money income, the small agricultural producers are able to keep more of their product and to expand their holdings, an expansion that takes place at the expense of both the large landholders and, on the other side, of their less successful peasant neighbors.[24] It is thus the *rural* sector of the economy that is dynamic, and the solvent of feudal relations is neither merchant capital nor the trading activity it finances but a vigorous peasant economy; the crucial element in the collapse of feudalism is peasant resistance to the seigneurial extraction of surplus profit from the agrarian economy. What we have, then, to conclude this discussion with a highly schematic description, is a feverish consumer boom in luxury goods masking irreparable structural weaknesses and set against a powerful, self-confident peasant economy—a self-confidence visible throughout the latter medieval period and nowhere more dramatically than in the rising of 1381.[25]

---

22. Dobb, "A Reply," in *Transition from Feudalism to Capitalism*, ed. Hilton, 59.

23. For the classic discussion of "The Crisis of Seigneurial Fortunes," see Marc Bloch, *French Rural History: An Essay on its Basic Characteristics*, trans. Janet Sondheimer (Berkeley and Los Angeles: University of California Press, 1970), 112–26. The growth of the luxury trade, and its impoverishing effect upon seigneurial fortunes, is stressed by Miskimin, *Economy of Early Renaissance Europe*, 135–37 and *passim*.

24. It should be pointed out that both the existence and the nature of the late medieval improvement of peasant conditions remains a controversial issue among medieval historians. Postan, for example, disputes the squeezing out of the small landholder, and sees the whole process as one of the increasing prosperity of the peasant class as a whole (*Medieval Economy and Society*, 201–2), while Miskimin is very dubious about any improvement (*Economy of Early Renaissance Europe*, 50–51, 56–57).

25. For the rising as an effect of the seigneurial attempt to contain the growth of an independent peasant economy, see Christopher Dyer, "The Social and Economic Background to the Rural Revolt of 1381," in *The English Rising of 1381*, ed. R. H. Hilton and

## II

One clear effect of this account upon our understanding of Chaucer is that it should encourage us to dispense with the notion of the poet as ideologically free-floating. To begin with, the foundational distinction between noble and bourgeois, feudal and urban, while real and visible, cannot be drawn as sharply as this description requires. On the contrary, both sets of values, however different one from the other, are *together* part of the hegemonic ideology that dominates late medieval English society; and both are to be set against the largely inarticulate but nonetheless insistent pressure of rural commodity production and the political resistance it spawned. The crucial ideological distinction, in other words, is not between the seigneurial nobility and the urban merchant class, but between both of these elements of the exploiting class on the one hand and the increasingly independent and self-sufficient productive classes in the country on the other.

The unity of the ruling classes, whether seigneurial or mercantile, is especially visible in the case of Chaucer himself. Far from being simply an ordinary London citizen, Chaucer was in fact the son of one of the members of the mercantile patriciate who controlled the city, a privileged position that is certainly reflected in his early entrance into the household of the Countess of Ulster and in his successful career within the courts of Edward III and Richard II.[26] Moreover, as one of Richard's royal servants the poet did not, as is usually assumed, disclaim any interest or role in politics; on the contrary, he was very much the king's man in the crucial Parliament of 1386, suffered for his allegiance when the king's party failed, and was finally rewarded for his loyalty when the king regained power in 1389.[27] In other words, to see Chaucer as somehow caught between two worlds and therefore free of both is both to misunderstand the structure of late medieval English society and to

---

T. H. Aston (Cambridge, Eng.: Cambridge University Press, 1984), 9–42. As Dyer points out, "not just rising expectations, but actual achievements, were being exploited by a vigorous seigneurial administration" (36), an exploitation that finally generated an explosive peasant anger.

26. Chaucer's continued affiliation with the merchant patriciate has recently been stressed by Britton J. Harwood, "Chaucer and the Silence of History: Situating the Canon's Yeoman's Tale," *PMLA* 102 (1987): 339.

27. For this reading of Chaucer's role in the politics of the 1380s, disputed by some Chaucer Scholars, see T. F. Tout, *Chapters in the Administrative History of Mediaeval England*, vol. 3 (Manchester: Manchester University Press, 1928), 417.

underestimate the strength of the poet's political commitments, whether freely chosen or not. What this ultimately means, then, is that whatever signs of a turning away from the dominant ideology we recognize in the *Canterbury Tales*—and I believe there are a great many—should be understood not as a function of the instinctive pull of a natural origin (Chaucer returning to his bourgeois roots) but as a conscious and deliberate decision. Moreover, given the fact that the most powerful alternative to this dominance was embodied in a rebellious peasantry which we might expect Chaucer to have regarded with little natural sympathy, we can anticipate that any turn towards alternative values will be marked with a powerful ambivalence.

It is my argument that the *Canterbury Tales* first stages Chaucer's rejection of the cultic values of the courtly world in explicitly political terms with the Miller's *quiting* of the Knight. But this embrace of peasant self-confidence is immediately registered as threatening, and the subsequent development of the *Tales* serves to contain this threat—a containment that is accomplished first by the Wife of Bath, with her privileging of a socially undetermined (and politically inert) subjectivity, and then in the complementary tales of the Friar and Summoner, in which peasant self-assertiveness is both dissipated into internecine squabbling among ecclesiastical agents and appropriated, at the end of the *Summoner's Tale,* by seigneurial authority. In the first eight of the *Canterbury Tales* the break from social orthodoxy is staged not once but twice. If the order of the best manuscript tradition is correct (and I believe that recent scholarship has shown that it is), then the first eight tales fall into the following pattern:

| I: KNIGHT | II: MAN OF LAW |
|---|---|
| Monk, *interrupted by* | Parson, *interrupted by* |
| Miller | Wife of Bath |
| Reeve | Friar |
| Cook [unfinished] | Summoner[28] |

With the choice of the Knight as the first tale-teller, the initial movement of the *Tales* begins by affirming the conservative social ideology

---

28. An excellent discussion of this vexed issue, with persuasive arguments in favor of the authority of the Ellesmere order, is provided by Larry D. Benson, "The Order of *The*

of the three estates that has already governed, in however qualified a
fashion, the articulation of the portraits in the General Prologue.[29] Yet
when Harry Bailly—true to his name—tries to enforce this repressive
ideology by turning next to the Monk, the Miller interrupts, initiating
a countermovement of *fabliaux* revelry that comes to a precipitous halt
with the Cook's shameful anecdote. Then the process starts again, now
with the Man of Law as the voice of orthodoxy, an orthodoxy with
which Chaucer associates his earlier, now discarded poetic self by having this agent of the ruling classes be an admirer of precisely the *Legend
of Good Women*. After the *Man of Law's Tale* of the saintly and long-
suffering daughter of the Emperor of Rome (derived from a chronicle
written originally for one of the daughters of Edward I), Harry Bailly
attempts to continue this comfortable line of development by turning
to the apolitical Parson. Yet now the Wife of Bath interrupts, initiating
a line of development that will continue without interruption until the
definitive cancellation of the *Canterbury Tales* finally accomplished by
the long-deferred Parson.

The important point for our purposes is to recognize that the agents
of the break—the Miller and the Wife of Bath—are in both cases representatives not of the bourgeois mercantile world of the cash nexus
but rather of the aggressive rural economy that was threatening seig-
neurial/mercantile dominance. And the next question that arises is: why
does the interruption succeed in the second case while it fails in the
first? The reason is, I believe, political: in the first case the challenge is
class determined and as a result too explicitly threatening, while in the
second it is deflected into a traditional mode of ideological opposition—that is, into promoting the claims of a socially undetermined
subjectivity that stands apart from *all* forms of class consciousness. In

---

*Canterbury Tales,*" *Studies in the Age of Chaucer* 3 (1981): 77–120. For a dissenting view,
which argues that *no* order is authoritative, see Charles Owen, "The Alternative Reading
of *The Canterbury Tales*: Chaucer's Text and the Early Manuscripts," *PMLA* 97 (1982):
237–50. In the discussion that follows, I have also accepted the disputed authenticity of
the Man of Law's Epilogue and the argument that the interrupter of the Parson in that
Epilogue is indeed the Wife of Bath, whose Prologue and Tale then follow; for arguments
supporting this view, see E. Talbot Donaldson, "The Ordering of the Canterbury Tales,"
in *Medieval Literature and Folklore Studies: Essays in Honor of Francis Lee Utley,* ed. Jerome
Mandel and Bruce A. Rosenberg (New Brunswick, N.J.: Rutgers University Press, 1970),
193–204.

29. For the three estates scheme in the General Prologue, see Jill Mann, *Chaucer and
Medieval Estates Satire* (Cambridge, Eng.: Cambridge University Press, 1973).

other words, Chaucer begins by posing his opposition to the dominant ideology in terms of class antagonism, but then retreats by setting up as his privileged category subjectivity per se, the free-floating individual whose needs and satisfactions stand outside any social structure—in short, the transhistorical being that criticism has traditionally taken Chaucer himself to be. And while we may see this move as politically timid, it is nonetheless crucial to Chaucer's subsequent dominance of our literary tradition. For, as we have seen, it is as the great champion of the individual that Chaucer has displaced his rivals (like Gower and especially Langland, both of whom haunt the *Canterbury Tales* as rejected possibilities) and has established himself as the Father of English Poetry.

## III

One could argue that Chaucer chose a miller as his initial agent of disruption simply in order to set up the hostile Reeve's use of the traditional tale of the Miller and Two Clerks. But in fact millers played a crucial if still somewhat obscure role in the medieval rural economy. The millsoke—the toll paid by peasants who were required to have their grain ground at the seigneurial mill—was not only a significant source of income for the landlord but a bitterly resented imposition upon the rural producer and a central focus of peasant resistance to seigneurial authority.[30] But if the disruptive energy with which Chaucer

---

30. In *Land and Work in Medieval Europe,* trans. J. E. Anderson (Berkeley and Los Angeles: University of California Press, 1967), Marc Bloch provides a brief account of this history of landlord-tenant strife over the milling monopoly: "There were occasions when milling stones were seized by the lord's officials in the very houses of the owners and broken in pieces; there were insurrections on the part of housewives; there were lawsuits which grimly pursued their endless and fruitless course, leaving the tenants always the losers. The chronicles and monastic cartularies of the thirteenth and fourteenth centuries are full of the noise of these quarrels. At St. Albans they assumed the scale of a veritable milling epic" (157). Here Bloch refers to the extraordinary events that occurred at St. Albans during the rising of 1381, when the peasants both retrieved from the floor of the abbey the stones of their handmills that the abbot had seized and scornfully used as pavement and then extracted from him a charter relieving them of millsoke (a charter that was, of course, later revoked). The most recent discussion of this event is offered by Rosamond Faith in "The 'Great Rumour' of 1377 and Peasant Ideology," in *English Rising,* ed. Hilton and Aston, 66. For other examples of disputes over millsoke, see Richard Bennett and John Elton, *The History of Corn Milling,* 4 vols. (London: Simpkin Marshall, 1898–1904), 1:20–21 and 4:40–53. Bloch's account has recently been deepened and rendered more nuanced, but not contradicted, by Richard Holt, "Whose Were the Profits of Corn Milling?," *Past and Present* 116 (1987): 3–23.

endows his Miller derives from this general condition, we remain uncertain about the particular role that millers themselves played in the
struggle for peasant advancement. Since they are neither tenants of land
nor tillers of soil they cannot technically be considered peasants.
Rather, their vocation locates them within the artisanal class, like the
Miller's John the Carpenter. But their actual functioning within the
village community, like their economic status, remains uncertain. Were
they agents of seigneurial control, like bailiffs? Were they mediatory
agents, as reeves were supposed to be? Or were they themselves part of
the resistant village community, underlings who had their own grievances? We know that from at least the twelfth century mills were leased
out by landlords for a fixed rent, but to what extent the leasees were
themselves the millers is by no means clear.[31] We also know that
throughout the thirteenth century most of the previously "free" mills
that had been owned by nonseigneurial proprietors were brought back
under manorial control.[32] So too, that millers stole is confirmed by
both numerous documents and popular reputation, but were their vic-

31. For the leasing of mills, see Kosminsky, *Studies in Agrarian History*, 52. For an
example of the miller as himself the leasee, see Herbert P. R. Finberg, *Tavistock Abbey: A
Study in the Social and Economic History of Devon*, Cambridge Studies in Medieval Life and
Thought, n.s., 2 (Cambridge, Eng.: Cambridge University Press, 1951): "The practice of
farming the mills out at a fixed rate and leaving the miller to make a profit from the toll-
corn appears in the earliest surviving account rolls, and it became the rule again in the
fifteenth century; but for about a hundred years after the Black Death the mills were kept
in hand, and receipts from the sale of toll-corn figured regularly in the accounts" (195).
Indeed, a recent study of medieval milling reportedly claims that "mills became part of
peasant holdings by the thirteenth century rather than monopoly tools of exploitation by
the lords" (a summary by J. Ambrose Raftis ("Social Change versus Revolution: New
Interpretations of the Peasants' Revolt of 1381," in *Social Unrest in the Late Middle Ages*,
ed. Francis X. Newman [Binghamton: Medieval and Renaissance Texts and Studies,
1986], 7) of Christopher Dyer and John Langdon, "English Medieval Mills," *Bulletin of
the University of Birmingham* (23 January 1984): 1–2—an essay I have not been able to
consult). But for examples of the leasee as a nonresident who then either pays the miller
a salary or allows him to reimburse himself by taking a portion of the toll, see the discussion by Bennett and Elton, *History of Corn Milling*, 4:67–84, 136–43. Similarly, Tim Lo-
mas, "South-east Durham: Late Fourteenth and Fifteenth Centuries," in *Peasant Land
Market*, ed. Harvey, notes that "it was the more wealthy tenants who leased the village
ovens and in the later fourteenth century it was usually they who held the mills, but in
the fifteenth century most of the millers seem not to have been local people" (323). Since
these leasees or "farmers" were not local, they must not have in fact been the millers, that
is, the men who did the actual work. In the early fifteenth century Margery Kempe
invested in a mill: see *The Book of Margery Kempe*, trans. Barry Windeatt (Harmondsworth: Penguin Books, 1985), 44.

32. For this "reassertion of seigneurial monopoly," see Holt, "Whose Were the Profits," *passim*.

tims primarily the peasants or the lord?[33] Similarly, we do not really know how relatively prosperous millers were. There is some evidence to support the widespread opinion that "the miller was commonly one of the most considerable men in the village," and the sharp decline in mill rents in the postplague period suggests that millers were, like the other members of the peasant community, able to drive better bargains with mill owners—a sign of growing strength that doubtless contributed to their unpopularity.[34] Not coincidentally, then, millers were included in the various Statutes of Labourers whose fees the government sought to control.[35]

33. On the distasteful reputation of millers, see George Fenwick Jones, "Chaucer and the Medieval Miller," *Modern Language Quarterly* 16 (1955): 3–15, and Bennett and Elton, *History of Corn Milling*, vol. 3, *passim*. Holt records an instance on the estates of Glastonbury Abbey where a miller leased the mill from the abbey in exchange for the multure, which meant that any theft would be at the expense of the peasants who were having their corn ground ("Whose Were the Profits," 15–16). There is also evidence, however, that millers stole from mill owners: among the many accusations laid against millers in the legal records, there are a number that charge them with stealing mill parts—a theft obviously directed against the mill owner; see Barbara Hanawalt, *Crime and Conflict in English Communities, 1300–1348* (Cambridge, Mass.: Harvard University Press, 1979), 135. When the miller's "popular" image as a thief is invoked, it should also be remembered that the custodians of the documents that record this description were not the peasants whose grain was being ground but the governing classes who were extracting profit from the process over which the miller presided.

34. The common opinion is cited from George C. Homans, *English Villagers of the Thirteenth Century* (Cambridge, Mass.: Harvard University Press, 1941), 285, who unfortunately offers no evidence. According to William G. Hoskins, *The Midland Peasant: The Economic and Social History of a Leicestershire Village* (London: Macmillan, 1957), "Among the tradesmen of Wigston in the sixteenth century the miller was pre-eminent" (169); and in "Debt Litigation in a Late Medieval English Vill," in *Pathways to Medieval Peasants*, ed. J. Ambrose Raftis (Toronto: Pontifical Institute of Mediaeval Studies, 1981), Elaine Clark shows that in at least one instance millers served as village money lenders. On the other hand, in "Berkshire: Fourteenth and Fifteenth Centuries," in *Peasant Land Market*, ed. Harvey, Rosamond Faith provides a custumal drawn up in 1221 for the village of Woolstone that seems to show that the three millers living in the village were considered among the least substantial of the inhabitants (122–23). Holt, "Whose Were the Profits," tells of the prosperity of one Leuric the Miller on a Glastonbury Estate, but it appears that Leuric did not do the milling himself but simply leased the mill and then hired a servant to do it for him (18–19). On the question of mill income, Finberg points out that for the mills on the manors of Tavistock Abbey "the farm was appreciably lower in the fifteenth century than it had been before the Black Death" (*Tavistock Abbey*, 195). The fact that the mills were not farmed during the period 1350–1450 suggests that no tenants could be found. For other examples of falling rents from mills, see J. Ambrose Raftis, *Warboys: Two Hundred Years in the Life of an English Mediaeval Village* (Toronto: Pontifical Institute of Mediaeval Studies, 1974), the table on 260, and especially Bois, *Crisis of Feudalism*, 226–34.

35. Bertha Haven Putnam, *Enforcement of the Statute of Labourers* (New York: Columbia University Press, 1908), 81.

One thing we do know for certain, however, is that millers were participants in the Peasants' Revolt of 1381. One John Fillol, for instance, a miller from Hanningfield, Essex, was hanged for his part in the revolt, and the records indicate that other millers played a prominent role.[36] Furthermore, if names are any indication of occupation, it is significant that a John Millere of London was charged with being one of those who stole wine from the Vintry, a John Meller of Ulford was hung and his goods confiscated, and the eloquent leader of the rebels at St. Albans was William Grindecobbe.[37] Moreover, when the rebels of Bury St. Edmonds beheaded John Cavendish, a King's Justice who had enforced the Statute of Labourers with particular severity, the executioner was named Matthew Miller; given both the physical strength of millers and their reputation for violence, the name seems likely here to coincide with vocation.[38]

Most important, however, is the fact that the peasants themselves seem to have seen the figure of the miller as capable of embodying both their grievances and their desire for an almost apocalyptic reckoning. Two of John Ball's famous letters refer specifically to an allegorized miller:

> Johan the Mullere hath ygrownde smal, smal, smal;
> The Kyngis sone of heuene shalle pay for alle.
> Be war or ye be wo;
> Knoweth ʒour frend fro ʒoure foo,
> Haveth ynowe and seyth "Hoo":
> And do welle and bettre, and fleth synne,
> And seketh pees and holde therynne.

Jakke Mylner asketh help to turne hys mylne aright. He hath grounden smal smal; the kings sone of heven he schal pay for alle. Loke thy mylne

36. For John Fillol, see Christopher Dyer, "The Social and Economic Background," 38; for another anonymous miller, see Dyer, 16. In his hysterical account of the rebellion in *Vox clamantis,* John Gower also contemptuously testifies to the presence of millers among the rebels: "nor did the dog at the mill stay home" (*The Major Latin Works of John Gower,* trans. Eric W. Stockton [Seattle: University of Washington Press, 1962], 59). Francis R. H. Du Boulay, *The Lordship of Canterbury: An Essay on Mediaeval Society* (London: Nelson, 1966) mentions that one of the ringleaders of "Cade's" Rebellion in the midfifteenth century was a "malt-miller" (191).

37. On the two John Millers, see André Réville and Charles Petit-Dutaillis, *Le Soulèvement des Travailleurs d'Angleterre en 1381* (Paris: Picard, 1898), 224 and 232; on William Grindecobbe and his famous speech, see *The Peasants' Revolt of 1381,* ed. R. B. Dobson (London: Macmillan, 1970), 269–77.

38. Edgar Powell, *The Rising in East Anglia in 1381* (Cambridge, Eng.: Cambridge University Press, 1896), 13–14.

go aright, with the foure sayles, and the post stande in stedfastnesse. With ryght and with myght, with skyl and with wylle, lat myght helpe ryght, and skyl go before wille and ryght before myght, than goth oure mylne aryght. And if myght go before ryght, and wylle before skylle, than is oure mylne mys adyght.[39]

No doubt there is a scriptural subtext to these threatening words (see, for example, Matt. 21:44, Luke 20:18), but they more immediately witness to the long history of peasant anger towards the seigneurial monopoly of the power of the mill—a power that the rebels of 1381 here seek to appropriate and turn to their own, retributive uses. Chaucer's Robin the Miller would have called such retribution "quiting," and lest we think the analogy with John Ball's Jack the Miller is arbitrary, let us remember at the outset that Jack's message includes an ambiguous injunction—"Haueth y-now, and seith 'Hoo' "—that is also at the center of Robin's lesson:

> I have a wyf, pardee, as wel as thow;
> Yet nolde I, for the oxen in my plogh,
> *Take upon me more than ynogh* . . .
> . . . . . . . . . . . . . . . . . . . . . . . . . . . . . . . . . . .
> So he may fynde Goddes foyson there,
> Of the remenant nedeth nat enquere.
> (3158–66)[40]

Part of the peasant's claim to freedom, and what sets him apart from the extortionate lord who would bind him, is that he understands the natural fitness of things and knows when he has (and when he has had) enough.

---

39. The verse letter is cited from Thomas Walsingham, *Historia Anglicana,* ed. Henry Thomas Riley (London: Longman, 1864), 2:34; the second, from Knighton's *Chronicon,* is cited from *Peasants' Revolt,* ed. Dobson 381–82. For a bibliographical account of the various versions of these letters, see Rossell Hope Robbins, "Poems on Contemporary Conditions," in *A Manual of the Writings in Middle English 1050–1500,* ed. Albert E. Hartnung, vol. 5 (New Haven: Connecticut Academy of Arts and Sciences, 1975), 1513–14. For further discussion of John Ball's letters, see Rossell Hope Robbins, "Dissent in Middle English Literature: The Spirit of (Thirteen) Seventy-Six," *Medievalia et Humanistica* 9 (1979): 25–51, and Russell A. Peck, "Social Conscience and the Poets," in *Social Unrest,* ed. Newman, 113–48. These two texts have been recently put in relation to the *Miller's Tale* by Paul A. Olson, *The Canterbury Tales and the Good Society* (Princeton: Princeton University Press, 1986), 54–55, who sees the Miller as "cousin to the revolt's 'Jack the Miller' but seen through [Chaucer's] elite court eyes" (75).

40. All citations are from *The Riverside Chaucer,* ed. Larry D. Benson (Boston: Houghton Mifflin, 1987).

IV

There is thus a specifically political appropriateness to the fact that the *Miller's Tale* is a narrative staging of the vitality and resourcefulness of the natural world. In part, these values are embodied in Alisoun, whose vernal beauty serves to elicit the male desire that motivates the *Tale*. All three of the men attempt, with varying degrees of success, to constrain her to their needs: John holds "hire narwe in cage, / For she was wylde and yong, and he was old" (3224–25); to Absolon she is a prey to be caught—"if she hadde been a mous, / And he a cat, he wolde hire hente anon" (3346–47); and if Nicholas does manage to seize her, it is only for a moment: "she sproong as a colt dooth in the trave, / And with hir heed she wryed faste awey" (3282–83).[41] Yet the *Miller's Tale* does not in fact articulate an opposition between natural freedom and social constraint; on the contrary, it presents this opposition as itself mediated by a moderation that bespeaks a calm confidence in the just workings of natural law. The *Tale* everywhere displays an apparently flawless orderliness: not only does the seemingly random aimlessness of the plot reveal itself to be ordered by an exquisite logic, but the unthinking hedonism of the action leads to judgments of an impeccable exactness.[42] The dandified Absolon suffers a scatological humiliation, the too-clever Nicholas, who "thoughte he wolde amenden al the jape" (3799), becomes himself the butt of a jape executed by his intended victim, and the arrogantly know-nothing John is victimized by his violation of the natural law that "man sholde wedde his simylitude" (3228). Compared to the moral anarchy over which the Knight has (however unwittingly) presided, the *Miller's Tale* seems to articulate a world of perfect moral sense. Although the Miller's ludic festivity bursts into the pilgrimage

41. Implicit in the cage metaphor is the Boethian image of the caged bird who yearns for its woodland home—an allusion that serves to legitimize Alisoun; see George D. Economou, "Chaucer's Use of the Bird in the Cage Image in the *Canterbury Tales*," Philological Quarterly 54 (1975): 679–84. Absolon's attack with the coulter takes on a telling configuration in this context: in thinking to brand Alisoun he means both to efface the hairy sexual reality that she has forced upon him and to force her to the sexual cultivation appropriate to her femaleness (hence the coulter); but in instead branding/plowing Nicholas he reveals what a Boethian philosopher would call his true "ende." I take it that the Miller's purpose in establishing this pattern is to mock the homoerotic rivalry that binds Arcite and Palamon together in the *Knight's Tale*.

42. In a famous comment in *Poetry Direct and Oblique*, rev. ed. (London: Chatto and Windus, 1945), E. M. W. Tillyard tellingly described the climax of the *Tale* as arousing "feelings akin to those of religious wonder" (92).

with rude insistence, in other words, it appears to contain its own self-regulation. To attempt to control it is at once unavailing and unnecessary. The natural and the supernatural are in perfect harmony, the *Tale* tells us, and the "belle of laudes" (3655) that rings while the lovers are enjoying their sexual frolics harmonizes the "melodye" (3652) in Alisoun's and Nicholas's bed of love with the song of the friars in the chantry. The result is an unstinted hymn of praise: "what wol ye bet than weel?" (3370).[43]

Criticism has traditionally read this claim as either an end in itself—an effect of the benign naturalism of the *fabliau*—or as an expression of the Miller's philosophical naivete and spiritual culpability.[44] But in fact, I believe, the Miller's celebration of the natural—as a world of beauty, as a source of glad animal spirits, and (most important) as a principle of order—is best understood as a political statement that is consistent with the deeply political nature of the *Tale* as a whole.[45] Criticism has shown how the *Tale* launches a pointed attack upon the chivalric ideology so thoroughly, and critically, represented in the *Knight's Tale*. The heroic *Theseus artifex* is here represented by John the Carpenter, his astrological credulity inciting him, to his cost, to pry into "Goddes pryvetee" (3454, 3558), just as Theseus's hubristic oratories invoked planetary gods who then brought disasters down upon the world that worshipped them. In its largest sense, the *Tale* teaches a lesson about the impossibility of constraining either people or events to the kind of overmastering will that characterizes chivalry. Similarly, Nicholas and Absolon travesty two forms of the chivalric love ethic that underwrites the *Knight's Tale:* Nicholas is the predatory seducer who

---

43. As Alfred David says, "The counterpoint of the melody made by the lovers in bed and the song of the friars in the chantry beautifully illustrates the comic balance Chaucer has achieved between the sacred and the profane. Each in his own way is performing the office of praise and sending up his *Te Deum*" (*The Strumpet Muse* [Bloomington: Indiana University Press, 1976], 103).

44. For the first, see V. A. Kolve, *Chaucer and the Imagery of Narrative* (Stanford: Stanford University Press, 1984), 158–216; for the second, Morton Bloomfield, "The Miller's Tale—an unBoethian Interpretation," in *Medieval Literature and Folklore Studies,* ed. Mandel and Rosenberg, 205–11.

45. On this point I have been anticipated by Olson, *Canterbury Tales and the Good Society,* who also sees the Miller as promoting the rebellious prelapsarianism of John Ball (75–80); where we disagree is over Chaucer's attitude, which for Olson remains that of the court. Another consistently political interpretation of the *Tale* is the excellent article by Robert P. Miller, "The *Miller's Tale* as a Complaint," *Chaucer Review* 5 (1970–71): 147–60. Like Olson, however, Miller also sees the *Tale* as providing a critique of the Miller's insurrectionist misunderstanding of the proper role of the three estates. See also Knight, *Geoffrey Chaucer,* 90–93.

deploys the forms of courtly wooing in order to gratify his appetites, Absolon the narcissistic, inefficient dandy who plays at lovemaking without understanding how to do it. And here too the critique is not only mocking but includes as well a sharp sense of grievance: in directing their attentions to Alisoun, after all, Nicholas and Absolon seek to enact a characteristically seigneurial appropriation: "She was a prymerole, a piggesnye, / For any lord to leggen in his bedde, / Or yet for any good yeman to wedde" (3268–70).

Yet it is not only or even primarily the seigneurial class that is the target of the Miller's *quiting*. If the representations of Nicholas and Absolon serve to mock and subvert the Knight's chivalric culture, they are also vehicles for an attack upon an ecclesiastical establishment that is perceived as equally overbearing and exploitative; and given the fact, as Hilton has pointed out, that "the great ecclesiastical landlords [were] notorious for their bad relations with their tenants," the anticlericalism of the *Tale*, as of medieval peasant movements as a whole, is not to be wondered at.[46] To be sure, in the figure of the inefficient Absolon, a parish clerk who puts on snobbish airs, theatrically displays (in his role as Herod) a ferocity he clearly lacks in life, and laughably deforms the biblical text for seductive purposes, the Miller's critique is essentially mocking and contemptuous. But even here more than mockery is at issue. For by having Absolon use the *Song of Songs* as his text, the Miller is calling attention to a tradition of interpretation in which is visible perhaps more than in any other the coercive manipulation inherent in the institution of biblical exegesis per se. As the very frequency with which it was interpreted suggests (it was by far the most commonly interpreted book of the Bible throughout the Middle Ages), the *Song of Songs* was an especially provocative text to medieval exegetes, challenging them to rewrite a Hebrew love song into the dogmatic terms

46. *A Medieval Society: The West Midlands at the End of the Thirteenth Century* (London: Weidenfeld and Nicolson, 1966), 156. For the anticlericalism of peasant movements, see Hilton, *Bond Men*, 50–52, 101–3, 106–8, 124–25, 167–68, 198–206. According to Michel Mollat and Philippe Wolff, *Ongles bleus, Jacques et Ciompi: les révolutions populaires en Europe aux XIV^e et XV^e siècles* (Paris: Calmann-Lévy 1970), "Evêques et abbés ont été des seigneurs particulièrement vigilants et combatifs, parce qu'ils s'estimaient comptables du patrimoine qu'ils avaient reçu et qu'ils devaient transmettres intact" (Bishops and abbots were particularly vigilant and combative lords, because they considered themselves accountable for a patrimony that they had received and that they had to transmit intact, 288). One episode in the Peasants' Revolt that is particularly relevant to the *Miller's Tale* is the attack at Cambridge against the manor held by Corpus Christi College; for an account, see *Peasants' Revolt*, ed. Dobson, 240–42.

of church doctrine.[47] And yet, implies the Miller, if their fascination bespeaks an awareness of the *Song*'s destabilizing potential, it also witnesses to an unacknowledged pleasure in its seductive literality, a literality that Absolon here turns precisely to the purposes of seduction.[48] In other words, the Miller is arguing that Absolon's misuse of the *Song of Songs* is a characteristically clerical misappropriation: what exegetes typically do *to* the *Song of Songs*, Absolon here seeks to do to Alisoun *by means of* the *Song of Songs*.

If in the figure of Absolon clerical *dominium* is revealed as hypocritically self-regarding and yet comically ineffective, in the figure of Nicholas the ecclesiast is represented as a far more proficient manipulator. Here the instruments of manipulation are other forms of clerical culture—astrology to be sure, but also, and most tellingly, the mystery plays to which allusion is made throughout the *Tale*. For it is Nicholas who stages the entire production, using as his primary text the Noah play.[49] It is the appropriateness of this choice that I wish to examine.

47. For the popularity of the *Song of Songs*, see Jean Leclercq, *The Love of Learning and the Desire for God*, trans. Jean Misrahi (New York: New American Library, 1962), 90–93, and the works cited there.

48. This is not the place to provide full argumentation on this point, but for a telling and authoritative instance of the ambivalence with which the *Song of Songs* was regarded by medieval exegetes, see the well-known discussion by Augustine in *De doctrina christiana* 2.6, where the issue is precisely pleasure. This issue is in fact present in the exegesis of the *Song* from its very inception: Origen prefaces his *Commentary* by warning "everyone who is not yet rid of the vexations of flesh and blood and has not ceased to feel the passion of his bodily nature, to refrain completely from reading this little book and the things that will be said about it" (*The Song of Songs: Commentary and Homilies*, trans. R. P. Lawson [Westminster: The Newman Press, 1957], 23)—a threat from which Origen, as a castrate, was of course protected (which is perhaps why it is the effete Absolon who purveys the *Song* in the *Miller's Tale*). Evidence that the *Canticum canticorum* was indeed interpreted literally in the fourteenth century is provided by the complaint of Pierre d'Ailly: "Intentio Salomonis est hortari sponsam ad oscula et amplexus et ab omni amore adulterino revocari: unde patet falsitas errorum illorum quo dicunt Salomonem hunc librum composuisse ab amorem concubinae carnalis, quam fornicari dilegebat" (Solomon's intention is to encourage his spouse with kisses and embraces and to restrain her from all adulterous love; whence is evident the falsity of the errors of those who say that Solomon composed this book for the love of a fleshly concubine with whom he wished to fornicate, *Super Cantica Canticorum*, in *Opuscula spiritualia* [Douay: Wyon, 1634], 468–69; cited by Olson, *Canterbury Tales and the Good Society*, 154 n. 48). The standard reading of the allusions to the *Song* in the *Miller's Tale* is to see them as spiritually impeaching the Miller rather than as being part of his social critique of the Church: see Robert E. Kaske, "The 'Canticum Canticorum' in the 'Miller's Tale,'" *Studies in Philology* 59 (1962): 479–500, and James Wimsatt, "Chaucer and the Canticle of Canticles," in *Chaucer the Love Poet*, ed. Jerome Mitchell and William Provost (Athens: University of Georgia Press, 1973), 66–90.

49. The *Tale* also includes, as critics have shown, allusions to other scriptural stories—some dramatized, others not—such as Gabriel at the Annunciation, Satan's temp-

In one sense, since the play focuses on the theme of *maistrye* in the relationship of Noah to his wife, the play has a natural affinity for 'maister Nicholay" (3437, 3579), who, as his unnecessarily elaborate plot shows, is seeking not just to seduce Alisoun but to demonstrate in particularly spectacular fashion his superiority over "men that swynke" (3491).[50] But it has as well, I believe, another, deeper relevance to the political dynamic that controls the *Miller's Tale,* the exploration of which will return us to the question of peasant consciousness and the nature of nature.

V

When Richard II revoked his charters of manumission and suppressed the rebellion, he told the peasants, "Rustics you were and rustics you are still; you will remain in bondage, not as before but incomparably harsher."[51] Behind these chilling words lies what Rodney Hilton calls "the caste interpretation of peasant status"—the idea that serfdom is a permanent condition of moral inferiority inherent in the peasant's very being rather than a social status capable of being both assumed and (at least in theory) left behind.[52] The common medieval opinion that the grossly inequitable political order was a consequence of man's sinful nature, while implying a passive acquiescence in injustice, was not in a

---

tation of Eve, and St. Nicholas and the Pickle Barrel miracle, in which three clerks are resurrected from barrels into which their murderer had stuffed them. But that it should be above all the Noah play that Nicholas seeks to reenact is the textual detail that requires explanation. For an excellent discussion of the dramatic allusions in the *Tale,* see Sandra Pierson Prior, "Parodying Typology and the Mystery Plays in the Miller's Tale," *Journal of Medieval and Renaissance Studies* 16 (1986): 57–73. Refreshingly avoiding the spiritualizing readings of previous critics, Prior argues that Chaucer is criticizing a general human propensity to "presume too much upon God's *pryvetee* and unique power" (73). But the plays are not socially neutral, and Prior is closer to the mark when she more specifically claims that "the outcome of Nicholas's play and game teaches us that clerks who rewrite salvation history may burn (here if not in hell)" (73)—for their social rather than their theological transgressions.

50. For the play of Noah as about *maistrye,* see V. A. Kolve, *The Play Called Corpus Christi* (Stanford: Stanford University Press, 1966), 146–51.

51. This is Walsingham's account, as translated in *Peasants' Revolt,* ed. Dobson, 311. For the original, see Walsingham, *Historia Anglicana* 2:18. Dobson also prints a contemporary account of the revolt of the villeins of Darnall and Over in 1336, who are forced to swear to the Abbot of Vale Royal "that they were villeins, they and their sons after them to all eternity" (81).

52. Rodney Hilton, "Peasant Movements in England Before 1381," *Journal of Peasant Studies* 1 (1974), 207–19; reprinted in *Class Conflict,* 138.

crudely direct way an instrument to enforce specific class interests: for Augustine, the distinction between Cain, the founder of the *civitas terrena* (in which we all live) and Abel, the precursor of Christ and thus founder of the *civitas Dei* (to which we all aspire), was less historical than moral and spiritual, an opposition fought out within the soul of each Christian.[53] But later writers gave the distinction a specific social instantiation: as one late medieval cleric misleadingly claimed, "Augustine said that the miserable calamity of bondage hath reasonably been brought into the world because of the demerits of the peoples, so that bondage is now fitly rooted among peasants and common folk."[54] And this distinction could then be scripturally authorized by identifying Abel as the father of all nobility, Cain as the first *servus*.[55] The ultimate effect of this line of argument was not only to explain the peasant's subjection as a function of his sinfulness but to define the peasant as in effect belonging to another order of being, as a member of a different race, a nonhuman. Hence when Gower says, in book 5 of the *Vox clamantis,* that the peasantry "is a race without power of reason, like beasts," he is not only repeating a ubiquitous vilification but characterizing the peasantry as a race of subhuman creatures whose fallen nature requires subjection.[56]

53. As Augustine explained, before the fall there was no mastery or servitude because God "did not wish the rational being, made in his own image, to have dominion over any but irrational creatures, not man over man, but man over the beasts." But with the entrance of sin into the world all was changed: "The first cause of servitude is sin, whereby man was subjected to man in the condition of bondage" (*City of God* 19, 15; trans. Henry Bettenson [Harmondsworth: Penguin Books, 1972], 874–75. For an extended discussion of the medieval justification of social inequality, and specifically of sin as the source of the class of *laboratores,* see Georges Duby, *The Three Orders: Feudal Society Imagined,* trans. Arthur Goldhammer (Chicago: University of Chicago Press, 1980), 52 and *passim.*

54. Balthasar Reber, *Felix Hemmerlin von Zurich* (Zurich, 1846), cited by G. G. Coulton, *The Medieval Village* (Cambridge, Eng.: Cambridge University Press, 1925), 522.

55. David Williams, *Cain and Beowulf* (Toronto: University of Toronto Press, 1982); see also Coulton, *Medieval Village,* 21, 247; and for the representation of Cain in the Towneley *Mactatio Abel* as a husbandman, see G. R. Owst, *Literature and Pulpit in Medieval England,* 2d ed. (Oxford: Blackwell, 1961), 491–92. It is this enrollment of the peasant in the damned race of Cain that accounts for his designation in antipeasant writings as a Jew (see Paul Lehmann, *Parodistische Texte* [Munich: Die Drei Masken, 1923], where the peasant is described as being "ineptus et turpis ut Judeus" [21]), as a Christ-killer (see Francesco Novati, *Carmina Medii Aevi* [Florence: Libreria Dante, 1883], for a poem that asserts that "Christo fu da villan crucificò," [27 n. 1]), and as an *alter Judas* (Novati, 45).

56. *Major Latin Works,* trans. Stockton, 210; this is an identification that he later enforced by depicting the Peasants' Revolt as a rising of maddened animals. For other instances of the use of animalistic language to describe the participants in the events of 1381, see *Peasants' Revolt,* ed. Dobson, 138, 173, and *passim.* For examples of antipeasant

It was this definition of serfdom as an intrinsic and permanent condition of sinfulness, and not simply certain economic disadvantages attached to villeinage, that the 1381 rebels sought to efface. Froissart's well-known summary of the peasants' demands makes this abundantly clear:

> These unhappy people . . . said that they were kept in great servage, and in the beginning of the world, they said, there were no bondmen, wherefore they maintained that none ought to be bond without he did treason to his lord, as Lucifer did to God; but they said that they could have no such battle for they were neither angels nor spirits, but men formed to the similitude of their lords, saying why should they then be kept so under like beasts.[57]

As Hilton has said, the rebels "strove not merely for a reduction of rent but for human dignity"—a statement that can also be applied to virtually every late medieval peasant revolt.[58]

For all its comic tolerance, the *Miller's Tale* takes part in this struggle,

---

writings that stress the animal nature of the peasant, see Novati, *Carmina Medii Aevi*, 32 n. 1, 34–38; as Matteo Vegio said in the early fifteenth century, a peasant's ox has a more human appearance than does the peasant himself (31 n. 1). See also the medieval proverb, "Rusticus asello similis est" (Hans Walther, *Lateinische Sprichwörter und Sentenzen des Mittelalters und der Frühen Neuzeit*, ed. Paul Gerhard Schmidt [Göttingen: Vandenhoeck und Ruprecht, 1986], 9:511, item 223). The notion of the peasant as a creature capable not of love but only of lust is part of this identification of his fallen nature: as Andreas Capellanus famously said in his *De amore*, rustics "are impelled to acts of love in the natural way like a horse or a mule, just as nature's pressure directs them" (ed. and trans. P. G. Walsh [London: Duckworth, 1982], 223). See also the treatise on love included within *Li Hystore de Julius Cesar*, which describes the love of a villain as "comme une beste salvage" (ed. A. Långfors, *Romania* 56 [1930], 367).

Two well-known representations of the peasant as a subhuman, animal creature can be found in Chrétien de Troyes's *Le chevalier du lion* and *Aucassin et Nicolette;* a particularly bestial visual image of a miller may be found in the margins of the Luttrell Psalter, conveniently reproduced on the cover of the paperback edition of Postan's *Medieval Economy and Society*. Less prejudicial pictures that serve to link the peasant to the natural world can be seen in late medieval calendar illustrations, where the peasant serves as virtually a marker of the passage of the year. For examples, see Henrik Specht, *Poetry and the Iconography of the Peasant: The Attitude to the Peasant in Late Medieval English Literature and in Contemporary Calendar Illustration* (Copenhagen: Akademisk Forlag, 1983). Duby is by and large correct when he points out that the medieval world "still recognized only one value in manual labor: that of salutary punishment. Work was servitude. It debased, degraded" (*Three Orders*, 325–26). As Hilton says, "The gentry and the nobility regarded peasants as different creatures from themselves, almost as a different race" (*Bond Men*, 35).

57. *Peasants' Revolt*, ed. Dobson, 370; the translation is by Lord Berners. For the original, see *Oeuvres de Froissart*, ed. Kervyn de Lettenhove, vol. 9 (Brussels: Devaux, 1869), 387.

58. *Class Conflict*, 138.

and not least by subverting and mocking the very terms with which the reigning ideology sought to stigmatize and oppress peasants. For one thing, the Miller's witty, even elegant *Tale*—an achievement that not even modern critics, who continue to wonder at the presence of so intelligent a tale in the mouth of so obviously brutish a teller, have been quite prepared to grant him—both proves that the peasant is not the inarticulate and brutal figure that hostile representations had depicted and establishes a countervailing set of values. In place of the Knight's paranoid insistence on the continual need for supervision and constraint, the Miller describes (as we have seen) a world that shatters all efforts at confinement but that nonetheless contains its own principle of equilibrium in a sense of natural fitness and decorum. In locating at the thematic center of his *Tale* a benign, virtually prelapsarian *lex naturalis,* the Miller is thus reversing the terms of antipeasant defamation. Far from being fallen and degraded, nature here serves as a beneficent and supportive principle; far from being in need of compensation by the *lex positiva* created by men, the *lex naturalis* is seen as providing an unerring standard. And what is striking is that the Miller's rehabilitation of nature as a principle of moral order is itself profoundly expressive of his class consciousness. For he promotes a view of the natural world that was—so far as we can tell from the fragmentary evidence— common to peasant movements throughout the late Middle Ages. That nature provides a self-evident norm of fairness, an originary and still authoritative principle of equality, is implicit in the famous couplet of 1381, "When Adam dalf, and Eve span / Wo was thanne a gentilman?"[59] And in their political program the rebels sought to return England to a similarly prelapsarian condition, in which both a people's monarchy and a people's church could subsist without any intervening hierarchy.[60] Furthermore, both here and throughout the Middle Ages, one of the goals of peasant resistance was to achieve access to the bounty of the natural world—the woods, fish, and game—that they felt was theirs by right of being natural creatures like their lords.[61] In sum, stigmatized

---

59. Walsingham, *Historia Anglicana* 2:32. That this couplet was a traditional homiletic saying long before 1381 does not affect its utopianist meaning within the context of political rebellion; see Owst, *Literature and Pulpit,* 291–94.

60. For the program of the Peasants' Revolt, see Hilton, *Bond Men,* 229.

61. For examples, going back as far as the tenth-century peasants' war in Normandy, see Hilton, *Bond Men,* 71, 230; and for the peasant sense that the natural world should not be subjected to the tyrannical control entailed by private ownership, see 40. As the Ger-

by their opponents as beings who expressed with special and culpable directness the fallenness of nature—"they so till the earth, they are so utterly earthly, that we may truly say of them: They shall lick the earth and eat it," as one particularly vicious prelate put it, while an English celebrant of peasant humility described them as "grobbyng aboute the erthe"—peasants not only accepted this "natural" identity but re-deemed it by insisting, like the Miller in his *Tale*, upon nature's essential goodness.[62]

Far from being the result of either misguided optimism or spiritual turpitude, then, the Miller's rehabilitation of nature is part of a political program that turns against the governing classes one of its own instru-ments of ideological control. The same thing can be said about his use of the Noah story. We have already seen how the distinction between Cain and Abel was used as an aristocratic *Gründungsage* to justify the subjection of the peasant. The story of Noah was upon occasion used for the same purpose. When human history was refounded after the flood, the original division of peoples established by Cain and Abel now became a threefold distinction to be drawn among Noah's three sons, Japhet, Ham, and Shem. Once again, a distinction that for patris-tic writers existed at the level of the spiritual and ecclesiastical life be-came defined in the later Middle Ages in terms of social opposition. The first writer to make this definition explicit was, it seems, Honorius of Autun in his *De imagine mundi* (1133): "At this time humankind was divided into three: into freemen, knights, and serfs [*servos*]. Freemen

---

man peasants of 1525 said in the fourth of their Twelve Articles, "When the Lord God created man, he gave him dominion over all animals, over the birds of the air, and the fish in the waters" (Peter Blickle, *The Revolution of 1525: The German Peasants' War from a New Perspective*, trans. Thomas A. Brady and H. C. Erik Midelfort (Baltimore: Johns Hopkins University Press, 1981), 198). Similarly, as Hilton points out, the Robin Hood ballads express a "Utopian vision of free communities of hunters eating their fill of a forbidden food" (*Bond Men*, 72).

62. For the first citation, see Roderigo, Bishop of Zamorra, *Speculum Vitae Humanae* (c. 1465), cited by Coulton, *Medieval Village*, 518; for the second, see Owst, *Literature and Pulpit*, 553. Perhaps the most explicit peasant assertion of the authority of the *lex naturalis* (which they identified with the *lex divina*) now available to us is that found in the docu-ments produced during the German Peasants' War of 1524–25. For a discussion, see Blic-kle, *Revolution of 1525*, 168, and Heiko A. Obermann, "The Gospel of Social Unrest," in *The German Peasant War of 1525—New Viewpoints*, ed. Bob Scribner and Gerhard Benecke (London: Allen and Unwin, 1979), 39–51. Coulton is surely right when he says that the Twelve Articles "rest upon [an] appeal from oppressive human law and custom to natural law" (*Medieval Village*, 546).

[are descended] from Shem, knights from Japhet, serfs from Ham."[63] Ham's subjection was to be explained by the curse laid upon Ham's son Canaan by Noah when Ham mocked his drunken father's nakedness: "Cursed be Canaan, a servant of servants [*servus servorum*] shall he be unto his brethren" (Gen. 9:25). As exegetes had always insisted, Ham was of the race of Cain, and now this text identified that race with the *servi* who were so visible a part of medieval life.[64]

Needless to say, any argument that stigmatizes the vast majority of the population as damned beyond redemption—"curssed uppon þe grounde," as the York play put it—can hardly enter the mainstream of medieval political thought.[65] Yet there is evidence that, despite its exorbitance, this identification of the cursed Ham with rustics did achieve considerable currency. The popular *Cursor mundi*, first written in about 1300 and then rewritten into two other versions, appended to the usual geographical distribution of Noah's sons (Shem to Asia, Ham to Africa, and Japhet to Europe) Honorius's social analysis:

> Knyȝt & þral and fre man
> Of þese þre briþeren bigan:
> Of Sem fre mon, of Iapheth knyȝt,
> Þral of Cam, waryed wiȝte.[66]

63. Honorius of Autun, *De imagine mundi:* "Huius tempore divisum est genus humanum in tria: in liberos, milites, servos. Liberi de Sem, milites de Japhet, servi de Cham" (*Patrologia Latina* 172:166; hereafter *PL*). Duby argues that Honorius's distinction is governed by the model of the traditional three estates (*bellatores, oratores, laboratores*) that developed during the ninth through eleventh centuries, and points out that in his *Summa gloria* Honorius assigns Shem to the priesthood, Japhet to the kingdom, and Ham to the *populus*, which is subject to the others (*Three Orders*, 253–54). But in an earlier discussion, "Une enquête à poursuivre: la noblesse dans la France médiévale," *Revue historique* 226 (1961), reprinted in *The Chivalrous Society*, trans. Cynthia Postan (Berkeley and Los Angeles: University of California Press, 1980), 94–111, Duby sees Honorius' division as governed by a "'germanic' concept" of binarism that should be contrasted with the traditional ternary. It is surely this difference that accounts for the fact that the later development of the topos focused almost exclusively upon the subjection of Ham. See also the discussion by Jacques Le Goff, "A Note on Tripartite Society, Monarchical Ideology, and Economic Renewal in Ninth- to Twelfth-Century Christendom," in *Time, Work, and Culture in the Middle Ages,* trans. Arthur Goldhammer (Chicago: University of Chicago Press, 1980), 53–57.

64. For Ham as a member of the race of Cain, see Oliver F. Emerson, "Legends of Cain, Especially in Old and Middle English," *PMLA* 21 (1906): 925–26.

65. *Sacrificium Cayme and Abel,* in *The York Plays,* ed. Richard Beadle (London: Arnold, 1982), line 86.

66. *The Southern Version of Cursor Mundi,* ed. Sarah M. Horrall, col. 1 (Ottawa: University of Ottawa Press, 1978), 102–3. The *Cursor mundi* survives, in its various versions, in 8 mss.

More significant is the very popular *Liber de moribus hominum et officiis nobilium ac popularium super ludo scachorum,* written in the early fourteenth century by Jacobus de Cessolis and in the course of the century translated at least twice into French and then later four times into German and once (by Caxton) into English. For de Cessolis not only enforces the identification of peasants as members of the race of Cain, but he uses the story of Ham's mockery to introduce a discussion of the four kinds of drunkenness (like a lion, a lamb, a swine, and an ape), a vice that is then associated with the laborer and seen as a spur to social disturbance: wines (in Caxton's translation) "make the poure [man] riche as longe as the wyn is in his hed and shortly dronkenshyp is the begynnynge of alle euylles." [67] Ham is also designated the progenitor of serfs in *Dives and Pauper,* written in the first decade of the fifteenth century: "for scornynge & vnworchepe þat þe sone ded to his fadir began first bondage and þraldam & was confermyd of God," a designation that is reconfirmed, the text implies, by every subsequent act of scorning and unworship that unruly serfs perform. [68] And the currency of this account is also attested by the fact that Wycliff, in his discussion of dominion, goes out of his way to reject the "foolish" opinion that servitude was instituted by the cursing of Ham. [69]

But the text that is most interesting in terms of the *Miller's Tale* is the *Liber armorum,* a brief treatise on heraldry included in the early fifteenth-century *Boke of Seynt Albans.* [70] For here the antipeasant myth of Ham is deployed in a way that not only makes its relevance to the *Miller's Tale* evident but suggests that its late medieval currency was a response to the debate about the nature of serfdom that was at the center of the class struggle taking place in fourteenth-century En-

67. William Caxton, trans., *The Game and Playe of the Chesse,* 2d ed. (Westminster: Caxton, 1481[?]), reprinted in facsimile by William Figgins (London, 1855). For an edition of de Cessolis, see *Das Schachzelbuch Kunrats von Ammenhausen nebst den Schachbüchern des Jakob von Cessole und des Jakob Mennel,* ed. Ferdinand Vetter (Frauenfeld, 1892).

68. *Dives and Pauper,* ed. Priscilla Heath Barnum, EETS OS 275 (Oxford: Oxford University Press, 1976), vol. 1, part 1, p. 305.

69. *Opera Minora,* ed. Johann Loserth (London: Paul, 1913), 146.

70. According to E. F. Jacob, "The Book of St. Albans," *Bulletin of the John Rylands Library* 28 (1944): 99–118, the *Liber armorum* is in part dependent upon both Nicholas of Upton's *De officio militari* (late 1420s–early 1430s) and a "Book of the Lineage of Cote Armour," but I have not yet been able to determine either the precise lines of affiliation or the other sources that might be involved. The two other items in this compilation—treatises on hawking and hunting—are both based on early fourteenth-century sources. Even if the *Liber* was composed in the early fifteenth century, it clearly draws upon traditional materials.

The *Liber armorum* begins by demonstrating "how gentilmen shall be knowyn from vngentill men and how bondeage began first" specifically in order to counter peasant claims of natural equality: "A bonde man or a churle wyll say, 'All we be cummyn of Adam.' So Lucifer with his cumpany may say, 'All we be cummyn of heuyn.' "[71] For Lucifer and his rebel angels were the first group to be placed in bondage, followed by Cain, who was damned by God and by Adam for his fratricide: "By that did Cayn become a chorle and all his ofspryng after hym" (cci[v]). Noah was descended from Abel's son Seth, and he in turn

> had .iii. sonnys begetyn by kynde; by the modre .ii. were named Cham and Sem and by the fadre the thirde was namyd Jafeth. Yit in theys .iii. sonnys gentilnes and vngentilnes was founde. In Cham vngentilnes was founde to his owne fadre, dooun to discuver his preuytes and laugh his fadre to scorne. Jafeth was the yongist and repreued his brodre. Than like a gentilman, take mynde of Cham: for his vngentilnes he was become a chorle and had the cursyng of God and his fadre Noe. And whan Noe awoke he sayde to Cham his sonne, "Knowyst nott thow how hit become of Cayn, Adam['s] soon, and of his churlish blode? All the worlde is drownde saue we .viii. And now of the to begynne vngentilnes and a cause to destroye vs all—vppon the hit shall be and so I pray to God that it shall fall. Now to the I gyuve my curse, wycked kaytife for euer, and I gyuve to the the north parte of the worlde to draw thyn habitacion, for ther shall it be where [are] sorow and care, colde and myschef. As a churle thow shalt haue . . . the thirde parte of the worlde, wich shall be calde Europe, that is to say the contre of churlys".
>
> (ci[v]–cii[r])

Nothing could more vividly illustrate the writer's sense of contemporary urgency than his (or her) willingness to override the traditional geographical endowments. Far from being exiled to distant Africa, the damned race of Ham is ubiquitously present in the here and now of late medieval Europe, a presence that requires the gentle reader to learn, for his own self-protection, the way "to deseuer Gentilnes from vngentilnes" (ci[r]).[72] And so it is not surprising that aristocratic genealogies of the fifteenth century were careful to trace the descent of England's

---

71. *The Boke of Seynt Albans* (St. Albans, 1486), fol. ci[r]; further page numbers will be included in the text. I have supplied the punctuation. The *Boke* has also been discussed by Coulton, *Medieval Village*, 232–33, and by Thrupp, *Merchant Class*, 288–319.

72. The essentially racist nature of the myth of Ham was made odiously explicit in early nineteenth-century America, where it functioned as a justification for slavery; see Thomas Virgil Peterson, *Ham and Japeth: The Mythic World of Whites in the Antebellum South* (Metuchan, N.J.: Scarecrow Press, 1978).

noble houses from Adam through Japhet.[73] Finally, lest we doubt the
currency of this identification of the serf with Canaan and the children
of Ham, we actually find a somewhat inaccurate reference to it in that
most orthodox of late fourteenth-century texts, Chaucer's *Parson's Tale:*
"This name of thraldom was nevere erst kowth til that Noe seyde that
his sone Canaan sholde be thral to his bretheren for his synne"
(X.766).[74]

What the *Miller's Tale* does, then, is turn the myth of Ham against
the clerical culture from which it originally arose. For here the searcher
into hidden "pryvetee," far from being a peasant, is instead the
astrologer-cleric Nicholas, who uses his illicit knowledge to mock and
scorn John the Carpenter, the father Noah of the play he is staging.[75]
Moreover, the characteristics that are ascribed to the biblical Ham by
medieval clerical culture are here applied, with striking aptness, to
Nicholas. Ham's name means, according to the commentators, *calidus,*
and he represents a spirit that is *impatiens, inquietus,* and *commotior.*[76]
He also represents, according to Augustine's authoritative exegesis,

> those who boast the name of Christian and yet live scandalous lives. For
> it is certain that such people proclaim Christ's passion, symbolized by
> Noah's nakedness, in their professions, while they dishonour it by their
> evil actions. It was of such people that we read in Scripture, "You will
> recognize them by their fruits."[77]

Most centrally, Ham is the heretic who reveals that which ought to
remain a mystery, the *corporis mysterium* enacted in the passion and re-
enacted in the Eucharist: he "makes manifest that which was for the

73. Alison Allan, "Yorkist Propaganda: Pedigree, Prophecy, and the 'British History'
in the Reign of Edward IV," in *Patronage, Pedigree and Power in Later Medieval England,*
ed. Charles Ross (Gloucester: Alan Sutton, 1979), 172.

74. This sentence is not found in the text that apparently served as Chaucer's source:
Siegfried Wenzel, "The Source of Chaucer's Deadly Sins," *Traditio* 30 (1974): 368.

75. It is just possible that Chaucer derived the idea of having the role of Ham played
by a cleric from Gower's identification of Ham in the *Confessio amantis* as the inventor of
writing and the founder of *clergie* (*The English Works of John Gower,* ed. G. C. Macaulay,
vol. 1, EETS ES 81 [London: Oxford University Press, 1900], p. 366, book 4, lines 2396–
2400); according to Macaulay's note to the passage, Gower derived his information from
Godfrey of Viterbo's *Pantheon.*

76. See, e.g., Ambrose, *Liber de Noe et arca* (PL 14:435); Isidore, *Quaestiones in Veterum Testamentum: In Genesin,* 8.6 (PL 83:235–36).

77. Augustine, *City of God,* 16.2 (650–51). This interpretation is repeated throughout
the Middle Ages, as by Isidore, *Quaestiones in Veterum Testamentum: In Genesin,* 8.6 (PL
83:235–36), and Rhabanus Maurus, *Commentarius in Genesim,* 2.9 (PL 107:525–26). So too,
the interpretation of Noah's drunken nakedness as representing Christ's passion is the
standard exegesis.

prophets a secret," and with this illicit knowledge he "deceives the simple"—the sort of "lewed man," like John, "That noght but oonly his bileve kan."[78] As John succinctly says, with (as we know from his prologue) the Miller's approval, "Men sholde nat knowe of Goddes pryvetee" (3454–56). The relevance of these characteristics to the Miller's Nicholas is self-evident. In his picture of Nicholas, the Miller offers a biting exercise in cultural criticism, turning the materials of clerical culture against its proprietor, and revealing by his very act of criticism how defamatory—and self-protective—are its misrepresentations.

## VI

Yet we must also recognize that the *Miller's Tale,* in its animosity towards John the Carpenter, contains as well an act of peasant self-criticism. In part, of course, we may have an expression here of the stresses and strains within the peasant community itself: John is a "riche gnof," and Robin represents himself in the tale as a servant boy who can be packed off to London and (so John at least thinks) to death by drowning without a second thought.[79] But again, I think we do best to understand the Miller's scorn for John as political in a deeper, more serious sense. Despite being a successful village craftsman, John not only allows himself to be intimidated by his lodger but has, by marrying the youthful Alisoun, violated a natural law that he, of all people, ought to understand; and when the Miller says that John married Alisoun because "he knewe nat Catoun, for his wit was rude" (3227), he is mockingly invoking an *auctoritas* to support a truth that ought to be self-evident to the truly natural man.[80] As Langland had put it, "kynde

---

78. Rhabanus Maurus, *Commentarius in Genesim,* 2.9 (*PL* 107:525), and Remigius, *Commentarius in Genesim,* 9 (*PL* 131:78). Cassian identified Ham as a worker in secret arts: see Williams, *Cain and Beowulf* 30–31, and Gower, *Confessio amantis* 4:2396–2400, in *English Works,* ed. G. C. Macauley (London: Oxford University Press, 1901), 1:366.

79. Carpenters were prominent among those village artisans who profited from the economic conditions of the postplague years. For their inclusion within the Statutes of Labourers, see Putnam, *Enforcement,* 75, 80–81, and for instances of carpenters accused of overcharging, see the appendix, 163 and 214. According to Du Boulay, "The possession of land was a touchstone, and already 'every gentleman flyeth unto the country.' Our rentals of fifteenth-century Gillingham and Wrotham are rich in the names of tenants who were also masons, carpenters, shinglers, glaziers, tanners and poulterers"—but, apparently, no millers (*Lordship of Canterbury,* 163). That Robin represents himself in so helpless a role in his *Tale* provides some evidence that although others saw millers as prosperous (hence the antimiller literature), millers thought of themselves otherwise.

80. See Tillyard, *Poetry Direct and Oblique,* 88.

wit" is the companion of the commons and teaches "ech lif to knowe his owene."[81] Moreover, and more reprehensibly, he has also betrayed his class interests by handing himself over to a smooth-talking clerical con man.[82]

Thus it is John who is most severely punished at the end of the *Miller's Tale:* his wife is "swyved," his arm is broken, and his reputation as a man of probity is ruined. Yet even here, significantly enough, the Miller cannot finally withhold his sense that this punishment, however merited, is nonetheless enacted in the distasteful form of class victimization:

> The folk gan laughen at his fantasye;
> Into the roof they kiken and they cape,
> And turned *al his harm unto a jape.*
> For what so that this carpenter answerde,
> It was for noght; *no man his reson herde.*
> With othes grete he was so sworn adoun
> That *he was holde wood* in al the toun;
> *For every clerk anonright heeld with oother.*
> They seyde, *"The man is wood,* my leeve brother";
> And every wight gan laughen at this stryf.
>
> (3840–49)

Before beginning to rehearse the *Miller's Tale,* a nervous narrator had warned the "gentils" "nat [to] maken ernest of game" (3186); now at the end the Miller reverses the terms—and meaning—of the warning: when a group of clerks turn "al [a rustic's] harm unto a jape," more is at issue than simple comedy. The point is not only that the clerks band together against the rich artisan—an opposition that figures not just the traditional medieval antagonism between clerks and peasants but also, in an oblique but nonetheless historically corroborated fashion,

---

81. *Piers Plowman: The B Text,* eds. George Kane and E. Talbot Donaldson (London: Athlone Press, 1975), Prol. 121–22. See also the poem written in 1392 by John Berwald of Cottingham, in which he insists that it would be "vnkind" (that is, unnatural) for a villein to suffer "any villan hething" (that is, the oppression or derision of any other villein); *Historical Poems of the 14th and 15th Centuries,* ed. Rossell H. Robbins (New York: Columbia University Press, 1959), 61; and see *Peasants' Revolt,* ed. Dobson, 383–84.

82. An instance of clerical contempt for peasants with special relevance to the plot of the *Miller's Tale* is the widespread parodic prayer against rustics: "Deus, qui multidudinem rusticorum congregasti et magnam discordiam inter eos et nos seminasti, da, quesumus, ut laboribus eorum fruamur et ab uxoribus eorum diligamur" (O God, who brought forth a multitude of rustics and sowed great discord between them and us, grant, we beseech, that we may live off their labors and enjoy their wives). Lehmann, *Parodie im Mittelalter* (Munich: Drei Masken, 1922) 178; see also 117, and Lehmann, *Parodistische Texte,* 22.

the larger conflict between the classes that was the central social phenomenon of Chaucer's England. Rather, it is that the terms the Miller uses here to represent the carpenter's oppression bear a powerful political valence and force us to attend to the class consciousness to which the tale witnesses.

The clerks do not here merely silence John's arguments—"no man his reson herde"—but deny him rationality itself.[83] In twice insisting that the clerks considered John mad, the Miller is again invoking a terminology typical of medieval commentators (most of them, of course, clerics) on peasant behavior. And this madness is nowhere more visible than when the peasant seeks to promote his own interests. For the early fourteenth-century chronicler of the Abbey of Vale Royal, the "bestial men of Rutland" who had recourse to the courts and the king in a vain effort to prove that they were not the abbot's serfs were *rabicanes*—mad dogs.[84] And as we should perhaps expect, the chroniclers of the Peasants' Revolt consistently use the language of insanity to describe the rebels. For Walsingham, the Revolt as a whole is an expression of the *insania nativorum*—the madness of bondmen—and his account is both saturated with terms like *dementes, irrationibile,* and *stulti* and invokes throughout the language of satanic possession: the rebels are *ganeones daemoniaci* (children of the devil), perhaps even *pejores daemonibus* (worse than devils).[85] Gower also describes the Revolt as an expression of bestial madness: the rebels "were swine into which a cursed spirit had entered, just as Holy Writ tells of," and "just as the Devil was placed in command over the army of the lower world, so this scoundrel [Wat Tyler] was in charge of the wicked mob."[86] And even less vindictive observers invoke the language of madness and folly: a relatively disinterested macaronic poet calls the rebels "folus" and *stultes*, Knighton

83. Not, of course, that this silencing is insignificant. In *Literature and Pulpit*, Owst provides a summary of a fourteenth-century sermon that attacks just this inability of the rich to hear the poor: "if a poor man . . . were to come asking help of some rich neighbours, 'for the love of his father and mother and all those dear to him,' they would deign neither to hear nor see him. If, redoubling his entreaties, he were to beg, 'My Lord, for the love of Christ crucified and all the saints of God, help me, lest I be destroyed unjustly by my adversaries,' still there would be 'neither voice nor hearing'" (315–16).

84. A long extract from the *Ledger Book of Vale Royal Abbey* (Lancashire and Cheshire Record Society, 1914), is translated by Coulton, *Medieval Village*, 132–35; for *rabicanes*, see 133.

85. Walsingham, *Historia Anglicana* 1:457–60, 472, 2:13, 16; *Peasants' Revolt*, ed. Dobson, 169–74, 272–75, 307–10.

86. *Major Latin Works*, trans. Stockton, 58, 65.

calls them *stultes* and refers to them as servants of the devil, Froissart compares them to devils from hell, and the monk of Westminster re-invokes *rabicanes*.[87]

"The man is *wood*," say the clerks about John when he tries to tell "his reson"—a designation important enough that the Miller first invokes it in his own voice and then has the clerks repeat it. As we shall in a moment see in detail, the use of the language of folly and demonic possession to describe peasant resistance surfaces again in the *Canterbury Tales:* the lord in the *Summoner's Tale* begins by assuming that the churl John is a "fool" (2292) or—a term that is applied twice and implied once—a "demonyak" (2240, 2292; and cf. 2221). The point is that these are not simply terms of causal abuse but are derived from the language of moral censure with which the governing classes of medieval Europe, and particularly of fourteenth-century England, tried to stigmatize, and so to control, peasant protest. In having the unified mockery of the clerics pervert John's "resons" into the irrationality of madness, then, the *Miller's Tale* offers a bitter commentary not just upon the Peasants' Revolt but upon the official language that sought to censor peasant resistance at the level of discourse as effectively as the instruments of government suppressed it politically.

## VII

In searching for an ideological posture by means of which to distance himself from the cultic and increasingly caste-defined aristocratic culture of his time, Chaucer almost inevitably turned to the most vigorous oppositional force within his society—the rural world of peasant culture.[88] In the General Prologue the Miller is represented in the conventional terms of peasant caricature: he is grossly ugly, with a flat nose, a huge mouth, and swinishly red hairs that protrude from a wart and match a beard also red "as any sowe or fox"—in sum, a threatening figure of peasant animality who uses his head not for rational thought

87. For these terms, see *Peasants' Revolt,* ed. Dobson, 144, 183, 189, 199, 278.
88. It should be stressed that while the caste definition of the aristocracy, which of course entails an analogous caste definition of the peasantry, was increasingly insisted upon in late fourteenth- and fifteenth-century England—see, for example, McFarlane, *Nobility,* 268–78, and Thrupp, *Merchant Class,* 288–319—it is also a feature of other periods and places in medieval history, specifically twelfth- and early-thirteenth-century France; see Georges Duby, *Chivalrous Society, passim.*

(of which peasants are in any case incapable) but to enact invasive acts of violence: "Ther was no dore that he nolde . . . breke it at a rennyng with his heed" (1.550–51).[89] And when he then invades the tale-telling game, he displays two of the most characteristic of peasant vices— drunkenness and a contempt for order.[90] In sum, the essential terms of the Miller's representation are not moral and psychological but social and political; and the consciousness articulated by his *Tale* is derived from the politics of late medieval English society.

It is a consciousness, moreover, to which Chaucer grants remarkable scope and force, allowing it both to counter the oppressive hegemonic culture of the aristocracy and to subvert the language of class hatred promoted by certain forms of clerical discourse. Yet as we should expect, this authority is immediately, and severely, circumscribed. For as soon as the claims of peasant class consciousness are put forward they are countered. The *Reeve's Tale* accomplishes this subversion in two ways. One is to reveal the disunity within the peasant class itself, not simply by the antagonism between the Reeve and the Miller but by the Reeve's own betrayal of class interests. He is himself an agent of seigneurial control, and he has social ambitions: he began life as a carpenter, is now a reeve, and his dress and diction reveal his clerical ambitions.[91] In short, he shows that the social identity asserted by the Miller

89. For a discussion of the conventions governing the representation of peasants, see Alice M. Colby, *The Portrait in Twelfth-Century French Literature* (Geneva: Droz, 1965), 73–81. See also Beatrice White, "Poet and Peasant," in *The Reign of Richard II,* ed. F. R. H. Du Boulay and Caroline Barron (London: Athlone Press, 1971), 58–74. The sense of the Miller's threatening demeanor is enforced by the oppressive immediacy with which he is observed; as Mann acutely observes, "The most striking aspect of the description of his face is the effect of 'close-up' that it gives; we can see the hairs on his wart, and his nostrils and mouth gape hugely at us. This is not a face observed from the distance normally observed in polite conversation; it is two or three inches away" (*Chaucer and Medieval Estates Satire,* 162).

90. Indeed, he is even given a name that is not only itself lower-class—the male protagonist of the *pastourelle,* for instance, is typically called Robin—but that seems to have carried implications of subversion and illegality: a number of fourteenth-century texts, including *Piers Plowman,* refer to criminals as Roberdesmen, and the term, perhaps like the Miller's own name, was probably derived from the stories of Robin Hood; see J. C. Holt, "The Origins and Audience of the Ballads of Robin Hood," *Past and Present* 18 (1960), reprinted in *Peasants, Knights and Heretics,* ed. R. H. Hilton (Cambridge, Eng.: Cambridge University Press, 1976), 241. For Chaucer's familiarity with the Robin Hood rhymes, see *Troilus* 5.1174, where Pandarus refers to "haselwode, there joly Robyn pleyde."

91. In theory the reeve was chosen by the tenants to represent them and should therefore be distinguished from the bailiff, who was the lord's agent; but in practice the reeve often functioned as a bailiff: see H. S. Bennett, "The Reeve and the Manor in the Fourteenth Century," *English Historical Review* 41 (1926): 358–65. In the later Middle Ages,

is a fiction, that there is no class unity among the peasantry but only individuals. The second point is that Chaucer endorses this position by requiring us to read the *Reeve's Tale* as the expression of an individual psyche. By a whole variety of means, which criticism has well analyzed, the *Reeve's Tale* expresses a meaning that is not political or social but psychological and spiritual, thus undoing the reversal accomplished by the Miller. And this assertion of the primacy of the individual serves, of course, to depoliticize the *Tale* by moving it from the realm of history to that of psychology.

The stigmatizing of the Miller's interruption is then carried to its inevitable conclusion in the *Cook's Tale*. Although he means to recoup the disruptive energies of the *Miller's Tale,* the Cook unwittingly reveals them to be not enlivening but destructive, not a necessary alternative to the hegemonic ideology of the *Knight's Tale* but a riotous excess that threatens the social order as a whole. Hence his fragmentary *Tale* is itself about degeneration followed by ejection: it tells of the apprentice Perkyn Revelour whose ludic festivity declines into criminal riot and leads to his expulsion from his master's house. The principle that governs the action of this *Tale* is phrased by the Cook as a proverb: "Wel bet is roten appul out of hoord / Than that it rotie al the remenaunt" (4406–7), a principle that is then revealed to be relevant as well to his own performance, which is terminated before it can defile the *Tales* as a whole. In locating this social menace in the figure of the Cook, Chaucer is stigmatizing not only the urban wage laborers (the very group who scandalously welcomed the rebellious peasants when they invaded London in 1381) but the craft guilds whose representatives are presented, within the fiction of the General Prologue, as the Cook's employers.[92] In other words, in making the Cook the voice of lower-class criminality, a criminality sponsored, however unwittingly, by the small, relatively powerless craft guilds, Chaucer places his poetry in the service of the dominant merchant patriciate from which he himself originally derived.

How, then, is the second effort at escaping from the tyrannical em-

---

according to Father Raftis, "The inability of the villagers to depend upon officials (reeves, for instance) as their 'men' left the peasant exposed to demands such as the poll tax" ("Social Change versus Revolution," 16).

92. For the distinction between the powerful trade guilds or merchant companies and the far weaker craft guilds, see Thrupp, *Merchant Class,* 27–41. For a different account of the *Cook's Tale,* which sees it as expressing the attitude of a conservative guildsman, see Kolve, *Chaucer and the Imagery of Narrative,* 257–85.

brace of the dominant ideology accomplished in the next group of tales? The role of the establishment previously filled by the Knight is now played by the Man of Law, a sociologically appropriate choice given the ease with which lawyers entered into the world of the aristocracy.[93] Moreover, the Man of Law is both a familiar companion of merchants (he learned the tale he is now about to tell, he informs us, from them) and a reader of Chaucerian poetry and specifically of the *Legend of Good Women,* a text he cites in his Prologue and that provides the paradigm for the tale of the saintly and long-suffering Constance he then tells. The Man of Law represents, in short, that earlier Chaucerian self that is now to be rejected. If we think of Chaucer as a man with mercantile social origins, whose economic security depends upon fulfilling ministerial functions for the king, and who may even have himself received legal training, then we can see the way in which the *Man of Law's Tale* scrutinizes, and ironically inflects, the very social identity that led Chaucer to retreat from the experiment of Fragment I. Conversely, the Wife of Bath, who now fills the role previously played by the Miller, is one of those rural commodity producers—specifically, one of the independent weavers who were springing up all over England with the sudden growth of the English cloth industry—who were contributing so heavily to the threatening strength of an economy independent of seigneurial control.[94] The scene is thus set for a replay of the Knight-Miller confrontation.

93. As Postan has said, with perhaps unconscious irony, "it is difficult to overestimate the continuous social advancement of lawyers and their ability to break into the upper ranks of society" (*Medieval Economy and Society,* 175). Postan adds: "All through the middle ages, but perhaps more in the later centuries than in the earlier ones, legal education and the opportunities it offered for bureaucratic and political employment provided the easiest and best-trodden path to the advancement of individuals. . . . It is not therefore surprising that lawyers descending from families of merchants or petty landlords or of even humbler provenance should have been able to climb into the upper reaches of society more frequently and with greater ease than most other men" (175–76). As for the sons of merchants becoming lawyers, Thrupp comments on "the fascination that the legal profession was coming to hold for wealthy citizens' sons" in the early fifteenth century—a trend that may have some bearing on the tradition that Chaucer studied at the Inns of Court, as well as on the connection that the Man of Law draws in his Prologue between himself and the merchants who supplied him with his *Tale* (*Merchant Class,* 246). The choice of the Man of Law as the voice of authority is also given special point by the rage toward the legal system expressed by the rebels of 1381.

94. See Mary Carruthers, "The Wife of Bath and the Painting of Lions," *PMLA* 94 (1979): 209–22, and D. W. Robertson, Jr., "'And for my land thus hastow mordred me?': Land Tenure, the Cloth Industry, and the Wife of Bath," *Chaucer Review* 14 (1979–80):403–20. The independent commodity producer is postfeudal not because he or she

Yet this is not quite what we get. On the contrary, just as the *Reeve's Tale* drained away the political meaning of the *Miller's Tale* by an act of privatization, so the Wife of Bath's performance accomplishes a similar internalization of value. To be sure, the issue now is not spiritual salvation but psychological wholeness; and the topic is not social ambition but marriage. But the Wife of Bath's *social* challenge as an independent, postfeudal commodity producer is here set aside. Unlike the Miller, she insists upon the rights not of her class but rather of her selfhood. It is subjectivity per se that she promotes, a subjectivity that Chaucer (like many medieval writers) associates both here and throughout his work with women.[95] In other words, in substituting for the political threat posed by the Miller the Wife of Bath's insistence upon the priority of the individual self, Chaucer makes what we have come to recognize as the characteristic liberal move. What the Wife wants is not, despite her truculent tone, political or social change; on the contrary, the traditional order is capable both of generating her independent selfhood and of accommodating the marital happiness that would accomplish its fulfillment. To be sure, to acknowledge that the basic unit of social life is a socially undetermined selfhood has crucial political implications—beginning with the recognition of the equality of all people—that carry the possibility (but by no means the necessity) of social change. And to see that the bearers of this message are women is also a political statement. But the direction in which the politics of the individual moves is of course opposed to that dictated by the class consciousness of the Miller: after all, the socially undetermined selfhood privileged by individualism is by definition already common property. Thus the Wife avoids the kind of economic transformations entailed by the Miller's antagonistic social consciousness—transformations that were in fact overtaking late medieval England but were prevented from coming to

---

produces commodities (which is true to some extent of all agrarian production throughout the Middle Ages), but because the mode of production is independent. The essential and defining characteristic of the feudal mode of production is that it is *dependent*, as Postan points out: "Dependent cultivation, and the lords' power behind it, were so characteristic of the prevailing system and were so seldom to be found in other, nonmedieval, types of rural society, that they must be accepted as the distinguishing economic and social features, the true *differentia*, of the manorial order"(*Medieval Economy and Society*, 88).

95. For a reading of the Wife's *Prologue and Tale* as a progressive discovery of the subject, and its staging of questions of poetic authority and gender, see my "'For the Wyves love of Bathe': Feminine Rhetoric and Poetic Resolution in the *Roman de la rose* and the *Canterbury Tales*," *Speculum* 58 (1983): 656–95.

fulfillment by the final destruction of the peasant economy in the sixteenth and seventeenth centuries.

The successful completion of the subversive process initiated by the
Wife of Bath is possible, therefore, because her opposition is generated
from a position that does *not* correspond to the most vigorous oppositional forces at work in Chaucer's historical world. On the contrary, her
invocation of the rights of the subject derives its force from a dense and
widespread web of precedents found in earlier medieval writing.[96] For
precisely the familiarity of her challenge, however brilliantly innovative
the form in which it is articulated, makes it appealing and useful to
Chaucer. Moreover, the final two movements of this staged, four-act
drama of rebellion—the *Friar's* and the *Summoner's Tales*—are also
constructed from highly traditional materials that while, again, brilliantly reaccented, nonetheless remain comfortably within the settled
structures of medieval social ideology. Just how comfortably can be
briefly indicated by a final glance at the key member of this pair, the
*Summoner's Tale*. This tale plays here, in the *Canterbury Tales'* second
movement, the role that fell to the disgraced and excluded *Cook's Tale*
in the first movement. Far from being chastened by the apparent failure
of Fragment I, then, Chaucer seems defiantly to return here to the
churlish world of mockery and retaliation that was forced into the pilgrimage by the Miller's interruption, the world of *quiting* that came to
such a bad end in the *Cook's Tale*. The *Summoner's Tale* enacts *quiting* to
an almost quintessential degree: not only does the *Tale* retaliate against
the pompous Friar by deploying all of the traditional antifraternal arguments, but it even mocks fraternal propaganda by subjecting it to
merciless ridicule.[97] *Quiting* is thus definitively recuperated, and in order to enforce the parallelism with Fragment I Chaucer chooses as his
spokesman for this recuperation the one other diseased pilgrim among
the group, the scabrous Summoner whose inflamed face seems an appropriate counterpart to the disgusting "mormel" or ulcer that adorns
the Cook's leg.

Now our question becomes truly pressing: why does Chaucer complete this process with the Summoner while he apparently felt himself

---

96. For a discussion of these precedents, see my "'For the Wyves love of Bathe,'"
*passim.*

97. For full discussions, see Penn R. Szittya, *The Antifraternal Tradition in Medieval
Literature* (Princeton: Princeton University Press, 1986), 231–46, and references cited
there.

unwilling to go forward with the Cook? If the argument of this paper is correct, the answer lies in the realm of politics. And in terms of the conditions of fourteenth-century life, the Cook and the Summoner do indeed represent two very different worlds. The Cook derives from the threatening urban proletariat that stands as the economic and ideological counterpart to the emergent rural producers—a degraded urban version, in other words, of the Miller—while the Summoner, for all his gross immorality, is part of the apparatus of social control imposed upon medieval society by the Church.[98] The Summoner, like the Reeve, is a bailiff, although in this case for the archdeaconal court that punished various spiritual and moral offenses, especially sexual ones. In other words, as his agent of successful subversion Chaucer has chosen not a genuinely rebellious figure but instead a representative of one of the most repressive forces in medieval society.

This conservatism is also thematized in the *Tale* itself. As is appropriate for its place within the *Tales* as a whole, the *Summoner's Tale* is a recuperation of the churlish irreverence introduced into the *Tales* by the Miller; and it does tell how a pompous representative of clerical learning is undone by the churlish wisdom of his intended victim. Yet the very traditional nature of the Summoner's attack—its deployment of the well-worn topoi of antifraternal satire—functions to remove the *Tale* from the specific context of late fourteenth-century English history. As Penn Szittya rightly says about antifraternalism, "The poets, like the polemicists before them, are writing less about the friars than about an idea about the friars, less about men they have seen begging on the streets in London than about numberless and placeless figures who are the sons of Cain and allies of Antichrist, men whose final significance lies not in history but at its End."[99] Moreover, Thomas's churlish triumph is displaced from the peasant locale in which it is initially enacted to a seigneurial context: after receiving his insult from Thomas, the friar retreats to the manor house, where the insult is completed by the squire. For one thing, then, the lines of social opposition are here drawn not along class lines (as in the *Miller's Tale*) but instead according to the traditional division of lay versus clerical. And for another, Thomas's churlish wit is revealed to be in need of a supplementary

98. See Thomas Hahn and Richard W. Kaeuper, "Text and Context: Chaucer's *Friar's Tale*," *Studies in the Age of Chaucer* 5 (1983): 67–101.
99. *Antifraternal Tradition*, 230.

interpretation that can be provided only within the context of aristo-cratic play.

It is quite true, of course, that the *Tale* leads us to think that the gift always contained within it the wonderfully deflating meaning that the squire makes explicit, that—to put it crudely—the seigneurial class lives off the humor of its agricultural workers as well as off their labors. This is part of the recuperation of churlishness that the second four tales seek to accomplish. Yet live off it they do, and nothing in the *Tale* suggests that this is an arrangement that can or should be called into question. Far from there being any question of peasant independence or class antagonism, the *Summoner's Tale* presents us with a rural world united in its opposition to the fraternal orders—orders that had origi-nally, of course, preached a dangerously radical social message but that are now represented as hopelessly, laughably corrupt.[100] The true forces of social change abroad in Chaucer's historical world are thus defini-tively disarmed, and we retreat into a world of aesthetic appreciation, in which peasant energy, however potentially threatening, is reduced to a playful manipulation of the images of the official culture that leaves the realities firmly in place.

Yet even here Chaucer does not wholly suppress the political. On the contrary, it returns at the end of the *Summoner's Tale* in a passage that both recalls (as I have already suggested) the end of the *Miller's Tale* and invokes, in an oblique but I think unmistakeable fashion, the radi-cal political program that informed late medieval peasant belligerence.

---

100. Again, one of the means by which the fraternal orders are divested of social force, both here and elsewhere in fourteenth-century satire, is the relentlessly dehistori-cized apocalypticism of the traditional criticism; see note 97 above. It was not always the case that antifraternalism relied upon these traditional topoi; for a survey of contempo-rary complaints against friars, see Carolly Erickson, "The Fourteenth-Century Francis-cans and Their Critics," *Franciscan Studies* 35 (1975): 107–35; 36 (1976): 108–47. That the fourteenth-century fraternal orders still had the capacity to participate in movements for social justice is suggested by objections early in the century to their participation in peas-ant protests against monastic landlords at Bury St. Edmunds, at Christ Church, Canter-bury, and at Sandwich (see A. G. Little, *Studies in English Franciscan History* [Manchester: University of Manchester Press, 1917], 98–99); similarly, complaints that they supported the rebels of 1381 (by Walsingham, for instance [*Historia Anglicana* 2:13], and by the au-thor of the *Fasciculus Zizaniorum*, ed. W. W. Shirley [London: Longmans, 1858], 292–95) are probably antifraternal slanders, but they may just point to a shred of historical truth. Certainly, as Charles Oman long ago suggested, the social gospel preached by the friars—although in no sense only by them—must have contributed to the sense of the intolera-bility of social injustice that was a sine qua non of the revolt; see Charles A. Oman, *The Great Revolt of 1381* (Oxford: Clarendon Press, 1906), 20; see also Little, *English Franciscan History*, 155–57, and Owst, *Literature and Pulpit*, 548–93.

Presented with the churl's problem of how to divide a fart equally among a convent of thirteen friars, the seigneurial household is itself divided. The lady is instantly dismissive: "I seye a cherl hath doon a cherles deed" (2206). But the lord is intrigued, and when the terms of his puzzlement are located within the political context of rural discontent they take on a startling relevance:

> The lord sat stille as he were in a traunce,
> And in his herte he rolled up and doun,
> "How hadde this cherl ymaginacioun
> To shewe swich a probleme to the frere?
> Nevere erst er now herde I of swich mateere.
> *I trowe the devel putte it in his mynde.*
> In ars-metrike shal ther no man fynde,
> Biforn this day, of swich a question.
> Who sholde make a demonstracion
> That *every man sholde have yliche his part*
> As of the soun or savour of a fart?
> *O nyce, proude cherle, I shrewe his face!*
> Lo, sires," quod the lord, "with harde grace!
> *Who evere herde of swich a thyng er now?*
> *To every man ylike? Tel me how.*
> *It is an inpossible; it may nat be.*
> Ey, *nyce cherl*, God lete him nevere thee!
> The rumblynge of a fart, and every soun,
> Nis but of eir reverberacioun,
> And evere it wasteth litel and litel awey.
> Ther is no man can deemen, by my fay,
> *If that it were departed equally.*
> What, lo, *my* cherl, lo, yet how shrewedly,
> Unto *my* confessour to-day he spak!
> I holde hym certeyn a *demonyak!*
> Now ete youre mete, and lat the cherl go pleye;
> *Lat hym go honge hymself a devel weye!*"
>
> (2216–42)

Taken aback by signs of mental power in a creature thought to lack the capacity, the lord is intrigued but finally retreats into typical defamations: the churl is either foolish ("nyce") or crazy ("a demonyak"—and see the squire's words when he solves the puzzle: "He nys no fool, ne no demonyak" [2292]). At issue, of course, is the burning peasant demand for equality: "To every man ylike? Tel me how. / It is an inpossible, it may nat be." Not only a fart cannot be "departed equally," but neither can the goods of this world; and the lord closes with a curse on any who would think otherwise—"Lat hym go honge hymself a devel weye!"—and returns to his meat, itself one of those goods with which

he is so abundantly supplied but which peasants like Thomas conspicuously lack. In short, Chaucer presents a brief allegory of the seigneurial reaction to peasant demands, and then shows, in the squire's translation of Thomas' challenge back into the dehistoricizing language of
antifraternal discourse, how those demands are displaced and finally
appropriated to the traditional structure of medieval society. And finally, of course, this is an allegory of Chaucer's own practice of articulating but finally silencing the voice of peasant protest.

# 4

# "Whan She Translated Was"

## A Chaucerian Critique of the Petrarchan Academy

### David Wallace

Truth is violent, it controls minds.
                    Petrarch, *Familiares* 17.10.18

The state decides what poets may or may not write—that is a
nightmare as old as the Occident.
                    Hans Magnus Enzensburger,
                                *Critical Essays*

What did Petrarch mean to Chaucer? Our best chance of answering this
question lies in considering what Chaucer's *Clerk's Tale* makes of Petrarch's story of Griselde, a tale that Petrarch borrowed from Boccaccio.
But before turning to texts we might consider the broader implications
of this opening question. The name of Petrarch has come to mean
much more than the sum of texts that Petrarch wrote: it suggests a
cultural movement called humanism. But the minute we admit the term
humanism into any question the entire discussion threatens to escape
all historical limits. Nobody knows where humanism begins or ends,
although it seems to include writers as far apart as Mussato, Petrarch,
Salutati, Bruni, and Valla. The problem becomes more chronic when
we employ humanism as a term bridging English and Italian cultures.
Most scholars of English literature who concern themselves with Petrarch work in the English Renaissance: it often seems as if Petrarch
were of the same historical generation as Wyatt and Surrey. Petrarch is
sometimes played off against Chaucer to lend definition to those ne-
bulous terms "Renaissance" and "medieval." But Petrarch was, of
course, a generation older than Chaucer. To achieve some sense of what
Petrarch meant to Chaucer we must, then, recover the historical specificity both of the Petrarchan texts and of Chaucer's reading of them.

   This essay will briefly note the images of Petrarch that were fash-
ioned and circulated in late medieval Europe before narrowing its focus

to consider Chaucer's historical experience of Italy. Through his visit to Florence in 1373 and to Milan in 1378 Chaucer came to understand both sides of a fierce ideological debate that pitted Republican *libertas* against dynastic despotism. Boccaccio and Petrarch locate themselves on opposite sides of this ideological divide: their differing political and aesthetic allegiances clearly impress themselves upon their differing treatments of the Griselde story. Having seen how Petrarch fits Boccaccio's text to the exigencies of his humanist Academy, we will see how Chaucer, in turn, critiques Petrarch in restoring Griselde to the vernacular, the mother tongue. Certain aspects of the cultural critique mounted by the *Clerk's Tale* grew ever more urgent for Chaucer as Richard II grew ever more tyrannical. This essay ends by considering how, in both versions of the Prologue to *The Legend of Good Women*, Chaucer's developing critique of the tyrant is bound up with a critique of the poet who serves him.

To seek the historical origins of a Petrarchan text is not to aspire to some ideal of originary meaning that may be discovered within the text and then proclaimed as authorial intention. Textual meaning has its own history: no author better exemplifies this than Petrarch. Nicholas Mann has shown that fifteenth-century north Europeans knew and revered a "medievalized" Petrarch.[1] Petrarchan texts were shorn of their stoicism and their more exotic classical instances were replaced by commonplace medieval dicta. The urge to read Petrarch as a Church Father accounts for his appearance in some manuscripts as "Franciscus Patriarca." This was the Petrarch that Lydgate revered: the orthodox medieval moralist. This Petrarch was always a Latin author: the only evidence of Petrarch's vernacular works circulating outside Italy before 1500 is Chaucer's translation of "S'amor non è" which forms part of *Troilus and Criseyde*.[2] And even this stray sonnet was later translated into Latin by Coluccio Salutati as "Si fors non sit amor."[3]

While north Europeans were striving to make Petrarch more medieval, Italian humanists such as Salutati were working in the opposite

1. "Petrarch and Humanism: The Paradox of Posterity," in *Francesco Petrarca: Citizen of the World* ed. Aldo S. Bernardo (Padua and Albany: Editrice Antenore and State University of New York Press, 1980), 287–99.
2. Mann, "Petrarch and Humanism," 295; B. A. Windeatt, ed., Geoffrey Chaucer, *Troilus and Criseyde. A New Edition of "The Book of Troilus"* (London: Longmans, 1984), 110–13; Piero Boitani, "Petrarch's *Dilectoso Male* and its European Context," in *Zusammenhänge, Einflüsse, Wirkungen: Kongressakten zum ersten Symposium des Mediävistenverbandes in Tübingen, 1984*, ed. Joerg Fichte et al. (Berlin: Walter de Gruyter, 1986), 299–314.
3. E. H. Wilkins, "Cantus Troili," *ELH* 16 (1949): 169.

direction. The early history of humanism, itself precarious and (excepting Salutati) devoid of forceful leadership, struggled with Petrarchan texts that were delicately poised between opposite tendencies: between, for example, a yearning for monkish seclusion and a determination to intervene in public affairs.[4] And Florentine humanists under Salutati's leadership often found it disconcertingly difficult to reconcile Petrarch's political and cultural ideals with the values of Florentine Republicanism. Petrarch had censured Cicero for his excessive fondness for public controversy, for valuing *negotium* above *otium*: in 1394 the humanist educator Pier Paolo Vergerio was moved to reply in Cicero's name.[5] Petrarch's own pronouncements on public affairs, while concerning themselves with historical particulars, were always liable to balloon away into Augustinian metaphysics. His traditionalist distrust of and contempt for worldly wealth required vigorous modification by later humanist figures; and his distaste for marriage, coupled with a notion of woman as "l'aura," the airy object and cipher of romantic quest, proved equally baffling. When speaking of women Petrarch was always liable to take a sharp turn into medieval misogyny, a tradition that differed markedly from the misogyny of later writers.

For Petrarch life was (to draw from the brilliant sequence of almost two hundred epithets he compiled on 29 November 1370) "imbecille potentia, pulchra deformitas, nuge serie" (feeble strength, beautiful deformity, serious foolishness).[6] But what are the historical and political implications of this tendency to escape or evaporate from the pressures of a concrete historical moment? Such a dualistic, paradoxical habit of mind, where one half of the mind hides from the other, is generously invoked by critics wishing to explain Petrarch's political thinking. Margaret Schlauch, for example, in considering why Petrarch "labored and wrote for a *renovatio imperii*," argues that he did this "for reasons probably unclear to himself."[7] Nobody would say this of Dante on empire. Perhaps this is because Dante's thought is taken as a historical terminus, whereas Petrarch's forms an origin, a point of departure. The true destination of Petrarchan thought, unclear to Petrarch himself, is made clear by the subsequent history of the movement he is bringing to light.

4. See Ronald G. Witt, *Hercules at the Crossroads: The Life, Works and Thought of Coluccio Salutati* (Durham, N.C.: Duke University Press, 1983), 416.

5. See Quentin Skinner, *The Foundations of Modern Political Thought. Volume One: The Renaissance* (Cambridge, Eng.: Cambridge University Press, 1978), 108.

6. *Seniles* 11.11, as excerpted by E. H. Wilkins, *Petrarch's Later Years* (Cambridge, Mass.: The Medieval Academy of America, 1959), 196–97.

7. "Chaucer's Doctrine of Kings and Tyrants," *Speculum* 20 (1945): 148.

This tendency to interpret the origins of humanism by reference to its ends has proven virtually irresistible. Perry Anderson, even as he attempts to trace "the lineages of the absolute state," seems unwilling to connect a vatic Petrarch ("Petrarch's passionate call, at the threshold of the new age, proclaimed the vocation of the future") with the absolutist regimes he actually worked for.[8] Some effort must be made, then, to recover the historical moment of each given Petrarchan utterance.

But if we could locate such moments, how close would this bring us to Chaucer? Chaucer's engagement with Petrarch precedes those Italian and north European traditions of reception that we have just adumbrated. But culturally and geographically medieval England seemed like a strange and distant planet to its Italian contemporaries. Leonardo Bruni could marvel at the enterprise of Florentine merchants, whose profession could lead them as far away as Britain, "which is an island in the ocean almost on the edge of the world."[9] Petrarch marveled at English successes in war against the French, but only as examples of how Fortune could allow a lesser kingdom to humiliate a greater one.[10] He was depressed to note, in the course of a diplomatic mission for the Visconti in 1360, how war with England had ruined the French countryside and brought the intellectual life of Paris to a standstill (*Fam.* 22.14). Petrarch later expressed his vigorous contempt for French intellectual traditions. The English had no traditions that could claim his attention, although he did acknowledge acquaintance with the *Architrenius* of the Englishman Jean de Hanville. This Petrarch described as the most tiresome thing he had ever read.[11]

---

8. *Lineages of the Absolutist State* (London: Verso, 1979), 149. Later in this chapter Anderson describes the sovereignty of the *signoria* (the model of polity Petrarch dedicated himself to) as being "always in a deep sense illegitimate," resting "on recent force and personal fraud" (162).

9. From Bruni's *Oration* of 1428, translated by Skinner, *Foundations,* 74. See also Wendy Childs, "Anglo-Italian Contacts in the Fourteenth Century," in *Chaucer and the Italian Trecento,* ed. Piero Boitani (Cambridge, Eng.: Cambridge University Press, 1983), 65–87.

10. *Familiares* 15.7 (dating from 1352); *Seniles* 10.2 (from 1367), translated and slightly abridged in Morris Bishop, *Letters from Petrarch* (Bloomington: Indiana University Press, 1966), 270. For the Latin text of *Familiares,* see Francesco Petrarca, *Le Familiari,* ed. V. Rossi, 4 vols. (Florence: Sansoni, 1933–42). For English translations, see Francesco Petrarca, *Rerum familiarum libri,* trans. Aldo S. Bernardo, 3 vols. (Albany: State University of New York Press, 1975, vol. 1; Baltimore: Johns Hopkins University Press, 1982–85, vols. 2–3).

11. See Wilkins, *Later Years,* 236, 239; *Invectiva contra eum qui maledixit Italie,* ed. P. G. Ricci, in Francesco Petrarca, *Prose,* ed. G. Martellotti et al. (Ricciardi Editore: Milan and Naples, 1955), 768–807; Winthrop Wetherbee, *Platonism and Poetry in the Twelfth Century* (Princeton: Princeton University Press, 1972), 242–58 (for the *Architrenius*).

On the other hand, the English, despite being perched at the edge of the world, had ample opportunity to learn about Petrarch. Avignon provided one source of information, and the imperial court at Prague (with which Petrarch maintained strong ties) provided another.[12] Contacts between London and Prague were strengthened in 1382 when Richard married Anne of Bohemia.[13] Anne had special reason to remember Petrarch since she was named after Anne, third wife of Charles IV, the only woman known to have received a letter from Petrarch. This letter, *Familiares* 21.8, took the form of a short treatise *de laudibus feminarum,* a legend of good women.

Chaucer stood little chance of coming across Petrarch manuscripts in London since Petrarch exerted extremely tight control over the production and diffusion of his works. At the same time, he did nothing to discourage the spread of his own fame. Fame had been the theme of the oration he had delivered on being crowned poet laureate at Rome in 1341. In 1373 he received a letter from Boccaccio urging him to give up writing since he had written quite enough already; his younger admirers could take over. Petrarch found such a suggestion abhorrent: if (as Boccaccio maintained) he had now become world famous this could only serve to spur him on to greater things.[14] The cult of Petrarch's fame was nurtured and spread by the curious institution alluded to in my title, the "Petrarchan Academy." By this I mean a small, consciously exclusive, masculine group of intitiates dedicated to the pursuit of Latin culture: just such a group, in fact, as Petrarch describes in framing his Griselde story.[15] The two differing receptions of this story recorded by *Seniles* 18.3 both took place in Petrarch's presence. Most such gatherings

12. In 1357 two of Petrarch's most trusted associates found themselves in London. Bernabò Visconti had convinced himself that Pandolfo Malatesta (to whom Petrarch sent a copy of the *Canzoniere* in 1373) was fooling with one of his *amours.* Pandolfo managed to escape to Prague, and Sagremor de Pommiers, one of Petrarch's most trusted messengers, was sent in pursuit to uphold the Visconti honor. Sagremor pursued Pandolfo from Prague to London and challenged him to single combat at court on seventeen successive days. Pandolfo failed to show up, and Edward III signed a document recording these events. See E. H. Wilkins, *Petrarch's Eight Years in Milan* (Cambridge, Mass.: The Medieval Academy of America, 1958), 132–34, 148–49.

13. See Janet Coleman, "English Culture in the Fourteenth Century," in *Italian Trecento,* ed. Boitani, 59.

14. *Seniles* 17.2; Bishop, *Letters from Petrarch,* contains a short translated excerpt (301–2). This letter announces *Seniles* 17.3, containing the Griselde story, which proves (says Petrarch) "how far I am from accepting counsels of inactivity" (302).

15. See Anne Middleton, "The Clerk and His Tale: Some Literary Contexts," *Studies in the Age of Chaucer* 2 (1980): 130–35; Charlotte Morse, "The Exemplary Griselde," *Studies in the Age of Chaucer* 7 (1985): 55–66.

around Petrarchan texts, however, took place in his absence, although Petrarch liked to think of himself as metaphysically present through the body of his text.[16]

I employ the term "Petrarchan Academy," then, to denote a complex cultural phenomenon that was in part historical (Petrarch's admirers held meetings) and in part imaginary, expressive of a desire to escape history entirely: Petrarch dreamed of producing finalized texts of permanent value.[17] Petrarch formed the center of this cultural entity and his followers formed its periphery. The most important of these peripheral Petrarchan groups were located at Florence and Naples. Although not formally constituted, these groups exhibited many institutional features. Membership was difficult to come by. Petrarch warned his followers against being imposed upon by men who claimed to be his friends (*Fam.* 20.5). When Francesco Bruni sought admission to the Florentine circle it took some vigorous petitioning from Pandolfo Malatesta and then Francesco da Carrara before Petrarch would write Bruni a letter.[18] Petrarch maintained a policy of not writing to anybody who did not first write to him: but he answered every letter.[19] Writing to Petrarch, of course, subjected any command of Latinity to the severest scrutiny: correspondents such as Francesco Nelli suffered acute embarrassment on realizing their mistakes.[20] The best way of improving your *Latinitas* was, of course, to get hold of a collection of Petrarchan epistles; Petrarch's letters were eagerly copied and hoarded away, and many were stolen en route to their addressee. The dearest ambition of any Petrarchan circle was, paradoxically, to defeat the Petrarchan policy of *tarditas,* the postponed circulation of texts.[21] In 1361 four admirers at Sulmona decided to appeal to Petrarch for the pre-posthumous release of his Latin epic *Africa.* This appeal, penned by Barbato da Sulmona and transmitted via Boccaccio (who added a covering letter) was turned down flat. Petrarch had already entrusted Barbato with one passage of

16. See *Familiares* 18.10, a letter in which Petrarch lays down the conditions for an ideal social and literary gathering or *convivium.*

17. This phenomenon might be compared in some ways to the peculiar cultural entity that organized itself, both imaginatively and institutionally, around Lacan: see Catherine Clément, *The Lives and Legends of Jacques Lacan,* trans. A. Goldhammer (New York: Columbia University Press, 1983).

18. Wilkins, *Later Years,* 13–14.

19. *Seniles* 16.3; Wilkins, *Later Years,* 14, 221.

20. Henry Cochin, *Lettres de Francesco Nelli a Pétrarque* (Paris: Champion, 1892), 24–26.

21. Petrarch explains this policy in *Seniles* 6.5.

*Africa,* in 1343, on condition that he would not release copies. Barbato had broken his promise, and Petrarch, some eighteen years later, was still aggrieved.[22]

Petrarch was further troubled by what we might call a number of anti-Academies: the French cardinals who reacted against Petrarch's belittling of France, for example, or the Aristotelians at Venice who decided that Petrarch was illiterate ("sine litteris").[23] It was the task of Petrarch's followers to keep him posted of all such murmurings.[24] What profit did such followers derive from their devotion? A number of them obtained important offices in Church or secular administrations (Petrarch complained in 1371 of having written endless letters of recommendation).[25] But many seemed content, like many adherents of more recent critical movements, to bask in the reflected glory of their distant master. And what benefit did Petrarch obtain from the demanding task of keeping these groups together through the nexus of his correspondence? The Academy provided a framework within which Petrarch could perpetuate the new philological standards he had established and at the same time secure the conditions of his own transmission to posterity. We see Petrarch committing himself to this process through his diligent editing, arranging, and rewriting (missive and final forms often differ) of his own letter collections. The *Familiares* opens with an address to posterity and closes with a letter to a friend of Petrarch's known as Socrates. This final letter opens up, toward the end, into a plural form of address and comes to rest with the individual reader: "te in finem, lector." As individual readers we recognize, of course, that we are interchangeable with any other member of the posterity that Petrarch is addressing. As he composed the final letter Petrarch knew its first addressee to be recently dead. But many Petrarchan letters are addressed to men who had been dead for a millenium; and all Petrarchan letters, in their final form, were designed to outlive their addressees.

---

22. Wilkins, *Later Years,* 33–34.
23. Wilkins, *Later Years,* 161, 92.
24. It was Salutati, then stationed at Avignon, who reported to Petrarch on the reception of his letter deriding the French and warned him that the French cardinals planned to commission a rejoinder; see Berthold L. Ullmann, *The Humanism of Coluccio Salutati* (Padua: Editrice Antenore, 1963), 80–81. A young Florentine monk informed Petrarch of criticisms leveled at the Mago passage of *Africa* by certain Florentines; this occasioned the lengthy and indignant *Seniles* 2.1, addressed to Boccaccio (who was not one of the critics).
25. Wilkins, *Later Years,* 209.

Petrarch typically wrote not to solicit opinions or initiate debate, but rather to publish finalized ideas.

Petrarch's epistles, though full of historical detail, tend to escape or erase the specific moment of their historical origin. The same may be said of Petrarch's other works, which, through a series of minute revisions extending over decades, conceal the chronology of their making. Petrarch's practice here forms an instructive contrast with that of Salutati (chancellor of the Florentine Republic from 1375 to 1406) who elected to let his works stand once written, thus revealing the lineaments of a personal history. Salutati also preferred to develop his ideas dialectically, through conversation, rather than announcing them in writing.[26]

The formation of the Petrarchan Academy, then, represents an attempt at self-classicizing, of exempting texts from the erosions of time. Time had been an urgent preoccupation for Petrarch since his youth, when he habitually marked passages in his reading relating to the flight of time.[27] Throughout his life Petrarch was constantly striving to stretch time out, to profit from every minute. Like the Emperor Augustus, he read while being shaved or having his hair cut; he slept with pen and paper by the bed and sometimes wrote on horseback (*Fam.* 21.12). He felt compelled to calculate and account for how his time was controlled and spent, and he even struggled to erase the natural demarcations of daylight and darkness by working right through them: the "solitary man," Petrarch said in *De Vita Solitaria*, "knows how to join on night to day and day to night, and when the occasion demands it to combine the two, and in other ways to interchange the duties incident to each division."[28] This passage goes on to contrast the life of such a man, "whose whole year passes happily and peacefully as though it were a single day," with that of "voluptuous men of the city," who "in the midst of their wines and feasts, their roses and ointments, their songs and their plays . . . think a single day longer than a year and can scarcely pass a few hours without grumbling and annoyance." Petrarch himself was a professed lover of solitude who was forced to live in cities for most of his life. His attitude to time strangely couples an Augustinian yearning for transcendence (we should seek to escape time by sending

26. See Witt, *Hercules*, 417–18.

27. See *Familiares* 24.1, in which Petrarch refers to his own youthful marginalia.

28. Francis Petrarch, *The Life of Solitude*, trans. Jacob Zeitlin (Urbana: University of Illinois Press, 1924), 180. All English translations of *De Vita Solitaria* refer to this work.

our souls ahead of us to heaven) with an outright commodification of
time that allies him with those Florentine merchants whom he so
fiercely condemned.[29] His final work, appropriately enough, was the
*Triumphus Eternitatis,* which was to succeed the Triumph of Time and
rediscover Laura in heaven. This last poetic sequence, which Petrarch
worked on for some thirty years up to his death at Arquà on 18 July
1374, systematically opposes the triad of forces that threaten the Academy to those that ensure its continuance: Physical Love, Death, and
Time versus Chastity, Fame, and Eternity.[30]

This struggle in the life and writings of Petrarch between the limits
and frustrations of earthbound time and the airy expanses of fame and
eternity is formulated with extraordinary precision by Chaucer's Clerk
of Oxenford:

> I wol yow telle a tale which that I
> Lerned at Padowe of a worthy clerk,
> As preved by his wordes and his werk.
> He is now deed and nayled in his cheste;
> I preye to God so yeve his soule reste!
> Fraunceys Petrak, the lauriat poete,
> Highte this clerke, whos rethorike sweete
> Enlumyned al Ytaille of poetrie,
> As Lynyan dide of philosophie,
> Or lawe, or oother art particuler;
> But Deeth, that wol nat suffre us dwellen heer,
> But as it were a twynklyng of an ye,
> Hem bothe hath slayn, and alle shul we dye.
>                                         (IV.26–38)[31]

Here we have Petrarch discovered as a living source of poetic inspiration; Petrarch as a corpse; Petrarch as a poet laureate whose rhetoric
illuminates a nation; and Petrarch laid low by death, a fate that unites
him with us all. The cultural achievement of Petrarch is here accorded

---

29. See *De Vita Solitaria,* ed. G. Martellotti, in Petrarca, *Prose,* liber 2: "dum corpora
nostra peregrinatur ab urbibus, peregrinentur a corporibus animi, premittamus illos ad
celum" (while our bodies are far from cities, our souls are far from our bodies; let us send
our souls ahead to heaven, 586). For important discussions of changing conceptualizations of time in this period, see Jacques Le Goff, *Time, Work, and Culture in the Middle
Ages,* trans. Arthur Goldhammer (Chicago: University of Chicago Press, 1980), esp. 29–
52; J. G. A. Pocock, *The Machiavellian Moment: Florentine Political Thought and the Atlantic Republican Tradition* (Princeton: Princeton University Press, 1975), esp. 53–55.

30. See Kenelm Foster, *Petrarch: Poet and Humanist* (Edinburgh: Edinburgh University Press, 1984), 19.

31. All citations from Chaucer follow *The Riverside Chaucer,* ed. Larry D. Benson
(Boston: Houghton Mifflin, 1987).

great respect, but is insistently brought up hard against the brute facts of mortality. The tone and logic of this passage are uneasy, unstable, almost tortuous: qualities which, in fact, are typical of Petrarch's own musings on life, on death, and on textual afterlife.

II

How was Chaucer able to formulate such a complex and detailed reaction to Petrarch? The fame of the Italian poet, we have noted, was universal; his friends reported that Petrarch's name could open doors "in extrema terrarum."[32] In 1361 Petrarch was wooed with invitations from the king of France, the emperor, the pope, and the queen of Naples.[33] On 25 May 1368 Petrarch set out from Padua to assist his former political master, Galeazzo Visconti, in negotiating a peace treaty with the emperor. He then traveled north to Milan to attend the marriage of Galeazzo's daughter, Violante, to Lionel, Duke of Clarence, on June 5. Unfortunately, however, Petrarch missed most of the festivities because he was confined to bed with an ulcerated leg.[34] Chaucer, who was active on the continent in 1368, may have traveled south to attend the wedding of Lionel, his earliest patron.[35] He must in any case have heard various reports of this extravagant and ultimately tragic affair (Lionel died just a few months later and was buried at Pavia) from the huge English retinue that descended on Milan. News of Petrarch might have mixed reports of great cultural celebrity, top-level political involvement, and physical infirmity.

The year 1368 may, then, have provided Chaucer with an initial image of Petrarch to work with; beyond this we need not speculate. Of vastly greater consequence for Chaucer's subsequent development, and for his understanding of Petrarch, were his two lengthy visits to Italy in the 1370s. Both of these are securely documented.[36] The first, during which he spent about one hundred days on Italian territory, took him first to Genoa and then to Florence. At this time Florence defined itself, in its

---

32. Wilkins, *Eight Years*, 208.
33. Wilkins, *Later Years*, 9–20.
34. Wilkins, *Later Years*, 144–45.
35. See M. M. Crow and C. C. Olson, eds., *Chaucer Life Records* (Oxford: Oxford University Press, 1966), 29–30.
36. See Crow and Olson, 32–40, 53–61, who provide references to many of the earlier articles that their edition effectively supersedes.

own city records, as a "stato popolare, Guelfo e libero."[37] The Florentine state could claim to be "popolare" in that its government took the form of a Republican system, underpinned by groupings of guilds and (much less importantly) confraternities. The traditional powers of the aristocracy had been severely curtailed by the development of the guild system in the thirteenth century. The absence of that class traditionally considered to embody honor caused great difficulties for the Florentines, especially in their dealings with northern Europeans; what other embodiment of truth and honor could there be besides nobility?[38] Such questions generated debates among Florentines over many generations about the nature of true (as opposed to inherited) nobility. And if nobility could be renegotiated, what was its relation to wealth, and of wealth to the commonwealth? Positive aspects of this new nobility are discussed in Dante's *Convivio,* book 4 (which the Wife of Bath found much to her liking); its negative underside is graphically exemplified in the lower reaches of Dis, the infernal city. The various strains of civil and ecclesiastical corruption found in the deeper pockets of the Dantean Malebolge are generously illustrated by Boccaccio's *novelle.* By turning such corruption into narrative entertainment that is socially cohesive, Boccaccio's *Decameron* best expresses the optimism, vigor, and regenerative civic pride of mid-Trecento (postplague) Florence.

The fact that Florence declared itself Guelf did not imply a slavish obedience to Rome, or to Rome in Avignon. In 1375 Florence went to war with Gregory XI. The most remarkable feature of this war was the alliance contracted between the Florentines and Bernabò Visconti. Just five years earlier Bernabò had employed the English *condottiere* Sir John Hawkwood and his mercenary company against Florence. This opposition between Florence and Milan was one of the most powerful and enduring features of Italian political life. When Florence thought of itself as a "stato libero," a free Republic practising the virtues of *libertas,* it inevitably defined itself against Milanese despotism. Physical warfare broke out periodically as Florence fought to keep the Visconti out of Tuscany; but ideological warfare raged continuously, as each regime attempted to expose and deride the weaknesses of the other.

---

37. N. Rubenstein, "Florence and the Despots: Some Aspects of Florentine Diplomacy in the Fourteenth Century," *Transactions of the Royal Historical Society,* 5th. ser., 2 (1952): 31.

38. See Richard C. Trexler, *Public Life in Renaissance Florence* (New York: Academic Press, 1980), 18.

Political theorists who concerned themselves with Republican government had always felt obliged to consider the nature of tyranny, the chief threat to such government. Bartolus of Sassoferrato (a jurist of European fame whose teachings on *utilitas publica* gained a hearing at Oxford through Albericus Gentilis, an exiled Perugian) complemented his treatise on city government with a treatise on tyranny.[39] Such analysis of tyranny in the postclassical world is as old as Isidore of Seville.[40] But there is a fresh urgency behind Bartolus's account, reflected by his more complex taxonomy: tyrannies may be open (*manifesti*), disguised (*velati*) or concealed (*taciti*), categories that are further subdivided and subjected to detailed analysis.[41] Such analyses served the Florentines well in their ideological battles with the Milanese. They were finally subsumed into the most famous treatise of all, Coluccio Salutati's *De Tyranno* of 1400. This was completed just as ideological warfare was turning, once again, into open physical conflict.

In 1373, however, Chaucer's Florentine hosts must have taken great pleasure in the serious crisis the Visconti were suffering: the Emperor deprived them of their Vicariate; Amadeus VI, Count of Savoy, marched to the gates of Pavia, ravaging the countryside, and defeated Galeazzo's army; and a papal force, with Florentine support, entered Bernabò's territories from Bologna.[42] Chaucer was forced to interest himself in such matters since his route home had to be chosen with great care if he was to return to England safely.[43]

Five years later, in the summer of 1378, Chaucer returned to Italy. This time he was briefed to seek out Bernabò Visconti and Sir John Hawkwood and help negotiate "aucunes busoignes touchantes lexploit de nostre guerre," the war in question being, of course, the interminable conflict with France.[44] Chaucer had already heard Florentine at-

---

39. Skinner, *Foundations,* 62–65; Walter Ullmann, *Law and Politics in the Middle Ages* (Ithaca: Cornell University Press, 1975), 108–10.

40. Ullmann, *Law and Politics,* 233.

41. Schlauch, "Chaucer's Doctrine," 147; Ullmann, *Law and Politics,* 110; Skinner, *Foundations,* 53–56. See also Ephraim Emerton, *Humanism and Tyranny: Studies in the Italian Trecento* (Cambridge, Mass.: Harvard University Press, 1925), which contains translations of Salutati, *De tyranno* and Bartolus, *De tyrannia.*

42. D. M. Bueno de Mesquita, *Giangaleazzo Visconti* (Cambridge, Eng.: Cambridge University Press, 1941), 8.

43. George B. Parks, "The Route of Chaucer's First Journey to Italy," *ELH* 16 (1949): 174–87. Parks notes that Chaucer had to worry about three wars in 1373: England against the French, Padua against Venice, and the war against Milan.

44. *Chaucer Life Records,* ed. Crow and Olson, 54.

tacks on the tyrannical Visconti. Now he was able to observe the Visconti for himself and to hear the other side of the ideological debate. The Viscontian court had no shortage of poets who, like Francesco di Vannozzo, were willing to urge their lord to rule "with marble heart and the severity of Nero."[45] Each new public or private act of Bernabò was greeted with acclaim (and in Tuscany with commensurate derision and abuse).[46] Milan had been subjected to continuous Visconti rule since 1277, the year in which the Milanese Republic was dissolved and Orto Visconti proclaimed "perpetual lord of Milan." The chief political argument advanced for the emergent Italian *signorie* is that they guaranteed peace: peace was surely preferable to the liberty promised by Republican regimes, which typically degenerated into chaos and misrule. Early Republican theorists, such as Brunetto Latini, opposed such despotic claims by developing the idea of common profit ("commun proufit") as the basis of civic liberty.[47] But Florentine theorists such as Latini (and later Boccaccio) were forced to admit that Republics were prone to ruinous factionalism.[48] Chaucer's Milanese hosts were no doubt willing to detail the dozens of riots and insurrections that had broken out at Florence in recent decades.[49] On July 20 (the very day that dissident cardinals opened the papal schism by declaring the elec-

45. "Con cuor di marmo e piglio di Nerone"; see Natalino Sapegno, *Il Trecento,* 4th ed., vol. 5 of *Storia letteraria d'Italia,* ed. A. Balduino (Padua: F. Vallardi, 1981), 440. Vannozzo served despots in Padua, Verona, and Venice before entering Visconti service at Milan in 1389. In 1374 he actually composed a *canzone* condemning tyrants; but his most famous political piece was the *Cantilena pro Comite Virtutum,* composed of eight sonnets, in which Italy and the cities of Padua, Venice, Ferrara, Bologna, Florence, Rimini, and Rome beg Gian Galeazzo Visconti to subject them to his control and to bring order and peace to the Italian peninsula. See Sapegno, 441.

46. See Sapegno, *Trecento,* 446.

47. See, for example, Brunetto Latini, *Li Livres dou Trésor,* ed. Francis Carmody (Berkeley and Los Angeles: University of California Press, 1948), 224, 392. See also Bianca Ceva, *Brunetto Latini: L'Uomo e l'Opera* (Milan-Naples: Ricciardi, 1965), 155–56.

48. See *Trésor,* ed. Carmody, 394. See also *Trattatello in laude di Dante,* ed. P. G. Ricci, in *Tutte le opere di Giovanni Boccaccio,* ed. V. Branca, 12 vols., incomplete (Milan: Mondadori, 1964–), where Boccaccio censures Dante for factionalism: "it is widely known in Romagna that any half-grown woman or little child could move him to such mad fury by speaking of political parties and condemning the Ghibellines that he would have ended up throwing stones had they not fallen silent" (vol. 3, version 1, paragraph 170).

49. From his study of Florentine criminal archives, Samuel Cohn, Jr., calculates that some forty-three riots and insurrections took place between 1343 (when records began) and 1385. They "must have involved thousands of men and women" ("Florentine Insurrections, 1342–85 in Comparative Perspective," in *The English Rising of 1381,* ed. R. H. Hilton and T. H. Aston [Cambridge, Eng.: Cambridge University Press, 1984], 148).

tion of Urban VI void) a popular revolt broke out at Florence; within three days the republican regime had toppled. On August 4 Galeazzo Visconti died, leaving Bernabò in a very powerful position. All this happened while Chaucer was at Milan.

E. P. Kuhl, writing in 1947, speaks of Chaucer's "momentous mission" to Lombardy as "one involving a crisis in the history of western civilization, involving in fact the very fate of England itself." Kuhl, warming to his subject, speaks of the top-level decision "to send Chaucer into a labyrinth of intrigues in seething Italy, to entrust him with England's welfare, economical, political, religious." Such trust in Chaucer attests to his "suavity, urbanity, casualness; tact, patience, spirit of compromise such as does not appear in the Nordic vehemence of Wycliff; astuteness and knowledge of men, a divine commonsense," and so on (featuring further comparisons with Langland and Gower).[50] Kuhl's inflated estimate of Chaucer's role in the hands-on making of history drastically oversimplifies the relationship between poetic style and public utterance. But he is right in suggesting that Chaucer's 1378 journey to Lombardy spanned a critical period in fourteenth-century history, a period in which Chaucer's understanding of political process must have developed rapidly. On 21 June 1377 England had passed from the senility of Edward III to the minority of the ten-year-old Richard. The English, particularly those in the south who felt exposed to French attacks, were becoming increasingly skeptical about the direction of the war and increasingly resentful of the growing burden of taxation. During the summer of 1377 many villagers offered organized resistance, often arguing for individual freedoms by reference to the Domesday Book.[51] A petition presented to Parliament in October 1377 speaks of fears of civil war, treason, and a general peasant uprising.[52] Chaucer must have heard of, or witnessed, disturbing evidence of popular resentment on returning from Lombardy, since Canterbury (which lay on the principal route between London and Europe) had recently been suffering

---

50. "Why was Chaucer sent to Milan in 1378?", *Modern Language Notes* 62 (1947): 43. Kuhl believed Chaucer to be "the most important member of the mission," but the mission was in fact headed by Sir Edward de Berkeley.

51. See Rosamond Faith, "The 'Great Rumour' of 1377 and Peasant Ideology," in *English Rising*, ed. Hilton and Aston, 43–73.

52. For a convenient translation see R. B. Dobson, ed., *The Peasants' Revolt of 1381*, 2d ed. (London: MacMillan, 1983), 76–77.

from social unrest.[53] If something like the Florentine Ciompi revolt were to break out in England, royal officials like Chaucer would become prime targets.

Such a revolt did, of course, break out three years later. Recent historians prefer to call the events of 1381 the "English Rising," since there is now greater awareness of urban (as well as peasant) involvement.[54] This has invited more detailed comparisons between the Ciompi and the English rebellions. Both certainly exhibited a high degree of organization. The Ciompi, for example, exploited the associational forms of their industrial organization.[55] The English rebels exploited the organizing principles of the commissions of array: where before they had been assembled to enforce the Statute of Labourers or to guard against the French, they now assembled to march on London. The energy that powered the English rising, it is now realized, had important political as well as social and economic sources.[56] There were, of course, a number of private vendettas and attacks upon local tyranny. But there is also plentiful evidence of an ability to visualize tyranny in broader terms, demanding a more generalized (and organized) response. Freedom was the great rallying call: freedom for the commonwealth against any form of seigneurial domination, whether national or local.

The language of political life in England was in no sense as developed as its counterpart in Italy.[57] But the fundamental debate conducted between Florence and Milan, one that opposed the freedoms and liberties of the commonwealth to the exigencies of despotism, was also of fundamental importance in Chaucer's England. There is, in both countries, a firm understanding that the opposition of tyranny to commonwealth is not God-given but is seen to evolve historically: tyranny brings itself into being by gradually eating away at civic liberties. Chaucer had seen how the Milanese were anxious to accelerate this process in Italy; and how the Florentines were desperate to resist and even reverse it. During the last two decades of his life Chaucer witnessed an increasingly desperate struggle in England as the king he served inched towards tyranny. His experience of the Florence-Milan conflict, and his

53. See A. F. Butcher, "English Urban Society and the Revolt of 1381," in *English Rising*, ed. Hilton and Aston, 105. On 16 July 1378 bailiffs at Canterbury were commissioned to investigate malefactors assembling, stirring up trouble, and defying authority.
54. See R. H. Hilton, "Introduction," in *English Rising*, ed. Hilton & Aston, 1.
55. See Cohn, "Florentine Insurrections," 146–47, 162–63.
56. Hilton, *English Rising*, 7–8.
57. See Ullmann, *Law and Politics*, 299.

reading of Boccaccio and Petrarch within the structure of this conflict, helped prepare him both as poet and political subject for English conflicts to come.

III

Before attempting to locate Petrarch and Boccaccio more precisely within this Florentine-Milanese framework we should acknowledge that the character of this ideological space has long been subject to heated historiographical debate.[58] More than a century ago Jacob Burckhardt spoke of the "natural alliance between the despot and the scholar, each relying solely on his personal talent"; the despot recruits the scholar and the poet so that the bare face of power may be ornamented by "a new legitimacy."[59] Hans Baron, writing in 1955, counters Burckhardt by proposing that Florentine civic humanism embodied, in the crucial years of its formation (1400–1402), a rearguard that struggled to resist the spread of tyranny across Italy.[60] This thesis has proved highly influential, although critics have drawn attention to earlier phases of the Florence-Milan conflict and to earlier traditions of rhetoric and political theory that contributed to the evolving humanist mentality.[61] Baron also sets out to break down "the time-honored identification of the Volgare tradition with the medieval Commune and of Humanism with the Tyranny of the Renaissance."[62] This identification proves difficult to break, since, as Lauro Martines has argued, humanist culture is inevitably elitist: the study of ancient eloquence provides "a

58. Readers who take exception to applying the term "ideology" to late medieval contexts might substitute the term "organizing myths" as employed by David McLellan, *Ideology: Concepts in Social Thought* (Minneapolis: University of Minnesota Press, 1986), 3. As McLellan notes, the term ideology "is less than 200 years old" (2), although its origins may be traced to the kinds of conceptual conflict we are examining: "the notion obviously has its roots in the general philosophical questions about meaning and direction with which the breakdown of the medieval world view confronted Western European intellectuals" (4).

59. *The Civilization of the Renaissance in Italy,* trans. S. G. C. Middlemore, 2 vols. (New York: Harper Torchbooks, 1958), 1:27–28, 229.

60. See *The Crisis of the Early Renaissance: Civic Humanism and Republican Liberty in an Age of Classicism and Tyranny,* rev. ed. (Princeton: Princeton University Press, 1966), esp. xxvi.

61. See Pocock, *Machiavellian Moment,* 55–66 (with its references to Seigel, Garin, Struever, Martines, Becker, Molho); Skinner, *Foundations,* 71–112; P. O. Kristeller, *Studies in Renaissance Thought and Letters* (Rome: Edizioni di storia e letteratura, 1956), 38, 359.

62. Baron, *Crisis,* xxvii.

recipe for ruling classes"; Latinity and the ideal of empire are intertwined; opposition to either ideal can seem to assume (in the minds of
princes) the dimensions of political conspiracy.[63]

The relationship of humanism to tyranny is still, in short, subject to
vigorous debate, a debate that inevitably highlights the political predi-
lections of each participant. All critics agree, however, in affirming the
importance of the Florentine-Milanese divide. Of course, qualifications
must always be made; some will be briefly noted here to counter the
impression that Florentine Republicanism was always a progressive and
enlightened force in its struggle against despotism. Florentine *libertas*
meant, above all, liberty for Florence; and since Florence embodied
liberty, any policy she chose to follow could be represented as the pursuit of *libertas*.[64] Such liberty was concentrated within the walls of the
city and did not extend to the countryside; Florence exerted unques-
tioned political and economic control over its *contado*.[65] (Current political theory sanctioned such control since *politia*—as derived from Aristotle—confined itself to the structure of relationships between city-
dwellers.) Florence also contrived to rob conquered cities and its own
countryside of their holy places, shrines, and relics, thereby arrogating
a centralized religious authority to itself as "a holy enclave surrounded
by a desacralized country."[66] Within Florence power tended to concen-
trate itself into fewer and fewer hands as the new Ciceronian Republicanism distanced itself from its origins in the guild structures of earlier
times.[67]

These qualifications are intended not to discredit Florentine political
ideology but to recognize its historicity, its deployment within a pro-
tracted historical struggle. Petrarch entered this struggle when he left
Provence for Italy in 1353. His crossing of the Alps seemed, in his own
mind, hardly less momentous than the imperial descent into Italy envisaged by Dante: Petrarch figures himself as an Aeneas, carrying a precious burden on his back; this patrimony is his library, which includes
some of his own compositions (*Fam.* 15.3). Petrarch had no definite idea
of his final destination in Italy; Mantua and Padua seemed promising.

63. Lauro Martines, *Power and Imagination: City States in Renaissance Italy* (Harmondsworth: Peregrine Books, 1983), 264, 269, 275.
64. See Rubinstein, "Florence and the Despots," 31–36.
65. See Cohn, "Florentine Insurrections," 145.
66. Trexler, *Public Life*, 4.
67. Antony Black, *Guilds and Civil Society in European Political Thought from the
Twelfth Century to the Present* (London: Methuen, 1984), 96–103.

But he got as far as Milan and found himself suddenly and utterly seduced. Like his own Griselde, Petrarch is reduced to shyness and silence on being courted by a despot: "I blushed and remained silent; and by doing so I consented or seemed to have consented. There was nothing, or at least I could find nothing, to say against it" (*Fam.* 16.12). The previous year Petrarch had spoken of Lombardy as "oppressed by an undying tyranny," a region where "you will not find one place where a lover of virtue and tranquillity may seek repose" (*Fam.* 15.7). But it was the promise of repose that convinced Petrarch to remain at Milan: the Visconti could guarantee him time and security for his writing (*Fam.* 16.11).

Petrarch offers the most detailed defense of his decision to accept Visconti patronage in *Familiares* 17.10, written to Giovanni Aretino, Chancellor of Mantua, on 1 January 1354. The letter is highly digressive (Petrarch admits to "evading and rambling"), but its digression and evasion may be read as part of its political statement. Its chief theme addresses a central mystery of human behavior: why do we desire and intend to do one thing and then do another? Paul and Augustine are Petrarch's chief authorities in this exploration of the divided self.[68] The outcome of the "internal warfare" suffered by Augustine was his decision to be baptized by Ambrose at Milan. This allows Petrarch to mythologize the scandal of his own presence at Milan as a temporary liminal paralysis; the suggestion is that he will soon cross the threshold and be free to move elsewhere. Petrarch further explains his paralysis by quoting from Paul, "the greatest of men in every respect": "'I do not do the good that I wish to do, but rather the evil that I do not wish to do.'" He suggests that the cause of this tragic divorce between action and volition "lies in the mysterious punishment that has come upon men and some deeply hidden flaw in the sons of Adam." The "root" of this monstrousness lies in the fact that although the mind can command the body it cannot command itself: "the mind commands the mind to will, the mind is itself, but it does not do it." We can but hate ourselves: "nothing is more vile to man than himself, nothing more venal than liberty."

The extreme political pessimism of this letter makes any form of

---

68. Petrarch's *Secretum* stages an energetic dialogue between Franciscus, a personification of Petrarch, and Augustinus. See Enrico Carrara's edition in *Prose*, ed. Martellotti, 22–215.

social action seem pointless and self-defeating. We hardly need defend liberty from external threats since it is bound to be undermined and defeated from within:

> We are not struck down from the outside, nor is it even necessary; for believe me, there is no need for well-trained troops or machines to attack the walls or secretly dig tunnels. Each man possesses within himself a destructive enemy, his companion amidst his pleasures, whom he surprisingly obeys and obstinately supports against himself.
>
> (*Fam.* 17.10)

Petrarch cannot obey his better self; but he can obey a better man, one who exerts "the power over me of an absolute command and the force of imperial majesty." This man is, of course, Archbishop Giovanni Visconti, the absolute ruler who can defend the physical walls of Milan and hence protect the metaphorical walls of Petrarch's selfhood. In this letter, then, Petrarch discovers himself to be a natural subject for despotic rule.

Petrarch joined the Visconti in 1353 just a matter of months after they had concluded a war with Florence. His Florentine friends were quick to voice their sense of outrage and betrayal. Most such protests came in the early months of Petrarch's residence at Milan, but they never stopped coming: Salutati wrote from Rome in 1369 attempting to prise Petrarch away from his despotic patrons, and Boccaccio wrote along similar lines in 1360 and again as late as 1373.[69] Some of Petrarch's Florentine critics were bluntly or ingeniously insulting. One Gano del Colle sent Petrarch a sonnet in which, according to a manuscript note, he exhorts Petrarch "to discharge himself from the tyranny of the lords of Milan and come to a place of liberty." Gano added insult to injury by sending a minstrel to sing the sonnet to Petrarch.[70] Petrarch hated minstrels and anything that smacked of minstrelsy and lower-class art: he changed the wording of one of his own *ballate* on realizing that it echoed a "plebeian song," and he censured Dante for writing verse that could be taken up by "ignorant oafs in taverns and market places."[71]

Petrarch claimed that the Visconti had offered him patronage and protection without formal responsibilities. In fact he was about to enter the most intensive and time-consuming period of his political life;

---

69. Wilkins, *Later Years*, 171, 173–74, 243; *Eight Years*, 207–8.
70. Wilkins, *Eight Years*, 9.
71. See Wilkins, *Eight Years*, 116–17; *Fam.* 21.15, as translated by Foster, *Petrarch*, 29.

when he wrote to Giovanni Aretino he was already contemplating a winter crossing of the Alps on Visconti business. Petrarch found himself composing numerous letters for the Visconti, representing them on long and exhausting diplomatic missions, negotiating with the emperor (on many occasions), the French, the English, the Venetians and other minor powers. When Giovanni Visconti died on 5 October 1354 Petrarch was called upon to deliver an oration commemorating the passage of power to the three new lords of Lombardy: Matteo, Bernabò, and Galeazzo. On 18 June 1358 Petrarch rode into Novara, recently recaptured from the Marquis of Monferrato, with Galeazzo and proceeded to deliver an oration to the nervous populace. His text was "Convertetur populus meus hic" (*Psalms* 72:10). "Convertetur" (*convertere*, meaning to convert, to exchange and—in Ciceronian usage—to translate) indicates the importance of repentance. "Populus" is a designation that not every group of men deserves; the Novarese are found deserving. "Meus" represents the status of Novara in relation to the Visconti. "Hic" is an emphatic adverbial form denoting special affection; Galeazzo has forgiven the city its faults and will henceforth take a close interest in its affairs.[72]

In the following year, 1359, the Augustinian friar Iacopo Bussolari took over the city government of Pavia and ousted the Visconti. He particularly outraged Bernabò by ordering the slaughter of all dogs: such creatures (wrote Petrarch at Bernabò's behest) deserved to meet a nobler death through hunting.[73] On being commanded to negotiate with Bussolari (by exchanging letters), Petrarch predictably exploits his familiarity with Augustine, particularly his doctrine of the two cities, earthly and heavenly (*Fam.* 19.18). He also makes careful distinctions between the literal and allegorical senses of certain Biblical verses (such as " 'I have not come to bring you peace but the sword' ") and offers a detailed profile of the true orator (who must unite rhetorical skill with concern for the public good). In deriding Bussolari's "ridiculous appetite for tyranny" Petrarch follows the example of other Viscontian propagandists who deflected a political lexicon habitually employed against the Visconti onto the Visconti's enemies.[74] He had done this before, some six years earlier, in speaking of the "oppressed masses" of

---

72. Wilkins, *Eight Years,* 167–69.
73. See Wilkins, *Eight Years,* 197–98; W. F. Butler, *The Lombard Communes: A History of the Republics of North Italy* (London: T. Fisher Unwin, 1906), 462–64.
74. Rubinstein, "Florence and the Despots," 35.

Genoa who turned to Giovanni Visconti, "this truly righteous prince," for assistance in resisting the establishment of a tyranny (*Fam.* 17.4).

## IV

The sharpest and most consistent criticisms of Petrarch's associations with despots came from Boccaccio, Dante's most dedicated admirer. Boccaccio first met Petrarch in 1350 when Petrarch stayed with him en route to and from Rome. In March 1351 Boccaccio traveled to Padua with official letters that revoked the notice of exile served on Petrarch's father in 1302, promised the restoration of confiscated patrimony, and offered Petrarch a University chair.[75] Petrarch declined this opportunity to return to Florence. Boccaccio's *Ut huic epistole,* dated 15 August 1353, is bitterly reproachful of Petrarch's move to Milan; it reminds Petrarch of the damning things he had said of Giovanni Visconti in Boccaccio's presence at Padua just two years before.[76] Petrarch never answered this letter. His meetings with Petrarch certainly exerted a powerful influence on Boccaccio's artistic development: he gave up composing vernacular verse and dedicated most of his mature energies to Petrarchan-inspired Latin encyclopedism. And yet Boccaccio always retained an impressive independence of political judgment. He turned down Petrarch's offers of patronage (even though he was often indigent) and maintained a long and active interest in the civic and diplomatic affairs of Florence. Whereas Petrarch maintained an uneasy, ambiguous attitude toward Dante, Boccaccio envisioned his Dantean discipleship as an integral part of his civic politics.[77] In 1350 (immediately before his first meeting with Petrarch) he traveled to a convent at Ravenna to present Sister Beatrice, Dante's daughter, with ten gold florins on behalf of the Florentine Compagnia di Or San Michele. In the summer of 1373, following a public petition, he was called upon by the Florentine civic authorities to deliver the world's first *lecturae Dantis.* And between these dates he composed three versions of his short treatise in praise of Dante, the *Trattatello in laude di Dante.*

---

75. Vittore Branca, "Giovanni Boccaccio: Profilo biografico," *Tutte le opere,* ed. Branca, 1:83–87.

76. See Giovanni Boccaccio, *Opere Latine Minori,* ed. A. F. Massèra, Scrittori d'Italia, III (Bari: Laterza, 1928), 136–40.

77. See Foster, *Petrarch,* 27–30.

Boccaccio's *Trattatello* makes a noteworthy contribution to Florentine political thought by tracing the originary interdependence of priesthood, poetry, and political dictatorship. In establishing the earliest religions, Boccaccio tells us, the priestly class set themselves apart from the populace by their manner of dress and by their development of an artificial and elevated form of speech, later called poetry (1:128–32). Later on, certain ingenious individuals attempted to set themselves over and above the populace, representing their superiority in their public appearances through their use of slaves and of ornaments ("ornamenti," 1:133–34). Not trusting too far in their own powers, such individuals began deliberately to exploit religious emotions and "to secure by oaths the obedience of those they would not have been able to constrain by force" (1:135). To keep the commoners in awe these rulers elected to deify their ancestors; this, they realized, could not be done without the aid of poets. Poets, like their political masters, dazzled the populace by embellishing the plain truth with ornaments—in this case ornaments drawn from that style of writing previously reserved for the praise of God. Through such rhetorical means poets managed to surround their masters with a mystifying religious aura and, says Boccaccio, to "cause to be believed that which the princes wished to be believed" (1:136).

The poet cannot legitimate the rule of a despot, but he can gild it with the semblance of legitimacy by exploiting his rhetorical skill to tap veins of religious feeling. Boccaccio's thesis, first devised somewhere in the period 1351–55, certainly invites us to view Petrarch's alliance with the Visconti in a harsh, clear light. It is, above all, the use of ornament that unites the poet and the prince in their bedazzling of an impressionable public. The prince recognizes in the poet the same skill that he has employed in establishing his own power; it is quite natural that he should attempt to appropriate such power to further his own purposes. This sense of mutual recognition forms an interesting subtext to the famous story about Gian Galeazzo Visconti who, when present as a boy at one of his father's banquets, was asked to name the wisest man present: he singled out Petrarch without hesitation.[78] And Petrarch himself also created a highly successful myth of his relations to power. On the one hand, he claimed total independence. "What am I then?" he asks himself in the course of *Seniles* 1.6: "a learner, but hardly even

---

78. See Bueno de Mesquita, *Giangaleazzo,* 10–11.

that; a lover of the woods, wont to utter insipid words amid tall birches, or ply a frail pen."[79] This accords with the famous poetic image of a Petrarch wandering "solo e pensoso" through "i più deserti campi" before expiring through the force of internal paradox.[80] But other letters suggest a different relationship to landscape, a landscape of power. Here, late in 1367, Petrarch recalls his youthful habit of wandering through Vaucluse at night:

> You wonder at my confidence? I have never feared ghosts and shadows; I never saw a wolf in my valley; I had no apprehension of man. Plowmen sang in the fields, fishermen watched silently by the stream; they greeted me at whatever hour, knowing well that their lord was more than a friend to me, he was a dear brother, a father. Thus they were always my well-wishers, never hostile.[81]

The "lord" with whom Petrarch allies himself in this early case is Philippe de Cabassoles, a powerful French landowner who later became a Cardinal at Avignon. Petrarch's insistence on this alliance ensures that his encounter with the rural laborers is not natural but hierarchical. Indeed, the notion of natural encounters in a natural landscape seems foreign to Petrarch: nature serves not to erase social distinctions but to help play them out. In 1372 he reminds Cabassoles of how, many years before, they would wander in the woods, far beyond the reach of the servants who came hunting for them at dinner time.[82] And in *Familiares* 19.16 he speaks of the "freedom" he is enjoying during a short spell of country life, of how "my humble neighbours eagerly bring me fruits from their trees, flowers from the meadows, fish from the streams, ducklings from the brooks, birds from their nests, hedgehogs from the fields, as well as hares and goats and wild pigs." Such energetic activity, here admired by the eye of a consumer, becomes elsewhere a cause for complaint: "for often celebrated lakes are disturbed by fishermen's nets, often famous forests are invaded by barking dogs" (*Fam.* 17.10). Such contradictions suggest that the ideal landscape Petrarch sought

79. Translated by Wilkins in *Later Years*, 18.
80. Francesco Petrarca, *Rime sparse*, ed. Giovanni Ponte (Milan: Mursia, 1979), 35 (p. 83).
81. *Seniles* 10.2, translated in Bishop, *Letters from Petrarch*, 268.
82. *Seniles* 16.4. Petrarch exhibits a strange compulsion to advertise his control of eating habits. Strange, but medieval: see H. L. Dreyfus and Paul Rabinow, *Michel Foucault: Beyond Structuralism and Hermeneutics*, 2d. ed. (Chicago: University of Chicago Press, 1983), 229.

throughout his life as the locus for his contemplation existed only in his verse or in his memory of Vaucluse.[83]

The country landscape of Petrarch's day was actually a dangerous place to inhabit; it was frequently traversed by armies and mercenary bands. Petrarch was therefore forced to spend most of his time among the restless and agitated city-dwellers he so despised. The city, for Petrarch, is (in a tortured imagistic inversion) a tempest, a sea of miseries; the countryside is our true harbor. Petrarch frequently yearns to set sail for this harbor, especially when buffeted by the rude shocks incident upon the urban division of labor:

> Arise, come, hasten, let us abandon the city to merchants, attorneys, brokers, usurers, tax-gatherers, scriveners, doctors, perfumers, butchers, cooks, bakers and tailors, alchemists, fullers, artisans, weavers, architects, statuaries, painters, mimes, dancers, lute-players, quacks, panderers, thieves, criminals, adulterers, parasites, foreigners, swindlers and jesters, gluttons who with scent alert catch the odor of the market-place, for whom that is the only bliss, where mouths are agape for that alone. For on the mountains there is no smell of cookery.
>
> (*De Vita Solitaria,* 312)

Petrarch here recoils from a whole Canterbury pilgrimage (or Langlandian tavern) of urban professions; but there can be no permanent escape to the countryside. This sad fact induced Petrarch to attempt one of his most audacious maneuvers: to turn the country and the city inside out. At Milan he took up gardening (with little success) and attempted to live as if he were, indeed, living in the country. At Padua in 1373 (having completed the Griselde story) he composed his own treatise on city and princely government. This treatise, which contains a good deal of random grumping, objects to roving pigs, women who wail too loudly at funerals, and wheeled carts (that is, the vehicles that facilitate urban trade).[84] Elsewhere Petrarch objects to one further source of urban blight—slaves:

> The disasters of Greece are long past, but those of the Scythians recent. From them we used to receive the annually great cargo of grain; but now the ships come loaded with slaves, whom their wretched parents sell

---

83. The real, historical Vaucluse offered Petrarch no hope of refuge in later years; his old home there was burned down. "Now venture to hope for safety in the dark recesses of the Closed Valley! Nothing is closed, nothing is too high or dark for thieves and bandits!" (*Seniles* 10.2, in Bishop, *Letters from Petrarch,* 269.)

84. See *Seniles* 14.1; Wilkins, *Later Years,* 252–56.

under the pressure of hunger. Now an unwonted multitude of slaves of both sexes, offscourings of their race with horrid Scythian faces, invade this lovely city, as a turbid torrent flows into a sparkling river. If their purchasers were not more indulgent than I, with eyes less offended by ugliness than are mine, these repulsive youths would not crowd our streets, nor would they revolt visiting foreigners, accustomed to better sights, by their hideous aspect. They would still be plucking with their nails and gnawing, pale with hunger, the scanty produce of their stony fields, which Ovid once described. But enough of this.[85]

This passage, for all its arrant inhumanity, deserves some scrutiny as an authentic testimony to Petrarch's hard-core humanism, or neoclassicism. As Perry Anderson has observed, "it was precisely the formation of a limpidly demarcated slave sub-population that . . . lifted the citizenry of the Greek cities to hitherto unknown heights of conscious juridical freedom. Hellenic liberty and slavery were indivisible: each was the structural condition of the other."[86] Just such a dyadic system seems to structure Petrarch's sensibilities here: it is his acute perception of the exceptional ugliness of the slaves that confirms his sense of his own exceptional vision. Ordinary eyes are not so sensitive to ugliness. It is entirely appropriate that Petrarch should end here with a footnote from Ovid: he is turning his eyes from ugliness towards the Academy, the institution where men of exceptional vision meet. Such men, it would seem, are drawn together across the centuries by uncommon powers of perception. But for Petrarch (as later for English humanists like Arnold and Leavis) this acute sense of separateness is founded, we might suspect, upon a radical inability, or unwillingness, to countenance the harsher aspects of an urban, mercantile culture upon which he depends.

Perhaps the most disturbing aspect of this passage is Petrarch's willingness to view certain human beings as non-subjects, as mere objects for unbridled hatred and disgust. It is additionally disturbing to recognize that his attitude to slaves, the purest expression of political nonentity, has much in common with his attitude to women. The only letter that Petrarch wrote to a woman was to the Empress Anne, congratulating her on the birth of a girl and assuring her that "better fortune often follows upon a weak beginning" (*Fam.* 21.8).[87] Women are

---

85. *Seniles* 10.2, a letter to Bruni probably written in November or December 1367; translated in Bishop, *Letters from Petrarch,* 273.

86. *Passages from Antiquity to Feudalism* (London: Verso Editions, 1978), 23.

87. The anxiety for a male heir was and is, of course, a harsh fact of life for any woman in monarchical society. But a reading of *Fam.* 21.8 does suggest that, for Petrarch, wom-

figured in Petrarch not as participants in a social discourse but as scattered fragments, as an idea, disembodied, posthumous, or metaphorical.[88] And yet when women are present only by way of analogy, or incidental metaphor, the female body is often figured as the object of social or commercial exchange or, more commonly, violence: " 'Remove the frontlet from horses that are for sale,' is an old caution. No sane man wants to marry a misfeatured girl because she is well dressed. If we tear off the frontlet, or the mask rather, from those who are so gay in their purple, we shall clearly see their wretchedness" (*De Vita Solitaria,* 312).[89]

Such imagery of dressing and undressing, masking and cosmetic face-painting, a familiar feature of classical demonstrations or critiques of the function of rhetoric, is a recurrent feature of Petrarch's polemical prose. Petrarch himself recognizes that the pursuit of rhetoric will inevitably color social practice: "what is advantageously taught in the art of oratory, the art, that is, of speaking with propriety and elegance, has in our time been mischievously applied to the art of wicked and disgraceful living" (*De Vita Solitaria,* 172–73). When imitation shifts from the literary to the social sphere the self becomes hopelessly dislocated: "no one is of a clear mind as to his costume, his speech, his thought— in short, as to what sort of man he would like to be, and therefore every man is unlike himself." Far from a denial of the social character of oratory, this is an argument for its social control, its policing. In the right hands, the hands of the prince or Academician, oratory may be practised to advantage. In *Familiares* 22.1, dated 11 September 1362, Petrarch turns his attention to marriage (a subject of which, he freely admits, he has no experience). In evaluating a prospective wife one should consider "not so much her dowry and wealth as her family line and upbringing, not so much her elegant attire as her devotion [*non tam ornatus elegantiam quam pietatem*], and above all, not so much her bodily beauty as her mind." Petrarch is here advocating a kind of masculine

---

en's power has diminished over the centuries. Women figure importantly at the beginnings of literacy, art, and history, but their power recedes in the Christian epoch; history becomes masculine, recovering from its own "weak beginning."

88. See Nancy J. Vickers, "Diana Described: Scattered Woman and Scattered Rhyme," in *Writing and Sexual Difference,* ed. Elizabeth Abel (Chicago: University of Chicago Press, 1982), 95–109.

89. See the Wife of Bath's Prologue, 289–92. The "old caution" derives from Jerome; see Robert P. Miller, *Chaucer: Sources and Backgrounds* (New York: Oxford University Press, 1977), 412.

*inventio* which, in gazing at or through the female body, may lay bare the essential qualities beneath. The female mind is valued, but only for its willingness to cast off any "ornatus elegantiam" it brings with it, laying bare the essential "pietatem" that may be subjected to masculine molding. It is best to select a young virgin from a distant community:

> For a noble maiden, devoted to you from an early age and distanced from her people's flatteries and old women's gossipings, will be more chaste and humble, more obedient and holy; quickly casting off her girlish frivolity, she will don the seriousness of a married woman. In short, whether a virgin or a widow, once she joins you in the nuptial bed, hearing, seeing and thinking of you alone, she will be transformed into your image alone and will adopt your ways.
>
> (*Fam.* 22.1)

As a woman assumes the lineaments of her master's control she attests ever more impressively to the excellence of his original choice, his judicious reading of her inner qualities. She functions as a semiotic object that points to a higher union, the marriage between the humanist and the landscape he inhabits. This is the mysterious alliance that is celebrated at the very end of *De Vita Solitaria*. Nature voices its approbation of everything that Petrarch has said: "These things I have addressed to you with such affection of mind that every rustle of the branches breathed upon by the wind and every ripple of the waters gushing from the ground about me seems to say a single thing: 'You argue well, you counsel uprightly, you speak the truth'" (312).

The Florentine humanists who were quick to praise Petrarch's championing of rhetoric were puzzled and disturbed by the antisocial character of his writings on women.[90] But the most sophisticated and extensive critique of this cultural complex—the relationship of the humanist enterprise to civil society, natural landscape, and the female body—is supplied by a Boccaccian text, *Decameron* 5.8. Nastagio degli Onesti, a noble, loves a woman of superior social rank. She despises him. At the urging of his friends, Nastagio leaves the city (Ravenna); but instead of seeking out a new city he camps in the countryside. One morning toward the beginning of May Nastagio, like a good Petrar-

---

90. See Skinner, *Foundations,* 88–89. Buonaccorso da Montemagna's Latin debate on nobility, translated by John Tiptoft as *The Declamacioun of Noblesse,* takes a more enlightened view of a woman's rights, particularly her right to study. See R. J. Mitchell, *John Tiptoft (1427–1470)* (London: Longman, 1938), which includes Tiptoft's translation (215–41).

chan, dismisses his servants and wanders off into the landscape, lost in thought:

> The fifth hour of the day was already spent, and he had advanced at least half a mile into the woods, oblivious of food and everything else, when suddenly he seemed to hear [*gli parve udire*] a woman giving vent to dreadful wailing and ear-splitting screams. His pleasant reverie [*dolce pensiero*] being thus interrupted, he raised his head to investigate the cause, and discovered to his surprise that he was in the pinewoods. Furthermore, on looking straight ahead he caught sight of a naked woman, young and very beautiful, who was running through a dense thicket of shrubs and briars towards the very spot where he was standing. The woman's hair was dishevelled, her flesh was all torn by the briars and brambles, and she was sobbing and screaming for mercy.[91]

The woman is pursued and then overtaken by a mounted knight and two huge dogs. Nastagio steps forward to defend her, but the knight (who identifies himself as a fellow-citizen) explains that Nastagio is witnessing a God-given torment: the woman is being punished for scorning his love and rejoicing at his death. Nastagio steps back and the woman, kneeling and sobbing, is duly torn to pieces; the knight slashes open her back with a dagger, digs out her innards, and throws them to the dogs. Soon, however, the girl rises to her feet as if nothing has happened and the hunt begins again. This happens every Friday. Nastagio realizes that this "ought to prove very useful to him" and arranges an outdoor banquet for the following Friday. The whole sequence is acted out again in front of Nastagio's lady and her family. The lady is so terrified that she manages (Boccaccio tells us) to turn her hatred for Nastagio into love; they marry without delay and settle down "to a long and happy life together" (462).

The potency of this myth for its masculine Renaissance readers is perhaps best attested by the four paintings Botticelli made of this narrative, a sequence that spawned countless imitations.[92] The myth's predatory, unbridled energy seems to express the emotions of a period when the rapid conquest of new texts (through a new humanist discipline) promised to liberate a power that could reshape the social world.[93] No detailed allegoresis can be attempted here; but a prelimi-

---

91. Boccaccio, *The Decameron*, trans. G. H. McWilliam (New York: Penguin, 1972), 458. Translations from the *Decameron* follow McWilliam; references to the Italian follow the edition of V. Branca in *Tutte le opere*, vol. 4.

92. Vittore Branca is compiling a catalogue.

93. See Pocock, *Machiavellian Moment*, 60–64.

nary reading of the novella can be offered. Masculine desire (of a specific social and educated level) finds itself locked out of social and erotic fulfillment and exiles itself from the city. While the male protagonist is lost in thought (within a humanist landscape) a text comes to mind: one that sees the female body pursued by masculine desire.[94] This text is captured, transcribed (with a dagger), and consumed. The knowledge of this text, gained in private, may then be exploited to influence behavior within the public domain. Control of the text, figured as a woman, determines control of the real woman in society.

V

Boccaccio's most extreme example of such masculine control of a female body is provided by his *Decameron*'s very last tale. This sees a female villager subjected to extreme mental and emotional torments by her political overlord, a Lombard dictator. Petrarch, finding himself "delighted and fascinated" by "so charming a story" (*tam dulcis ystoria*), suddenly snatched up his pen one day in 1373 and, he tells Boccaccio, "attacked this story of yours" (*ystoriam ipsam tuam scribere sum aggressus*).[95] By this time Petrarch had moved from Lombardy (although he remained on good terms with the Visconti) to Padua, the city that is justly celebrated as the cradle of humanism. The early Paduan humanists, or prehumanists, such as Lovato Lovati (1241–1309) and his disciple Alberto Mussato (1261–1329), had seen their dedication to the revival of literary culture as part of their service to City Republicanism. Mussato's Latin *Ecerinis*, hailed as the first secular drama to be written since antiquity, deliberately set out to celebrate the fight for liberty and self-government against the forces of tyranny.[96] Mussato was crowned with laurel by the *commune* of Padua in 1315 (an event that set the precedent for Petrarch's coronation at Rome in 1341), and a civic decree was passed that required an annual reading of *Ecerinis* before the assembled

---

94. When Actaeon gazes upon the naked Diana bathing he is torn apart by his own desires (hounds); see Vickers, "Diana Described," 97–99. The Nastagio story draws energy from this myth, which Renaissance men found so compelling, both by mirroring it and by exacting revenge upon it; here men watch in safety and woman is torn to pieces.

95. Quotations from *Seniles* 17.3 follow the edition of J. Burke Severs, *The Literary Relationships of Chaucer's "Clerk's Tale"* (New Haven: Yale University Press, 1942), 254–327. Translations from this text follow Miller, *Chaucer: Sources and Backgrounds*, 136–52.

96. See Roberto Weiss, *The Dawn of Humanism in Italy* (London: H. K. Lewis, 1947), 1–10; Skinner, *Foundations*, 38–39.

populace. In 1328, however, the Republic fell to the da Carrara, a dynastic dictatorship that remained in control of Padua until 1425.[97] Petrarch moved to Padua in 1368, serving Francesco da Carrara in many capacities. Petrarch's treatise on city government (or on princely government, since the prince now ruled the city) was written for Francesco da Carrara in November 1373, just months after the completion of the Petrarchan Griselde story. Francesco had been urging Petrarch to write something for him for some time. He was no doubt delighted to receive such a prestigious legitimation of his rule from Italy's new poet laureate. Padua could now forget Mussato and the ideal of civic self-government he stood for.

For Petrarch and the various audiences described in *Seniles* 17.3, the meaning of the Griselde story is not, apparently, problematic. Petrarch acknowledges that the story "differs entirely from most that precede it" in the *Decameron,* but also notes that the rules of rhetoric dictate that the most important parts of a work come first and last. The first part of the *Decameron* describes, Petrarch notes, "that siege of pestilence which forms so dark and melancholy a period in our century." On turning to Boccaccio's account we discover that the Black Death has precipitated the complete breakdown of city law and familial obligations. Boccaccio's first story continues this theme of civic, judicial, and religious collapse as a city rejoices in the canonization of Ser Cepperello of Prato, "perhaps the worst man ever born" (71). The second story sees a Parisian Jew riding to Rome to discover the pope and his clergy "doing their level best to reduce the Christian religion to nought and drive it from the face of the earth" (85). The hero of these first two stories, in which the authority of all civic and religious institutions is severely problematized, is God, whose truth stands above all this as "something immutable" and (since the human eye is "quite unable to penetrate the secrets of divine intelligence" [69], utterly mysterious.[98] Filomena, in opening the third story, proposes that since "we have heard such fine things concerning God and the truth of our religion, it will not seem inappropriate to descend at this juncture to the level of men" (86).

97. See John Larner, *Italy in the Age of Dante and Petrarch* (London: Longman, 1980), 137–38.

98. Proponents of the "descending" theme of government claimed that their temporal or spiritual authority devolved directly from God; see Ullmann, *Law and Politics,* 31. But in these narratives the downward chain of command would seem to be utterly broken: authority can only originate (in accordance with the "ascending theme of government") from below, in the human (civic) world.

Storytelling remains at this more modest, human level for the duration—for as long, that is, as the *brigata* continues to occupy the temporary, provisional, marginal space it has mapped out for itself.[99]

Many critics, however, have read *Decameron* 10.10 as a return to a
more exalted sphere, a world in which God works his purposes through
patient Griselde and the god-like Walter.[100] Such a reading is, to a
greater or lesser extent, Petrarchan. It is, of course, very difficult for
readers (especially readers of Chaucer) to approach Boccaccio's *novella*
without crossing the lines of Petrarch's interpretation. We should recall,
however, that Boccaccio's narrator here is Dioneo, "a youth of matchless charm and readiness of wit" (64) who has invited the ladies to join
him in "laughter, song and merriment" and to forget their troubles:
"my own I left inside the city gates when I departed thence a short
while ago in your company" (64). All tales told by Dioneo are, accordingly, comically critical of any authority that takes itself too seriously.
Dioneo exploits his privilege of speaking last to ironize, subvert, or
disperse the theme that has supposedly unified the day's storytelling.
The theme proposed for the tenth and final day is liberality and magnificence.[101] The term "magnificenza" (as *Decameron* 10 defines it) de-
notes a form of liberality or giving that serves to enhance rather than
deplete the power and resources of a great lord. In combining the mystifying suggestiveness of religious transcendence with the stark realities
of social and economic power, magnificence is innately theatrical, a virtue realized though public spectacle.[102] The drama of magnificence represents a liminal moment in which a lord offers some revelation, gift,
or transfer that delights his subject and binds her closer to him. Walter

99. See Wesley Trimpi, *Muses of One Mind* (Princeton: Princeton University Press,
1983), 328–29; Glending Olson, *Literature as Recreation in the Later Middle Ages* (Ithaca:
Cornell University Press, 1982), 164–204.

100. For a succinct critique of past critical attitudes (and of Walter's claims to divinity), see Giuseppe Mazzotta, *The World at Play in Boccaccio's "Decameron"* (Princeton:
Princeton University Press, 1986), 122–30.

101. "si ragiona di chi liberalmente o vero magnificamente alcuna cosa operasse in-
torno a' fatti d'amore o d'altra cosa" (the discussion turns upon those who have performed liberal or munificent deeds, whether in the cause of love or otherwise [733], 10.1,
rubric).

102. English readers will associate magnificence with the person, court, and theater
of Elizabeth I, although Skelton's *Magnyfycence* forms an interesting evolutionary stage
between medieval morality drama and the court politics of Henry VIII. See John Skelton,
*The Complete English Poems,* ed. John Scattergood (New Haven: Yale University Press,
1983), 140–214. For backgrounds to sixteenth-century magnificence, see Rosamund Tuve,
*Allegorical Imagery: Some Mediaeval Books and Their Posterity* (Princeton: Princeton University Press, 1966), 57–60, 79–82, 98–99.

proves himself magnificent in Boccaccio's tale in the crucial, climactic scene in which he presents Griselde with her own children. The closest equivalent scene in *Decameron* 10 comes in the fourth *novella,* where a lover restores a lady (buried while pregnant and presumed dead) and her child to her husband. But Walter is only restoring what he himself has taken away: Dioneo's exemplification of a lord who acts "liberalmente o vero magnificamente" is characteristically perverse.

A second, ancillary virtue exemplified in *Decameron* 10 is the restraint of desire by lords of high degree when the pursuit of such desire would threaten the *bonum commune.* The moral world of *Decameron* 10.5 (the *Franklin's Tale* analogue) is held together by this virtue. In the next story (10.6) an elderly king gazes upon a near-naked girl, falls in love with her, and arranges for her *raptus* but then (after heeding the advice of a noble follower and at great personal cost) restrains his desire. The following story (10.7) sees an "exquisitely beautiful" (768) girl of low degree fall in love with King Peter of Aragon. Far from exploiting her vulnerability, Peter collaborates with his queen to cure the girl of love sickness and then sees her married "in truly magnificent style" (775).[103] He then jousts in the lists "as her loyal knight for as long as he lived." Such virtuous restraint is rarely exemplified by modern despots:

> By deeds such as these, then, does a sovereign conquer the hearts of his subjects, furnish occasions to others for similar deeds, and acquire eternal renown. But among the rulers of today, there are few if any who can train the bowstrings of their minds upon any such objective, most of them having been changed into pitiless tyrants.
>
> (775)

Such talk of "'signori . . . crudeli e tiranni'" (10.7.49) could only make a Florentine audience think of those "tirauntz of Lombardye" who threatened their borders. After two more tales the scene actually shifts to Lombardy, as Dioneo proposes not one more example of magnificence but a counterexemplum:

> I want to tell you of a marquis, whose actions, even though things turned out well for him in the end, were remarkable not so much for their munificence as for their senseless brutality [*non cosa magnifica ma una matta bestialità*]. Nor do I advise anyone to follow his example, for it was a great pity that the fellow should have drawn any profit from his conduct.
>
> (813)

103. See Mary F. Wack, "The Measure of Pleasure: Peter of Spain on Men, Women, and Lovesickness," *Viator* 17 (1986): 173.

Dioneo has no sympathy for Walter, who is described by his own subjects as a "cruel tyrant" (819) and as "'a cruel and bestial tyrant'"
(823).[104] Walter's tyrannical tendencies are actually signaled by the very
first sentence of the storytelling proper, which states that he "spent the
whole of his time hunting and hawking, and never even thought about
raising a family, which says a great deal for his intelligence" (813). Walter, in short, strives "moore for delit than world to multiplye"
(VII.3345); the comparison with Chauntecleer is appropriate since, in
Dioneo's view, Walter's behavior amounts to "matta bestialità," a thorough confusion of the rational and the animal. This pursuit of personal
pleasure at the expense of "comune profyt" identifies Walter quite
clearly, for a late medieval audience, as a tyrant: "for the tyrant strives
for a pleasurable [*delectabile*] good, whereas a true king strives for an
honorable one . . . for the tyrant, in that he despises the common good,
cares for nothing but his own pleasures." These precepts are taken from
Aegidius Romanus, *De Regimine Principum,* a text that circulated
widely in both Latin and French; their sentiments are echoed in Nicholas Oresme's *Livre de Politiques,* written for King Charles V of France
in the 1370s.[105] Oresme argues that "anyone who governs for his own
benefit and against the common good, whether alone or in a group,
can be called a tyrant."[106] For Aegidius and Oresme, as for Aquinas and
Brunetto Latini, the fate of the *bonum commune* remains the key issue.[107] Aquinas noted that a king becomes tyrannical in governing "for
his own good, and not for the good of his subjects." And Henry Bracton, the thirteenth-century legal commentator, maintains that a ruler so
guided by arbitrary will (*voluntas*) is no longer a king: "for there is no

---

104. McWilliam's translations of the phrases "crudele uomo" (10.10.39) and "'crudele
e iniquio e bestiale'" (10.10.61) are accurate because the epithet "cruel" was routinely
applied to tyrants: see J. D. Burnley, *Chaucer's Language and the Philosophers' Tradition*
(Cambridge, Eng.: D. S. Brewer, 1979), esp. 29–43; Susan M. Babbitt, *Oresme's "Livre de
Politiques" and the France of Charles V* (Philadelphia: American Philosophical Society,
1985), 80–81.

105. Excerpts from *De Regimine* translated from Latin text as quoted in Schlauch,
"Chaucer's Doctrine," 139 (my translation). Aegidius notes that the unbridled pursuit of
*delectabilia* may induce a tyrant to violate a subject's rights by violating his wife or daughter (140).

106. Babbitt, *Oresme,* 81. Babbitt translates here from Oresme's gloss to Aristotle,
*Politics* 2.22.

107. See Schlauch, "Chaucer's Doctrine," 137–140; Skinner, *Foundations,* 44–48; Babbitt, *Oresme,* 69–97. For the importance of the *bonum commune* to fourteenth-century
English writers, see Anne Middleton, "The Idea of Public Poetry in the Reign of Richard
II," *Speculum* 53 (1978): 94–101; Carol Falvo Heffernan, "Tyranny and *Commune Profit* in
the *Clerk's Tale*," *Chaucer Review* 17 (1983): 332–40.

king where will [*voluntas*], not law, holds sway."[108] Such a conflict between the law of the land and kingly will and pleasure, subjected to detailed analysis in late medieval writings on tyranny, was to be played out most dramatically in the final years of Richard II.[109]

Once Dioneo's story has run its course, Panfilo, Boccaccio's tenth and final monarch, feels obliged to renounce his own power and to propose the dissolution of the *brigata*. In doing this, however, he is moved to commend the company for their disciplined maintenance of social order: "from what I have seen and heard, it seems to me that our proceedings have been marked by a constant sense of propriety, an unfailing spirit of harmony, and a continual feeling of brotherly and sisterly amity. All of which pleases me greatly, as it surely redounds to our communal honor and credit" (825). Such concern for the common good requires a sacrifice of selfish interests. The depressing circumstances of the plague license an exceptional indulgence in singing, dancing, feasting, and storytelling—anything within reason that will nurture cheerfulness and keep terror at bay.[110] Such strong medicine may, of course, "encourage unseemly behavior among those who are feeble of mind" (825); but as the king has observed, nobody has betrayed the *brigata* by following selfish impulses. Such vigilant concern for the integrity of the *brigata* suggests that this temporary institution represents more than a convenient framework within which to wait out the plague. It represents, rather, an active response to the moral, social, and political collapse of Florence: the communal spirit must be kept alive outside the city walls until the city is once more healthy enough to support its growth.[111]

The effect of the Black Death on Florence is rather like the effect of tyranny on any city: it is a disease that runs out of control, feverishly devouring the body politic. Such an association between plague and tyranny is at least as old as the *Oedipus Rex* of Sophocles. In *Paradiso* 19.115–32 Dante denounces European princes, whose selfishness, vio-

---

108. Translated from Schlauch, "Chaucer's Doctrine," 137, 136.

109. See Michael Wilks, "Chaucer and the Mystical Marriage in Medieval Political Thought," *Bulletin of the John Rylands Library* (Manchester, England) 44 (1962): 571, for references to John of Salisbury, Aquinas, Bracton, and Ockham.

110. See Olson, *Literature as Recreation*, 165–83.

111. Bruneto Latini, in discussing Aristotle's views of city government, emphasizes at the outset that "if each man follows his own individual will, the government of men's lives is destroyed and totally dissolved" (*Trésor*, ed. Carmody, 223; translated by Skinner, *Foundations*, 44).

lence, and tyranny spells out (in acrostic form) "LUE": pestilence. Similar associations are relied upon in the prescription Aquinas writes for the Christian subject afflicted by tyranny: "sin must therefore be done away with so that the plague of tyrants may cease."[112] This course of treatment is followed most faithfully by Griselde, who cultivates an inner purity that finally outlasts the torments with which Walter plagues her. Boccaccio's Griselde is the faithful and enduring Christian subject, and while Walter is not to be compared to God, he might be seen as God's agent. He might, as a tyrant, be compared to the Black Death.

The plague of 1348 must have reminded Boccaccio of an earlier phase of that "decade of disaster": the tyrannical regime of the Duke of Athens.[113] This duke, proclaimed *signore* of Florence for life in September 1342, was driven out of Florence by a united effort of all social classes in July 1343. It is particularly fitting that the *Decameron* should close with the defeat of Walter's tyranny since (Boccaccio's fellow Florentines would recall) the Duke of Athens was also a Walter (Gualtieri)—Walter of Brienne. The defeat of tyranny, like the cessation of plague, signals a return to Florence—a return to those liberties that Griselde and the Boccaccian *brigata* have endeavored to keep alive.

## VI

My argument does not assume that Chaucer knew the Boccaccian Griselde story, although it is quite possible that he did. I am suggesting, however, that the political dimensions of Boccaccio's *novella*, its embeddedness in contemporary ideological debate, do have an important bearing on our reading of the *Clerk's Tale*. Petrarch's translation certainly tends to conceal the historical character of Boccaccio's story. Griselde is classicized, mythologized, and moralized as an exemplum of obedience to God: Petrarch's readers are advised to "submit themselves to God with the same courage as did this woman to her husband" (138). This implied analogy between Walter and God can be taken seriously in Petrarch's text because Walter's tyrannical proclivities are played down or passed over without comment. But Petrarch's Latin cannot entirely erase the historicity of Boccaccio's Italian text: signs of contra-

112. "Tollenda est igitur culpa, ut cesset a tyrannorum plaga"; cited by Schlauch, "Chaucer's Doctrine," 138. For a more extensive extract from this passage of *De Regimine Principum*, book I, see *The Political Ideas of Thomas Aquinas*, ed. Dino Bigongiari (New York: Hafner, 1953), 192.
113. Gene A. Brucker, *Florentine Politics and Society 1343–1378* (Princeton: Princeton University Press, 1962), 3. Brucker is referring to the period 1338–48.

diction bubble to the surface when Petrarch's story is subjected to a historical reading. Chaucer, I am suggesting, was excellently qualified as a historical reader of Petrarch through his experience of Florence and Milan, his participation in political events in England, and his evident familiarity with the metaphors, tropes, and general rhetoric of ideological debate. Contradictions detected in the Petrarchan story are not just smoothed away but are critiqued or carried over into English and made part of the meaning of the Chaucerian *Tale*.

Part of Chaucer's meaning in translating Petrarch is that there can be no final translation. Despite the studied casualness with which he announces his own translating, Petrarch evidently sees his own work as a literary and historical terminus: future translation is obviated by a text that is good for all times and all places. Chaucer, I am arguing, sees the Petrarchan text as a response to a particular historical and political moment. As that moment recedes Chaucer needs to translate Petrarch into his own cultural present. Chaucer, unlike Petrarch, does not see his own narration as a unitary moment that can save itself from past and future translations. Once the Clerk's voice falls silent it will be supplanted by other voices that contest his individual pronouncements on politics, religion, and marriage and hence place them within the larger interpretive framework of the Canterbury pilgrimage. But even as the Clerk speaks we hear ghostly voices from earlier versions of the story: Boccaccio's politics reverberate within Petrarch's dehistoricized spirituality; Petrarch's unworldly allegorization struggles with the domestic exemplarism of the French tradition. Chaucer's Clerk tells a very crowded *Tale*. The Petrarchan Griselde occupies a classicized, perpetual present that displaces past and future and so exempts itself from historical contingency: Chaucer's text questions the very possibility of occupying a "present" moment in its own narrating. Chaucer's translation restores Griselde to the movement of history.

Petrarch begins *Seniles* 17.3 with *inventio*, a detailed account of how he came across the Griselde story. The effect here is extremely odd, since Petrarch evidently wishes to distance himself from Boccaccio's *novella* even as he appropriates it. Petrarch recoils from the circumambient pressure of historical events, yet he cannot allow Boccaccio's Italian to make any serious claim on his attention:

> Your book, written in our mother tongue [*nostro materno eloquio*] and published I presume, during your early years, has fallen into my hands, I know not whence or how. If I told you that I had read it, I should deceive you. It is a very big volume, written in prose and for the multi-

tude [*ad vulgus et soluta scriptus oratione*]. I have been, moreover, occupied with serious business, and much pressed for time. You can easily
imagine the unrest caused by the warlike stir about me, for, far as I have
been from actual participation in the disturbances, I could not but be
affected by the critical condition of the state. What I did was to run
through your book, like a traveller who, while hastening forward, looks
about him here and there, without pausing.

(137)

Boccaccio's book merges here with the busy, vulgar world that Petrarch
can attend to only intermittently and distractedly. Petrarch's expert eye
rests long enough on Boccaccio's text, however, to identify the one
portion that merits isolation, translation, and the promise of a greater,
less localized audience. Petrarch draws attention here to his exceptional
insight, his ability to see through the plain clothes of Boccaccio's text
to the naked beauty beneath. This beauty will be made visible to others
by the rhetorical garments in which Petrarch will dress it.

This characterization of humanist vision, which sees the naked
beauty of a woman beneath whatever rudiments of style an author has
laid upon her, had been developed in detail many years before in a letter
Petrarch wrote in Milan to a friend in Florence:

> Your letter, written in haste and on the spur of the moment, was
> nevertheless pleasing to my eyes and mind, indeed even more so; its
> appearance was that of a rather disheveled woman to her eager lover. I
> sighed, saying, "What would this have been had it seen itself in the mir-
> ror!" It bore witness to its hasty stuffing into an everyday dress and to
> its command to come to me in that fashion, as you were rising from
> dinner with Ceres and Bacchus struggling within you, to use your joking
> phrase. Yet its style revealed a sober and fasting author: nothing could
> be more modest or abrupt; the seriousness of the ideas was suitable for
> the occasion, the tone of the words sweet and tender. It behooved many
> women caught unawares to make use of shame, a trembling voice, un-
> combed hair, ungirt breasts, bare feet, and casual dress; often a casual
> simplicity has been preferred to fancy dress. Thus did the disheveled
> Cleopatra sway the imperial firmness of Caesar's spirit.[114]

Here, once again, a Petrarchan discussion of reading and textuality sees
the strangest confusion of the erotic, the rhetorical, the authoritarian,
and the violent: the Petrarchan eye sees into everything; a male author
rises drunkenly from the table, brings a disheveled woman into existence, and is pronounced "sober"; a female body is stuffed into a dress,
commanded, dispatched, and then scrutinized by a man who gazes like
"her eager lover"; and the persuasive power exerted by such surprised,

---

114. See *Fam.* 18.7, addressed to Francesco Nelli and dated 1 April 1355.

half-naked women over masculine rulers is duly noted. Such Petrarchan passages are especially unsettling because they slip or drift between the metaphorical and the historical, between figures of speech and the experience of actual women. The final part of this passage does, apparently, move more decisively into history: the example of Cleopatra and Caesar is followed by that of Phaedra and Hippolytus, Sophonisba and Masinissa, Lucretia and Sextus Tarquinius. Griselde and Walter may obviously be added to this list. And yet the historical couples of *Familiares* 18.7 are bracketed within the limits of *comparatio*, existing only as parts of an extended rhetorical figure: what Petrarch is really talking about is his reading of the letter to which he is currently writing a reply. Similar uncertainties have (at some level) unsettled most readers of *Seniles* 17.3 and the tale Chaucer made from this "rhetorike sweete." Is Griselde rhetorical or real? Does her suffering have any historical basis or is it just pointing at something else?[115]

Petrarch's emphatic representation of the powers of his own eye finds an obvious equivalent within the *Seniles* story as Walter gazes upon Griselde. This scene, developed from a casual phrase in Boccaccio, is faithfully preserved in Chaucer's account:

> Upon Grisilde, this povre creature,
> Ful ofte sithe this markys sette his ye
> As he on huntyng rood paraventure;
> And whan it fil that he myghte hire espye,
> He noght with wantown lookyng of folye
> His eyen caste on hire, but in sad wyse
> Upon hir chiere he wolde hym ofte avyse,
>
> Commendynge in his herte hir wommanhede,
> And eek hir vertu, passynge any wight
> Of so yong age, as wel in chiere as dede.
> For thogh the peple have no greet insight
> In vertu, he considered ful right
> Hir bountee, and disposed that he wolde
> Wedde hire oonly, if evere he wedde sholde.
>
> (232–45)

Walter's steady and deliberate gaze ("sette his ye") aligns and crosses between two carefully articulated social spaces: court space (extended

---

115. The two readings that Petrarch appends to his tale answer such questions in precisely opposite ways. The friend from Padua is so moved by tears of compassion that he cannot continue reading. The friend from Verona refuses to weep a single tear because he believes "'that this is all an invention.'" Petrarch himself, not uncharacteristically, refuses to accept responsibility for the tale's fictional or historical status: readers wishing to know whether all this is "a history or a story" (*an historiam an fabulam*) will be referred to the author, Boccaccio.

through "huntyng"—Walter gazes down from the saddle) and village space.[116] Walter's superior "insight" detects in Griselde a "vertu" that remains hidden to "the peple." Walter decides to appropriate such "vertu" by drawing it into his own immediate sphere. He has a dress and "other aornementes" made, estimating Griselde's physical dimensions from a girl of similar "stature" (253–59). He then rides to the village, secures Griselde's total obedience in thought, word, and deed, and then has her stripped of her old clothes. The effect of Griselde's new, court-manufactured clothes causes a public sensation:

> Unnethe the peple hir knew for hire fairnesse
> Whan she translated was in swich richesse.
>
> (384–85)

Chaucer's use of the verb *translaten* here emphasizes Walter's power as both ruler and rhetor. As a ruler he is empowered to move Griselde across territorial boundaries. The means by which he demonstrates the exercise of this power are rhetorical: he first invents—comes across—Griselde, then reads her, and finally lays upon her the ornate clothes that make the excellence of his reading visible. This procedure is, of course, analogous to Petrarch's translation of Boccaccio's vernacular text into the *ornatus difficilis* of humanist Latin. Both Walter and Petrarch, who gaze with a court-trained eye, know that village or vernacular virtue is blind to itself. Such virtue can only be made visible if it is translated to court space in court language. Village or vernacular virtue achieves meaningful social existence only when gilded by the transforming power of the poet-potentate.

Such affinities of *modus operandi* perhaps help explain why Petrarch was so assiduously (and successfully) courted by Italian despots. They return us to Boccaccio's theorizing, in his *Trattatello in laude di Dante*, of the function of poets within the first despotic regimes: both poets and princes hold the populace spellbound through their use of ornament. The source of such spellbinding, as Boccaccio explains, lies in religion, specifically in the symbols and sentiments of religion that

116. John of Salisbury argues that in nurturing wild beasts for hunting the lordly hunter deprives "farmers of their fields of grain, tenants of their allotments, the herds and flocks of their pasturage." John notes that some hunters "inspired by this form of vanity have gone to such extremes of madness as to become enemies of nature [*hostes naturae*], forgetting their own condition and scorning divine judgment by subjecting God's image to exquisite torture" (John of Salisbury, *Policraticus,* trans. M. F. Markland [New York: Ungar, 1979], 6–7; Ioannis Saresberiensis, *Policraticus,* ed. C. C. I. Webb, 2 vols. [Oxford: Clarendon Press, 1909], 1:4.396 a-b).

poets and princes have annexed to their own spheres of influence. Religion, we have noted, plays no significant part in Boccaccio's Griselde story. But in Petrarch's translation it becomes (as it became in the political speeches Petrarch wrote for the Visconti) both powerfully intimidating and nebulously vague: a potent tool for tyranny. Walter is not God, but (as Griseldes, his political subjects) we would be well advised to treat him as if he were. We should all, says Petrarch, strive to be Griseldes (138)—an injunction that usefully distracts us from considering Petrarch as a Walter.

The cultural strategies of the Petrarchan Griselde story show signs of brittleness and inconsistency; they form their own internal and unconscious critique. Let us, for a moment, take Petrarch at his word. What would happen if we did strive to become Griseldes, and some of us succeeded? In Italian debate of the late fourteenth century the *signoria* justifies its own historical inevitability by pointing to the factious, unruly, and disobedient character of the body politic. Citizens cannot rule themselves and so the despot steps in to rule them. Despotism exists to enforce obedience. But what happens when a despot confronts a subject who is utterly obedient? Such a subject undermines despotic self-justification; this is why Griselde unhinges Walter. Fortunately for Walter, however, nobody can see Griselde's singular qualities (except Petrarch, who describes them before Walter gets to the village) without his mediation, dressing, and translating. Once Griselde is relocated within Walter's court structure Walter can explore the limits of her obedience at his leisure, as his *delectabilia* dictates. If Griselde breaks, Walter can relax and be generous: no subject is perfect; despotism recovers its ideological self-justification. But Griselde does not break, and this, for despotism, is scandalous. Fortunately, however, Walter is able to reincorporate Griselde into his political structure by taking her back into marriage. And this is, indeed, a formidable alliance: despotic power is wedded to natural virtue through the force of its own exceptional vision.

Just how sensitive is Chaucer to this complex of humanistic vision, religious mystification, and tyrannic power? I would like to conclude my discussion of the *Clerk's Tale* by proposing five ways in which it might be read as an explicit critique of its Petrarchan source.[117] First,

---

117. For a detailed comparison of Chaucer's *Tale* and the Petrarchan source, see Severs, *Literary Relationships*, 215–48, and the works cited in John Leyerle and Anne Quick, *Chaucer: A Bibliographical Introduction* (Toronto: University of Toronto Press, 1986), 158–60. Derek Pearsall remarks on Chaucer's exceptional fidelity to Petrarch's Latin (*The Can-

and fundamentally, Chaucer reverses the direction of Petrarch's literary translating. Although he locates the discovery of his source text at the very center of the Petrarchan Academy—the Clerk learned it from Petrarch in Padua—Chaucer chooses to restore this text to the vernacular. All the mysteries that Petrarch's Latinity conceals are laid open for general inspection.[118] Specific attention is drawn to this policy of removing obstacles that stand between the story and the common reader. The Host requests the Clerk to save his *ornatus difficilis* until he needs to impress the king at court:

> "Youre termes, youre colours, and youre figures,
> Keepe hem in stoor til so be ye endite
> Heigh style, as whan that men to kynges write.
> Speketh so pleyn at this tyme, we yow preye,
> That we may understonde what ye seye."
>
> (16–20)

The Clerk immediately declares himself obedient to the Host's temporary authority ("Ye han of us as now the governance") and applies himself to his chosen "tale" (56). Before he can get to Petrarch's "tale," however, he must cut a path through Petrarch's "heigh style" preface. Those high hills and mountains, which form "the boundes of West Lumbardye," function like a cultural frontier that none but the gifted Latinist may cross. Chaucer's Clerk has no use for them:

> And trewely, as to my juggement,
> Me thynketh it a thyng impertinent,
> Save that he wole conveyen his mateere;
> But this his tale, which that ye may heere.
>
> (53–56)

The fact that the Clerk actually translates much of Petrarch's geography (44–51) before questioning its relevance (52–55) focuses attention upon the business of critiquing Petrarch: we see what deserves cutting before

---

terbury Tales [London: Unwin, 1985], 265–66). This certainly makes Chaucer's infidelities easier to spot.

My proposal that the *Clerk's Tale* forms a critique of Petrarch and Italian humanism parallels Renate Haas's reading of the *Monk's Tale*. The Monk, who acknowledges Petrarch as "my maister" (VII.2325), takes great pride in introducing the humanist-revived genre of tragedy to England, a cultural innovation that enjoys little success among the Canterbury pilgrims. See Haas, "Chaucers Tragödienkonzept im Europäischen Rahmen," in *Zusammenhänge,* ed. Fichte, 451–65.

118. On the importance of the Clerk's *sermo humilis,* see Robin Kirkpatrick, "The Griselde Story in Boccaccio, Petrarch and Chaucer," in *Chaucer and the Italian Trecento,* ed. Boitani, 246–48.

the cut is signaled. This suggests, as we approach Petrarch's "tale," that the translation to come will be actively critical rather than passively faithful.

Chaucer's Clerk is translating a tale whose most dramatic events are enacted across a threshold of translation. Chaucer's use of the verb *translaten* to describe Griselde's movement from village to court attire deserves some pondering. The Chaucerian use of *translaten* and *translation* generally refers to movement between languages. The one exception, besides that of the *Clerk's Tale*, comes in the *Boece*, where it refers to the movement of money.[119] Translation in Chaucer is a term that is customarily hedged with nervous qualifications: it is an activity that calls for some sort of apology or explanation.[120] Most complete manuscripts of *The Canterbury Tales* end with a Retraction, in which Chaucer abjures "my translaciouns and enditynges of worldly vanitees." Subsequently, however, "the translacioun of Boece de Consolacione, and othere bookes of legendes of seintes, and omelies, and moralitee, and devocioun" (X.1084–87) are pulled out of the fire. It is not clear whether the *Clerk's Tale* is to be numbered with these works or with "the tales of Canterbury, thilke that sownen into synne." Every translation contains a trace of impurity because no translator can guarantee a perfect transfer between languages: nobody, that is, except Christ, the "perfect translator of God's will to man."[121] Perhaps this is why Griselde puts down a signifier that points us to Christ at the very threshold (Chaucer insists on the term by repeating it) that divides her from Walter:

> And as she wolde over hir thresshfold gon,
> The markys cam and gan hire for to calle;
> And she set doun hir water pot anon,
> Biside the thresshfold, in an oxes stalle.
>
> (288–91)[122]

The Incarnation sees the translation to the world of Christ, the unique and perfect sign whose signified is the Father. No gap divides the Father from the Son: they are consubstantial and without difference.[123]

119. See *Boece*, 2, pr. 5, 21.

120. See *The Legend of Good Women*, (F) 324, 329, 370, 425, (G) 341; *Astrolabe*, intro. 63. The Second Nun defines her "translacioun" as "feithful bisynesse" (VIII.24–25).

121. Eugene Vance, *Mervelous Signals: Poetics and Sign Theory in the Middle Ages* (Lincoln: University of Nebraska Press, 1986), 316.

122. See James I. Wimsatt, "The Blessed Virgin and the Two Coronations of Griselde," *Mediaevalia* 6 (1980): 188–92.

123. See Vance, *Mervelous Signals*, x.

Chaucer's allusion to the Incarnation here (an addition to Petrarch's text) emphasizes the imperfection of the translation that Walter is about to make across the threshold that divides him from Griselde. We recall that the dress and ornaments that represent this translation cannot fit Griselde exactly or perfectly: they are transferred from the lineaments of another woman (256–57). All "heigh style" language has, of course, this property of transferability: the tropes and figures that praise one king can easily be turned to the praise of another.

Griselde fascinates Walter because no gap shows between her public face and her private feelings: she is "ay oon in herte and in visage" (711). This gap between face and feelings, which is observed in Walter throughout his testing of Griselde, is of course a defining feature of life at court.[124] The innocent who fails to perceive the rhetoricity of court behavior lays herself open to deception and betrayal. We may recall here, by way of example, the young falcon in the *Squire's Tale,* who is betrayed by a tercelet who "dyed his colors" (511) so skillfully that she mistook them for nature.[125] Griselde suffers a similar ordeal of rhetorical betrayal, an ordeal she survives without once indicating that she is speaking or behaving rhetorically herself. Her face agrees with her thoughts and feelings; she is as "constant as a wall" (1047). Is Griselde unrhetorical? Is she made of stone? Once her ordeal is terminated Griselde drops to the ground. Her public face falls with her and some time elapses before she "caught agayn hire contenaunce" (1110). It seems, after all, that Griselde contains a world of private feeling, an individuality, that Walter, operating through the methods and assumptions of a courtly rhetor, cannot comprehend or take possession of. Walter's experience here of his own imprisonment within the confines of artificial language parallels that of the early part of the *Vita nuova* as Dante struggles to realize his love for Beatrice through the tired tropes and mechanical formulae of conventional love poetry (7–16). Eventually, from within a circle of women, Dante learns how to praise (rather than invent) Beatrice. A marvelous period of poetic creativity follows, in which Dante sees that Beatrice is possessed of an individuality too brilliant to be looked on (20–27). Beatrice then surprises Dante once again (she dies) and everything again changes (27–42). Dante knows that he

124. See IV.512–15, 671–72, 892–93, 1030–31.
125. See V.558–61. This account of treachery through courtly rhetoric is offered by a young Squire who is himself betrayed by the complexities of rhetorical art.

cannot "have" Beatrice in any language; and Walter can never "have" Griselde.

For Petrarch, we have noted, the fact that Boccaccio's text is written "in our mother tongue" ("nostro materno eloquio") can only diminish its power. Chaucer reverses the direction of Petrarch's translating because, as I have argued elsewhere, he shares Dante's profound conviction that the vernacular is uniquely adequate to human experience.[126] True enough, Dante feels compelled, in the pit of hell, to renounce the language learned at the breast in favor of a more artificial form of expression:

> for it is not a task to take in jest
> to show the base of all the universe—
> nor for a tongue that cries out, "mama," "papa."[127]

As soon as he returns to the light, however, Dante resolves to put such "dead poetry" ("morta poesia") behind him.[128] The last two *cantiche* see a return to the "lingua materna," the mother tongue that must somehow serve Dante for his ultimate vision:

> What little I recall is to be told,
> from this point on, in words more weak than those
> of one whose infant tongue still bathes at the breast.
>                                   (*Par.*33.106–8)

The tongue learned at the breast must prove weak in the face of eternity, although, Dante notes in his *Convivio,* it was the exercise of such a *lingua materna* that brought his mother and father together and hence brought him into being.[129] Dante opens *De vulgari eloquentia,* his treatise on the vernacular, by defining the vernacular as "that language which infants learn from those around them, when they first begin to articulate sounds; or, more briefly, that which we acquire by imitating

126. See David Wallace, "Chaucer's Continental Inheritance: The Early Poems and *Troilus and Criseyde*," in *The Cambridge Chaucer Companion,* ed. Piero Boitani and Jill Mann (Cambridge, Eng.: Cambridge University Press, 1986), 33–34; Wallace, *Chaucer and the Early Writings of Boccaccio* (Cambridge, Eng.: D. S. Brewer, 1985), 15, 103–4, 137–40.

127. *Inferno* 32.7–9 in the translation of Allen Mandelbaum. All translations from the *Commedia* follow *The Divine Comedy of Dante Alighieri,* trans. Mandelbaum, 3 vols. (New York: Bantam, 1982–86).

128. *Purgatorio* 1.7.

129. See *Convivio* 1.13.4 in the edition of G. Busnelli and G. Vandelli, 2 vols. (Florence: Le Monnier, 1934–54).

our nurses without needing any rule."[130] We later learn a secondary, artificial language "which the Romans called *grammatica.*" Of these two the vernacular is the nobler language: "nobilior est vulgaris." This nobler language, the mother tongue, structures the primary linguistic community that Griselde governs. Griselde is "fair of eloquence": the people who "hire loved that looked on hire face" are happy to accept this as something "hevene sente" (410–13, 440). Walter, of course, cannot accept this. In estranging Griselde from her own children Walter is violating that primary linguistic community. By doing this he hopes to crack Griselde's "eloquence" and discover the "Griselde" within. The utter failure of this enterprise is followed by the reunion of Griselde and her children with Walter. This new linguistic community, which marries the natural virtues of the mother tongue to the artificial skills of the courtly rhetor, promises to generate an ideal language, an illustrious vernacular that will prove uniquely capable of serving the common good.[131]

Chaucer's second critique of Petrarch is coupled with the first: for as he restores the narrative to the vernacular, the language of the commons, he also restores the commons to the narrative. The English poet shows an interest in the details and mechanisms of politics and government that goes way beyond his sources. This is evident from the first as the people try to divert Walter from "his lust present" to his responsibilities in securing the future: without this intervention there would be no Griselde story, just pages of hawking and hunting. The commons, who seem every bit as nervous as the mice in Langland's Westminster, work through a representative Speaker, who begins by appealing to Walter's "humanitee" (92). This term, a unique Chaucerian usage, translates Petrarch's *humanitas* and brings with it some of the doubleness of the Petrarchan usage: the ruler is linked to his subjects by a common humanity, but is also divided from them by a more authentic understanding of what humanity is. This tension of affinity and difference is felt throughout this first political exchange between Walter and his subjects, particularly in their conflicting presuppositions about the origins of power. The people presume upon their right to initiate an affair of state (Walter must marry) but they presume too far in offering to choose a bride. Walter rebukes them for this second presumption,

---

130. *De vulgari eloquentia* 1.1.2 in the edition of P. V. Mengaldo, in Dante Alighieri, *Opere Minori,* ed. Mengaldo et al. (Milan-Naples: Ricciardi, 1979).

131. The reunion of Griselde and Walter, in other words, forms the core of the linguistic community ideally envisaged by Dante's *De vulgari.*

claiming that the right to make his own choice (in this as in all else)
descends upon him from God:

> "I truste in Goddes bountee, and therfore
> My mariage and myn estaat and reste
> I hym bitake; he may doon as hym leste."
> (159–61)

Does Chaucer's text mount any challenge to this descending model of
authority? Walter, we have noted, lives "in delit" (68). But so does Griselde:

> Noght fer fro thilke paleys honurable,
> Wher as this markys shoop his mariage,
> There stood a throop, of site delitable.
> (197–99)

The "delit" that Griselde lives in is that of an austere and time-honored
simplicity. This is the "blisful lyf, a paisible and a swete" of Chaucer's
"Former Age," a simple life that preceded the rapacity of "tyraunts" and
the building of "paleis-chambres."[132] The tranquility of this "Etas
Prima" was ruined by ambitious tyrants such as Nimrod, who, being
"desirous / to regne" (58–59), precipitated the fall of Babel and the
confusion of tongues:

> Allas, allas, now may men wepe and crye!
> For in oure dayes nis but covetyse,
> Doublenesse, and tresoun, and envye,
> Poyson, manslawhtre, and mordre in sondry wyse.
> (60–63)[133]

Griselde's life of moral, economic, and dietary simplicity evidently
has a longer pedigree than Walter's life at the palace, with its "houses
of office stuffed with plentee" (264). Walter's invasion of village space
recalls the original, ruinous disruption to the life of "the peples in the
former age" (2); his courtly rhetoric, structured on "doubleness," is an
instrument of torture for Griselde as it is for many "men . . . in oure
dayes" (60–61). Walter employs such rhetorical doubleness most skillfully in dividing Griselde from his (her) subjects. The commons recognizes that Griselde is concerned with its collective interests, "the
commune profit" (431). But Walter informs Griselde that the commons

132. See "The Former Age," lines 1, 33, 41 (*Riverside Chaucer,* 650–51).
133. For Nimrod as tyrant, see Michael Wilks, *The Problem of Sovereignty in the Later
Middle Ages* (Cambridge, Eng.: Cambridge University Press, 1963), 540. See also *Inferno*
31.34–81.

have turned against her: they complain, says Walter, that "the blood of Janicle" will succeed to power (634); they constrain him to take another wife (800). Walter must take such words seriously; he is not free to behave like a commoner:

> "Swich wordes seith my peple, out of drede.
> Wel oughte I of swich murmur taken heede,
> For certeinly I drede swich sentence,
> Though they nat pleyn speke in myn audience."
> (634–37)

> "I may nat doon as every plowman may."
> (799)

Walter pretends to respect, to be constrained by, an ascending model of power; but this is, of course, a fiction, an invention to legitimize his own perverse designs. Not only, then, does Walter invent, appropriate, Griselde; he also invents the people by speaking for them a fiction of his own devising. The commons are roundly condemned for their fickleness within Chaucer's text; but this critique is voiced by another part of the same social body across a line of rupture drawn by the tyrannical Walter himself. The people criticize the people since Walter stands beyond open criticism:

> O stormy peple! unsad and evere untrewe!
> Ay indiscreet and chaungynge as a vane!
> Delitynge evere in rumbul that is newe.
> (995–97)

The commons is not sentimentalized in the *Clerk's Tale*, but it is concretely realized as a political force that can initiate political policy and then keep a watchful and critical eye on its execution. It is powerful enough to warrant impersonation by the despot. In restoring the commons to Petrarch's narrative Chaucer was perhaps mindful of the impressive organizational abilities that enabled the 1381 marchers to confront the king in London; and he may have recalled the efforts of the House of Commons to curb the king's tyrannical tendencies. Chaucer's commoners may not be pretty but they can exert a beneficial social influence. The common birds in *The Parliament of Fowls* justly question the naturalness of aristocratic sexual practice (or non-practice); and the *Physician's Tale* suggests that an aristocracy might save itself from tyranny (and from its own worst fatalistic and self-destructive tendencies) by counting upon the sound instincts of "the peple" at moments of social crisis. No such suggestion is to be found in Petrarch.

Thirdly, having restored the commons to the body politic, Chaucer restores the female body to itself. Griselde's suffering begins when she becomes the object of the tyrannical gaze: but self-realization begins here too since, as Sartre observes, to realize that you are being looked at is to realize yourself.[134] It follows that Walter's perceptions, Walter's gazing out into the world, must remain scattered throughout the world: there is nobody who can look out at him and tell him who he is. This, then, is the tragedy of the tyrannic gaze: that it cannot be met. Through his perpetual gaze at the Other-as-object the tyrant (and the tyrannic humanist) excludes himself from the possibility of human community.

Griselde contains the effects of Walter's gaze, and later of his acts, within herself; she never gratifies tyranny by becoming a spectacle of its own effects. Petrarch's Valterius gazes wonderingly ("admirans") at Griselde's constancy as he robs her of her second child. In Chaucer, however, the gaze drops as Griselde finishes speaking:

> "Deth may noght make no comparisoun
> Unto youre love." And whan this markys say
> The constance of his wyf, he caste adoun
> His eyen two.
>
> (666–69)

"Constance" means more of the same, the same as before. Walter sees this when he gazes at Griselde; and yet this sight, something he has seen all along, suddenly becomes unbearable. Perhaps he has seen, in Griselde's "constance," a mystery that he cannot fathom or possess; or perhaps he cannot countenance any visual sign of his own "senseless brutality." Walter, as he casts down his eyes, does not know what he has seen.

Valterius adheres quite closely to Petrarch's own prescription for a happy marriage: find a devoted, good-hearted girl from far away who will wish to see, hear, and think of you alone and so be transformed into your image.[135] *Familiares* 22.1, addressed to a single man, recognizes no autonomous significance in female thought and feeling; and neither does Petrarch's *Seniles* story. The mental and bodily hurts of the Petrarchan Griselde apparently vanish into thin air; but in Chaucer they

---

134. Jean-Paul Sartre, *Being and Nothingness,* trans. Hazel E. Barnes (New York: Washington Square Press, 1966), 340–400, esp. 352, 384. But see also Jacques Lacan, "Of the Gaze as *Objet Petit a,*" in *The Four Fundamental Concepts of Psycho-Analysis,* ed. J-A. Miller, trans. Alan Sheridan (New York: Norton, 1978), 74–77.

135. See *Familiares* 22.1 (and p. 182 above).

achieve powerful physical discharge just as soon as tyranny admits to final defeat. Griselde locks her own children back into herself in a fierce and passionate moment of physical reintegration (1079–1101). Although enacted publicly, and at court, this is a wholly private moment from which (as Griselde swoons) Walter is hopelessly excluded. The next narrative moment, in which Griselde's children are drawn from her body with great care and difficulty (1102–3), has all the physical intensity of childbirth. The release or rebirth of these children signals the final expiration of the masculine fantasy (as old as *Genesis*) that a man might mother or "bring forth" his own children without female participation.

Chaucer's fourth critique of Petrarch is formed by putting this Petrarchan narrative into the mouth of a logician. The essential opposition between the Oxford logician and Petrarch the rhetor is initially obscured by the fact of kinship beneath a religious dress: each is described as a "worthy clerk" (IV.21, 27). But no logician, especially one bred on "Aristotle and his philosophie" (I.295), could happily tolerate the slippages of meaning that characterize Petrarchan rhetoric. In the winter of 1365–66 Petrarch learned that a group of Aristotelians at Venice had concluded that he was a good man but an illiterate ignoramus.[136] Petrarch responded in 1367 with *De sui ipsius et multorum ignorantia,* a treatise that characterizes current speculative philosophy as "petty, arid, pedantic, an endless exercise in dialectic punctuated by absurd and boring genuflections to a quasi-divinized Aristotle."[137] It seems, then, that in giving the Griselde story to an emaciated Aristotelian, Chaucer is enjoying an academic joke at Petrarch's expense. There is one member of the Canterbury pilgrimage who bears all the hallmarks of a rhetor: the Wife of Bath.[138] The Wife is, in some sense, the author (or grandmother) of the *Clerk's Tale:* she spurs the Clerk into narrating and makes a dramatic guest appearance in the last stanza of the story proper (1170–76). We should note that the Wife is not only the most rhetorical of pilgrims but also the most tyrannical in her headlong pursuit of *delectabilia.*

136. "Virum bonum, ydiotam ferunt"; "me sine litteris virum bonum." Quoted from the *De ignorantia* by Wilkins, *Later Years,* 92. For the Latin text, see *Opere Latine di Francesco Petrarca,* ed. Antonietta Bufano, 2 vols. (Turin: UTET, 1975), 2:1025–1151. For a convenient translation, see *The Renaissance Philosophy of Man,* ed. Ernst Cassirer et al. (Chicago: University of Chicago Press, 1948), 47–133.

137. Foster, *Petrarch,* 151 (summarizing from passages of *De ignorantia*).

138. See John A. Alford, "The Wife of Bath versus the Clerk of Oxford: What Their Rivalry Means," *Chaucer Review* 20 (1986): 108–32. See also Tzvetan Todorov, *Theories of the Symbol* (Ithaca: Cornell University Press, 1982), 74–77.

The fifth and final aspect of this Chaucerian critique concerns questions of framing and closure. The manifold ways in which the *Clerk's Tale* fails to enforce its own closure have been widely recognized. The final events reported by the narrative—the death of the peasant Janicula in court space and the assumption to power of his grandson—are fraught with political and ideological difficulties; these are simply not discussed. We then have successive attempts at equating the readership to the figures in the text. The narrator first takes his cue from "Petrak" and his "heigh stile" story (1147–48) in proposing that we are all (or should be) Griseldes. We should steel ourselves "ful ofte to be bete" by the "sharp scourges of adversitee" that God sends us "for oure exercise" (1142–62). But then it appears that Griseldes are women, although only two or three are to be found in each town (1163–69). Finally, in a song sung "for the Wyves love of Bathe" (1170), we surprisingly rediscover the original Petrarchan formula: we are all Griseldes (1177–1212). But this time the we (as in the Petrarchan Academy) is exclusively masculine: all wives are Walters, tyrants who torture our Griselde-like bodies. By now it is not clear whether this is Chaucer speaking or Chaucer's Clerk. But by now it has ceased to matter. What does matter is that these terminating contradictions and incoherencies are seen to issue from similar qualities within the tale itself and, by extension, from within its acknowledged Petrarchan source.

Although the letter of Chaucer's closing stanzas restates an allegiance to Petrarch, the tone and spirit of this closure is Boccaccian. Whereas Petrarch's Walter ends "happy in his wife and his offspring" (151), Boccaccio's Dioneo ends by wishing that Griselde "had found some other man to shake her skin-coat for her, earning herself a fine new dress in the process" (824).[139] This conjunction of sex and commerce is most powerfully embodied by the last person named in Chaucer's story, the Wife of Bath. In pointing us back to the Wife, the Clerk, we have noted, is recognizing the true source of his impulse to narrate. He is also directing us to an ironic gloss on his own narration, particularly to that tyrannico-humanist act of vision. The *Wife of Bath's Tale* opens with a comparable act of seeing and translating: a mounted knight sees a woman and rapes her. The remainder of the Wife's *Tale* traces the lengthy and difficult process, under female judicial governance, of un-

139. Joy Hambuechen Potter observes that with this "change of theme and register" Dioneo "blows the noble frame of the tenth day stories wide open" (*Five Frames for the "Decameron": Communication and Social Systems in the "Cornice"* [Princeton: Princeton University Press, 1982], 151).

doing or unwilling this tyrannical masculine act. The masculine weeping and wailing with which the *Clerk's Tale* closes is, for the Wife, the beginning of masculine wisdom.

Such "wepyng and waylyng" (1213) forms an immediate point of departure for the Merchant, another masculine Griselde who suffers the "passyng crueltee" of a wife. It is the *Merchant's Tale* that performs the most comprehensive critique of the *Clerk's Tale* and hence of its Petrarchan origins. The Merchant's opening line makes it clear that we have not yet left Lombardy: we have, to be precise, moved just ninety miles east-north-east, from Saluzzo to Pavia. His *Tale*'s opening sentence also informs us that we are to consider (once again) a man who "folwed ay his bodily delyt / On wommen." The narrative then plays out the familiar pattern: a tyrannical male sees a female body, commands it, takes possession of it. But here the determining act of vision, likened to a sighting in a mirror in a market place, is seen as one of blindness, not of insight: "For love is blynd alday, and may nat see" (1598). Here, as in the *Clerk's Tale,* such deliberate gazing at a female object is presented as the legitimate outcome of a consultative political process. But here that process, the consulting of Placebo and Justinus, is evidently a crude facade that covers a naked act of will.

John of Salisbury initiates his discussion of tyranny in his *Policraticus* by emphasizing the great dangers of flattery at court. The victory of Placebo over Justinus signals a failure of vision and an unwillingness to hear the truth:

> The flatterer is the enemy of all virtue and forms as it were a cataract over the eye of him whom he engages in conversation. He is the more to be avoided, as he never ceases harming under guise of friendship, until he has blinded keen vision and put out the modicum of light that seemed present. Added to this he stops up the ears of his listeners that they may not hear the truth. I hardly know of anything more disastrous than this.[140]

May is first seen in the *Merchant's Tale* as the familiar voiceless and (apparently) volitionless female object of masculine vision. But as the narrative progresses our perspective changes: we are invited to lie down on our backs with May in her marriage bed, gazing up at her tyrannizing spouse (1849–54). Later, of course, May discovers her voice and

---

140. John of Salisbury, *Policraticus,* ed. Markland, 35; ed. Webb, 3.4.481a.

January loses his vision. And when January recovers his eyesight (just as May is recovering her sexuality up a pear tree) a new interpretive order is established: men will see, but women will explain what men see.

What I am proposing, then, is that Chaucer's two tales of Lombard tyranny be considered as the kind of narrative sequence formed by the *Knight's Tale* and the *Miller's Tale*: the second tale, through judicious use of structural parallelism and grotesque realism, performs a humorous critique of the first. The somber, claustrophobic, courtly societies of Theseus and Walter yield to the cheerful, mobile market economies of Alisoun and May. It was, of course, a stroke of genius to locate two Lombard tyrannies within such a unified narrative sequence: tyranny cannot tolerate two tyrants any more than it can tolerate two Griseldes. But when Chaucer traveled to Lombardy in 1378 he discovered two tyrants: there was Bernabò Visconti (Petrarch's former patron) with whom Chaucer did business at Milan; and there was Bernabò's nephew and son-in-law, Gian Galeazzo Visconti, twenty miles south at Pavia.[141] This state of affairs could not last for long. Eventually it was January's townsman, the tyrant of Pavia, who won out against his "double allye" (VII.2403). Bernabò, once the "scourge of Lombardy," *flagellum Dei*, dies an obscure death that merits just one stanza from Chaucer's Monk. In Fragment IV of *The Canterbury Tales* one foolish Lombard tyrant succeeds another; and in Fragment VII the most famous Lombard tyrant of all just dribbles away through the cracks ("why ne how noot I") of narrative history:

> Off Melan grete Barnabo Viscounte,
> God of delit and scourge of Lumbardye,
> Why sholde I nat thyn infortune acounte,
> Sith in estaat thow cloumbe were so hye?
> Thy brother sone, that was thy double allye,
> For he thy nevew was and sone-in-lawe,
> Withinne his prisoun made thee to dye—
> But why ne how noot I that thou were slawe.
>
> (2399–2406)

---

141. Chaucer may have visited Pavia in 1378 for business, literary, and sentimental reasons; see W. E. Coleman, "Chaucer, the *Teseida* and the Visconti Library at Pavia: A Hypothesis," *Medium Aevum* 51 (1982): 92–101; R. K. Delasanta, "Chaucer, Pavia and the Ciel d'Oro," *Medium Aevum* 54 (1985): 117–21. Galeazzo Visconti, brother of Bernabò and father of Gian Galeazzo, died on 4 August 1378, while Chaucer was in Lombardy.

## VII

To what extent does Chaucer's account of a tyrannized Lombardy function as a veiled critique of England under Richard II? As he composed *The Canterbury Tales* Chaucer was, of course, well placed to observe Richard's descent into tyranny. In 1386, when southeast England was again facing the threat of French invasion, Chaucer served as Member of Parliament for Kent. The Commons assumed exceptional political power and importance in that year by forming an alliance with a magnate (Thomas of Woodstock, youngest surviving son of Edward III); a reform commission was set up to examine Richard's rule.[142] This was repudiated by Richard; eleven years later he had its proponents declared guilty of high treason. This 1397 parliament was held in a special open-sided building in the precincts of Westminster. According to the chronicler Adam of Usk, Richard surrounded this assembly with archers who were ready to shoot and on one occasion drew their bows to the ear.[143] In 1398, according to another chronicler, Richard spent his crown-wearing days sitting on his throne in silence; if anyone chanced to meet his gaze "the person had to bow the knee."[144] In 1399 Richard was deposed. The articles of deposition of 1399 play out this conflict between the laws of the land and the arbitrary will and pleasure of the king in dramatic fashion. Richard, it is claimed, ignored the laws and customs of the realm since "according to the whim of his desire he wanted to do whatever appealed to his wishes."[145] Sometimes, speaking with "harsh and determined looks," he claimed "that the laws were in his own mouth, sometimes he said that they were in his breast, and that he alone could change or establish the laws of his realm."[146] This crude formulation, in which Richard arbitrarily claims that his own body and the body politic are one and the same, implicitly rejects the metaphor

---

142. See Anthony Goodman, *The Loyal Conspiracy: The Lords Appellant under Richard II* (London: Routledge & Kegan Paul, 1971), 14; Anthony Tuck, *Richard II and the English Nobility* (London: Edward Arnold, 1973), 104–8; R. H. Jones, *The Royal Policy of Richard II: Absolutism in the Later Middle Ages* (Oxford: Blackwell, 1968), 33–35; Anthony Steel, *Richard II* (Cambridge, Eng.: Cambridge University Press, 1962), 120–40.

143. Steel, *Richard II*, 234.

144. Steel, 278, translating from the *Eulogium Historiarum*.

145. *Rotuli Parliamentorum* 3:416, as translated in *English Historical Documents 1327–1485*, ed. A. R. Myers (New York: Oxford University Press, 1969), 410.

146. Myers, *English Historical Documents*, 410. Richard is perhaps appealing to an English royal tradition which held that the king's government proceeds from mere will ("mera et spontanea voluntate," a phrase that was expunged from the reissue of Magna Carta in 1216). See Wilks, "Mystical Marriage," 509.

by which Chaucer had urged him to imagine his relationship to his subjects: "Dred God, do law, love trouthe and worthinesse, / And wed thy folk agein to stedfastnesse." [147] In this marriage the people play the bride to Richard's "stedfastnesse," the virtue that holds *voluntatis arbitrium* in check. The adverb "agein" is significant here since it suggests that the sacramental bond uniting this ruler to his subjects as *sponsus regni* has come unraveled. [148] Walter, of course, welcomes Griselde as his wife "agein" once he has renounced his "merveillous desir his wyf t'assaye" (454). This second union surpasses the first in ceremonial splendor and symbolic importance:

> For moore solempne in every mannes syght
> This feste was, and gretter of costage,
> Then was the revel of hire mariage.
> (1125–27)

Tyranny is not a terminal disease, an irreversible state of mind; it may be renounced as quickly as it is assumed. Walter finally overthrows his own tyrannizing of Griselde. The *Canterbury Tales* contains much intelligent commentary on the dynamics of tyranny. Theseus, for example, is offered several opportunities to step into tyranny when his personal desires conflict with the needs of his subjects. In waging war on Thebes, Theseus resists tyranny not only by destroying the tyrant Creon but also by acting against his personal desire to return home with his new wife. Such voluntary restraint allies Theseus with the great lords in the *Decameron's* tenth day who, with the notorious exception of Walter, sacrifice personal desires for the good of their subjects and for the political health of their kingdoms. [149]

Chaucer's most extensive commentary on the responsibilities of a monarch (and the rights of an individual subject) appears in the Prologue to *The Legend of Good Women*. Here Chaucer figures himself as the accused, standing between Alceste, "the worthyeste queene," and

---

147. "Lak of Stedfastnesse," 27–28. Laila Z. Gross notes that "in Shirley's MS R.3.20 the poem is called "Balade Royal made by our laureal poete then in hees laste yeeres" and the envoy is headed "Lenvoye to kyng Richard" (*Riverside Chaucer*, p. 1085). See also Wilks, "Mystical Marriage," 500–504.

148. For the concept of *sponsus regni*, see Wilks, "Mystical Marriage," 500–501; E. H. Kantorowicz, *The King's Two Bodies: A Study in Medieval Political Theology* (Princeton: Princeton University Press, 1957), 221–26.

149. See p. 187 above.

the forbidding God of Love. There is no need to press for absolute correspondences here in associating Alceste and her husband with Anne and Richard: indeed, Chaucer would have been foolish to be anything more than generally allusive. It is worth noting, however, that in F 185 Alceste is termed an "emperice" (an epithet canceled in the G version, which was evidently written after Anne's death); she also exhibits a learned familiarity with the ways of the imperial court:

> "Envie ys lavendere of the court alway,
> For she ne parteth, neither nyght ne day,
> Out of the hous of Cesar; thus seith Dante."
>                                    (F 358–60)

Anne of Bohemia (cited as dedicatee of the work in F 496–97) was, of course, the daughter of an empress; she grew up in "the hous of Cesar." It may be that Chaucer was attempting to color Alceste's political advice with a suggestion of higher authority. He was certainly exploiting, once again, the political and allegorical suggestiveness of marriage, the institution within which this advice is being offered. Alceste's defense of her hapless subject, Chaucer, before the God of Love sees a most interesting elision from poetics to politics, historical and theoretical:

> "He ne hath nat doon so grevously amys,
> To translaten that olde clerkes writen,
> As thogh that he of malice wolde enditen
> Despit of love, and had himself yt wroght.
> This shoolde a ryghtwis lord have in his thoght,
> And nat be lyk tirauntz of Lumbardye,
> That han no reward but at tyrannye.
> For he that kynge or lord ys naturel,
> Hym oghte nat be tiraunt ne crewel,
> As is a fermour, to doon the harm he kan.
> He moste thinke yt is his lige man,
> And is his tresour, and his gold in cofre.
> This is the sentence of the Philosophre."
>                                    (F 369–81)

No king should diminish himself by becoming a tyrannical tax-gatherer; his subjects are his true treasure. This discourse on true royalty and nobility (which might have been dictated by a civic-minded Florentine in the face of those "'tirauntz of Lumbardye'") runs on for another two dozen lines before coming back to its author, Chaucer, the erring subject. Its topical force is strengthened in the later text: after the "lige man" line, for example, we discover a more detailed account of how a king should "treasure" his subjects:

> "And that hym oweth, of verray duetee,
> Shewen his peple pleyn benygnete,
> And wel to heren here excusacyouns,
> And here compleyntes and petyciouns,
> In duewe tyme, whan they shal it profre.
> This is the sentence of the Philosophre."
>
> (G 360–65)

It is difficult to think of a passage that speaks more eloquently to the political needs of Richard's later years, a relevance that has been explored in detail by Margaret Schlauch. But the presence of Chaucer *as poet* in the midst of this "miniature political essay," as Schlauch calls it, requires some pondering.[150] Does the practice of poetry have something in common with, or bear some relation to, the practice of government? Boccaccio's *Trattatello*, we have noted, suggests that it does: poets were first drawn into the service of princes to serve premeditated political ends. Chaucer's Prologue to *The Legend of Good Women* has often been considered as some sort of poetic manifesto.[151] Robert O. Payne's *The Key of Remembrance* offers a fine account of the rhetorical foundations of Chaucer's poetics.[152] Payne takes his title from a line in the Prologue (F 26; G 26): the key discovered here is that of "olde bokes," the starting point for the writing of both history and poetry where experience and living memory fall short. The instrument that enables both history and poetry to be written is rhetoric.[153] Rhetoric, moreover, is fundamental to the formation of civil society as well as to poetics and history. Even before the word "politics" enters the vocabulary of the Latin west we find the historian John of Salisbury pondering the function of eloquence in the original framing of society.[154] In

150. "Chaucer's Doctrine," 151.

151. See John H. Fisher, "The *Legend of Good Women*," in *Companion to Chaucer Studies*, ed. Beryl Rowland, rev. ed. (New York: Oxford University Press, 1979), 464–76; Lisa J. Kiser, *Telling Classical Tales: Chaucer and the "Legend of Good Women"* (Ithaca: Cornell University Press, 1983).

152. *The Key of Remembrance: A Study of Chaucer's Poetics* (New Haven: Yale University Press, 1963).

153. Poetry and history require a present exercise of rhetoric that recoups the exercise of rhetoric in the past. Such current rhetorical exercise translates past utterances to the (poetic and historical) language and understanding of the present.

154. The first Latin translation of Aristotle's *Politics* was completed by William of Moerbeke O.P. soon after 1250. See Walter Ullmann, *The Individual and Society in the Middle Ages* (Baltimore: Johns Hopkins University Press, 1966), 119–20.

his *Policraticus* John proposes that in Eden there was at first no speech at all. Then speech came and men could praise God. Soon, however, man became "verbosior," talked with the tempter, and fell.[155] John's *Metalogicon,* however, begins by claiming that eloquence gave rise to civilization. Here John is following Cicero and Quintilian in the commonplace belief that right reason and cultivated speech enabled man to distinguish himself from animals and so organize cities and nations. Eloquence for John may prove either conducive to society or destructive of it: it all depends on the good or evil intent of the speaker. We discover a comparable ambiguity at the opening of Cicero's most widely known work, the *De Inventione.*[156] Whether or not men and communities have received more good or evil from oratory and a consuming devotion to eloquence is still a matter for debate (1.1.1). Before there was eloquence there could be no marriage, no family, and no law (1.2.2). But once reasoned eloquence had established city life, corrupt eloquence proved able to destroy it. On balance, then, men should study eloquence, since "from eloquence the state receives many benefits, provided only it is accompanied by wisdom, the guide of all human affairs" (1.4.5).

This traditional cleft between wisdom and eloquence is, I believe, the awkward place upon which Chaucer situates himself in the Prologue to *The Legend of Good Women.* There is no doubt that Chaucer has been eloquent: the catalogue of his works takes up over a dozen lines (F 417–30; G 405–20). But has he been wise? This is problematic. According to Alceste, Chaucer has been ignorant rather than wise: he "taketh non hed of what matere he take"; he wrote the *Rose* and the *Troilus* "Of innocence, and nyste what he seyde" (G 343–45). This writerly rationale is, of course, a familiar one: the Chaucerian persona simply offers a verbal report (is eloquent) and wisdom is brought to this text by his readers. Such a collaboration, which the Prologue explicitly exposes, confirms the peculiarly public character of Chaucer's art: its meaning is not locked away in authorial intention but is rather shared between the audience that receives the text and the patrons who

155. See Roger Ray, "Rhetorical Scepticism and Verisimilar Narrative in John of Salisbury's *Historia Pontificalis,*" in *Classical Rhetoric and Medieval Historiography,* ed. Ernst Breisach (Kalamazoo, Mich.: Medieval Institute Publications, 1985), 63–64. For Chaucer's knowledge of the *Policraticus,* see Leyerle and Quick, *Chaucer,* 78.

156. References to the *De Inventione* follow the Loeb edition of Cicero, trans. H. M. Hubbell (Cambridge, Mass.: Harvard University Press, 1949).

set it in motion.[157] In this account the initiating act of patronage assumes considerable importance as rhetorical *inventio*. Chaucer *may* have written the *Rose* or the *Troilus* on his own initiative, but it is more likely that

> hym was boden make thilke tweye
> Of some persone, and durste it not withseye;
> For he hath write many a bok er this.
> (G 346–48)[158]

Such textual production is firmly embedded within a structure of power and authority. The authorial hand must sometimes move upon command; the moral authority of the hand's commander may then help determine the character and value of the text produced. In this particular text the God of Love (deflected from tyrannical obdurateness by the intervention of Alceste) envisions a good end for Chaucer in writing *The Legend of Good Women*. But what if such a ruler were to persist in tyranny: can a good literary end be made from a corrupt point of origin? What is the moral standing of a poet whose "rhetorike swete" is expended in the service of " 'tirauntz of Lumbardye' "? And what of the poet who traveled as emissary to such tyrants, serving a king considered (by the articles of deposition of 1399) "so variable and dissimulating in his words and writings, especially to popes and rulers outside the realm, that no one could trust him"?[159] Such questions, concerning institutional power, politics, and authorial responsibility, do not imperil the *Legend*'s status as a poetic manifesto: they simply confirm that rhetoric and poetics cannot isolate themselves from such issues. They also suggest that the questions asked of Petrarch through the *Clerk's Tale* were questions Chaucer felt compelled to ask of himself through his own cultural practice.

VII

Our opening question of what Petrarch meant to Chaucer remains difficult to answer. This is not surprising since the question of what Petrarch meant to Petrarch was typically answered in paradoxes and confessed contradictions. Paradoxes and contradictions are, of course,

---

157. For more on this, see Middleton, "Public Poetry," 94–114.
158. F 368 (rewritten as G 348) reads, "Or him repenteth outrely of this."
159. *English Historical Documents,* ed. Myers, 411.

organizational forms; through them the self contains itself within a closed circle of neat, binary opposites, saved from the chaotic flux of historical experience. Chaucer, I have attempted to argue, recognized Petrarch's impulse to save himself and his texts from temporal erosion. The Petrarchan self sets itself apart through the superiority of its "insight," its ability to read through the garments of Nature. Chaucer was familiar, from his reading of Macrobius, with the notion that "only eminent men of superior intelligence gain a revelation of her truths"; the rest are excluded and must settle for less.[160] Chaucer sees into Nature, to some extent, in his dreams, where we encounter talking eagles, Macrobian guides, and even Nature herself. But the Chaucerian dreamer cannot translate what he sees to his own understanding, let alone to his life outside the dream. In the Petrarchan world the walls between dream and reality are extremely thin.[161] But although Petrarch may achieve "insight," his ability to translate this into historical action remains problematic, since history itself is so fleeting and illusory.

It was Petrarch's instinct for self-preservation that induced him to accept the patronage of north Italian despots. The Visconti, in particular, promised him the physical security that would free him to write. Ironically but inevitably, Petrarch found himself busier than ever before at Milan, employing all his Ciceronian skills in defending and advancing Visconti interests. Chaucer must have heard a lot about all this during his dealings with Bernabò in 1378. It must have disturbed him that in exchange for the liberty to write, Petrarch had worked for tyrants against the principles of *libertas* and *commune profyt* embodied by Boccaccio's Florence. The Prologue to *The Legend of Good Women* suggests that a work's patron has a share in the work's meaning. The meaning of Petrarchan humanism, for Chaucer, could hardly be divorced from the tyranny that had nurtured, protected, and exploited it.

Petrarch's efforts at self-preservation extended to the organization of his textual afterlife, to what I have termed the Petrarchan Academy, the place where men of insight gather around Petrarchan texts. Chaucer's Clerk recognizes the efficacy of this institution: Petrarch's "rethorike sweete" has "enlumyned" all of Italy (IV.32–33). Chaucer obviously

---

160. *Commentary on the Dream of Scipio*, translated in Miller, *Sources and Backgrounds*, 47.

161. See David Wallace, "Chaucer and the European *Rose*," in *Studies in the Age of Chaucer. Proceedings, No. 1. 1984: Reconstructing Chaucer*, ed. Paul Strohm and Thomas J. Heffernan (Knoxville, Tenn.: New Chaucer Society, 1985), 67.

spared some thought for his own posterity: he pauses before the ped-
estaled poets in the House of Fame, attaches his *Troilus* to an illustrious
line of poets, and then places the same text in the hands of "moral
Gower" and "philosophical Strode" (V.1856–57). But Fame's House
stands on a rock of ice, and the *Troilus* is repeatedly threatened by the
"negligence and rape" of "Adam scriveyn"; what will become of the
text when Chaucer is no longer around to "renewe" the work of old
Adam?[162] Such reflections in Chaucer are never entirely gloomy: they
are lightened by an edge of humor that accepts physical decay as the
inevitable future of both texts and the people who make them. The
vernacular is the language of time. Its works are to be enjoyed in a
Boccaccian *brigata*, a Chaucerian *compaignye*, or a Dantean *convivio*, a
banquet to which everybody is invited. We can, alternatively, gather
ourselves with our texts behind the high walls of the Academy, but one
fate still awaits us all:

> "He is now deed and nayled in his cheste;
> I prey to God so yeve his soule reste!"
> (IV.29–30)

The coffin's lid comes down on Petrarch before his text can be revived
through Chaucer's Clerk: the most definitive act of closure takes place
before Petrarch's story has even begun. It is a nice Chaucerian touch
that the last worldly sound associated with "the lauriat poete" should
be not the applause of the Academy but the hammering of the artisans
who nail down his coffin.

---

162. See "Chaucers Wordes unto Adam, His Owne Scriveyn," in *Riverside Chaucer*,
650.

# 5

# The King's Two Voices

*Narrative and Power in Hoccleve's*
Regement of Princes

*Larry Scanlon*


## PROLOGUE: THE DEPOSITION OF RICHARD II

Thomas Hoccleve's *Regement of Princes,* written between 1410 and 1412 for the future Henry V, is something of a forgotten masterpiece.[1] A witty, subtle, and relentlessly self-conscious poem, its language is magisterial, modulating effortlessly between the philosophical and colloquial with a Chaucerian fluency. Its numerous exempla and extended autobiographical petitions to the prince make it predominantly narrative, but it draws on nonnarrative philosophical genres as well—the complaint, the dialogue, and chiefly, the *Fürstenspiegel,* or Mirror of Princes. Indeed, it takes its title, as well as some of its content, from Aegidius Romanus's widely influential *De Regimine Principum.* The poem situates these philosophical genres narratively, producing both a coherent moral vision of kingship and an examination of the rhetorical means by which that vision has been itself produced.

The work has been forgotten because the ideology of kingship is not a problem modern scholarship has considered very interesting. Literary scholars have been particularly remiss in this respect, despite the constant preoccupation of medieval poets with the subject.[2] Dante, Petrarch, and Boccaccio all wrote major works dealing with kingship, which modern scholars routinely ignore: respectively, *De Monarchia, De*

---

1. Since the work is addressed to Henry as the Prince of Wales, it would have to have been written before 21 March 1413, the date of his coronation. Its allusion in the Prologue to the 1 March 1410 execution of the Lollard John Badby places it after that date. Furnivall settles on 1412 because the Court Rolls seem to indicate an interruption in Hoccleve's annuity in that year (*Hoccleve's Works: I. The Minor Works* [London: pub. for the Early English Text Society by Kegan Paul, Trench Trübner & Co., 1892], xiii). This date, however, depends on a strictly literal reading of the poem's begging stance.

2. One recent exception to this trend is David Lawton's excellent article, "Dullness and the Fifteenth Century," *ELH* 54 (1987): 761–99.

*Viris Illustribus,* and *De Casibus Virorum Illustrium.* In addition, Petrarch also wrote a short *Fürstenspiegel, De Re Publica Optime Administranda.*[3] The last major treatment of Chaucer and kingship appeared in 1945.[4] It is generally acknowledged that the three major poets following Chaucer in the Chaucerian tradition, Gower, Hoccleve, and Lydgate, remain underexamined, and it seems hardly accidental that the *chef d'oeuvre* of each, the *Confessio Amantis,* the *Regement of Princes,* and the *Fall of Princes,* centrally concerns kingship.

Why was kingship such a dominant concern in later medieval literature? At first glance, the answer to this question seems straightforward and not particularly interesting. Secular literature needed to differentiate itself from the discourse of the Church without directly challenging ecclesiastical authority. In the figure of the king, secular writers found a single, central source of authority analogous to the figure of God in ecclesiastical discourse and yet fully secular.

There is, however, much more to say about the matter than this. Secular authority, political or literary, was an extremely fluid category at this time, dependent on the very ecclesiastical traditions from which both secular rulers and secular writers were attempting to wrest it. Throughout this process of secularization the political and the literary interpenetrated—kings were as ideologically dependent on their writers as the writers were politically dependent on kings. For as poets like Hoccleve staked out the claims of a new vernacular tradition, what they encountered in kingship was not some fully formed and uncontested institution. Rather, they encountered a dynamic political structure in the midst of defining itself ideologically in order to maintain and extend its power politically.[5] The representation of kingship in works like the

---

3. Wilhelm Berges, *Die Fürstenspiegel des hohen und späten Mittelalters* (Stuttgart: Hiersemann Verlag, 1938), 352–53.

4. Margaret Schlauch, "Chaucer's Doctrine of Kings and Tyrants," *Speculum* 20 (1945): 133–56.

5. That ideology reproduces relations of power is a Marxist truism. Cf. Karl Marx and Friedrich Engels, *The German Ideology,* ed. C. J. Arthur (New York: International Publishers, 1970), esp. 42–68; Gyorgy Lukács, "What is Orthodox Marxism?" in *History and Class Consciousness,* trans. Rodney Livingstone (Cambridge, Mass.: MIT Press, 1971), esp. 15–18; and Louis Althusser, "Ideology and Ideological State Apparatuses," in *Lenin and Philosophy,* trans. Ben Brewster (New York and London: Monthly Review Press, 1971), 127–86. For a succinct, incisive history of the term "ideology," see Stuart Hall, "The Hinterland of Science: Ideology and the 'Sociology of Knowledge,'" in *On Ideology* (Birmingham: Centre of Contemporary Cultural Studies, 1977; London: Hutchinson, 1978), 9–33. The concept of ideology I use throughout this essay is drawn mainly from Althusser.

*Regement of Princes* was part of this larger ideological project. For this reason consideration of the formal integrity of such works will continue to be impossible until it is grounded in an understanding of kingship as an ideological structure. We cannot hope to understand the discursive strategies whereby kingship was represented in literature until we understand the ideological strategies whereby its power relations were reproduced within the social structure.

On this point historians have been as remiss as literary scholars. While they have hardly ignored kingship, they have generally kept its ideology separate from its practice. Perhaps as a reaction to the teleological excesses of constitutional history, regnal biographers and administrative historians have tended to view the administrative growth of medieval kingship in preponderantly local terms (a series of practical solutions to immediate problems) while resisting any appeal to larger theoretical conceptions. On the other hand, comprehensive accounts of medieval theory, such as the classic works of Ernst Kantorowicz and Michael Wilks, treat their subject as an intellectual drama in which the only actors are ideas, and in which the primary motivation is the purely ratiocinative desire for ever clearer solutions to logical dilemmas. The agency that is always missing is power. Because these scholars are interested in ideas rather than ideology, they have little to say about the way medieval ideas about kingship functioned culturally, how they maintained the power structure they conceptualized.

A particularly striking illustration of this point can be found in one of the central political documents of Hoccleve's time: the Articles of Deposition of Richard II. One of the most famous articles defines the problem of royal power as precisely a problem of representation.

> 33. ITEM, the same King, did not wish to preserve or protect the just Laws and Customs of his Reign, but to make whatever decision occurred to him according to the judgment of his own will. Whenever the Laws of his Reign were explained and declared to him by the Justices and others of his Council, and according to these Laws justice for the suitors exhibited, he would say expressly with a stern and shameless countenance, that his Laws were in his mouth, and several times, in his heart, and that he himself alone was able to change or institute the Laws of his Reign . . . [6]

6. *Rotuli Parliamentorum*, ed. J. Strachey (London, 1767–83), 3:419: "33. ITEM, idem Rex nolens justas Leges & Consuetudines Regni sui servare se protegere, set secundum sue arbitrium Voluntatis facere quicquid desideriis ijus occurrerrit, quandoque & fre-

This story is usually read as a simple denunciation of tyranny, consistent with the standard constitutionalist view of the Deposition as "one more step in the transference of the centre of political gravity from ruler to people."[7] Indeed, more recent historians, who have been suspicious of this Whig teleology, also treat Article 33 as an essentially accurate depiction of Richard, even though, as Anthony Tuck concedes, there is no proof of its truth.[8] But the crucial point about this article is not its accuracy but its rhetorical debt to medieval conceptions of kingship and the practical power they lend to its ideological mission.

Before the article is a constitutional claim it is a narrative, and as a narrative it convinces fictively rather than referentially. For it recapitulates the complex of corporate and organological fictions that Kantorowicz's classic study has shown ultimately issue in the notion of the "King's Two Bodies." "The Prince (or Pope) has the laws in the shrine of his breast" was a maxim the canonists adopted from Roman law.[9] But in its earlier instances, the intent of the fiction seems to have been, at least in part, to constrain the royal *voluntas* by counsel. Thus, the jurist Cynus of Pistoia interpreted "shrine of his breast" to mean "Doctors of Law through whose mouths the most law-abiding Prince himself speaks."[10] Similar formulations occur in French jurists, and Bracton

---

quentius quando sibi expositi & declarati fuerant Leges Regni sui per Justic' & alios de Consilio suo, & secundum Leges illas petentibus justiciam exhiberet; Dixit expresse, voltu austero & protervo, quod Leges sue erant in ore suo, & aliquotiens in pectore suo: Et qd ipse solus posset mutare & condere Leges Regni sui . . ." (the translation is mine).

7. B. Wilkinson, *Politics and the Constitution 1307–1399*, vol. 2 of *Constitutional History of Medieval England 1216–1399* (London: Longmans & Green, 1952), 298. In fairness I should say that as constitutional history has become less fashionable, more recent accounts have become less explicitly teleological. Nevertheless they still treat Richard's deposition as primarily a matter of resisting tyranny and to this extent are guilty of a similar form of anachronism. By modern standards, all of the medieval nobility were tyrants in the sense that most of the populace lacked adequate redress against them. In this context to single out Richard's tyranny is to ignore the larger issue of class relations within which his relation to the rest of the nobility was played out. Even recent accounts do not address the issue of class and tend to reduce Richard's "tyranny" to personal traits: according to Anthony Tuck, he was arrogant and petulant (*Crown and Nobility 1272–1461* [Oxford: Basil Blackwell, 1986], 222); to May McKisack, vindictive and possibly insane (*The Fourteenth Century* [Oxford: Clarendon Press, 1959], 496–98); to A. B. Steel, definitely on the verge of insanity (*Richard II* [Cambridge, Eng.: Cambridge University Press, 1941], 278–79).

8. Anthony Tuck, *Richard II and the English Nobility* (London: Edward Arnold, 1973), 204.

9. Ernst H. Kantorowicz, *The King's Two Bodies: A Study in Medieval Political Theology* (Princeton: Princeton University Press, 1957), 153.

10. Cynus de Pistoia, *Commentarium in Codicem et Digestum vetus* (Frankfurt, 1578), 6, 23, 19. Cited in Kantorowicz, *King's Two Bodies*, 154.

exchanges the terms of the trope so that the Prince becomes the "mouth of the council," making laws "as he pleased" after hearing their advice.[11] In Article 33, however, this intent seems to have been reversed. Richard is depicted as claiming the law is in his breast or mouth precisely in order to free himself from counsel. This apparent inconsistency can be resolved by reconsidering the intent of the earlier instances and reinserting the missing term "power." A product of Roman thought, the fiction's first major instance occurs in Livy, where the patrician Menenius Agrippa uses it to quell a plebeian revolt.[12] Though it passed into the Middle Ages via the Pauline concept of the Church as *corpus Christi,* it was not actively applied to medieval institutions until the later growth of the papacy, when papalists began casting the pope as *caput* of the *ecclesia.*[13] It was soon taken up by royal apologists, as a way of both resisting the claims of the papacy and defining their own. In both cases its political value was the same: to reduce an aggregate of individuals to a single entity, imagined in one way or another as a single person, or a single body. It reinforced the unity and the preeminence of a central institution undergoing a massive administrative expansion. Accordingly, the point of the fiction is not to democratize a unitary form of power, but to enable that power to maintain its ideological unity as it is being institutionally diffused. And even as the fiction occurs in Bracton and earlier writers its point is not so much to neutralize the prince as it is to empower his council. In other words, the point of the metaphor is not to disperse power but to solidify it, not to hedge it about with constraints but to reinforce its stability and dominance. And the crucial line of demarcation is thus not between prince and his council but between the governing class and everyone else.

In more complex fashion, the same sort of empowerment is at work in Article 33. Appealing to the expanded notion of the king's council as embodied in Parliament, the narrative employs an expanded version of the corporate fiction.[14] It retains the ideal of a unified royal voice, even in disavowing Richard's right to it. For at the very moment Richard voices his ostensibly discredited claim, the narrative focuses not on the

---

11. See Kantorowicz, *King's Two Bodies,* 152–55.

12. Livy, *Ad Urbe Condita,* 2.32, 8–33, 2.

13. M. J. Wilks, *The Problem of Sovereignty in the Later Middle Ages* (Cambridge, Eng.: Cambridge University Press, 1963), 15–64, 455–78.

14. Parliament was originally conceived as an extension of the royal council. For a brief discussion and additional bibliography see Bryce Lyon, *A Constitutional and Legal History of Medieval England* (New York: Harper & Row, 1960), 408–30.

specific legal results of the claim, but on his body, on what his face looked like as he spoke: "with a stern and shameless countenance." The narrative returns to his merely physical body in order to dissociate him from the institutional royal body. Ironically, then, for the story to make its case against Richard it must concede to him the very power to embody the law it accuses him of illicitly claiming. In those cases so vaguely cited here, where Richard made this claim, his voice *did* have the force of law. He was able effectively to void precedent and nullify counsel simply by announcing, according to his own *voluntas*, that he wished to do so. If the story makes Richard out as a tyrant it is not because he violated some explicitly established constitutional principle. It is because he declined to live up to the ideal of the corporate fiction. He refused to embody counsel and legal precedent in a single unifying voice: he literalized the body politic and thus revealed monarchical theory to be a metaphor—that is, a fiction.

The story is also vague about the constitutional issues it raises. Which were the cases where Richard claimed his prerogative? What specific legal issues were at stake? How specifically should he have been limited by precedent and counsel? Should any prerogatives have been open to him at all? The article does not begin to address these questions. Instead it is entirely focused on the power of the king's voice. The article does not wish to do away with royal *voluntas*, but rather desires a *voluntas* at one with the law. If the law is imagined as the property of the realm as opposed to the king (which is what the phrase *Leges & Consuetidines Regni* implies), then what the article desires is a royal voice that is spoken by the realm, a king whose voice unifies the nobility's interests. The article resorts to narrative because any attempt to define this ideal juridically or constitutionally—that is, to conceptualize it—would destroy it. If the king is to be a living embodiment of the law, a *lex animata*, he must be so naturally and spontaneously. A *lex animata* produced entirely by prior external constraint is by definition not a *lex animata*. By presenting its case narratively, the article can dispose of Richard and yet retain the ideal it would have had him embody. And Richard *must* be disposed of, because his literalization of the metaphor has rendered it unavailable to the nobility as a whole.

In the first instance, the ideal was crucial to Bolingbroke and the other architects of the deposition. A usurper rather than a revolutionary, Bolingbroke wanted to replace Richard but not alter the structure of kingship. Indeed, he rejected out of hand the one tentative suggestion that he accept a parliamentary title.[15] But the practical value the ideal of a spontaneously lawful *voluntas* had for Henry was matched by its ideological value to the rest of the ruling class. In respect to those below him, the legislative and juridical prerogative of a nobleman was not essentially different from the royal prerogative to which Richard here lays claim.[16] In the main, medieval justice was indeed what the nobility said it was. It was instituted by them, interpreted by them, and administered by them as, in Maitland's phrase, "a proprietary right."[17] In the Middle Ages, justice was something the nobility *owned*. While one may not wish to go as far as Perry Anderson when he claims that medieval justice "was the ordinary name of power," it is hard to argue with Alan Harding's observation that medieval courts served a double function: "first, the maintenance of social peace by the settlement of disputes between individuals, and second, the maintenance of the social dominance of the king and noble who held the court. Practically, the two are inseparable."[18] While seigneurial justice was, by the end of the fourteenth century, being gradually displaced by royal justice, the manner of this displacement was such that it made the unity of the royal *voluntas* that much more attractive.[19] For the decline of seigneurial courts coincided with the advent of the justices of the peace. Though nominally an officer of the king, the justice of the peace was invariably a local landowner who would follow the local interests of his class. So what the nobility gave up in direct juridical control it regained through

15. The suggestion was made by Archbishop Arundel. See McKisack, *Fourteenth Century*, 494–96; K. B. McFarlane, *Lancastrian Kings and Lollard Knights* (Oxford: Clarendon, 1972), 54–58.

16. Record remains of at least one case in which the prerogatives of a lord were denounced in the same terms that the Articles of Deposition used to denounce Richard. In the 1320s Hugh Despenser was accused of *voluntrif seigneurie* by the English community of Glamorgan. See Alan Harding, "Political Liberty in the Middle Ages," *Speculum* 55 (1980): 441, and William Rees, *Calendar of Ancient Petitions Relating to Wales* (Cardiff: University of Wales Press, 1975), 279.

17. Sir Frederick Pollock and Frederick William Maitland, *The History of English Law Before the Time of Edward I*, 2nd ed., reissued with a new introduction and bibliography by S. F. C. Milsom (Cambridge, Eng.: Cambridge University Press, 1968), 527.

18. Perry Anderson, *Passages from Antiquity to Feudalism* (London: Verso, 1974), 153; Alan Harding, *The Law Courts of Medieval England* (London: Allen & Unwin, 1973), 13. I might add that when Harding claims in the next sentence that "kings, princes, and also priests, come onto the scene as the chosen arbiters of society," he comes perilously close to the kind of anachronism I noted above. For the vast majority of those who faced medieval justice, the judge was in no way chosen.

19. See Alan Harding, "The Revolt Against the Justices," in *The English Rising of 1381*, ed. R. H. Hilton and T. H. Aston (Cambridge, Eng.: Cambridge University Press, 1984), 167–68, for a brief discussion and additional bibliography.

its alliance with the bureaucracy of the crown. As Harding has said, "the sessions of the Justices of the Peace replaced the manorial courts as a means of social control as the relationship of peasant to landlord changed from a legal subjection to a purely economic subjection."[20]

The juridical power the nobility once exercised purely in its own name it now exercised in the name of the king. Though the form had changed, the fundamental ideological presumption had not. Legal authority was still the property of a single class, and the immediate effect of the change of form was to bring the prerogative of the nobility even closer to that of the king. When a justice of the peace spoke, he spoke with the king's voice. The result of this institutional diffusion of the king's voice was a more efficient concentration of the legal power of the ruling class as a whole. It also meant that the ruling class as a whole had a greater stake in defining how royal power was to be exercised. While this condition certainly does not explain Richard's deposition by itself, it does help explain the particular form the deposition took. The nobility was not likely to call for structural changes in the status quo, because the status quo was precisely the prize they were gaming for. By giving them control of Richard's voice the narrative of Article 33 helped them take control of the power structure without having to change it.

The power of this narrative thus inheres neither in its referential fidelity to some actual statement of Richard's, a correspondence that seems vague at best and an outright fabrication at worst, nor in its articulation of some constitutional principle. Its power inheres instead in a formal capacity that modern criticism has identified as one of narrative's central features: the capacity to speak convincingly in the voice of another. Older Anglo-American accounts of narrative treat this capacity, also identified as narrative's shifting point of view, as their primary object of study.[21]

More recently, under the influence of Continental narratology, Anglo-American criticism has moved from considerations of narrative voice to more theoretically rigorous considerations of the various forms of narrative discourse. I retain the older term here for two reasons.

---

20. *Law Courts,* 116. Harding observes somewhat earlier on that "a striking feature of English social history from the fourteenth century to the seventeenth century is the combined use of civil and criminal law by the members of the gentry class in order to gain local advantage" (93–94).

21. See Wayne Booth, "The Author's Many Voices," in *The Rhetoric of Fiction,* 2nd ed. (Chicago: University of Chicago Press, 1983), 16–20.

First, as Jonathan Culler has pointed out, the modes of inquiry are not that dissimilar.[22] To begin, as narratology does, with the distinction between the way a story is told ("discourse," or *sjuzhtre*) and the sequence of events it records ("story," or *fabula*) is in fact to study the problem of point of view. Indeed, narrative's capacity to speak convincingly in the voice of another is simply the most extreme instance of the more general capacity narratologists identify as narrative's power to make events "seem to tell themselves."[23] When a narrative shifts into the voice of one of its characters it is presenting that voice as pure event, as if an entirely distinct entity were now speaking. Narrative thus has the ideological power not only to present events neutrally, as if they were actually unfolding, but also to present equally neutrally other ways of viewing these events, as if the other viewpoints were speaking directly for themselves.

This is my second reason for retaining the term "voice": to foreground precisely this power to coopt other points of view. Despite its theoretical rigor, narratology's emphasis on event threatens to conceal narrative's ideological power rather than expose it. Unfortunately, it is a short step between observing with Roland Barthes that narrative "is simply there, like life itself," to assuming (as he later does in the same essay) that in its purest form, narrative is ideologically neutral.[24] On the contrary, narrative's ideological power inheres precisely in its illusion of neutrality, an illusion narrative produces as assiduously as a Petrarchan sonnet produces the illusion of artifice. Analyzing narrative as a matrix of voices penetrates the illusion at its most mystifying moment, the moment when it turns a point of view into an event.

In Article 33, the voice that the narrative constructs for Richard becomes *his* voice, which is how Article 33 makes moot the issue of its referential accuracy. The Lancastrian narrator can reproduce Richard's

22. "Story and Discourse in the Analysis of Narrative," in *The Pursuit of Signs* (Ithaca: Cornell University Press, 1981), 170–71.

23. The phrase is Benveniste's. For a brief discussion, see Hayden White, "The Value of Narrativity in the Representation of Reality," in *The Content of the Form: Narrative Discourse and Historical Representation* (Baltimore: Johns Hopkins University Press, 1987), 3–4.

24. "Introduction to the Structural Analysis of Narratives," in *A Barthes Reader*, ed. Susan Sontag (New York: Hill and Wang, 1982), 252. For example, Barthes declares that "'what happens'" in narrative "is language alone, the unceasing adventure of its coming" (295).

voice without needing Richard actually to have spoken the words assigned him. Were the issue sheer referential accuracy, then the question who is speaking here, Richard or his Lancastrian accusers, would have to be settled before the story could be of any use. But as the reaction of Tuck and other modern historians illustrates, whether Richard actually spoke these words is not finally the crucial question. What is more important is that the article gives Richard a voice that plausibly explains what the article perceives to be the basis of his actions, a plausibility that depends upon, and reproduces, the dominant ideology of kingship.

The plausibility thus produced is itself a fictional effect. The voice assigned to Richard is plausible because it recapitulates previous fictions of the royal voice. It is the very essence of these fictions to present a voice at once itself and the voice of others. The royal voice is thus incipiently narratorial in that it defines itself by its capacity to speak for others without losing its own specificity. The king both speaks the communal voice and is spoken by it. This broad structural similarity between the medieval ideology of kingship and narrative may well explain medieval political theory's preponderant dependence on fictions. This dependence has usually been viewed in teleological terms as a weakness. Medieval theorists are seen to have resorted to fictions and metaphors as stopgaps because they had not yet arrived at adequate conceptualizations. It may be, however, that the opposite is true, that medieval theorists preferred fiction because it was better suited to the ideological task at hand, a positive means of empowerment, rather than a stopgap.

Such certainly seems the case with the narrative of Article 33. To be able to tell this story of the royal voice was quite literally to usurp its authority. Narrative becomes a species of political power. Yet despite this convergence, the two categories are not completely interchangeable. Within medieval ideologies of kingship, narrative was precisely that species of power that could never know itself as such. The ideological fictions of kingship had always to be subordinated to the form of power they maintained. Article 33's story of Richard's voice, though primarily the product of previous traditional fictions, works precisely by suppressing its fictionality and presenting itself as the truth.

At the same time, this fiction was public in a way that its predecessors hadn't needed to be. The quasi-parliamentary status of the Articles of Deposition testify to the increased dispersion of the ruling class they

226     *Larry Scanlon*

were attempting to unify. For the Lancastrians this dispersion meant that kingship's dependence on public modes of legitimation was greater than ever before. They could not be satisfied simply to commission works in Latin; they needed legitimation in the vernacular. Here the needs of political authority and the needs of the newly emergent Chaucerian tradition converged, and royal patronage of vernacular poetry was an important item on the Lancastrian ideological agenda, particularly for Henry V.[25]

As an early example of this trend, the *Regement of Princes* emerges as a remarkable meditation on the relation between the literary and the political. Narrative, the rhetorical form common to both, provides the meeting ground. Like many *Fürstenspiegel,* the work consists of a series of moral discussions interspersed with exempla. But if these moral discussions constitute kingship's other voice—that is, the voice of counsel—they are framed by the larger narrative of Hoccleve's autobiography. The autobiography exposes Hoccleve's material dependence on Henry, subjugating the voice of counsel he embodies to the very power it would constrain. The effect of the narrative, then, is to present the Prince as at once constrained by the voice of counsel and independent of it.

The autobiography further complicates matters by introducing Chaucer into the poem as Hoccleve's "maister deere," an independent source of literary authority.[26] This complication is necessary to the legitimation of Henry even as it seems to transcend it. The vernacular legitimation of Henry requires a vernacular moral authority, and this is what the canonization of Chaucer provides. In effect, the very thoroughness with which Hoccleve pursues the celebration of Henry leads him to canonize Chaucer. Both aims are offered to an expanding ruling-class audience as complementary aspects of the same general project of cultural empowerment. I have already sketched this project's largest ideological outlines. It is now time to examine Hoccleve's text, and the specific models of authority with which it grapples, to see how he works out the project in detail.

25. G. L. Harriss, "Introduction: The Exemplar of Kingship," in *Henry V: The Practice of Kingship* (Oxford: Oxford University Press, 1985), 1–29.
26. Thomas Hoccleve, *Regement of Princes,* ed. Frederick J. Furnivall (London: 1897), 1961. All subsequent citations are from this edition and will hereafter be given in the text.

## THE VOICES OF TRADITION:
## CHAUCER AND THE *FÜRSTENSPIEGEL*

The *Regement* brings together the primarily Latin tradition of the *Für-stenspiegel* with the vernacular tradition presided over by Chaucer. Hoc-cleve's interest in kingship was anticipated by both Chaucer and Gower as well as by poets in the alliterative tradition. *Wynnere and Wastoure,* the early passus of *Piers Plowman,* and *Mum and the Sothsegger* all treat the king as society's moral center.[27] Gower returns to the problem of kingship throughout the *Confessio Amantis,* and he presents the seventh book of that work as a recapitulation of the *Secretum Secretorum,* per-haps the most popular *Fürstenspiegel* in fourteenth- and fifteenth-century England. The issue surfaces in the *Canterbury Tales* as well. Like Lydgate's *Fall of Princes,* the *Monk's Tale* is a *De Casibus* collection, a genre related to the *Fürstenspiegel.* And the tale Chaucer presents in his own voice, the *Tale of Melibee,* while not explicitly concerned with kingship, is a "serious and thoughtful address to the powerful on how to save their power."[28]

Many scholars still view the political concerns of these writers as regrettable concessions to public taste. What this view fails to recognize is that the audience that supported the tradition's explicitly political work, though perhaps larger, was basically the same audience that sup-ported the putatively apolitical Chaucerian tales modern scholarship has found more to its liking. This audience came from the newly em-powered strata of the ruling class, the gentry and the richest of the urban bourgeoisie, who looked to the royal court as the source of cul-tural as well as political authority.[29] For this audience, the growing con-

27. Indeed, discussions of kingship are so prevalent in fourteenth-century poetry of complaint that Janet Coleman has suggested such works "be classified *thematically* as mirrors for princes" ("English Culture in the Fourteenth Century," in *Chaucer and the Italian Trecento,* ed. Piero Boitani [Cambridge, Eng.: Cambridge University Press, 1983], 60).

28. Stephen Knight, *Geoffrey Chaucer* (Oxford: Basil Blackwell, 1986), 139.

29. For a general overview of the reading public in late medieval England, see Janet Coleman, *Medieval Readers and Writers 1350–1400* (New York: Columbia University Press, 1981); Richard Firth Green, *Poets and Princepleasers* (Toronto: University of Toronto Press, 1980); and Anne Middleton, "The Idea of Public Poetry in the Reign of Richard II," *Speculum* 53 (1978): 94–114. For Chaucer's audience, see Paul Strohm, "Chaucer's Audience," *Literature and History* 5 (1977): 26–41, and "Chaucer's Fifteenth-Century Au-dience and the Narrowing of the Chaucer Tradition," *Studies in the Age of Chaucer* 4 (1982): 3–32.

sumption of vernacular literature was no less an exercise in cultural entitlement than the growing participation in political discourse.

Chaucer's participation in this project was not restricted to *Melibee*
and the *Monk's Tale*. The entire Canterbury collection is built around
the dialectic between narrative voice and social position. As Jill Mann
has shown, the General Prologue is an estates satire.[30] As the frame tale,
it thus locates each of the many narrative voices of the *Tales* within a
social totality, a solidarity within which the apparently inexhaustible
capacity of Chaucerian narrative for shifting voices is played out. This
fact alone would seem to call into question the formalist assumption
that Chaucer's shifting perspectives signal his desire to transcend the
communal demands of his audience.

Mann herself reserves judgment on this point, preferring to see the
Prologue as a detached exercise in ethnography, rather than the rein-
forcement of the moral values associated with estates satire. As the narrative voice shifts from one character to the next, demonstrating that
each character's point of view is conditioned by his social position,
within which it is perfectly coherent, the reader recognizes the impossibility of any totalizing judgment.[31] But this view will produce an
apolitical reading of the *Tales* only if one assumes a complete separation
between the discursive and the political. If not, then to the extent that
the shifts in voice are rendered intelligible by the social categories the
frame tale imposes, the categories are themselves validated. It may be
impossible to judge the value of the Knight's point of view in relation
to the Miller's, but the very fact that the estates frame enables one view-
point to be recognized as a "noble" tale and the other as a "cherles" tale
gives the frame a heuristic validity that depends ultimately on its social
content. For this reason, Chaucer's ethnography is not ultimately any
more detached from estates ideology than the more explicitly evaluative
claims of earlier estates satires.[32]

---

30. *Chaucer and Medieval Estates Satire* (Cambridge, Eng.: Cambridge University
Press, 1973).

31. Ibid., esp. 187–202.

32. Mann as much as concedes this when she characterizes Chaucer's ethnography in
the following way: "This is how the world operates, and as the world, it can operate no
other way. The contrast with heavenly values is made at the end of the *Canterbury Tales*,
but it is made in such a way that it cannot affect the validity of the initial statement—the
world can only operate by the world's values" (201). The very force with which this
apparent tautology (the world operates as the world operates) asserts the indisputability
of the status quo conceals the validation of a particular status quo. So far as the General

This is particularly true when one considers the function Chaucer's ethnography would have had for his original audience. To an audience of the lesser nobility, the frame tale presents figures who are mostly inferior in social status. The estates frame is precisely what enables this audience to have access to these less privileged voices. It is politically empowering in that it assigns these voices their social meanings. As Article 33 gave the same audience access to the voice of the king, the *Canterbury Tales* gives it access to the voices of the socially excluded.

I am not suggesting that the contemporary political value of the *Tales* exhausts their meaning. But I am suggesting that this political value underlies the Chaucerian tradition's reading of Chaucer, and that it makes that reading of Chaucer as valid as any other. The modern cliché that the fifteenth-century's version of Chaucer was narrow or distorted is a purely ideological preference presented as an indisputable poetic law. That version of Chaucer is certainly no narrower than the modern view that celebrates Chaucer's romances and fabliaux and discards the *Melibee,* the *Monk's Tale,* and the devotional works. Modern commentators are as entitled to their ideological preferences as the fifteenth century was to its, but when they make those preferences the basis of their literary history, they have failed as historians. The fifteenth century was not a period of cultural decline. It was a period that carried on the cultural expansion that had begun in the last half of the fourteenth, an expansion about which texts like the *Regement of Princes* were entirely self-conscious.

The dialectic between narrative voice and social position that Chaucer achieved through estates satire, Hoccleve achieves through a generic mutation of another sort. In a Prologue that accounts for almost half the work's total length, he presents an extended dialogue with a beggar, whom he clearly intends as a surrogate (at one point the Beggar offers an autobiography reminiscent of the one Hoccleve himself offers in *La Male Regle* [596–742]). At the end of the Prologue the Beggar suggests Hoccleve write the *Regement* as a way of petitioning for an annuity. The next day Hoccleve sits down to write and places in the middle of

---

Prologue is concerned the claim "the world can operate no other way" always assumes "no other way" means "no other way than according to these categories, the categories of medieval estates satire." There are in fact lots of other ways to understand the way the world operates—as the teacher of Chaucer rediscovers each time he or she attempts to explain what a maniciple is to a survey class of college sophomores.

the work the request for an annuity the Beggar suggested he make (1842–2016).

Framing his *Fürstenspiegel* in this way counters the discursive authority Hoccleve assumes within the text with his social subordination to the prince outside of it. In fact, this framing breaks down the distinction between inside and outside, self-reflexively bringing into the text the projected exchange of the text itself for an annuity. This narrative in turn suggests Henry's actual presence, an impression Hoccleve reinforces throughout the poem by continually presenting his moral instruction in the second person. At least one of the manuscripts takes the fiction a step further still, inserting between the text of the Prologue and the text of the Proem, at the very point where Hoccleve begins to address Henry directly, an illustration in which a small, kneeling poet presents his book to a larger standing figure wearing a crown.[33]

The begging poem was a comparatively late genre, emerging in France in the fourteenth century.[34] It presupposes a court in transition from the personal to the bureaucratic, one sufficiently bureaucratized that petitions for small sums of money have become routine, but still sufficiently invested in the personal to want to see the granting of such petitions as the whimsical response to a *jeu d'esprit*. The begging poem postulates a royal *voluntas* that acts entirely at its own pleasure, and thus stands as a striking counterpoise to the didactic presumptions of the *Fürstenspiegel*, which posits a king who relies on counsel.

Nevertheless, yoking the two genres together simply underlines a tension already long established within the *Fürstenspiegel* itself. The compilers of *Fürstenspiegel* almost invariably display their dependence on a particular ruler. These works were customarily dedicated to a prince or ecclesiastical magnate on whom the compiler was dependent or from whom he wished preferment. Often, as in the *Regement of Princes,* the second-person address would continue within the body of the work. *Fürstenspiegel* also served as public celebrations of their dedicatees, appearing at moments of opportunity or dispute. For example, John of Salisbury's *Policraticus,* which commences the high medieval tradition, was dedicated to Becket while he was still chancellor to Henry II. The work is strenuously theocratic, arguing the king

---

33. Furnivall, ed., *Regement,* 73.
34. A. C. Spearing, *Medieval to Renaissance in English Poetry* (Cambridge, Eng.: Cambridge University Press, 1985), 111.

should be subject to the pope and should heed clerical counselors.[35] Similarly, the equally relentlessly royalist *De Regimine Principum,* one of the three sources Hoccleve names in his opening address to the prince (2038–2128), was compiled by Aegidius Romanus for Philip the Fair, whose later arrest of Boniface VIII would mark the beginning of the end for papal absolutism.[36] And the source that Hoccleve names first and seems to take as the model of the genre is the *Secretum Secretorum:* presented as if authored by Aristotle for Alexander, it opens with Aristotle's lavish praise of Alexander and frames the philosophical instruction to come as a means of inducing his subjects to obedience and lawful activity.[37] Widely circulated and translated in fourteenth- and fifteenth-century England, both these works stage the paradox of an omnipotent ruler who nonetheless requires advice, a royal *voluntas* from which proceeds reward and yet a royal ear eager to listen and so acknowledging its own insufficiency.

The *Fürstenspiegel* was a discrete generic expression of the larger medieval discourse of sovereignty. This discourse is generally seen as moving from theocratic absolutism to secular and constitutional monarchism, a movement through which, in the words of Wilks, "the Ages of Faith become transmuted into an Age of Reason."[38] As I have suggested, this Whig teleology ignores the deep attraction absolutist arguments had for both secular monarchs and their noble cohorts, the very attraction that in fact made the transition from the theocratic to the secular possible in the first place. The theocratic argument for papal

35. For the position of the *Policraticus* within the tradition, see Berges, *Die Fürstenspiegel,* 3–8. For John's relation to Becket, see Beryl Smalley, *The Becket Conflict and the Schools: A Study of Intellectuals in Politics* (Totowa, N.J.: Rowman and Littlefield, 1973), 87–108.

36. For a good, brief discussion and additional bibliography, see Richard Jones, *The Royal Policy of Richard II* (New York: Barnes and Noble, 1973), 154–59.

37. *Secretum Secretorum* as edited and glossed by Roger Bacon, ed. Robert Steele, fasc. 5 of *Opera hactenus inedita Rogeri Baconi* (Oxford: Clarendon, 1920), 40–42. The third source Hoccleve names, Jacob de Cessolis's *Libellus super Ludo Schachorum,* is the most important of the three for sheer bulk of material borrowed. (See William Mathews, "Thomas Hoccleve," in *A Manual of the Writings in Middle English 1050–1500,* ed. Albert E. Hartung, vol. 3 (New Haven: Connecticut Academy of Arts and Sciences, 1972), 749–50.) Though not dedicated to an actual monarch, it begins with a fictionalized scene of public instruction. The game of chess, it claims, was devised by a philosopher who needed an indirect stratagem to correct a tyrannical king. This work is generally considered an estates satire. However, Raymond D. Di Lorenzo, on the basis of this scene, argues it should be considered a *Fürstenspiegel* ("The Collection Form and the Art of Memory in the *Libellus super Ludo Schachorum* of Jacobus de Cessolis," *Medieval Studies* 34 [1973]: 206–9).

38. *Sovereignty,* 529.

sovereignty was not simply an argument for faith against reason, or the eternal against the temporal. It was an argument that wanted, on the basis of mutual consent (that is, shared belief in Christ), to center all communal authority in a single figure.

As medieval monarchy became increasingly institutionalized, this conception of authority became increasingly attractive, because it provided a way of intellectually concentrating the power that was being institutionally dispersed. The *Fürstenspiegel* enacted this concentration by its rhetorical celebration of its dedicatee. But it also acknowledged the fact of dispersion by its performance of public instruction. This may explain the popularity of the genre among an English ruling class continually seeking a greater share in royal power. It may also explain both the *Regement*'s specific political motivation and its ostentatious exploitation of the tradition's paradoxes.

For all of its ideological shrewdness, Bolinbroke's accession to the crown left him in a precarious position. The basis for his title was not and could not be made entirely clear. He faced revolts in 1400 and 1402, and by 1410 his ailments had forced him to leave the overseeing of the kingdom to councillors who were openly feuding with the prince.[39] Against this background the *Regement of Princes* can be seen as a direct attempt to secure the continuity of Lancastrian rule. By addressing a *Fürstenspiegel* to the future Henry V, Hoccleve effectively settles the question of dynastic rights by treating it as if it were already settled. He reinforces the point by scattering through the poem favorable invocations of the prince's patrimony: his father, the king (816–26, 1835, 3347–67), his grandfather, John of Gaunt (3347–67), and his great-grandfather, Henry of Lancaster (2647–53). This rhetorical representation of Henry as dynastically legitimate with a long, honorable patrimony and about to receive a *Fürstenspiegel* can appropriately be described as a narrative positioning. It is narrative because it historicizes: it not only locates the *persona* it produces within a preexistent social totality, indeed, but produces the *persona* precisely by so locating it.

The projected dynastic succession is thus implicit in the projected acceptance of a *Fürstenspiegel,* and both are framed by the projected exchange of begging poem for royal grant. These evocations of Henry

39. McFarlane, *Lancastrian Kings,* 106–12. See also Lawton, "Dullness," who reads the situation somewhat differently (776–77).

concretize the abstract set of moral lessons the text contains as the property of a specific, already established figure of supreme social authority. This narrative entails both idealization and coercion. There is the ideal of royal *voluntas* in general and Henry in particular as the personal embodiment of the text's commonly held moral principles. But there is also the coercion inherent in precisely this capacity of narrative to concretize: to present the ideal as if it were already embodied. In the equivocation between idealization and coercion lie both the risk and the aim of the *Regement of Princes*.

Hoccleve uses narrative's capacity for continually shifting point of view to resolve or bypass (to resolve by bypassing) the constitutional tensions surrounding the Lancastrian monarchy. Because of the severity of these tensions, he exploits his shifting point of view to the fullest, and thereby continually risks exposing its arbitrary, propagandistic aim. Yet he takes the risk precisely to convert it to his goal, which is to make his rhetorical construction of Prince Henry not simply a construction but the truth.

## THE VOICES OF AUTHORITY:
## CHAUCER AND THE PRINCE

One measure of the risk Hoccleve takes is the care he devotes to the frame tale that makes the *Regement* a begging poem. The Prologue is 2016 lines long, accounting, as I said before, for almost half the poem. It opens with an autobiographical detail that ties Hoccleve's fate to the prince's. "Musyng upon the restles bisynesse / Which that this troubly world hath ay on honde" (1–2) the poet spends a sleepless night at the Chester Inn. His reflections on the "brotlynesse" of Fortune (15–21) quickly become generalized:

> Me fel to mynde how that, not long ago,
> ffortunes strok doun threst estaat royal
> Into myscheef; and I took heed also
> Of many anothir lord that had a falle.
>
> (22–25)

Obviously this allusion to Richard is risky. Besides the more general presumption involved in comparing his situation to a king's, the allusion raises other awkward questions as well. Is he sympathizing with Richard? Is he presenting Richard as an unwitting victim of Fortune, when the logic of deposition assumes that Richard brought his fate entirely upon himself? Doesn't this recollection of the uncertainty of Richard's position call attention to the fragility of Henry's? All of these implicit questions give the passage an indefinite charge that stops just short of indecorous confrontation. For the topicality of the allusions is quickly absorbed into the conventional status of its context. This opening is similar to the moment of psychic disturbance that often opened dream visions. It is particularly close to the insomnia that opens the *Book of the Duchess:* what Chaucer finds in the Book of Ceyx and Alcyone, Hoccleve will find in the addition of another voice, the Beggar's.

In the place of a vision, the Beggar will provide the solution to Hoccleve's dilemma that addresses both its personal and its global dimensions. The appeal to Henry through the composition of a *Fürstenspiegel* will solve Hoccleve's financial problem at the same time it strengthens a threatened "estaat royal." The Prologue comes to this solution indirectly yet deliberately. After a long dialogue on Fortune and the many ways to protect oneself against it, and after several other suggestions, the Beggar finally broaches the appeal to Henry:

> "O my good sone, wolt þou yit algate
> Despeired be? nay, sone, lat be þat!
> Þou schalt as blyue entre into þe yate
> Of þi comfort. now telle on pleyn and plat:
> My lord þe prince, knowyth he þe nat?
> If þat þou stonde in his benevolence,
> He may be salue vnto þin indigence.
>
> No man bet, next his fadir, our lord lige."
> "Yis fadir, he is my good gracious lord."
> "Wel sone, þan wole I me oblige,—
> And god of heuen vouch I to record,—
> Þat if þou wolt be ful of myn accord,
> Thow schalt no cause haue more þus to muse,
> But heuynesse voide, and it refuse.
>
> "Syn he þi good lord is, I am ful seur
> His grace to þe schal nat be denyed;
> Þou wost wele, he benyng is and demeur
> To sue vnto; naght is his goost maistried
> With daunger, but his hert is ful applied
> To graunte, and nat þe needy werne his grace;
> To hym pursue, and þi releef purchace."
>
>                                    (1828–48)

This suggestion comes much more easily via the Beggar than it would have had it been made in Hoccleve's own voice. The Beggar's praise of

Prince Henry would have had the appearance of crass flattery had it been addressed to Henry directly by Hoccleve. But because it arises in the course of a conversation where the prince is not present, it acquires the givenness of an objective truth. When the Beggar offhandedly concludes, "No man bet, next his fadir," his very offhandedness increases the impression that Henry's virtue is a matter of both lineage and simple common knowledge, both now standing beyond any possible dispute.

Hoccleve links this assertion of Henry's virtue to the granting of his suit, leaving the onus of proof deftly and almost imperceptibly on Henry, but making such proof, by the very imperceptibility of the link, a matter of course. The suit is at once a test of Henry's generosity and a ratification of his future. For as Hoccleve's projected redeemer, Henry becomes a moral force standing outside the cycle of Fortune, impervious to the instabilities that undid Richard.

The Beggar enforces this impression with the specific suggestion that the appeal take the form of a *Fürstenspiegel:*

> "looke if þou fynde canst any tretice
> Groundid on his estates holsumnesse;
> Swych thing translate, and unto his hynesse
> As humbely as þat þou canst, present."
> (1949–52)

Hoccleve will appeal not simply to Henry's grace, but to his presumed enthusiasm for moral instruction. The Beggar precedes this final suggestion with a warning against flattery: "But of a thyng be wel waar in al wise, / On flaterie þat þou þe nat founde," adding that advisors are afraid to tell their lords the truth, and instead "thei stryuen who best rynge shal þe bell / Of fals plesance" (1912–13, 29–30). Lords are so continually surrounded by such flattery that it is impossible for them to learn their true condition, and therefore the greatest service Hoccleve can perform for Henry is to tell him the truth (1933–46).

The Beggar so firmly associates pleasant news with flattery that the measure of the truth becomes virtually its unpleasantness to princely ears. At this point the narrative frame for Hoccleve's authority has been fully articulated, providing the prince with moral grounds for granting his suit. By accepting the *Fürstenspiegel* Hoccleve offers, the prince will demonstrate that he is a ruler who prefers the truth to flattery—a virtue with which, of course, the Beggar has already endowed him. The Beggar's intervention transforms a self-interested petition into a fully moral exchange between a model ruler and a loyal subject. In return for moral instruction, Henry will award an annuity, not as mere compensation, but as a sign of his devotion to morality. The Prologue has transformed its terms of address, pretending all the while to have changed nothing.

Both the pretense and the transformation are specifically narrative products; both result from the addition of the Beggar's voice. Like the voice of any narrative figure, the Beggar's is at once his author's and his own, but Hoccleve intensifies the effect of this resemblance in difference precisely by identifying this voice as a Beggar's. This diffuses the begging position from which he himself speaks, making it more general and thus enabling him to present it favorably. The Beggar resembles Hoccleve in that both are beggars; he differs from Hoccleve in that Hoccleve is his social superior. This difference means that when he speaks to Hoccleve, and through Hoccleve to Prince Henry, both Hoccleve and the prince are now in the same position: social superiors being addressed by a subordinate.

Also, of course, Hoccleve uses this social positioning to affirm the Beggar's moral authority. When the Beggar first offers his assistance Hoccleve scoffs at his infirmity and meager appearance, concluding that "it moste be a greter man of myght / Þan þat þou art, þat scholde me releue" (176–77). In the long dialogue that follows, as the Beggar breaks down Hoccleve's resistance he implicitly breaks down the prince's as well. When he suggests the appeal to the prince at the end of the dialogue, the suggestion comes as if it were completely external. The considerable presumption involved in both begging poems and *Fürstenspiegel* is diffused, for the suggestion that the two are in fact one is made by a figure who has just demonstrated the independent moral authority beggars can possess.[40] And this independent authority has been produced by Hoccleve himself through his narrative, an act of production that has also, by means of the manipulation of narrative voice, been disguised.

This elaborate representational strategy is an extension of the begging poem's central ploy, the construction of a conceit whose intricacy will distract attention from the crassness of the request. The implication is that what the prince pays for is the elegance of the poetic structure:

40. Of course there was a powerful cultural precedent for this position in Langland's begging *persona* in *Piers Plowman*.

a begging poem always pays its patron the compliment of making him the arbiter of poetic value. In the *Regement of Princes,* the poetic structure is also a moral one. By being a *Fürstenspiegel* and begging poem at once, it defines Henry as the repository of moral as well as poetic value. This combination allows Henry to have it both ways. Accepting the *Regement* as a begging poem will certify his moral rectitude; acceding to it as a *Fürstenspiegel* will not diminish his social authority.

The tension this combination produces is one to which Hoccleve can return again and again. When after the Prologue ends Hoccleve finally addresses Henry directly, he can do so in the language of compliment, for that language now carries moral weight.

> Hye and noble prince excellent,
> My lord the prince, o my lord gracious,
> I, humble servant and obedient
> Vnto your estate hye & glorious,
> Of whiche I am full tendir & full ielous,
> Me recomaunde unto your worthynesse,
> With hert entier, and spirite of mekenesse.
>
> Right humbly axyng of you the license,
> That with my penne I may to you declare
> (So as that kan my wittes innocence,)
> Myne inward wille that thursteth the welefare
> Of your persone; and elles be I bare
> Of blisse, whan þat the cold stroke of deth
> My lyfe hath quenched, & me byraft my breth.
>
> (2017–30)

The tension between producing an effect and disguising it recurs here in the abandonment of will Hoccleve wants his writing to signify. As the very ornateness of these introductory lines make clear, direct address does not merely locate a *persona* but constitutes it as well. Hoccleve is not simply addressing a prince all of whose attributes are immediately available outside the text, but a prince whom he makes high, noble, and excellent by so addressing. To the extent this *persona* is perceived as simply Hoccleve's invention, the project fails. Asking for "license" from the very *persona* being produced at once acknowledges and disclaims the inventiveness, which is effaced under the sign of the real Henry. The textual *persona* of the model prince becomes an unnecessary recreation of virtues already embodied in Henry's actual personality.

As I have already noted, Hoccleve keeps his moral instruction in the second person, maintaining the fiction of Henry's personal presence throughout the poem. Hoccleve cannot assert his own independent moral authority without simultaneously reiterating his status as a dependent addressing a prince. His authority is always dependent on the central fiction of Henry's presence. This frame intensifies the personal component in the already heavily personalized conceptions of royal authority that Hoccleve inherits from the *Fürstenspiegel* tradition.

The poem proper is divided into fifteen sections with an envoy. The first four deal with the royal *voluntas*: royal dignity, the coronation oath, justice, and the observance of the laws. Next are five personal virtues: piety, mercy, patience, chastity, and magnanimity. After three on the management of wealth and two on counsel, there is a concluding section on peace. The emphasis throughout is on the power of the royal example, the social order that Henry will produce by assuming these virtues. Upon occasion Hoccleve explicitly invokes Henry's absolute freedom, making his acceptance of moral constraint an act of grace:

> Who-so þat in hye dignite is sette,
> And may do grevous wrong & cruelte,
> If he for-bere hem, to commend is bette,
> And gretter shal his mede and meryte be.
> (2843–48)

But even where this freedom is not made explicit, the aspect of Henry's personal moral restraint Hoccleve stresses most is the awe and respect it will arouse in his subjects. When moral restraint meets royal power, the result is social control, and the moral shades into the ideological.

The transaction is most evident where the personal and political are hardest to distinguish: royal speech. The discussion of coronation oaths returns this issue to a *locus classicus* of medieval tradition. The coronation oath was a symbolic instrument for finessing the ambiguities surrounding the problem of royal prerogative. In taking the oath, a monarch voluntarily constrains his own prerogative to the laws of his predecessors. Thus the oath was a ceremonial recognition of the practical constraint on royal prerogative that nonetheless left it theoretically absolute. Hoccleve trades on this ambiguity by stressing the performative aspect of oath-keeping, its prescription of internal consistency rather than its assertion of simple conformity to an external standard.

> And syn a kyng, by wey of his office,
> To god I-likned is, as in manere,
> And god is trouthe itself, þan may the vice

Of vntrouthe, naght in a kyng appeere,
If his office schal to god referre.
A besy tonge bringeth in swiche wit,
He þat by word naght gilteþ is perfit.

A! lord, what is fair and honurable,
A kyng from mochil speche him refreyne;
It sitte him ben of wordes mesurable,
ffor mochil clap wole his estate desteyne.
If he his tonge with mesures reyne
Governe, than his honur it conserveth.

(2409–21)

To what extent is the God-like king "trouthe itself"? Obviously royal speech is not absolutely performative in the way of divine speech; it cannot call truth into being simply by articulating it. And yet Hoccleve strongly implies that so long as "untrouthe" is avoided, royal speech may become God-like.

In this paradoxical formulation royal speech is performative within certain bounds, bounds that become clearer as the passage proceeds. The advice against speaking too often follows directly the warning against "untrouthe," as if the two were equivalent. To view royal speech as capable of excess is to assume that royal prerogative is safest when least evident, as if ultimately it were incapable of justifying itself in purely linguistic terms. It is to assume a status quo that operates best when least observed. "For mochil clap wole his estate desteyne": a king who speaks too much is likely to expose himself as no more in control of language than its other users.

A king can control his estate by controlling his tongue; the status quo provides the reference point against which "untrouthe" is to be judged. Royal speech becomes performative precisely by not seeking to be, by always seeking to submerge its effects in its preservation of royal power. It is as if the ideal of royal speech were silence. This is the reason kingship always needs another voice, like Hoccleve's. Justification spoken in another voice will always make royal authority seem to be a power beyond language, which it must always be in order to be justified at all.

This view of political authority is both profoundly conservative and yet self-consciously constructive at the same time. Contradictory as the combination may seem to a modern consciousness, the two tendencies are actually mutually reinforcing. Hoccleve's often spectacularly self-conscious poetic mastery continually serves his political conservatism, but just as significantly the conservatism is also what motivates the poetry. The Shelleyan view of poetry as politically redemptive runs extraordinarily deep in twentieth-century literary studies. It persists *mutatis mutandis* in the deconstructive tenet that a text's representational strategies will always subvert its explicit ideology. The *Regement* presents a strong counterexample to this view, demonstrating instead the capacity that Terry Eagleton has called "the cunning of the ideological"—the capacity of an ideological position to strengthen itself precisely by exposing its assumptions.[41]

Hoccleve's conservatism is so intertwined with his poetry that it motivates his most poetic of moments: his canonization of Chaucer. This canonization is another way in which Hoccleve makes authority narrative. Chaucer's is an authorizing voice more historically and linguistically continuous with Hoccleve's than those of classical or ecclesiastical authors. And Hoccleve consistently locates Chaucer's authority biographically. There are three discussions of Chaucer, which all follow essentially the same pattern. After a celebration of Chaucer's authority there is a lament for his death. In the last two discussions, there is also a prayer that he rest in peace. In several of the manuscripts this final invocation is accompanied by a portrait. The portrait in British Museum Harleian Manuscript 4866 (leaf 91) is the earliest known of Chaucer and is probably the source of most later portraits, including the equestrian portrait of the Ellesmere manuscript.[42] This fact, though it may seem no more than a charming bit of antiquarianism, signals a crucial change. It signals an increasing historicization of discursive authority, an increasing desire to locate authority within a personage historically and linguistically immediate.

The literary canonization of historically proximate, vernacular authors has traditionally been taken as the hallmark of Renaissance humanism. Though the trend predates Hoccleve, beginning in Italy with Boccaccio and Petrarch, Hoccleve is the first to articulate it fully in English. If, as A. C. Spearing argues, Chaucer invents "the possibility of a history of English poetry," Hoccleve makes that possibility actual

41. Terry Eagleton, "Text, Ideology, Realism," in *Literature and Society: Selected Papers from the English Institute, 1978,* ed. Edward Said (Baltimore: Johns Hopkins University Press, 1980), 153.

42. Jerome Mitchell, *Thomas Hoccleve: A Study in Early Fifteenth-Century English Poetic* (Urbana: University of Illinois Press, 1968), 110–15.

by establishing Chaucer as the source of such a history.[43] Of course, this canonization is not so much a break with older notions of authority as an attempt to recuperate them in a more usable way.

Hoccleve clearly presents Chaucer as the most immediate source of his own authority. The first invocation occurs in the Prologue directly after he agrees to write the *Regement* (1954–81) and begins with the regret that Chaucer is not available to lend "consail and reed" (1960). The second occurs in the discussion of his sources, where he makes it clear his access to these authorities, meager though it is ("Simple is my goost, and scars my letterure" [2073]), comes through Chaucer, who "fayn wolde han me taght" (2078). In both passages he is the center of traditional authority, like Cicero in rhetoric, like Aristotle (whom Hoccleve has just named as author of the *Secretum Secretorum*) in philosophy, and like Virgil in poetry (2085–90). This displacement of Latin authority into the vernacular authority of Chaucer is obviously meant to make the authority of tradition more accessible to Hoccleve's audience. But this broadening of textual authority has as its larger goal the solidification of royal authority.

For to the extent that the textual is historicized, immediate political authority is strengthened. As Hoccleve elevates Chaucer to the status of an *auctor,* his insistence on the biographical makes the textual even more dependent on the actualities of historical existence. Chaucer's authority inheres most fully in his person; it does not survive complete in his texts alone. Though he is "universel fadir of science" (1964) and "first fyndere of our fair langage" (4978), what Hoccleve learned from him he learned personally. The implication of the lament that Chaucer is no longer available for "consail and reed" is that once Chaucer is no longer alive and producing, the power of his texts to put the cultural world in order begins to fade. The final portrait, which abandons language altogether in favor of pictorial representation, takes this idea to its logical limit.

Vernacular authority is thus tied more directly to historical actuality than either the classical or the sacred. If authorizing the vernacular means a greater freedom from the past, it may also mean a greater subordination to the immediate status quo. These two tendencies are not necessarily opposed, for freedom from the past may be enabled by an

43. Spearing, *Medieval to Renaissance,* 34.

increase in political empowerment. This was the case for Hoccleve's audience, and his canonization gave them a new, vernacular authority in the guise of the old. As the "Mirour of fructuous entendement," the "universal fadir in science" (1963–64), Chaucer becomes the Aristotle to Henry's Alexander, the source of the communally held moral values to be embodied in the ideal prince.

The legitimacy of Henry is the cost of this new, vernacular access to discursive authority. Without an immediately available embodiment of moral order, Hoccleve cannot grant any moral privilege to the historically immediate. And if historical immediacy is without moral value, then so too is the vernacular. Hoccleve's celebration of the nascent English tradition embodied in Chaucer and the political authority embodied in Henry are the twin faces of the same moral vision. As this vision empowers itself by exposing the assumptions of the Latin traditions it inherits, it also solidifies its empowerment in the figure of Henry. Henry must become the guarantor of moral order because it is he who will become king. This is perhaps the one assumption of which the *Regement* can never become fully self-conscious. Like any *Fürstenspiegel*, it must assume that there is moral value in the very structure of kingship, regardless of the moral status of the individual who occupies it. Without this assumption, the *Fürstenspiegel* has lost its raison d'être.

## NARRATIVE POWER

I have already discussed many of the ways in which the *Regement* expresses this central tenet of the ideology of monarchy. Perhaps its most extreme expression occurs in the one aspect of the work I have not yet discussed: the exempla. In the exemplum medieval thought explicitly recognized the persuasive power of narrative. Early discussions of preaching recommended the use of exempla on the grounds that narrative was more immediately persuasive than doctrine. The first medieval exemplum collection was Gregory's *Dialogues;* Gregory remarks on several occasions that exempla touch the heart more directly than doctrine or rational argument.[44] Not surprisingly, the form was viewed as particularly suited to persuading the uninstructed or the unconverted. The sermon exemplum achieved its zenith during the great preaching

---

44. See J.-Th. Welter, *L'exemplum dans la littérature religieuse et didactique du Moyen Age* (Paris: Occitania, 1927), 14–15.

campaigns of the twelfth and thirteenth centuries, when the urban lower classes were being proselytized for the first time.[45]

The exemplum had a similar rhetorical profile in the *Fürstenspiegel*, though obviously its audience was different. John of Salisbury, whose *Policraticus* became a dominant repository of exempla both within and without the tradition, comments extensively on the form. In book 4, he buttresses the claim that the prince is an inferior minister of the priests with classical exempla, then justifies his appeal to the classical by asserting Paul used such exempla to preach to the Athenians.[46] This characterization of the form achieves a double purpose. It places John's royalist opposition in the position of uninstructed pagans, and then suggests that like Paul, John can convert them by his superior handling of their own forms. In a more general discussion elsewhere, he describes exempla as *strategemma* and *strategemmatica*, sites of polemical conflict.[47]

The exemplum thus came to secular writers like Hoccleve as a form charged with ecclesiastical authority, but also as a form suited to polemic. The latter capacity enabled these writers to turn the form against the Church and put it to the service of secular authority. Many of Hoccleve's exempla turn on a ruler's voluntary restraint of some power or prerogative otherwise freely available to him. While occasionally these are stories of self-sacrifice, such as that of Regulus, the Roman commander who convinced the senate to return him to execution in Carthage rather than complete an unfavorable exchange of prisoners (2248–96), more typically the restraint redounds to the ruler's advantage. For instance, there are two similar stories of Roman generals Camillus (2584–2646) and Scipio Africanus (3676–3710). A schoolmaster in a city Camillus is besieging kidnaps the children of the wealthy citizens who employ him and offers them to Camillus to use as a bargaining chip. Camillus refuses, and when the citizens discover this, they decide to surrender in recognition of his great virtue. In the other story, Scipio is offered a virgin betrothed to a lord in Carthage, and his refusal brings about the same result, the surrender of the city. In both cases

45. On the class significance of the preaching campaigns, see Barbara Rosenswein and Lester K. Little, "Social Meaning in the Monastic and Mendicant Spiritualities," *Past and Present* 63 (1974): 18–32.

46. *Policraticus* 4.3.

47. *Policraticus* 8.14, 2. Cited and discussed in Peter von Moos, "The Use of *Exempla* in the *Policraticus* of John of Salisbury," in *The World of John of Salisbury*, ed. Michael Wilks (Oxford: Basil Blackwell, 1984), 227–28.

moral restraint effects a significant gain in political power, producing a sovereignty that has not existed before. Camillus and Scipio bend a hitherto refractory population to their will through the ideological power of example, through their personal enactment of a public moral narrative, acts of virtue that cannot be separated from the political positions they reinforce.

An even greater interdependence of the moral and the political occurs in two successive exempla, Lycurgus and his Laws (2948–89) and the Phalarean Bull (3004–38), which end the section on Justice and begin the section on Piety. Both of these exempla were widely circulated in the later Middle Ages, both within the *Fürstenspiegel* and outside it. Both occur in the seventh book of the *Confessio Amantis*, which was probably Hoccleve's most immediate source.[48] He does all that he can to intensify the representation of kingship as the source of moral value already implicit in both exempla. He juxtaposes them, and adds dialogue to what had been primarily plot summary. He makes their protagonists anonymous, as if to focus attention on their political position. Private personal virtue is either moot, in the case of Lycurgus, or nonexistent, in the case of Phalaris. Moral order is something they produce simply through their manipulation of political authority.

In Hoccleve's version, Lycurgus becomes an anonymous knight who devises a new code of law. After his "sharp lawes" are read to the "froward peple," they are "wondir wroth," and "wold han artyd [compelled] þis knyght hem repele, / Makyng ageyn hym an haynous querele" (2950–61). The knight assigns the authorship of the laws to Apollo: "I mad hem naght, it was god appollo; / And on my bak . . . þe charge he leyde / To kepe hem; sires, what sey ye here-to?" (2963–65). But the people are unimpressed and still demand their repeal. He promises to ask Apollo about the matter, on the condition that no changes be made until he returns. Going off to Greece but not to Apollo, he stays there until his death, thus insuring that the code will remain unchanged.

While the story never calls into question the independent existence of Apollo, his introduction into political life as moral authority is purely the invention of the knight. The knight's position as the sole voice of law puts divine authority entirely at his disposal, and makes him the source of moral truth. He produces this truth through the narrative about Apollo, a narrative that is wholly fictitious. Moral truth

48. John Gower, *Confessio Amantis* 2917–3021, 3295–3332.

is thus produced not merely *through* but *as* narrative fiction, with the single constraint that the fiction can never acknowledge itself as such. The knight must always keep the referential accuracy of his story an open question. He must leave his state never to return. In exchange for this sacrifice of day-to-day control he gains an ideological control that is absolute. In effect, he replaces his person with his story, and controls the state not simply through the imposition of the story, but by having constructed a story that will always maintain the distance between the story and the reality it claims to represent—a story, that is, that will always maintain its fiction. The referential accuracy of the story is neither affirmed nor denied; it is always held in reserve. This holding in reserve enables the status quo, also the product of the knight (through his new laws), to remain in force. Indeed, the truth the story holds in reserve is precisely the truth of the status quo, and the story maintains the status quo precisely by holding it in reserve.

The same power is depicted in the next exemplum in a manner that corresponds even more closely to the ideological structure of medieval kingship. The exemplum of the Phalarean Bull presents an attempt to construct kingship's other voice. The wicked counselor of a cruel tyrant makes a brass bull as an instrument of torture. Victims are placed within it and roasted alive. Moreover, the device is so constructed that their cries of pain always sound like the lowing of a bull. The cruelty of this machine so offends God that he causes the counselor to be the first to use it:

> ffor whan þe kyng, his cruel werk had seyne,
> Þe craft of it commendith he ful wele;
> But þe entent he fully held a-gayne,
> And seyde, "þou þat art more cruel
> Than I, þe maydenhede of this Iuel
> Shalt preve anone; þis is my Iugement."
> And so as blyue he was þer-in I-brent.
>
> (3032–38)

While the counselor's cruelty is punished, the tyrant's is simply accepted as a given, providing the ground that gives the counselor's crime meaning. The building of the bull is an attempt, however misguided, to satisfy the tyrant's appetite for cruelty; the bull is a response to the prevailing standard of cruelty the tyrant has already established. The bull monumentalizes this standard precisely by depriving resistance to tyranny of its own voice. It destroys the tyrant's enemies by forcing them to speak their resistance in the voice he has ordained for them. The logic of this machine is so remorseless in its perfection that it can bring benefit to the tyrant alone, and accordingly destroys its maker. If the counselor is punished for his cruelty, he is also punished for his presumption, that is, for attempting to become more cruel than the tyrant. The structure of kingship makes it impossible for the tyrant to be surpassed in cruelty. The voice of evil counsel concretized in the bull is always subject to the modification of the tyrant's own voice. In this case the absolute privilege of the tyrannical voice has a restraining effect, producing moral order even as it aims at tyranny.

With this exemplum we are a far cry from modern platitudes about the bland morality of medieval *Fürstenspiegel*. The story defines a wholly arbitrary yet inevitable balance between ideology and power. The monarch's unconstrained political power gives him an unlimited control over ideological forms, yet the ideological and the political are still mutually constraining. Ideology's prior dependence on royal power will always give it a predetermined shape; monarchy's need to maintain the integrity of its ideology will influence its mode of action. The tyrant's need to be recognized as the cruelest restrains the cruelty of his ministers.

A society where tyranny is possible is by definition also a society where the politically empowered can impose ideological forms by fiat. In return for acquiescence to the authority of Henry's *voluntas*, Hoccleve's audience gets their own ideological empowerment. This exchange of royal prerogative for ideological control is not so much a logical unity as it is two divergent tendencies the narrative holds together. Like all the other reconciliations Hoccleve offers between royal interests and the common interests of the ruling class, it must remain implicit, half hidden within the manipulations of his narrative.

Yet implication does not lessen the power of ideological reconciliations; rather it enhances them. The exempla of Lycurgus and the Phalarean Bull are narrative expositions of the ideological power of narrative. To a lesser extent so are the other exempla, with their continual emphasis on the monarch's exemplary status. Like the larger narratives that frame them—the genealogy of Henry, the canonization of Chaucer, the placement of Hoccleve's *Fürstenspiegel* within his own autobiography—the knowledge they convey must remain within its narrative form. To this narrative knowledge the *Regement*'s moral teaching is always tied. Indeed, the work's most practical lesson may well have been its continual narrative framing of the moral. With this framing it showed its audience how moral authority could be submitted to ideological control.

For modern scholars, the *Regement* may still hold a similar lesson. Works like the *Regement* present a challenge both to our view of the past and to our sense of our own present. First there is the challenge to the sense that the past lacked the critical sophistication of the present. Where one expects piety, Hoccleve offers a shrewd meditation on the political value of moral authority. Where one expects bland didacticism, Hoccleve offers a complex set of narratives that make the ideological and the moral interdependent, producing the very authority by which they claim to be governed. And here Hoccleve indirectly challenges our view of ourselves. For his example shows that literary self-consciousness is itself historically variable, and that far from being proof against an ideological status quo, a self-consciously critical stance may often be its most powerful instrument. This is a particularly chastening lesson at a time when critical self-consciousness is next to Godliness—not that such self-consciousness should be abandoned, just that it should never be complacent about the power of the status quo.[49]

49. This essay grew from an MLA talk to its present length in large part because of the possibilities others saw in it. I would like to thank Winthrop Wetherbee, Charles Blyth, and Seth Lerer both for their helpful comments and for their bibliographical suggestions. I would also particularly like to thank Lee Patterson, whose extensive commentary in the later stages of the essay's preparation greatly strengthened it.

# 6

# Reading REED

## *History and the Records of Early English Drama*

### *Theresa Coletti*

The Records of Early English Drama, or REED as it is commonly known, is a dauntingly ambitious editorial project that aims "to locate, transcribe, and publish systematically all surviving external evidence of dramatic, ceremonial and minstrel activity in Great Britain before 1642." Founded in 1975 as an international project, REED from its beginning has involved the cooperative efforts of Canadian, British, and American scholars, joining its forces with Leeds Texts and Studies, the Malone Society, and the Early English Text Society.[1] Initially funded by a major grant from the Canadian government, REED has drawn the large measure of its material support, academic guidance, and human inspiration from the University of Toronto, where its ongoing editorial and bibliographical labors have made the project's office a mini-research center for the student of early English drama, culture, and society.[2] To date the REED project has published ten meticulously produced volumes of dramatic records; several more are nearly complete, thirty-two in progress.[3] It has also spawned a related series, Studies in Early English

---

1. Up to the time of REED's inception these three British institutions had been publishing dramatic records. For a brief history of the founding of REED, see Ian Lancashire, "Medieval Drama," *Editing Medieval Texts,* ed. A. G. Rigg (New York: Garland, 1977), 76–77.

2. See Theodore R. De Welles, "Bibliographic resources and research at Records of Early English Drama," *REED Newsletter* 9.1 (1984): 16–20. The *REED Newsletter* only began numbering its volumes with no. 8 (1983); my citations number the volumes consecutively, beginning with the first in 1976.

3. These REED volumes have appeared thus far, all published by the University of Toronto Press: *York,* ed. Alexandra F. Johnston and Margaret Rogerson, 2 vols. (1979); *Chester,* ed. Lawrence M. Clopper (1979); *Coventry,* ed. R. W. Ingram (1981); *Newcastle upon Tyne,* ed. J. J. Anderson (1982); *Norwich 1540–1642,* ed. David Galloway (1984); *Cumberland, Westmorland, Gloucestershire,* ed. Audrey Douglas and Peter Greenfield (1986); *Devon,* ed. John Wasson (1986); *Cambridge,* ed. Alan H. Nelson, 2 vols. (1988). The quotation in the first sentence of this essay is from *York* 1:vi. Subsequent references to REED volumes appear parenthetically in the text.

Drama (SEED), a semiannual newsletter, colloquia, and the microfiche publication of materials germane to dramatic records.[4] The sheer wealth of activity and resources thus far channeled into REED has given the recovery and editing of dramatic records high visibility among students of early English drama, for many of whom records research has become the preeminent mode of scholarly activity. Clearly, REED is a literary phenomenon to be reckoned with.

Implicit in the project's efforts is the idea that with the editing and publication of every guild indenture, inventory, or record of fines and payments, REED inches its way forward to a true and full history of English drama. The REED project sees itself as not only crucial but in some ways antecedent to the writing of that history. The York volumes proclaim that REED, "when complete, will provide the basis for the first accurate history of the English theatre before 1642." Dramatic records will furnish the "raw material" of that history (*York* 1:i, ix). To that end, the volumes compile and arrange in chronological order all evidence of dramatic, minstrel, and ceremonial activity to be found in surviving civic, guild, parish, and where relevant, cathedral, monastic, diocesan, county, and household documents. The REED volumes assert the noninterventionist mentality of their editorial policies.[5] The project takes pride in presenting its findings "without commentary in chronological order" (*York* 1:ix); it warns against "wholesale interpretation and speculation, especially at this early stage in the publication of the REED series" (*Norwich,* vii). One REED editor succinctly expresses the methodological purity the project strives for: "The aim of the Records of Early English Drama is to collect written evidence of drama, minstrelsy, and ceremonial activity, not to interpret it. The nature of the material gathered here invites interpretation; I hope that I have almost entirely succeeded in resisting that invitation" (*Coventry,* xiii).

REED exemplifies a mode of literary history that is sanctioned by particular conceptions of fact and objectivity; this mode embraces pres-

---

4. The first volume of SEED is Ian Lancashire's *Dramatic Texts and Records of Britain: A Chronological Topography to 1558* (Toronto: University of Toronto Press, 1984); see also *Records of Early English Drama: Proceedings of the First Colloquium,* ed. Joanna Dutka (Toronto: REED, 1979). Alan Somerset has compiled a computer-sorted index on microfiche to the scrapbooks of antiquarian Halliwell-Phillipps, which are now in the Folger Library, Washington, D.C.

5. REED's editorial procedures are set forth in the *REED Handbook for Editors,* compiled by A. F. Johnston and S. B. MacLean (Toronto: REED, 1980).

ervation, transmission, and completeness as key features of its mission. Though REED offers its methods and its findings as if they were self-evident, they are in fact underwritten by a powerful set of assumptions about the nature, conduct, and goals of historical scholarship. Given REED's massive effort at researching and recovering dramatic records and its preemptive claims for an authority certain to have a lasting impact on the writing of the history of early English drama, its guiding assumptions merit scrutiny.[6] For they champion a version of literary history that in recent years has been called into question by scholars of literature and history alike who increasingly have acknowledged "the historically conditioned character" of both the historical discipline and historical understanding.[7]

This revisionary historiography critiques the conventional distinction between facts and interpretation, recognizing the "difficulty of discriminating . . . between these two levels" of historical discourse.[8] It replaces traditional historicism's conception of fact and objectivity with the idea that facts are not simply "out there" but rather are constructed by the historical inquiry itself. Facts do not reside in some recuperable and neutral way in documents that refer to and convey information about empirical reality. Rather, the documents have their own historicity, their own relation to the processes that produced them. Historical knowledge, therefore, is always mediated, not only because the historical record is incomplete, but also because practitioners of the historical discipline are themselves historically situated.[9]

This essay examines REED as an instance of historical and literary scholarship, confronting its methods with the premises of a revisionary historiography. To that end, I address two facets of REED that are profoundly implicated in its conception of history. I look first at the project as a historical phenomenon in its own right, its relation to recent early drama scholarship, and the place of that scholarship in the

6. See the comments on REED's authority by Barry Dobson, review of *REED: York, Renaissance and Reformation* n.s. 6 (1982): 47–48.
7. Hayden White, *Tropics of Discourse: Essays in Cultural Criticism* (Baltimore: Johns Hopkins University Press, 1978), 29.
8. White, *Tropics of Discourse*, 107.
9. This description of the premises of a revisionary historiography is summarized from White, *Tropics of Discourse*, chaps. 1–3; Dominick LaCapra, *Rethinking Intellectual History: Texts, Contexts, Language* (Ithaca: Cornell University Press, 1983), 23–71; Paul Zumthor, *Speaking of the Middle Ages*, trans. Sarah White (Lincoln: University of Nebraska Press, 1986), 19–24, 80–81.

history of early drama studies since the nineteenth century. I am interested here in describing who historicizes in REED and why. I turn next to the manner in which REED writes literary history with a detailed look at its definition and treatment of evidence. In the final part of this essay I consider some alternative ways of reading both the evidence that REED brings to light and the data that it neglects.

Before proceeding further, however, I wish to address two matters that, though implicit in the following discussion, merit special notice here. The first concerns what I am *not* suggesting in the critique of REED set forth in this essay. My examination of REED's methodology in no way is intended as a criticism of archival research per se. That would be a foolish thing for a medievalist to do. I have no dispute with the REED editor who responded to the argument of this paper with the rejoinder, "But you find things when you search the archives." Yet, as Paul Zumthor states in support of "the slow, ungrateful labor of data gathering," it is

> not a question of denying the considerable gains of a century's erudition, whatever its distortions may have been. . . . The historian of "medieval literature" does not labor in vain when he succeeds in proving that around 1060, in Spain, a version of the *Chanson de Roland* was known. The discovery is not in question; what is in question is the fate of the knowledge it engenders, the awareness we must have that the factual data fulfills a necessary condition of every critical reading: the respective placement of the object and its observer.[10]

The fate—and the form—of the knowledge REED discovers, not a challenge to the archives, are my principal concerns in the following discussion. I am interested in the uses to which REED data may be put, the sorts of explanations it will make possible.[11]

---

10. Zumthor, *Speaking of the Middle Ages*, 79–80. On data gathering in relation to the philosophical implications of historical scholarship, see Lee Patterson, *Negotiating the Past: The Historical Understanding of Medieval Literature* (Madison: University of Wisconsin Press, 1987), 15.

11. The questions raised in this critique coincide (temporally though not substantively) with criticism of REED by the Social Sciences and Humanities Research Council of Canada (SSHRCC), which until recently had been a major and generous source of the project's funding. The funding crisis and REED's response to it are described by Sally-Beth MacLean, "REED Present and Future," *REED Newsletter* 12.1 (1987): 1–2. According to MacLean, the SSHRCC's decision to cut back on REED funding was based on an evaluation of the project as a "narrowly-defined medieval drama project with a relatively small group of users." As a recent REED brochure suggests, the project has responded to this development by stressing its potential usefulness to scholars "in a wide variety of fields." Further, REED is apparently meeting the challenge of this funding crisis with a

My second point follows from Zumthor's observation about the "necessary condition" of critical reading and is allied to my appeal in what follows that REED acknowledge its own historicity. If all acts of historical understanding are mediated by the historical position of the one engaged in the act, it seems appropriate that I situate myself in relation to the issues entertained in this essay.[12] I am motivated here by a desire to account for the present state of medieval drama studies, which in the last decade have increasingly turned away from considerations of dramatic texts and moved instead toward elaborating, explaining, or deploying various sorts of documentary evidence. To a field in which speculation and hypothesis have inspired both creative insights and misleading formulations, REED has brought the putative stability of verifiable data. My tacit agenda here is to suggest that this turn toward scientism has not had the most beneficent effects on early English drama studies. Apart from REED and its satellite enterprises, the field seems caught in a methodological vacuum: although it is no longer possible to speak about dramatic texts as we once did, alternative ways of shaping our discourse on these texts have only haltingly emerged. I would like to believe that the observable decline in the actual number of studies of early dramatic texts revealed by even a casual perusal of the standard bibliographies reflects not these texts' lack of significance for us, but rather our inability to formulate meaningful questions about them. This is a situation, I believe, that the REED enterprise can make only doubtful claims to ameliorate. My own bias in regard to the larger question of the fate of medieval drama studies advocates a return to the text, understood not in the conventional sense of the literary artifact distinguished from its "context," but in relation to the broadly con-

---

renewed commitment to its goals and a vigorous determination to continue its monumental effort with the help of the private sector. Leaving aside the question of REED's worthiness and the charge of "narrowness" imputed to the project by the SSHRCC, we should nonetheless entertain the larger significance of this official obstacle to REED's continuance. At issue here is the general commodification of scholarship and the growing realization that the marketplace of ideas is also a marketplace of dollars and cents. What are the prospects for enormously costly endeavors such as REED (each volume in the series costs $100,000 to produce)? Has the era of monumentality passed? Might it be reinvigorated by the advent of technologies that already are making possible the distribution of enormous quantities of information in forms other than that of the book?

12. On the role of the individual in relation to the recuperation of the medieval past, see Zumthor, *Speaking of the Middle Ages,* 32–33, 80–81, and Patterson, *Negotiating the Past,* 43–44. Zumthor speaks of the medievalist's reading as the point where "two historicities touch" (33).

strued complex of verbal, social, and symbolic representations which early drama literally enacted.

## I

Though REED's chronological purview covers dramatic activity in Great Britain before 1642, REED has in fact been seen mainly as a "medieval project"; that is the sense in which I understand it throughout this essay.[13] A look at REED's place in the history of early drama studies might begin, then, with a glance at its relation to present scholarly developments in Renaissance drama. In the same period that records editing and research have risen to preeminence, the study of Renaissance drama has significantly reconceived its relation to history. While the REED project pursues a traditional literary history that privileges fact, origin, chronology, wholeness, and development, much scholarship in Renaissance drama, like Renaissance studies in general, has increasingly turned to the medley of complementary approaches gathered under the umbrella of a revisionary historiography.[14] Conceiving of culture as a system of discursive and nondiscursive practices, the new history understands the literary text, indeed all texts, not as artifacts but as social and cultural events that are always and only partially accessible through a critical scholarship that is itself a culturally contingent part of the history of understanding.[15] Thus the revisionary historical reading of Renaissance drama engages its texts in their economic, political, and institutional settings; it sees them as produced for

13. On REED as a medieval project, see David Galloway, "Records of Early English Drama in the Provinces and what they may tell us about the Elizabethan Theatre," in *Elizabethan Theatre,* ed. G. R. Hibbard, vol. 7 (Hamden, Conn.: Archon Books, 1980), 86.

14. This characterization of REED's traditional history is informed by Foucault's critique of the "unities of discourse"; see *The Archaeology of Knowledge and the Discourse on Language,* trans. A. M. Sheridan Smith (New York: Pantheon Books, 1972), 21–30. For a succinct comparison of the old and new histories, see Herbert Lindenberger, "Toward a New History in Literary Study," *Profession 84,* ed. Phyllis Franklin and Richard Brod (New York: Modern Language Association, 1984), 16–23.

15. In the return to history in Renaissance studies the main players are the so-called cultural materialists, primarily British, and the new historicists, primarily American. For an overview of key figures and the distinction between their interests and methods, see Jonathan Goldberg, "The Politics of Renaissance Literature: A Review Essay," *ELH* 49 (1982): 514–42. On new historicism and Renaissance studies in general, see Louis Montrose, "Renaissance Literary Studies and the Subject of History," *ELR* 16 (1986): 5–12; Jean E. Howard, "The New Historicism in Renaissance Studies," *ELR* 16 (1986): 13–43; and Patterson, *Negotiating the Past,* 57–71.

and by their culture, a culture in which the texts themselves may mediate social relations and articulate contradictions.[16] The new historical reading of Renaissance drama examines both the way texts "work" in their culture and the successive reconstructions through which they have continuously been made available.

This historicizing of Renaissance drama proceeds at a great remove from the activities of REED. To exaggerate the differences for the sake of comparison, whereas the dramatic records editor engages in a custodial but noninterventionist reportage of data, doing the spade work for historians and critics to come, the new historian of Renaissance drama acknowledges both the "cultural specificity . . . of all modes of writing" and the "unavailability of a full and authentic past . . . that has not already been mediated by the surviving texts of the society in question." For the former, "literature" and "history," "text" and "context" exist; for the latter these are problematic categories that the scholarly endeavor constructs in the act of study.[17]

As developments in the historical study of early English drama, both REED and the turn to a new historicism, despite their marked differences, must be seen in part as responses to the same phenomenon: the decline of the formalist paradigm that had dominated literary studies until the early 1970s. Though the literary texts of early modern Europe may have only reluctantly given themselves over to a hermeneutics based on an aesthetic formed by nineteenth-century bourgeois culture, formalist models and ideas of literature nonetheless had a powerful impact on early drama studies.[18] In Renaissance drama and Shakespeare studies in particular, an emphasis on dramatic structure and unity and on the representation of timeless and universal truths about human nature and values had long claimed the critical edge over an enormous scholarly interest in the Shakespearean theater.[19] The new literary his-

16. Jonathan Dollimore and Alan Sinfield, "Foreword: Cultural Materialism," *Political Shakespeare,* ed. Dollimore and Sinfield (Ithaca: Cornell University Press, 1985), vii–viii; Goldberg, "Politics of Renaissance Literature," 526–28.

17. Montrose, "Renaissance Literary Studies," 8, 6; see also Howard, "The New Historicism," 22–25.

18. For an overview of the concepts of literature and English studies that contributed to the rise of formalism, see Terry Eagleton, *Literary Theory* (Minneapolis: University of Minnesota Press, 1983), chaps. 1–2. On the misalliance of medieval texts and formalist ideas of literature, see Zumthor, *Speaking of the Middle Ages,* 23–25.

19. For a brief description of the state of Shakespeare studies that helped usher in a revised literary history, see Robert Weimann, *Shakespeare and the Popular Tradition in the Theatre,* ed. Robert Schwartz (Baltimore: Johns Hopkins University Press, 1978), xi–xxii;

tory's attention to the Renaissance dramatic text as cultural practice is at least in part a specific and deliberate reaction to the ahistorical character of formalist models.

The same companion emphases on theater history and formalist analysis were evident in early drama studies prior to REED's inception. Formalism gave medieval drama two of its most important studies, V. A. Kolve's *The Play Called Corpus Christi* and Rosemary Woolf's *English Mystery Plays,* with Kolve in particular probably doing more to further the investigation of medieval drama than any other work before or since.[20] Kolve provided medieval drama with an aesthetic principle, based on his idea of *corpus christi,* a principle that posited the mystery cycle as a coherent ordering of episodes in which content and form constituted an obligatory unity. Kolve's idea of cyclic design, the "generic thing-in-itself" furnished an ideal structure against which the individual cycles and plays could be assessed.[21] Woolf's method was slightly different: she dismembered Kolve's *corpus christi* model to consider individual plays, not in terms of an overarching design, but in relation to each other according to distinctly formalist criteria. Both Kolve and Woolf were concerned with the integrity and value of the literary artifact. And although these books grounded their discussions in historical data, each at base approached the literary text as a thing apart, treating the social and historical auspices of the cycles in terms of the idealized abstractions of a universalized Middle Ages.[22]

Still, formalist analysis never took the firm hold in medieval drama studies that it had in the reading of the drama of Shakespeare and his contemporaries. For medieval drama, formalism's "critical readings" had always maintained a tense equilibrium with traditional literary historical studies of dramatic sources, analogues, language, and manuscripts. As early as 1969, David Mills voiced his discomfort with a for-

---

an account of what formalism brought to Renaissance drama studies is given by Richard L. Levin, *New Readings vs. Old Plays: Recent Trends in the Reinterpretation of English Renaissance Drama* (Chicago: University of Chicago Press, 1979).

20. V. A. Kolve, *The Play Called Corpus Christi* (Stanford: Stanford University Press, 1966); Rosemary Woolf, *English Mystery Plays* (Berkeley and Los Angeles: University of California Press, 1972).

21. *Play Called Corpus Christi,* 51.

22. These works both assured the continuance of an essentially formalist methodology that examined medieval dramatic texts in terms of various features of medieval culture, e.g., theology, spirituality, iconography. My own early work in medieval drama was largely informed by this approach.

malist or "literary" approach to early drama and made a plea for a scholarly method responsive to the social and theatrical conditions that contributed to the distinctive structure and form of the mystery cycles.[23] His appeal coincided with the lead already taken by Glynne Wickham in the first volume of *Early English Stages*.[24] In subsequent years the impulse to pursue "dramatic" or theatrical aspects of early drama issued in a spirited examination of local historical documents that, it was stated, might shed light on the original circumstances of medieval dramatic production. This is the scholarly ambience that led to the formation of REED, which imposed pattern, organization, and system upon the urge to recover early English drama's "true" past.

In the first volume of the *Revels History of Drama in English*, Mills has more recently observed that medieval drama studies currently bear witness to a major problem: the "disturbing distinction" between a scholarly approach concerned with "literary" questions of form and meaning and one primarily focused on the conditions under which early drama was produced. Though Mills rightly maintains that the "critic entering the field of medieval drama is uneasily aware of the absence even of agreed terminology, the considerable variety of critical attitude and the rapidly changing state of scholarship," recent work in the field reflects a greater homogeneity of interest than his statement would indicate.[25] That consensus is more accurately summed up in the description of current research in medieval drama proclaimed in a recent essay collection: "The two most important new areas of work are the systematic scrutiny of all surviving records relating to original productions and imaginative experimental *modern* productions based on careful treatment of the surviving texts."[26] With their mutual insistence on the local, contingent, materially specific aspects of early drama, both the historicism of records edited and the historically informed exercises in theatricality may be seen as specific substitutions for the timeless

23. "Approaches to Medieval Drama," *Leeds Studies in English* n.s. 3 (1969): 47.

24. *Early English Stages 1300–1660,* vol. 1 (London: Routledge and Kegan Paul; New York: Columbia University Press, 1959).

25. Mills, "Medieval and Modern Views of Drama," in A. C. Cawley et al., *Revels History of Drama in English: Medieval Drama*, vol. 1 (London: Methuen, 1983), 83. W. A. Davenport sees an identical dichotomy in medieval drama studies, *Fifteenth-Century English Drama: The Early Moral Plays and Their Literary Relations* (Woodbridge, Suffolk: D. S. Brewer, 1982), 3.

26. Paula Neuss, "Preface," *Aspects of Early English Drama* (Woodbridge, Suffolk: D. S. Brewer; Totowa, N.J.: Barnes and Noble, 1983), ix.

appropriation of the text offered by formalist analysis. These twin activities now largely dominate medieval drama studies.[27]

## II

The different ways that medieval and Renaissance drama studies have responded to the shifting ground of literary historical discourse reproduces the distinction, present in early drama studies from their beginning, that marginalized the position of medieval drama in the English literary canon. Coming into being as an offshoot of the nineteenth-century pursuit of Shakespeare's genius, medieval drama studies had their origin in an evolutionary-biased, positivist historicism that was antimedieval, anti-Christian, and anti-Catholic.[28] This historicism deemed early English drama worthy of attention to the extent that it served as a primitive precursor of the bard. Despite a recent statement that the study of medieval drama has finally outgrown its apologetic phase, the turn to history, theatricality, and origins epitomized in records editing may be seen as an effort to overcome—now and for all time—the marginalization of medieval drama in early drama studies and the English literary canon.[29] The REED project challenges the "un-

27. Though a number of American scholars are involved in records research and dramatic performance, the new hegemony of a theatrically based traditional historicism is largely an Anglo-Canadian endeavor, with its most important centers of activity at Toronto and Leeds. American scholars produced much of the formalist reading of medieval drama, and they have also produced the major interpretive studies of texts. The split between Anglo and American scholarship in medieval drama is articulated in Meg Twycross's review of Peter Travis's *Dramatic Design in the Chester Cycle* (see note 53), in "Sign, Symbol and Script," *English* 32 (1983): 253–56. Twycross berates Travis for succumbing to what she deems representative American critical transgressions: for using "abstract" "polysyllabic" terms, for exhibiting the "worrying characteristic of current American scholarship," "the desire to find a theoretical model," and for deciding "not to treat the plays theatrically, and thus fatally" unbalancing his discussion. For Twycross the truth emerges from dramatic performance, where "ingeniously-woven webs of literary and thematic exegesis melt into thin air."

28. The story of the relation of early drama studies and nineteenth-century historicism has been told by O. B. Hardison, Jr., *Christian Rite and Christian Drama in the Middle Ages* (Baltimore: Johns Hopkins University Press, 1965), 1–34. The seminal text for this characterization is E. K. Chambers, *The Medieval Stage*, 2 vols. (Oxford: Clarendon Press, 1903).

29. The optimistic assessment of early drama studies comes from John Hurt Fisher's essay on Middle English literature in *The Present State of Scholarship in Fourteenth-Century Literature*, ed. Thomas D. Cooke (Columbia, Mo.: University of Missouri Press, 1982), 22–23. Even though the evolutionary paradigm is long-departed from historical studies, its aftereffects still prevail in contemporary considerations of early drama. See, for example, the introduction to the drama section of a recent anthology of Middle English

wanted stepchild" status of medieval drama, aiming through its sheer scope, size, and ambition to dwarf all prior considerations as secondary to and dependent upon its own findings. Seeking to recover every available fragment of early drama's obviously fragmented history, REED in its definition of its task effectively defers all questions about the status and meaning of medieval dramatic texts with the very monumentality of its method.[30]

In its complete turn to origins REED realizes its connection with a mode of historical inquiry that contributed much to medieval drama studies in its early phases: the antiquarian activity of the nineteenth century. The REED volumes may appropriately be seen "as the culmination of a tradition of antiquarian and literary scholarship which is well over a century old."[31] REED's work is enabled by the nineteenth-century research of Robert Davies on York, Thomas Sharp on Coventry, and James Orchard Halliwell-Phillipps on the whole of England.[32] Inspired both by their rich findings and their mistakes, REED aims to consolidate, check, and build upon the scattered fragments of dramatic records collected by British antiquarians.[33]

The antiquarian career of Halliwell-Phillipps intersects with many aspects of early drama studies relevant to the history and method of REED. Though he may be best known for his involvement with several literary scandals—he was suspected of stealing manuscripts from Trinity College, Cambridge, and he got caught up in Furnivall's controversy with Swinburne over the editing of Shakespeare—Halliwell-Phillipps's most important contribution to early drama studies was his exhaustive examination of local records as part of his effort to unearth information

---

literature, *Medieval English Literature,* ed. Thomas Garbaty (Lexington, Mass.: D. C. Heath, 1984), 861, and the remarks by Derek Pearsall, *Old English and Middle English Poetry,* Routledge History of English Poetry, vol. 1 (London: Routledge and Kegan Paul, 1977), 252–58.

30. On the monumentalizations of traditional historicism in medieval studies, see Zumthor, *Speaking of the Middle Ages,* 41–42.

31. Dobson, review of *REED: York,* 48.

32. Robert Davies, *Extracts from the Municipal Records of the City of York* (London: J. B. Nichols, 1843); Thomas Sharp, *A Dissertation on the Pageants or Dramatic Mysteries, Anciently Performed at Coventry* (Coventry: Merridew and Son, 1825). Halliwell-Phillipps will be discussed below.

33. On errors in local history and antiquarian documents, see Galloway, "REED in the Provinces," 86–89; Lancashire gives a brief history of antiquarian precedents for REED and of dramatic record collecting in general ("Medieval Drama," 72–74). Ingram discusses problems with the antiquarian records of Coventry (*Coventry,* xxvii-xxx).

about the life of Shakespeare.[34] He was the first of Shakespeare's biographers to pursue this strategy, and to that end he examined local documents—wills, parish registers, subsidy rolls—with a zeal that made him, according to one judgment, "the greatest of the nineteenth-century biographers of Shakespeare in the exacting tradition of factual research."[35] Thus it is hardly surprising that Halliwell-Phillipps has been called "the first REED researcher"; certainly parallels may be drawn between the small army of REED editors laboring throughout Britain and the agents Halliwell-Phillipps "employed all over the country, men who spent their time peering into waste-paper baskets, old town records, and musty garretts where they sometimes made great discoveries."[36] The list of towns he is known or believed to have visited reads like a list of REED "work in progress."[37]

Yet more than a sentimentalized antiquarian gusto links the work of Halliwell-Phillipps and REED. Though he seems to have been both obsessed with the idea of gathering every possible scrap of information about Shakespeare and willing to go to any lengths to accomplish that goal, Halliwell-Phillipps's commitment to exhaustiveness in his own research must also be seen as a distinctive feature of a historical method.[38] His comments on the nature and aims of his work in many ways bespeak a historicism very similar to that currently voiced by REED.

Halliwell-Phillipps hardly disguises the fact that his extensive research on the life of Shakespeare is intended as a monument to the genius whose works "have exercised beneficial influences on the progress of mankind."[39] To accomplish that goal he vows to examine all

34. See the account of Halliwell-Phillipps in S. Schoenbaum, *Shakespeare's Lives* (Oxford: Clarendon Press; New York: Oxford University Press, 1970), 396–432. On the scandals involving the Trinity College manuscripts and Furnivall, see 396–400 and 429–30. Halliwell-Phillipps is also known for his damaging of manuscripts; J. A. B. Somerset, "James Orchard Halliwell-Phillipps and his Scrapbooks," *REED Newsletter* 4.2 (1979): 13–14.

35. Schoenbaum, *Shakespeare's Lives*, 407. For an account of the scrapbooks Halliwell-Phillipps compiled in the process of researching early drama, see Somerset, "James Orchard Halliwell-Phillipps," 13–14.

36. Rose E. Reynolds, "An Afternoon at Hollingbury Close. July 15, 1887," in *Reminiscences of J. O. Halliwell-Phillipps,* quoted in Somerset, "James Orchard Halliwell-Phillipps," 9.

37. Schoenbaum, *Shakespeare's Lives,* 425; Somerset, "James Orchard Halliwell-Phillipps," 14–15.

38. Halliwell-Phillipps even felt compelled to publish "A List of the Contents of the Drawers in my Study, and in two other Rooms" (London: J. E. Adlard, 1870).

39. J. O. Halliwell[-Phillipps], *The Life of William Shakespeare* (London: John Russell

documents of the slightest relevance, and makes particular claims for the originality of his own inquiry into local records that "have never yet been properly examined." Despite his obvious bardolatry, Halliwell-Phillipps nonetheless maintains he presents his facts "in the least presuming form, and no more is attempted beyond placing before the reader an unprejudiced and complete view of every known fact respecting the poet." His work serves several ancillary purposes: it reveals the "inexhaustible treasures of our English archives" and affirms "a belief in hidden stores of knowledge which destroys all reliance on the finality of previous enquiries, leading us to trust to no examinations but our own."[40] In a proposal for a subscription series of quarto facsimiles of Shakespeare's works, the antiquarian promises "accuracy and authenticity" in place of the errors of previous editions. More emphatically, he pledges a series "*absolutely reliable as a permanent reference and authority* . . . that . . . will form one of the most important contributions to English literature ever executed."[41]

Though there are obvious differences between the hoarding, compulsive research of a Halliwell-Phillipps, who "finally seems to have been overwhelmed by the intimidating mass of materials he had collected over his lifetime," and the REED researcher who is currently assisted by a well-organized program and a technology adaptable to the growing amount of material collected, the similarities between the two antiquarianisms are unmistakable.[42] Halliwell-Phillipps's belief in the primacy of fact and the importance of completeness, his faith in the value of searching for origins and objectivity, and his claims for absolute authority, permanence, and literary historical influence all proclaim assumptions about historical research that are also voiced by the REED project, as this notice from one of its brochures makes clear: "The es-

Smith, 1848), v. Schoenbaum observes that Halliwell-Phillipps presented Shakespeare as an "exemplar of thrifty bourgeois virtue" (*Shakespeare's Lives,* 415).

40. *Life of Shakespeare,* vii, x, xiv. On the revering of England's national treasures and the growth of antiquarian and learned societies in the nineteenth century, see Harrison Ross Steeves, *Learned Societies and English Literary Scholarship* (1913; reprint, New York: AMS Press, 1970), 98–203.

41. James Orchard Halliwell-Phillipps, "Proposals for issuing by subscription, amongst a very small number of subscribers . . . entire facsimiles in small quarto volumes, of all the editions of Shakespeare's dramas and poems printed before 1623," (n.d.), 4.

42. Somerset, "James Orchard Halliwell-Phillipps," 9; Ian Lancashire, "Records of Early English Drama and the Computer," *Computers and the Humanities* 12 (1978): 183–88.

timated 50 volumes of REED will provide a complete package for the scholar and student and will form a standard reference work of permanent value." These pointed resemblances between the self-descriptions of Halliwell-Phillipps's antiquarian research and REED reveal the extent to which REED inherits its historical method from the nineteenth century. In addition to sharing a common conception of historical data, REED and Halliwell-Phillipps also adopt similar stances toward their activities. In Paul Zumthor's characterization of nineteenth-century historicism, this stance takes its "unexamined positivism . . . [as] the very pattern of intellectual rectitude" and considers its objectivity "as a high moral value."[43]

## III

The scholarly reaction to the homogenizing tendencies of formalist analysis and the resurrection of an earlier century's antiquarian ventures both came into play in early English drama's scholarly circles in the years leading up to the formation of REED. In 1968 Alan Nelson set out to challenge the assumption that the York cycle of biblical plays had been staged processionally, at multiple locations, on pageant wagons; using York civic records, he argued instead for performance at a single indoor site.[44] Nelson's motivation was twofold: his principal aim was to challenge Kolve's argument that the content and form of the mystery cycles originated in the theology of the Feast of Corpus Christi.[45] He was also responding to Kolve's observation that surviving dramatic records could not explain the origin of the mystery cycles; as Kolve had put it, in the face of such "documentary silence" "our only recourse is to theory."[46] Nelson contested the need for formal analysis; he argued that the documentary evidence that did exist would show that the mystery cycles developed out of festival processions. In the next few years

43. *Speaking of the Middle Ages,* 16–17.
44. This theory, first presented in an MLA paper and later published in *Modern Philology* 67 (1970): 303–20, was incorporated into Nelson's *The Medieval English Stage: Corpus Christi Pageants and Plays* (Chicago: University of Chicago Press, 1973), 15–81. For an assessment of the influence of theories of staging on prevailing conceptions of the medieval cycle plays, see Martin Stevens, "The York Cycle: From Procession to Play," *Leeds Studies in English* n.s. 6 (1972): 37–61. I share this analysis of the genesis of REED with Clifford Davidson, review of *REED: York, Comparative Drama* 14 (1980): 80.
45. Nelson, *Medieval English Stage,* 1–14.
46. Kolve, *Play Called Corpus Christi,* 38–39.

there followed a series of exchanges in which Nelson's theory was challenged by Alexandra Johnston and Margaret (Dorrell) Rogerson, whose study of the civic records of drama and ceremonial in York had supported assumptions about the cycle's processional performance.[47] These exchanges coincided with discussions among early drama scholars of the need to coordinate and support ongoing research in dramatic records, which issued in the founding of REED in 1975.[48]

Despite their differences of opinion about the staging of the York cycle, Nelson and Johnston and Rogerson agreed on the methodological importance of basing all statements about medieval drama on documentary fact. Their method was put to the ultimate test in 1977, when under the auspices of a newly formed REED and the guidance of Johnston, its executive director, the University of Toronto Center for Medieval Studies produced the entire York cycle on pageant wagons in an effort to stage the cycle "as closely as possible" to the conditions the records describe.[49] The controversy over the staging of the York cycle had a profound and long-term impact on medieval drama studies: it led to the intersection of record editing and contemporary performance for which Toronto and REED have subsequently become known.[50] More important, it concretely posited that the study of dramatic records must precede any theorizing about dramatic production and textual interpretation. The outcome of Nelson's critique of Kolve, then, was to render any and all "theories" suspect.[51] The REED volumes are a monument to this polarization of "fact" and "theory."

Since REED's inception, research in English dramatic records has

47. Margaret Dorrell [Rogerson], "Two Studies of the York Corpus Christi Play," *Leeds Studies in English* n.s. 6 (1972): 63–111; Alexandra F. Johnston, "The Procession and Play of Corpus Christi in York after 1426," *Leeds Studies in English* n.s. 7 (1973): 55–62, and "The Medieval English Stage," review of Nelson's *Medieval English Stage, University of Toronto Quarterly* 44 (1975): 238–48.

48. *REED Newsletter* 1.1 (1976): 1–3.

49. Alexandra F. Johnston, "The York Cycle: 1977," *University of Toronto Quarterly* 48 (1978): 2.

50. Since 1977 the Center for Medieval Studies, in conjunction with the *Poculi Ludique Societas* and other interested groups, has mounted a major dramatic production, usually accompanied by a symposium, every two or three years.

51. Johnston repeated this idea when she observed that "we can no longer rely only on theories since we are in growing command of the facts about the performance of early drama in England," which we would do well to approach in terms that grow "from the plays themselves" and not in relation to an "alien theoretical concept" ("The Critics and the Idea of the Cycle," paper delivered at the Twentieth International Congress on Medieval Studies, Kalamazoo, Michigan, 1985). Professor Johnston kindly provided me with a copy of this paper.

uncovered much information relevant to early dramatic entertainments and spectacles and the society in which they flourished. This information has challenged many received ideas about the kinds, numbers, and locales of early plays and entertainments; it has also shed light on the production, organization, and style of the early English theater. In perhaps its most important contribution thus far, REED research has significantly revised our understanding of the chronology and so-called development of the Corpus Christi play.[52] Lawrence Clopper's meticulous reading of the Chester records has succeeded in locating that city's cycle as we know it in its proper historical moment, with the discovery that the Chester plays constitute a preeminently Tudor cycle.[53] The REED volumes also present many random pieces of antiquarian information, quaint and often amusing, such as the York records' detailing of food prepared for the local eminences of York at their banquet on Corpus Christi Day 1520 (*York* 2:821–22), or their account of how the York Saucemakers settled disputes with "persons from other crafts" who sold mustard without authorization (*York* 2:716). The records attest to the cross-dressing of male actors in Coventry who played female roles, and to the cost of a bear named Chester (for baiting or performing?) in 1622.[54]

With REED now well into its second decade, its discoveries to date must be considered in light of the goals the project initially defined for itself: to uncover evidence relevant to the production of early drama; to provide data that will enable the identification of auspices and dates for extant dramatic texts; to furnish information that can be employed in the interpretation of surviving texts.[55] We should note first that the

---

52. For an early assessment of the contributions of REED along these lines, see John Wasson, "Records of Early English Drama: Where they are and what they tell us," *REED: Proceedings of the First Colloquium,* 128–44.

53. "The History and Development of the Chester Cycle," *Modern Philology* 75 (1978): 219–46. Clopper's important work interpreting the Chester records, though underwritten by REED, does not appear in the *Chester* volume. Peter Travis used Clopper's work on the Chester records and cycle text to argue that the late reshuffling and expansion of the cycle bespeak a purposive, thematic design (*Dramatic Design in the Chester Cycle* [Chicago: University of Chicago Press, 1982], 30–69).

54. Meg Twycross, "'Transvestism' in the Mystery Plays," *Medieval English Theatre* 5 (1983): 123–80; David George, "Records of interest at the Lancashire Record Office," *REED Newsletter* 4.2 (1979): 2.

55. John Astington, "Commentary," *REED: Proceedings of the First Colloquium,* 93; and see in the same volume, Peter Meredith, "'Item for a grone—iij d'—records and performance," 28; Lancashire, *Dramatic Texts and Records,* xxii–xxiii, xxxii, and "Medieval Drama," 71–72.

close connection between dramatic records, dramatic performance, and dramatic text that originally underwrote much of REED's endeavor is relevant only in certain contexts. Since the scrutiny of possible evidence of performance is greatly enhanced by the actual existence of extant texts, it is hardly surprising that the first REED volumes were devoted to locations in which a substantial body of civic records happens to accompany the survival of whole or partial cycle play texts—York, Chester, Coventry. The REED project appropriately began its publication with these locales, for which much of the work of editing and gathering was already well underway when REED was founded. These early volumes suggest the extent to which the nature and in some instances chance survival of documents have determined the way REED has formulated its central concerns. When carried over into contexts where the documentary evidence is less rich, the aspirations of REED become less clear, as the records of Newcastle upon Tyne suggest. We know that Newcastle had a cycle play, produced by the guilds after the manner of York, Chester, and Coventry. But few civic records survive, and the ones that do are primarily extracts from the Chamberlains' Account Books; thus the Newcastle dramatic records reveal very little about that town's dramatic activities, since they are largely given over to the enumeration of dozens of payments for clothing for the town's fools (*Newcastle upon Tyne*, xx).

The example of Newcastle upon Tyne points up the limitations of REED's overarching rationales, suggesting the extent to which the enormous labor and collaborative effort that records editing entails may hardly be commensurate with whatever light dramatic records are likely to shed on plays in performance, homeless plays, and dramatic texts. Hypotheses built on the detailed enumeration of costs the Coventry Drapers incurred while repairing their Doomsday pageant will not bring back their Doomsday play in its authentic originality. As the Coventry Weavers' accounts show, even in cases where records and play survive, there is not always a clean fit between the two.[56] Even in Chester an abundance of dramatic records, antiquarian commentary, and multiple manuscript copies of the cycle still do not provide us with a

56. R. W. Ingram, "'To find the players and all that longeth therto': Notes on the Production of Medieval Drama in Coventry," *Elizabethan Theatre,* ed. G. R. Hibbard, vol. 5 (Hamden, Conn.: Archon Books, 1975), 38.

text as performed.[57] Excepting the cycle plays of York, Chester, and to a lesser degree Coventry and Norwich, most of the records already or soon to be published furnish production details for plays and entertainments no longer extant. The fact that there are many extant dramatic records from all of England and many unidentified surviving play texts does not mean that those two will necessarily mesh. As much as "a knowledge of dramatic auspices [has] . . . become an essential prerequisite for the interpretation of a text," it seems doubtful that available or forthcoming records will provide "an historical matrix of place and time" for important play texts whose precise origin and auspices are still unknown.[58] Most students of medieval drama agree, for instance, that the records that might conclusively identify the auspices of the N-Town plays simply do not exist.[59]

REED had in fact anticipated objections such as these with its founding conception of an idealized and total history that sanctions the deferral of conclusions until all the "facts from everywhere are in."[60] Accordingly, REED is intended for the literary historians to whom "the task of providing the interpretation" will be left when more REED volumes are published.[61] REED presents its volumes as reference tools, sources of information to assist and inspire further research not only about drama but also "musicology, paleography, linguistics, social history, and medieval and Renaissance studies in general."[62] In a position

57. See R. M. Lumiansky and David Mills, *The Chester Mystery Cycle: Essays and Documents* (Chapel Hill: University of North Carolina Press, 1983).

58. Lancashire, *Dramatic Texts and Records*, xxiii, xxxii.

59. Two of the most provocative and wide-ranging efforts to provide a "local habitation" for dramatic texts—Gail Gibson's hypothesis of a Bury St. Edmunds origin for the N-Town compilation and Milla Riggio's reading of *Wisdom* as a banquet masque for monastic and royal patronage—have both been accomplished without the salutary assistance of relevant dramatic records (Gail McMurray Gibson, "Bury St. Edmunds, Lydgate, and the *N-Town Cycle*," *Speculum* 56 [1981]: 56–90; Milla B. Riggio, "The Staging of *Wisdom*," *Research Opportunities in Renaissance Drama* 27 [1984]: 167–76). For a rich demonstration, also with a dearth of dramatic records, of the importance of the locale of dramatic texts, see Gibson's study of East Anglian drama and culture, *The Theatre of Devotion: East Anglian Drama and Society in the Late Middle Ages* (Chicago: University of Chicago Press, 1989).

60. Lancashire, *Dramatic Texts and Records*, x; Davidson, review of *REED: York*, 81.

61. Lancashire, *Dramatic Texts and Records*, x.

62. On the REED volumes as reference tools for interdisciplinary research, see Alan Nelson, review of *REED: Chester, Modern Language Review* 78 (1983): 131–32; and Sheila Lindenbaum, review of *REED: York, Modern Philology* 80 (1982): 80. A recent REED brochure assesses the project's potential as a reference work: "It is of major significance to everyone interested in the culture of the English-speaking world."

now to take stock of the work of its first decade, REED has more recently deemphasized its initial mandate to illuminate connections between dramatic record and dramatic text, highlighting instead the wide-ranging value of data uncovered by REED research. REED editors are also acknowledging that forthcoming volumes may require more commentary than originally planned.[63] But despite these adjustments, which would necessarily be expected of a massive and long-term project finding its way in its crucial early years, REED's founding assumptions remain intact. Its most recent promotional material states: "We know what needs to be done and we know how to do it. Our methodology guarantees a complete and accurate survey of all evidence that remains from the period."

## IV

Though REED deems its proliferation of data an end sufficient in itself, a crucial discontinuity exists between the project's goals and claims and the material available to it. The records present both local and methodological problems in the state in which they survive and the manner in which they are appropriated, problems that fundamentally belie REED's aspirations to neutrality and to exhaustiveness of recovery. Since REED's conception and treatment of evidence are central to the idea of literary history on which it is founded, a critique of REED as historical scholarship must necessarily examine the evidence out of which it is constituted.

Some of the problems the records contribute to REED's historical goals are fairly simple. Occasionally it is impossible to tell exactly what the records say; for example, did the Chester Painters' Company buy eels or candles when then purchased "snyges" in 1575?[64] In other cases, we lack the criteria for interpreting information the records provide, such as the meaning of payments to actors in relation to other valuations in the society.[65] Or variable patterns of dating in civic documents destabilize REED's intention to present its evidence chronologically (*Cumberland, Westmorland, Gloucestershire*, 45–48).

---

63. In a discussion following the presentation of a version of this paper at the Twenty-Third International Congress on Medieval Studies, Kalamazoo, Michigan, 1988, Alan Nelson observed this difference of his Cambridge volumes recently published by REED.

64. Meredith, "'Item for a grone,'" 26–27.

65. Astington, "Commentary," 94–95.

More complex problems attend the number and kind of records that do and do not survive. REED epitomizes the difficulty inherent in any historical endeavor: that the "historical record is both too full and too sparse."[66] Even when the REED volumes are complete, one editor remarks, "they will still but dimly reflect a small fraction of the total dramatic activity that went on in Britain before 1642."[67] On the one hand, REED's aspirations toward exhaustiveness must confront the fact that, even after its county-by-county survey of Britain is complete, there remain an enormous number of documents from other auspices yet to be searched.[68] On the other, REED ironically labors under the discontinuous, fragmentary, and partial state of its primary evidence. REED's goal "to collect systematically the known historical evidence" must acknowledge the massive destruction of early records, the ephemeral nature of plays and pageants that left no record, the uneven distribution of surviving materials, and the existence of some records only in unreliable versions.[69] REED research has also made obvious how some relevant dramatic records are only fortuitously brought to light.[70] REED editors increasingly recognize that the records report some sorts of dramatic activity only because they involved infractions of law, which points up the fragile ground on which REED's evidence is gathered.[71] They also acknowledge the so-called "gaps" in the records and the extent to which REED's irrevocably partial findings may make any generalization impossible (*Devon*, xxvii–xxviii). One particularly ostentatious absence in the records is of evidence of dramatic activities connected with religious institutions, the obvious result of the enormous destruction of ecclesiastical documents during the dissolution.[72]

---

66. White, *Tropics of Discourse*, 51.

67. Galloway, "REED in the Provinces," 102.

68. Lancashire, *Dramatic Texts and Records*, xxxi–xxxii.

69. Lancashire, *Dramatic Texts and Records*, x. For notice of the loss of records relevant to locations covered in REED volumes to date, see *Coventry*, li–lii; *Newcastle upon Tyne*, xx.

70. For an account of relevant documents uncovered by a reboxing exercise in the Warwick County Record Office, see David George and Monica Ory, "Six payments to players and entertainers in seventeenth-century Warwick," *REED Newsletter* 8.1 (1983): 8–9.

71. Wasson notes that we know of the existence of the Exeter Corpus Christi cycle only because of a record of a summons to the mayor's court in 1414 (*Devon*, xxvii); Douglas makes a similar point (*Cumberland, Westmorland, Gloucestershire*, 17).

72. Wasson wonders how the surviving records from "ten abbeys, two collegiate churches, and numerous priories" would have altered the picture of dramatic activity offered by the Devon records (*Devon*, xxvii). Ingram notes the "virtual obliteration" of

While the REED editor must confront the obstacles created by these accidents of survival and discovery, still more disturbing are the problems resulting from REED's founding rationale and the interventions of the editing process itself. The critical issue here involves selection, of documents to be searched and the kinds of information to be culled from them: what exactly is a dramatic record? REED gives priority to all items relating to actual dramatic, mimetic, and musical activity and generally eschews references to ceremonial behaviors and public festivities unless they are accompanied by these.[73] The REED editor transcribes, and where necessary translates, the portions of the documents recording such dramatic activity. The typical REED entry is brief, such as the 1566–67 notice in the Plymouth Receivers' Accounts for five shillings "paied for a breckfast for the moryshe daunce pleers on may day" (*Devon*, 238); or this from the Chester Mayors List of 1515–16: "the shepards play & the Assumption of our lady was played in St Johns churchyard" (*Chester*, 23–24). Obviously, many entries are much longer, but only rarely does REED transcribe an entire document in which notice of dramatic or similar activity is recorded.

These procedures have been established by editorial guidelines in which REED has set forth certain hierarchies of documentary evidence and of items recorded. Thus a researcher begins with financial accounts because "experience has shown that the most accessible evidence for dramatic or musical activities" is found there.[74] As the example of Newcastle illustrates, this policy results in one of the most notable features of the REED volumes: a significant and sometimes major portion of each is constituted by lists of payments. Just as problematic are the criteria by which a "dramatic record" is identified. REED's policy of including only specific notices of dramatic activities has at least two important consequences: it results in the exclusion of potentially relevant items that lie outside its conception of the dramatic and mimetic; and, more important, it assumes that a dramatic record will self-evidently be identified according to REED's criteria. Sometimes the line dividing relevant and nonrelevant evidence is murky, as in REED editor Wasson's explanation that court cases "involving individual en-

---

the ecclesiastical records of the churches and priories of Coventry (*Coventry*, li); and Clopper makes a similar observation about Chester (*Chester*, xi).

73. *REED: Handbook for Editors*, 13–15.

74. Ibid., 21.

tertainers are transcribed only if the case relates to the performance of their art." Thus John Fool, the juggler who was arrested for assaulting a Spaniard, does not make it into the records, but the harper who lost his harp does (*Devon*, lxiii).

The case of John Fool, whose assault and arrest may in fact have had something to do with his occupation as an entertainer, typifies the difficulties that ensue from the policies of selection and extraction in which REED engages. A number of REED's reviewers have objected to these policies for the manner in which they disguise interpretive judgments and for the way they ubiquitously permit the selective quoting of brief references to dramatic activity from documents whose unquoted portions might provide a much fuller picture of the social framework of such activity.[75] They have suggested REED might find a partial way out of this dilemma by offering more interpretation and commentary or by proceeding henceforth with photographic facsimiles of all original documents from which the records are excerpted.[76]

To its credit, the REED project has made gestures acknowledging the problems generated by its method. An article published in the *REED Newsletter* admits that extracts from dramatic records "cannot always be trusted in isolation" but rather "must be studied in the context of the whole document, and if possible in relation to other events recorded at the time."[77] At least one REED editor has on several occasions admitted that the "historian creates the 'facts' of history" (*Norwich*, lxxv).[78] In part REED circumvents these criticisms by maintain-

75. Anne Hudson, review of *REED: Coventry, Review of English Studies* n.s. 35 (1984): 523. Hudson made a similar point in her review of *REED: Chester, Review of English Studies* n.s. 33 (1982): 314. See also Richard Axton, review of *REED: York, Modern Language Review* 78 (1983): 894.

76. Thus Peter Clark laments that in the Chester records "there is no real attempt either in the introduction or the extracts to present any picture, however bald, of the urban context" that would make sense of the records' relation to civic ritual and urban society. Clark recommends that the REED project more firmly ally itself with "a growing wave of interest among urban and social historians on both sides of the Atlantic"; review of *REED: Chester, Renaissance and Reformation* n.s. 5 (1981): 239. See Axton, review of *REED: York*, 894; Hudson, review of *REED: Coventry*, 523. It should be noted, however, that the REED volumes have also been praised for providing "primary materials edited scrupulously, accurately and in bulk" at a time "when so many local historians prefer analysis and interpretation" (D. M. Palliser, review of *REED: York, Northern History* 18 [1982]: 292).

77. Eileen White, "The Girdlers' pageant house in York," *REED Newsletter* 8.1 (1983): 7.

78. See also Galloway's remarks on the difficulty a REED editor faces, "REED in the Provinces," 101. Galloway and Wasson are the most methodologically self-conscious of

ing that its volumes are partly intended as an impetus to study the records' host documents in more detail. But in the main the REED endeavor has not expressed any strong anxiety about these challenges to its basic methods; the volumes are appearing at regular intervals, and nearly all the counties of England have been assigned to a REED researcher.

Yet my main point is not that the REED volumes should offer more interpretation of the evidence they gather together; nor is it that this already massive project should become even larger by reproducing companion sets of photographic facsimiles of its sources. Rather, it is that REED needs to acknowledge that its editorial policies and procedures have profound implications both for its own historical scholarship and for the literary history to which it hopes to contribute. Like all acts of historical understanding, REED's mandate to select and excerpt certain kinds of records of early drama from the documents in which they occur constitutes an interpretive intervention of a high order: what this activity offers as the representation of fact is already an explanation of historical structures, based on the editorial and selection processes themselves.[79]

Such decontextualizing of the evidence is at odds in obvious ways with REED's fiction of its own neutrality. In fact REED epitomizes a mode of historiography which, in situating its work in terms of its factual reference to empirical reality and in eschewing interpretation, has the "bizarre consequence" of presenting

> historical truth in an essentially nonhistorical way, for by attempting to restrict historiography proper to the description and analysis of verifiable facts (ideally in the form of a definitive and exhaustive account), it strives for an unchanging representation of changing "particulars" that would itself transcend the historical process. . . . The narrowly historicist and the ahistorical are extremes that meet in the ideal of a purely documentary historiography.

As long as REED continues to approach its documents "as a quarry for facts in the reconstruction of the past," they are unlikely to reveal their

---

the REED editors. But statements like that of Galloway just quoted would appear to be qualified by his vision of the cautiously prepared incremental history of drama that will result from REED (*Norwich,* vii).

79. See White's comments on the implications of the historian's processes of selection, *Tropics of Discourse,* 57, 90, 95.

own historicity.[80] They will thus inevitably misrepresent whatever evidence they do offer, because they offer it in a form that sets aside crucial questions about the documents' sociohistorical motivations, their place in a structure of communication, and their writers' relation to those in power.[81]

REED's treatment of its evidence thus ironically results in a dehistoricizing and detemporalizing of the records of early drama that make impossible the very act of recovery in which REED is engaged. Seeking an "inconceivable" completeness, REED nonetheless commits itself to an endeavor whose methodological assumptions may only succeed in gathering information of dubious value.[82] Now over a dozen years into its mission, REED has inspired only one major study focusing on the history and interpretation of early English drama.[83] Indeed, the one thing that seems clear is that REED research has the tendency to beget more REED research. The situation that currently faces the REED project is not unlike that of late eighteenth-century German textual scholars of the Bible and the Greek classics who, in pursuing acts of historical scholarship aimed at recovering these texts in their original form, historicized them to a degree that made an idea of origin impossible. They illustrate the "painful irony that the very means by which historicism recovers the past all too often renders it unusable."[84]

V

To what uses, then, can we put the past that REED has uncovered? An assessment of REED's present and probable contributions to the study of early English drama must consider two things: first, how REED's positivism results in a social and historical decontextualizing of the drama that is in its own way as radical as anything accomplished by the formalist readings it was originally intended to oppose; and second,

80. LaCapra, *Rethinking Intellectual History*, 30, 62, 31.

81. Zumthor, *Speaking of the Middle Ages*, 81.

82. Zumthor, *Speaking of the Middle Ages*, 82; and see his comments on traditional historicism's accumulation and extraction of data from "any living interest" (41).

83. Clopper, "The History and Development of the Chester Cycle."

84. Lee Patterson, "The Logic of Textual Criticism and the Way of Genius: The Kane-Donaldson *Piers Plowman* in Historical Perspective," in *Textual Criticism and Literary Interpretation*, ed. Jerome J. McGann (Chicago: University of Chicago Press, 1985), 77; see also Patterson's comments on the relationship between this obsessive historicizing of the literary text and the emergence of formalism (80–81).

how REED's historical method undermines its effort to illuminate dramatic activities and play texts. REED's conception of evidence risks divorcing that evidence from the very information that would make sense of it. The REED entries do tell a story, but despite what REED claims, they do not tell it on their own. Or if they do, they tell it unwittingly and without effect. Though REED has programmatically maintained that its evidence in its present form awaits the ministrations of future interpreters, the burden of proof is still upon it. And it is important to recognize that the most significant interpretive work relevant to the interests of REED—that of urban and social historians studying patterns of communal civic ritual in early modern Europe—has largely been achieved without REED's assistance.[85]

In their present form the records of early English drama are effectively excised from the "institutional settings" to which they bear witness.[86] As the work of social historians has shown, this was a setting in which "what we nowadays unhesitatingly label *drama* . . . was not always and regularly distinguished from other activities," but rather was deeply woven into the fabric of an everyday life that was regulated by visual and public ceremony expressive of an ideal cultural and social organization.[87] Members of the late medieval urban communities in which the Corpus Christi drama flourished did not distinguish among behaviors—religious, economic, social, recreational—that students of the Middle Ages have been inclined too readily to differentiate. Nor, it seems, did they distinguish between "ceremonial ideal and reality." Instead, these were "fused into their total life experiences" in overlapping spheres of interaction and influence.[88]

Though the dramatic records encode a complex social text of myth, ceremony, and spectacle, REED's method and principles of selection

85. See, for example, Charles Phythian-Adams, "Ceremony and the Citizen: The Communal Year at Coventry 1450–1550," in *Crisis and Order in English Towns 1500–1700*, ed. Peter Clark and Paul Slack (Toronto: University of Toronto Press, 1972), 57–85; "Urban Decay in Late Medieval England," in *Towns in Societies*, ed. Philip Abrams and E. A. Wrigley (Cambridge, Eng.: Cambridge University Press, 1978), 159–85; and *Desolation of a City: Coventry and the Urban Crisis of the Late Middle Ages* (Cambridge, Eng.: Cambridge University Press, 1979). See also Mervyn James, "Ritual, Drama and Social Body in the Late Medieval English Town," *Past and Present* 98 (1983): 3–29.

86. Rainer Warning, "The Alterity of Medieval Religious Drama," *New Literary History* 10 (1979): 266.

87. The quotation is from Mills, *Revels History*, 79; see also Axton, review of *REED: York*, 893. This ceremonial culture is discussed in the seminal work of Phythian-Adams, especially his "Ceremony and the Citizen," and *Desolation of a City*, 112, 170, 179.

88. *Desolation of a City*, 180.

do not sufficiently communicate the deep embedding of early drama in other social behaviors.[89] REED procedures tend rather to fragment aspects of this integrated cultural text, perhaps nowhere more pointedly than in the whole manner in which they treat the phenomenon of Corpus Christi. York Corpus Christi ceremony and spectacle were central to the founding of REED, yet REED research has thus far contributed very little to our understanding of this important social and religious concept.[90] This situation results from REED's self-conception and format, which hardly provide the opportunity to probe the meaning of Corpus Christi even though such a large portion of the records detail its cultural preeminence. It is also a by-product of a more general feature of the records: few of those thus far uncovered come from religious institutions, and few speak directly (at least in their present form) to the interplay of religious and dramatic phenomena. Thus the inevitably skewed evidence of the records paints an oversecularized portrait of ceremonial and dramatic activity. REED itself reproduces the records' unwitting bias in its general reluctance to embrace the centrality of religion and myth to the cultural activities they record, a bias that may be a subliminal vestige of records researchers' initial reaction to Kolve's theological "theories."

This reluctance is important because a major feature of the urban societies to which some of the REED volumes are devoted is the extent to which "the structure of organised religion conspicuously" underpins their stratification.[91] In these societies religion functions as a language, part of the cultural system of symbolic forms that "describe, mark and interpret urban life, . . . urban space, urban time and the urban community." Religion—its forms of worship, supplication, and sacrifice— provides metaphors for social relations and deeply held beliefs.[92] In

---

89. On the difficulty of recovering life as lived from "factual data . . . numbers, relationships, occupations, wealth," see D. M. Palliser, "Civic Mentality and the Environment in Tudor York," *Northern History* 18 (1982): 78. And on reconstructing social behaviors of the past when there are no records of "thoughts and feelings," see Peter Burke, "The Virgin of the Carmine and the Revolt of Masaniello," *Past and Present* 99 (1983): 4.

90. James, who has probably done more than anyone to advance our understanding of the Corpus Christi myth and cult, has noted that Nelson, Johnston, and Dorrell [Rogerson] seemed to lack "anything more than a very generalized idea of the late medieval social background against which the cult was practised and the plays performed" ("Ritual, Drama and Social Body," 3–4).

91. Phythian-Adams, *Desolation of a City,* 137.

92. Natalie Zemon Davis, "The Sacred and the Body Social in Sixteenth-Century Lyon," *Past and Present* 90 (1981): 41–42. This formulation of the role of religion in

many urban communities of late medieval England, the interaction of "the sacred and the body social" was evidenced in the civic cult of Corpus Christi, which through an elaborate program of festive activities and a highly developed public mythology linked the towns' governmental structure and hierarchy with an idealized theological conception of social organization and identity.[93]

Central to the civic cult of Corpus Christi is the idea of society as a body. Though the cult obviously takes its name from the multivalent theological symbol of the body of Christ, the religious idea of *corpus christi* is but one of many realizations of a more ubiquitous conception of society as "an integrated and yet articulated . . . organism."[94] Shaped by classical models, scriptural pronouncements, and early Christian theological teachings, the idea of a uniform yet differentiated social body prevailed in medieval sociopolitical thinking.[95] Essential to it is a particular conception of structure—"separate parts related to each other within a larger whole."[96] Specifically, this idea of society "developed a concept of *membership* which assigned to each and every individual his particular place and task within the superior organism."[97] To the late medieval urban community, this idea of the social body offered a means for conceiving of social order and social difference. In these communities the cult of Corpus Christi projected a myth of order and wholeness that attempted to contain and regulate deep-seated social conflicts and competition.[98] The mythic ideal and the social reality were articulated in the festive, cultic Corpus Christi procession and play, which must thus be understood in relation to a certain form of town life.[99]

---

shaping urban societies in early modern Europe should put to rest the old arguments insisting on either the essential "religious" or "secular" character of civic dramatic and ceremonial activity in England.

93. My discussion of the civic cult of Corpus Christi is greatly indebted to James, "Ritual, Drama and Social Body."

94. Anton Hermann Chroust, "The Corporate Idea and the Body Politic in the Middle Ages," *Review of Politics* 9 (1947): 424.

95. Chroust, 424, 431. For a fuller account of this idea and for anthropological explanations of it, see the works cited in James, "Ritual, Drama and Social Body," 4 n. 6.

96. James, "Ritual, Drama and Social Body," 6.

97. Chroust, "The Corporate Idea and the Body Politic," 441.

98. James, "Ritual, Drama and Social Body," 8. Richard Homan anticipated James in understanding the structure and function of the Corpus Christi plays in relation to the late medieval town's economic and political structure, but he did not explore the Corpus Christi ideology ("Ritual Aspects of the York Cycle," *Theatre Journal* 33 [1981]: 302–15).

99. Noting towns where Corpus Christi drama never developed or where it had a hard time hanging on, James observes the close connection between this drama and a

As a symbolic system and a structure of social relations, the cult of Corpus Christi provides the informing context for many of the records of early English drama. For example, the York records for 1432 contain an agreement between the city and the Corpus Christi guild regarding their shared access to and mutual keeping of the keys of a sumptuous Corpus Christi shrine that the guild offered for the city's honor and ceremony. Since the guild had the entire city in its membership, it cut across the social boundaries most fully represented by the hierarchically restricted groups of mayor, council, and citizenry (*York* 1:xiv-xv). In this agreement the city grants the wardens of the Corpus Christi guild the "freedom" and the "power to go to the aforesaid shrine each year as often as there is occasion"; it also grants them the keys to the shrine. In return, the city keeps "one key of the outer covering and veil . . . in the Council Chamber . . . under the control of the mayor . . . so that that mayor . . . without question or delay for the other keys, may cause that shrine to be shown when he wishes . . . so that . . . devotion may grow from this and the honour of the said city increase" (*York* 2:735–36). The agreement bespeaks the willingness of guild and city government to unite efforts to promote the city's honor at the same time that it clearly outlines the respective power and privileges of each. It illustrates what James terms the "final intention" of the civic cult of Corpus Christi: "to express the social bond and to contribute to social integration."[100]

The cult's mythological integration of benign social wholeness and uncontentious social differentiation is most directly conveyed in the prologue to the ordinances of the York Corpus Christi guild, founded in 1408.[101] The Corpus Christi guild had no direct connection to the dramatic cycle with which it shares its name.[102] REED's policy of including only those items that make explicit reference to dramatic activities may account for the omission of this document from the REED York volumes. The omission effectively illustrates the difficulties inherent in REED's principles of selection as well as the limitations of the

---

"specific kind of community—one in which there existed a certain tension and free play of political and social forces, and in which order and unity needed therefore to be continually affirmed in terms of shared rite and ritual" (24).

100. James, "Ritual, Drama and Social Body," 4.

101. The prologue, which appeared in R. H. Skaife's edition of *The Register of the Guild of Corpus Christi in the City of York* (Durham, Eng.: Surtees Society, 1872), has been newly edited and translated by Paula Lozar, "The 'Prologue' to the Ordinances of the York Corpus Christi Guild," *Allegorica* 1 (1976): 94–113.

102. Alexandra F. Johnston, "The Plays of the Religious Guilds of York: The Creed Play and the Pater Noster Play," *Speculum* 50 (1975): 55–90.

project's operative assumptions about "religious" auspices of the guild and the "secular" auspices of the civic, craft-sponsored plays. For the prologue to the ordinances of the York Corpus Christi guild provides telling examples of the late medieval tendency to use the metaphors of religious language to talk about social relations; of all the surviving evidence relevant to the civic cult of Corpus Christi, the prologue offers one of the fullest expressions of the ideology of this civic myth. Far from being ancillary to the records of early English drama, it is critical to their frame of reference.

The prologue takes as its theme Matthew 26:26, *Hoc est corpus meum* (this is my body), and traces the history of mankind as a unified body whose concord has been disrupted by rebellion, anger, envy, and discord. It laments the breach of human brotherhood (*confraternitas*) but finds hope for the restoration of order in the body of Christ, tellingly named the "city of refuge" (*urbs refugii*).[103] Drawing an analogy between the unity of Christ's mystical body and a harmoniously ordered social body, the prologue frequently employs metaphors that express the paradoxical relation of wholeness and differentiation that was central to the civic mythology of Corpus Christi. Thus "the unity and concord" of the brotherhood "are rooted in love, which is one in its root and sevenfold in the carrying out of works of mercy." The unity of the Church, an analogue of the guild, is built "on one man, although after His resurrection," Christ "granted equal power to all the Apostles"; it is like the sun, which has many rays but one light, or an oak tree, which has many branches but one "tenacious root."[104] As these quotations suggest, the York Corpus Christi guild's founding statement articulates the same image of diversity in unity as the Corpus Christi play, the cycle as a whole projecting "the honour of the town community in relation to the world outside" and the individual play units defining the identity and projecting the honor "of the particular occupational group in relation to the social body in which it was involved."[105]

The ritual language of the York Corpus Christi guild's founding statement reappears in guild ordinances from other locations, attesting to the ways urban documents make use of reiterated phrases to "desig-

---

103. Lozar, "'Prologue' to the Ordinances," 100–103.
104. Lozar, "'Prologue' to the Ordinances," 105, 107.
105. James, "Ritual, Drama and Social Body," 17. For an early opinion on the effect of play production in distinct parts, see Mills, "Approaches to Medieval Drama," 58.

nate the social bond."[106] The records of the craft fellowships from Newcastle upon Tyne in the first half of the fifteenth century speak repeatedly, as the Barbers' Ordinary of 1442 puts it, of the resolve to eschew "dissencion & discord that now late hath been among diuerse crafts of the . . . Towne" (*Newcastle upon Tyne,* 5). A casual perusal of the dramatic records of York, Chester, and Coventry indicates the extent to which such appeals to the Corpus Christi cult's mythic order complemented its more practical functions. The cult, and its accompanying procession and play, provided a structure for articulating the subordination of guilds to the authority of the city government and a means for expressing rising or declining guild fortunes in the face of financial pressure, foreign and nonguild competition, and the desire for status and prestige.[107]

Viewing the records of early English drama from the sociohistorical foundation from which they have been cut loose thus sets in relief the problems with REED's "documentary history," which, in giving its due to every scrap of evidence of dramatic activity, disregards the informing principles, contexts, and motivations that endow that evidence with value. REED's exclusion from the York volumes of the prologue to the ordinances of the York Corpus Christi guild illustrates the sort of historical intervention constituted by REED's hierarchies and selection of admissible evidence. Though the Corpus Christi guild may have had no role in the dramatic plays with which it shared its name, the document explaining the Corpus Christi mythos should nonetheless find a place in a massive and frequently repetitive collection of records in which the words "Corpus Christi" resonate on nearly every page.[108]

The example of the Corpus Christi guild prologue suggests the extent to which REED not only belies its ideal of neutrality but also fails to provide appropriate documentary evidence that would help make better sense of the copious data it does present. The two surviving Coventry Corpus Christi plays, the pageants of the Shearmen and Taylors

106. James, "Ritual, Drama and Social Body," 10.

107. For example, see the York Girdlers' petition to the City Council in 1485 (*York* 1:136–137); the Chester Cappers' petition of 1523 (*Chester,* 25–26); and the Coventry records' reflection of the rise and fall of guild fortunes (*Coventry,* 129–33).

108. Lozar's edition was published shortly before the REED *York* volumes appeared. But since the REED volumes frequently include their own versions of material published elsewhere, and since they aim for a kind of documentary inclusiveness, the prior publication of Lozar's edition does not seem sufficient reason to omit the "Prologue" from the *York* volumes.

and of the Weavers, furnish still another example, in this case calling into question the REED premise that the findings of the records will eventually help elucidate play texts.[109]

The REED volume's flat if intriguing sketch of that late medieval town's ceremonial activity has been immeasurably enriched by the work of Charles Phythian-Adams, whose account of Coventry's "desolation" furnishes the essential context for making sense of the dramatic records. The REED Coventry volume records the ceremonial activities of the craft fellowships and governing councils of the city; it tells of procedures, offices, disputes, and agreements of central importance to the city's mounting of its Corpus Christi play. But necessarily because of REED's editorial prescriptions, only rarely does the volume speak of the complex social organization from which the play cycle was born. Though they report the many changes in pageant financing in the early decades of the sixteenth century as guild after guild experienced economic hardship, the Coventry dramatic records as edited only hint at the town's critical, even disastrous decline.[110] The editor of the Coventry volume is careful to point out that Coventry, despite its economic decline, maintained regular production of its Corpus Christi cycle even in the lean years (*Coventry,* xix); but this view, which inevitably informs the selection and presentation of the Coventry records, necessarily skews the portrait of the city's dramatic records, favoring the idea of a continuous tradition of ceremonial over the tumultuous social circumstances that were inseparable from it.

Confined as they are to presenting only information that is directly related to ceremony and spectacle, the Coventry records reveal their limitations when Phythian-Adams's less systematic but more comprehensive reading of the evidence proves particularly relevant to Coventry's extant Corpus Christi plays. Phythian-Adams notes that in Coventry ceremony was "a valued instrument through which basic divisions of humanity, by sex, age, and wealth, could be related to the structure of the community."[111] One critical aspect of that community structure was its gerontocratic system. Life expectancy, the structure of guild membership, the rate of progress through the civic office-holding struc-

---

109. *Two Coventry Corpus Christi Plays,* ed. Hardin Craig, EETS ES 87 (1902; 2d ed., London: Oxford University Press, 1957). All citations appear in the text.

110. See, for example, the order from the Leet Book of 1494 requesting crafts to assist each other (*Coventry,* 78–79).

111. "Ceremony and the Citizen," 63–64.

ture, and the composition of the civic councils all contributed to a system which, through a two-tiered structure in the crafts as well as the city, vested authority in older men.[112] Ex-senior craft officers were known as "ancients" or, as in the case of one craft, " 'the Eldest & discretest of the feliship.' " A sixteenth-century recension of the Weavers' ordinances states "this ideal of gerontocratic authority": " 'honor unto Euery elder, Auncient And gouernor is due. And thereby both gouernment, Sivilytie and dutie to all degrees is mayntayned.' " In late medieval Coventry, "wealth, status and the gerontocratic ideal were fused together in a social institution" which, according to Phythian-Adams, went unchallenged until the late sixteenth century, when conflicts between "young" and "old" occurred "at all the structural levels of society."[113]

If, as the REED project has regularly assumed, knowledge of local circumstances of dramatic production will illuminate play texts, the extant Coventry plays may furnish a case in point, for they offer dramatic corollaries to this portrait of the city's gerontocratic ideal. The pageants of the Shearmen and Tailors and the Weavers are both multiepisodic: the first depicts the Annunciation, Joseph's "trouble" with Mary, the Shepherds, the Three Kings, and Herod's slaughter of the Innocents; the second includes the Presentation in the Temple and Purification and Christ's disputation with the Doctors. Both plays contain long dialogues between two figures called "profeta." In their collocation of scriptural scenes, their use of characters, and what must have been their iconographic emphases, both plays foreground aspects of the seniority, privilege, and limitations of the older male. The central conflict in each is between youth and age.

In the Shearmen and Tailors' pageant a befuddled old Joseph is moved by an angel to accept Mary's divine pregnancy, and three kings humble themselves before the child who is king. Discussing the meaning of the Incarnation, the prophets, such as Isaiah, who introduces the play, act as repositories of ancient wisdom. All these willingly accept the youthful god and king, contrasting with Herod's enraged response to the child's challenge to his rule. In place of the accommodation and worship exemplified by Joseph, the three kings, and the prophets, Herod orders a violent end for the upstart who threatens him. The

112. *Desolation of a City,* 114–15, 122–24.
113. *Desolation of a City,* 114–115, 122, 273.

Weavers' pageant furthers these patterns of characterization and theme. Here too the prophets confirm the teachings of ancient wisdom. Remembering these teachings, an aged and feeble Simeon prays for and receives sight of the "babe . . . borne of dyngnete" (327). Joseph laments the physical infirmities of old age and complains of having married a young wife, only to be brought into line again by another angel. He and Mary take the twelve-year-old Jesus into the city, then lose and later find him among the doctors whose laws he expounds better than they (1001–4). Their affirmation of his success—"Ys not thys a wondurs case, / Thatt this yonge chylde soche knolege hase? / . . . Thatt we wyche nobull docturs be, / And gradudis gret of old antequete, / And now on this place with yonge infance / Ageyne ar sett to larnyng" (1161–68)—echoes Joseph's response to the wit of his son: "Lord God, benedicete! / Yong chyldur now more wyser be, / . . . then an olde mon" (795–97).

Though the emphasis in these plays on youth and age is inherent in the scriptural story, it may nonetheless also reflect the social order in the fabric of everyday life in late medieval Coventry.[114] Particularly when viewed in light of the Weavers' assertion that "honor vnto Euery elder, Auncient And gouerner is due," the plays' portrait of youthful challenges to authority, first violently addressed, then peacefully accommodated, points up the ways that late medieval drama appropriated the Christian story to speak in powerfully relevant ways to the local citizenry. If the plays highlight the divine power of the infant king and the young boy, they also show mature authority either in possession of the right information or able to accept it when it comes along. Thus the elders are not simply superceded; they are incorporated into the new order and truth signified by the birth of Christ. In the Weavers' depiction of Jesus winning the respect of his aged father and mature teachers, the image of the triumphant youth upsetting the traditional hierarchies of family and society may have functioned in creative tension with Coventry's actual gerontocratic social hierarchy. It is, perhaps, very important that all this occurs in the "sytte" (852), a point that identifies the dramatic setting with a social setting in which scriptural event is transformed into the socially resonant practice of the dramatic text. Though the city of Coventry did not witness open challenges to

114. Kolve notes the customary resonances of Luke 1:52: "He hath put down the mighty from their seat, and hath exalted the humble" (*Play Called Corpus Christi*, 156–57).

its gerontocratic structure until the late sixteenth century, its surviving Corpus Christi plays may register more subtle probing of that structure by and for a citizenry that must have been profoundly aware of the length of time it took for the young man to progress up the rungs of the ladder of guild and civic office holding.[115]

VI

This brief reading of the Coventry plays points up the extent to which the current agenda of the REED project, even with a neglected play text under foot, may obscure rather than clarify relationships between dramatic record and dramatic text. Under its present conception REED seems likely to perpetuate and even encourage that "disturbing" distinction between dramatic and literary approches to medieval drama noted earlier. That distinction is related to the far more disturbing one between "fact" and "theory" from which REED drew its founding inspiration. The "fact" is, that every mode of historical procedure has its theory, even one, like REED's, that is based on fact. Developments in literary, language, and historical theory have increasingly impressed upon us the limitations of operations that proceed according to traditional conceptions of a clear-cut difference between facts and interpretation. They prompt us to consider what that "true" and "final" history of early English drama that REED anticipates would look like, and indeed, whether it would be worth writing.

This essay has looked at REED's past and examined its plans for the future, but aspects of REED's immediate present are also interesting for the light they shed on its brand of historicism. In a sense, REED bespeaks an ideology resembling that reflected in many of the documents it combs. Like the late medieval towns it studies, REED projects its own ideal myth of community. Its participants join forces in the shared purpose of finding and preserving records of early drama before

---

115. These texts invite more extensive exploration of their symbolic mediation of relations between the old and the young in late medieval Coventry. In that regard the following would be helpful: Keith Thomas, "Age and Authority in Early Modern England," *Proceedings of the British Academy* 62 (1976): 1–46; Susan Brigden, "Youth and the English Reformation," *Past and Present* 95 (1982): 37–67; Louis Adrian Montrose, "'The Place of a Brother' in *As You Like It*: Social Process and Comic Form," *Shakespeare Quarterly* 32 (1981): 28–54.

they are lost.[116] They pursue their daunting job as a service to scholarship, performing acts of paleographic heroism that would truly be impossible without the intense collaborative effort that the REED project involves.[117] Indeed, REED provides an analogue to the late medieval urban mythology of Corpus Christi: the project, like the towns it studies, constitutes an integrated whole that is greater than the sum of its parts. Like other scholarly endeavors steeped in as much erudition as this one, REED adopts a posture of tolerance and humility in the face of its daunting aims. But continuing my late medieval analogy, it has also taken upon itself something of a preferred guild status whose visibility and presence and practical ability to produce what it promises would seem to preempt any questioning of its stated goals. Along side of REED's literary historical mission lies the more immediate problem of perpetuating itself.

REED is engaged in the process of coming to terms with the evidence it brings to light, evidence that increasingly underlines the fragmentary variety of the early English drama that it skeletally preserves. As John Coldewey in his study of the Nottinghamshire waits puts it: "There is no standard or formula to 'fix' the often quite distinct dramatic traditions of English counties. They are as diverse and unpredictable as the society they mirror, and they must finally be taken on their own terms."[118] This essay has suggested that taking the evidence "on its own terms," a rhetorical gesture that encodes REED's historical method, is neither possible nor desirable. The evidence and the researcher confronting it are already historicized. REED has been shaped by the history of scholarly methods, the habits of literary canonization, assumptions about historical periods, and perhaps even by a desire to promote early drama that has striven to accomplish by the myth of inclusiveness the ideal state that formalist analysis failed to provide in more patently evaluative terms. Similarly, the so-called records of early drama do not simply yield themselves up to some sort of objective search. History does not reside in archival phenomena; rather, it is cre-

116. On the danger of record dispersal and the haphazards of record survival, see Mark Pilkington, "Dispersal and REED," *REED Newsletter* 6.2 (1981): 12; see also David Klausner and Alexandra F. Johnston, "Research in Progress," *REED Newsletter* 4.1 (1979): 19–24.

117. See Anne Lancashire's description of working with the records of the London craft guilds ("London craft guild records," *REED Newsletter* 3.2 [1978]: 1–9).

118. "Some Nottinghamshire waits: their history and habits," *REED Newsletter* 7.1 (1982): 47.

ated by historians constructing and selecting the object of their work. The editing of the records of early English drama and the records themselves are social and cultural events that are deeply implicated in the symbolic and discursive practices of their society; they interpret rather than reflect social reality. The records and the acts that recover them "are engaged in constructing the world and in accommodating their writers, performers, readers, and audiences to positions within it."[119]

Records research, indeed all early drama studies, is appropriately positioned to begin thinking about itself in these terms. Having seen nearly all of the so-called "facts" about early English drama, "(including the classification of it as 'medieval') . . . questioned in the light of recent research," scholars in the field should be prepared to accept a revised historiography's challenge to the very ideas of fact and objectivity.[120] They are also already familiar with, if not sufficiently self-conscious of, the concept of the literary work as social practice, having understood all along that early English dramatic texts are collective enterprises in every sense. Early English drama scholars should welcome a historiography that will enable the recovery of texts and records in their social and cultural life. Never easily accommodated to the hermeneutic paradigm formed by ideas of "the character of written tradition, the singularity of authorship, and the autonomy of the text," early drama, which was aural, public, ephemeral, is more appropriately understood as an "anthropological space" for the enactment of its culture's "most basic values and innermost codes."[121] Accustomed to thinking about composite texts of multiple, anonymous authorship, palimpsests created over time, the early drama scholar should be no stranger to a revised historiography's destabilizing of the text in terms of origins and ends, its discomfort with authorial authority, and its suspicion of hermeneutic certainty.

---

119. Montrose, "Renaissance Literary Studies," 9.

120. Neuss, "Preface," *Aspects of Early English Drama*, ix; Wasson, "Records of Early English Drama," 128–44. My favorite instance of a challenge to the facts of literary history is Martin Stevens's persuasive argument that the so-called Wakefield Master's signature—the nine-line stanza—is the result of editorial tampering with the more common thirteener ("Did the Wakefield Master Write a Nine-Line Stanza?" *Comparative Drama* 15 [1981]: 99–119).

121. The characterization of the hermeneutic paradigm is from Hans Robert Jauss, "The Alterity and Modernity of Medieval Literature," *New Literary History* 10 (1979): 188; on the medieval literary work as an anthropological space, see R. Howard Bloch, *Etymologies and Genealogies: A Literary Anthropology of the French Middle Ages* (Chicago: University of Chicago Press, 1983), 15.

From its current hegemonic position in early drama studies REED offers an appropriate focal point for such a methodological self-examination. Confronted with its own methods, REED emerges not as a prolegomenon to some future history but as a literary historical act in its own right, part of a historiography that issues in no final object but rather provides only interim reports. The possibilities for the redirection of REED's goals suggested here are in fact already implicit in the project's inspired choice of a logo. All of REED's publications feature an image from an early printed copy of *Friar Bacon and Friar Bungay*, showing a shelf on which clasp-bound books rest.[122] Emerging directly from the top of one book, and seeming to float over the entire shelf, is a human head, from whose mouth flare out three banderoles, one inscribed with "Time is," another with "Time was," the third with "Time is past." The head's simultaneous voicing of all three pronouncements suggests the complex relation between the time that was and the time that is, the interaction of which produces what we know as history. In asserting the pastness of the past, the image offers a reminder that all perspectives on the past are precisely that, perspectives, products of human mediation. The REED logo's talking head growing from a shelf of books is a fitting image of the historical process that reading the records of early English drama—and the construction of all versions of the past—truly entails.

122. The logo is identified in the *REED Newsletter* 1.1 (1976): 25.

# 7

# Narrative and Capital
# in Late Medieval Scotland

## Louise Fradenburg

This essay explores how late medieval Edinburgh—at that time newly preeminent among the royal burghs of Scotland—functioned as an imaginative figure in the political culture of the late fifteenth and early sixteenth centuries.[1] In trying to understand the role of the city in late medieval imagining, it is necessary that we recognize how in different texts and at different times figurations of the city have often involved a problematic of origins. The idea of the city seems so often to raise the specter of ontological crisis. It provokes us to ask what it is we mean when we say that something "begins," and to ask about the kinds of values we attach to the concept of "beginning." Does "beginning" mean continuity or rupture?[2] Modern scholarship on the development of the Scottish burghs, for example, has long participated in the discourse of origins exemplified by Henri Pirenne's work and pursued by Marxist theorists concerned with the transition from feudalism to capitalism.[3]

---

1. Royal burghs were those burghs whose charters of privileges originated from the crown, and whose privileges, in actuality, tended to be more extensive than were those of the burghs of barony or the ecclesiastical burghs (for example, in the area of monopolies of foreign trade). Andrew Gibb and Ronan Paddison, "The Rise and Fall of Burghal Monopolies in Scotland: The Case of the North East," *Scottish Geographical Magazine* 99 (1983): 130–40, discuss the monopolistic practices of the royal burghs and the competition they entered into with other types of burghs.

2. See Edward W. Said's contrast between a notion of beginning as "dynastic," bound to sources and origins, mimetic, or as fraternity, complementarity, adjacency, break, in *Beginnings: Intention and Method* (Baltimore: Johns Hopkins University Press, 1975), 66.

3. For a review of different theories of the origins of Scottish towns, see Ian Adams, *The Making of Urban Scotland* (Montreal: McGill-Queen's University Press, 1978), 20; see also George Gordon and Brian Dicks, eds., *Scottish Urban History* (Aberdeen: Aberdeen University Press, 1983), "Prolegomena," and Dicks's essay on "The Scottish Medieval Town: A Search for Origins," 23, for his review of the debate on medieval town origins between "supporters of legal origins on the one hand and those of economic origins on the other." See Henri Pirenne, *Medieval Cities: Their Origins and the Revival of Trade*, trans. Frank B. Halsey (Princeton: Princeton University Press, 1925), and the collection of essays edited by Rodney Hilton in *The Transition from Feudalism to Capitalism* (Lon-

Modern historians want to know who, or what, gave rise to the medieval city; who, or what, sustained it; whether it was part of the country
surrounding it, or whether it was different. Their questions are framed
most often in economic terms, particularly in terms of a discourse of
production. In a number of modern texts, the discourse of production
proceeds by way of a return to the authority of theoretical categories—
hence by way, on the level of method, of a return to preoccupation with
legitimacy and illegitimacy. These texts ask: is the medieval city the
product of forces "internal" or "external" to feudalism? Is the medieval
city part of the feudal or the capitalist "mode of production"?[4]

If the city functions as an ontological problem in historical narrative,
we need to try to understand why this is so. First, the city poses the
problem of change—of the changes giving rise to the city as well as the
changes for which the city is often held responsible (sophistication,
alienation, the devaluing of rural and familial experience, the making of
money from money, the making of new things).[5] Change brings new-
ness into being; the imagination is as much at work in our economic
life as it is in our poetry. For this reason, the city—not exclusively, but
with a particular kind of power—poses the problem of how human
beings construct and produce their world. The artisanal or fictive eco-

---

don: Verso Editions, 1978; reprint, 1984), essential reading for anyone interested in the
debate on merchant capital (hence towns) and its role in the transition from feudalism to
capitalism. The definition of these two "modes of production" is, needless to say, as
problematic within Marxist theory as without. A provocative theoretical treatment is that
of Barry Hindess and Paul Q. Hirst, *Pre-capitalist Modes of Production* (London: Routledge and Kegan Paul, 1975).

4. John Merrington, "Town and Country in the Transition to Capitalism," in *Transition from Feudalism to Capitalism*, ed. Hilton, attempts to use these categories in a flexible
way by positing merchant capital as an "internal externality" to the feudal mode of production (177–78). But this attempt—like Perry Anderson's notion of the structure of the
centralized state as "secondarily *over-determined*" by the urban bourgeoisie (*Lineages of the
Absolutist State* [London: Verse Editions, 1979; reprint, 1984], 22–23)—remains locked
within categorical imperatives. The debate over the relation of feudalism to capitalism
and of country to town is badly in need of deconstruction.

5. See Pierre Bourdieu, *Outline of a Theory of Practice*, trans. Richard Nice (Cambridge, Eng.: Cambridge University Press, 1977; reprint, 1985), who links "the emergence
of a field of discussion"—of a culture's inclusion and discussion of competing opinions—
with "the development of cities": "this is because the concentration of different ethnic
and/or professional groups in the same space, with in particular the overthrow of spatial
and temporal frameworks, favours the confrontation of different cultural traditions" (233
n. 16). Bourdieu thus links the city to "crisis, which, in breaking the immediate fit between . . . subjective structures and . . . objective structures, destroys self-evidence practically" (168–69)—in other words, destroys what we take for granted, and makes its
arbitrariness apparent. See also his discussion of "genesis amnesia" (79).

nomic activities pursued within the city are figured in the very construction of the cityscape itself. It is possible, though still a profound misrecognition, to forget the extent to which nature—the country outside the city walls—has been constructed by human curiosity, presumption, intervention, labor. It seems to be more difficult to forget the fact of the city's construction, a fact that implies human creativity and a decentered human responsibility for the shape of the world. Indeed, forgetting this fact will often require, in one historical form or another, the fantasy of a city plan that reinscribes the superreal in the form of royal or divine creativity.[6] It is not surprising, then, that the figure of the city has so often been "split" in two: the city must either locate its origins in superreality or become the site of abjection, even of plague; it becomes a figure either of the upholding or dissolution of boundaries.[7] And, as that which threatens to reveal and therefore undo the createdness of cultural constructs, the city can become a figure for crises of belief—for crises in our ascription of superreality to various privileged cultural constructs.

6. This discussion relies heavily on the inspiration of Elaine Scarry's treatment of human making and unmaking in *The Body in Pain: The Making and Unmaking of the World* (Oxford: Oxford University Press, 1985), in which she links the "unequivocally negative consequences to city dwelling" in the Old Testament (Babel, Sodom and Gomorrah, the destruction of Jericho) to the Old Testament's prohibition of "human acts of making, creating, working" (221). One New Testament example is the story of the prodigal son. Scarry discusses the "unrecoverable" createdness of the superreal, of institutions whose contingent human origin is, within the context of a particular culture and a particular moment, hidden from view (312). I also explore a number of the issues raised by Scarry's work in my article "Criticism, Anti-Semitism, and the *Prioress's Tale*," *Exemplaria* 1 (1989), 69–115.

7. In the psychoanalytic literature on "borderline" cases, which involve disturbances in subject-object relations and in the differentiation between mother and child, "splitting" is one of the most important defense mechanisms. By splitting off the aggressive from the libidinal impulses, splitting protects the "good" mother from the "bad"—that is, from the dangers threatened by (internal) aggression. See Edward R. Shapiro, "The Psychodynamics and Developmental Psychology of the Borderline Patient: A Review of the Literature," *American Journal of Psychiatry* 135 (1978): 1307. On "abjection," see Julia Kristeva, *Powers of Horror: An Essay on Abjection* (New York: Columbia University Press, 1982), in which the experience of abjection is explained as follows: "It is . . . not lack of cleanliness or health that causes abjection but what disturbs identity, system, order. What does not respect borders, positions, rules. The in-between, the ambiguous, the composite" (4). Abjection, in Kristeva's thought, is particularly brought out through the collapse of subject-object distinctions, and hence is important in the relation of the child to the figure of the mother. The dissolution of distinction is also crucial to René Girard's understanding of the plague: "The distinctiveness of the plague is that it ultimately destroys all forms of distinctiveness. The plague overcomes all obstacles, disregards all frontiers" ("The Plague in Literature and Myth," *Texas Studies in Literature and Language* 15 (1974): 834). Scarry also discusses how the "dissolution of the boundary between inside and outside" is one of the most important aspects of physical pain (*The Body in Pain*, 53).

In his analysis of the ontological implications of the "primal scene," Ned Lukacher foregrounds the problem of memory: the "ontological self" depends upon "the notion of a subject for whom 'reality' inheres only in the self-presence of perception and recollection."[8] Lukacher's critique of the ontological self suggests that remembering can become a way of attempting to repair the relation of the human creature to superreality, a way, for example, of recovering an external origin—the agency of the Creator—within the interiority of the creature. Thus the ideal city of St. Augustine, who was writing at a time of extreme cultural crisis, is imagined in much the same way as is Augustine's own memory. In Augustine's *Confessions,* the memory is called both *sinus* and *aula.* Kenneth Burke, in *The Rhetoric of Religion,* notes that "in the Latin dictionaries the range of the meanings for the word [*sinus*] is given as: curve, fold, hollow, coil, bosom, lap, purse, money, bay, gulf, basin, valley; figuratively: love, affection, protection, intimacy, innermost part, heart, hiding-place."[9] The memory is closely associated in Burke's reading of the *Confessions* with strongly maternal and "infantile" strands of meanings and images, with "plenitude" and "manifoldness."[10] But the memory, through its identification as *aula,* is also to be associated with the paternal strand of meanings in Augustine, with the

---

8. *Primal Scenes: Literature, Philosophy, Psychoanalysis* (Ithaca: Cornell University Press, 1986), 39. Lukacher uses the term "primal scene" to refer to "an intertextual event that displaces the notion of the event from the ground of ontology." "Rather than signifying the child's observation of sexual intercourse, the primal scene comes to signify an ontologically undecidable intertextual event that is situated in the differential space between historical memory and imaginative construction" (24). Lukacher bases much of his reading of the primal scene on the ontologically uncertain status of the primal scene in Freud's case history of the Wolf Man; the primal scene, the "origin" of the Wolf Man's neurosis, could never be "remembered" by the Wolf Man, and yet Freud's reconstruction of the scene has the truth-status of an interpretive construction—an imaginative creation.

9. *The Rhetoric of Religion: Studies in Logology* (Berkeley and Los Angeles: University of California Press, 1970), 126.

10. I will quote from one passage at length to give a sense of the richness of Burke's reading of the infantile strand in the *Confessions:* "At first, [Augustine] . . . says, all he 'knew' (*noram*) was how to suck (*sugere*), to rest (*adquiescere*) and to cry (*flere*). The term 'fill,' that in the opening invocation had been applied to God (in His plenitude filling all Creation) is here applied literally to the milk that filled the breasts (*ubera implebant*) of the women who had nursed him. (I, vi) . . . A similar bridge between infancy and adult motivation is also explicitly supplied by a parallel he draws between the 'consolations' of God's mercies (*consolationes miserationum tuarum*) and the 'consolations' of human milk (*consolationes lactis humani*). . . . In the opening invocation of Book IV, when deriding Manichaean views on food and holiness, he speaks of himself as sucking God's milk and eating of Him as a food that does not perish. Characteristically, when speaking of the Word made flesh (VII, xviii), he calls it a food whereby God's Wisdom (*sapientia*) might give milk (*lactesceret*) to our infancy" (*The Rhetoric of Religion,* 66).

separations and discriminations of order celebrated most explicitly in the *City of God.*[11] The range of meanings for *aula* is: "court, forecourt, inner court, yard, hall, palace, royal court, residence, courtiers, princely power, royalty."[12] The notions of protection, domesticity, recess, secrecy, are thus linked with the plenitude of Augustine's "free maternal city" of God and with the architecture (and architectonics) of *potestas.*[13] The idyll that Augustine discovers hidden away within himself is imagined as a princely palace, an inner temple of grandiosity.

Augustine's identification of *aula* with memory takes place within the context of a profound meditation on the simultaneous proximity and mystery of the inner self; estrangement and restoration are imagined in terms of place. For Augustine, the perfect place is the free maternal city of peace, imagined as indistinguishable from the court of the absolute judge and ruler; the city of God, in its absolute form, is the result at once of an eternally nurturing, loving proximity, and of the severity of righteous discrimination—for the city of man lies far below it, split off, projected, separated. On earth, only the ignorant fail to see where the city of man ends and the city of God begins.

Augustine thus tries to make one, and make good, plenitude and discrimination; at stake in this process of atonement and reparation is, for Augustine, the nature of the relations between maternity and paternity, love and aggression, nurturance and punishment. His texts suggest a felt discordance between the maternal strand of meanings and the paternal strand; and they suggest how this discordance may be eased by the appropriation of the maternal strand for the paternal strand, whereby plenitude becomes associated with a peaceful city that

11. It might be said that whereas in the *Confessions* Augustine tries to work out absolute reunion with maternal love, in the *City of God* he tries to work out, through a penitential subjection to God, an identification with the paternal judge. See, for example, the passage beginning "even now God judges, and has judged from the beginning of human history" (*The City of God by Saint Augustine,* trans. Marcus Dods [New York: The Modern Library, 1950], 20.1.710–11), in which Augustine celebrates the omnipresence of judgment in the workings of salvation history, especially the principle of discrimination and its ability to separate the deserving from the undeserving. Thus categories—boundaries, distinctions—are absolutely restored. In Augustine, the fixing of responsibility through injurious punishment is essential to the substantiation of belief. See Scarry, *The Body in Pain,* for an account of how the "vibrancy," "incontestable reality," "certainty" of pain, "can be appropriated away from the body and presented as the attributes of something else," something that lacks this kind of material certainty—such as a cultural construct or belief (13–14).

12. Burke, *The Rhetoric of Religion,* 126.

13. Burke, 122, 141, 165.

is nonetheless the product of warfare and repudiation. Augustine's texts, in short, suggest some further ways in which the concept of the primal scene might be useful in our exploration of the figure of the city. As William Kerrigan has argued, the primal scene is a way of encountering one's own createdness, mortality, and finitude—the finitude, too, of one's creators; it is, at least potentially, an uncovering of the createdness of superreality.[14] The concept of the primal scene finally speaks to the experience of loss in relation to maturation and familiality—to the project of growing up, of situating oneself in a generational chain; to one's sense of the times one lives in, and the changing ways in which those times are to be lived in.

The rendering in familial terms of traumatic confrontation with the contingency of origins is not, however, exclusive to modern psychoanalysis (though psychoanalysis, in contradistinction to many earlier myths of origin, orients itself toward the dissolution of the "subject's" dependence and the analysis of his resistance to such dissolution). We have seen the importance of familial images to Augustine's treatment of historical crisis; the later Middle Ages was also a critical time in which the difficult relation of creature to Creator was imagined in strongly familial terms. The later Middle Ages increasingly recognized, both in theory and in practice, the secularity—the human reality—of the grounds, purposes, and practices of production. At the same time, theology located the Creator at an increasing distance from human cre-

---

14. William Kerrigan has concentrated more intently than most psychoanalytic critics on the relations between the primal scene and the question of origins. His work has the advantage—in contrast to Lukacher's—of retaining a sensitivity to the ontological crisis provoked by the primal scene without displacing issues of sexuality and the cultural construction of gender. He argues that, through the primal scene, the child mourns the loss of the fantasized parent—the loss of absolute protection, of union with the All—and encounters the contingency of the child's own being. The meaning of the primal scene, in Kerrigan's terms, is the "mourned passing of the narcissistic ego"—of fantasies of union, of omnipotence—"translated into the love, jealousy, and terror of the Oedipus complex." The primal scene is a blow to narcissism not only because it means that the mother is "not-with" the child, or that, instead of being the source of all things, she is instead a part and participant of desire, but also because "the image of parental intercourse . . . foretells the end of narcissism in the knowledge of contingency and createdness: the imaginer is as nothing before the fully revealed meaning of his image—there in the image, he was *not.* . . . An awesome revelation of one's own nothingness must be encountered." Seeing becomes a way of including oneself in the scene from which one has been excluded; the figure of the paternal gaze as benign can function as a defense against—or, in Kerrigan's analysis of Milton, as a triumph over—the implications of the primal scene. See *The Sacred Complex: On the Psychogenesis of Paradise Lost* (Cambridge, Mass.: Harvard University Press, 1983), 164–67.

ation, and brought Him back through the corporeal excesses of affective piety. Belief in the Real Presence was attacked, and was resubstantiated not only through the bodily pain of tortured heretics but also through the emphasis, in late medieval communion ritual as well as Corpus Christi spectacle, on the beholding of the sacrament.[15] The intensification of monarchical spectacularity—of visual representation of the king's magnificence—was also part of the attempt, in the later Middle Ages, to remake belief in medieval icons of superreality.

We have said that in modern historical narratives the question of production—of which economic forces produced the city and were in turn produced by it—has been uppermost. But in a number of medieval narratives of the city—partly because, as Philippe Ariès has put it, the "idea of childhood was bound up with the idea of dependence"— the paramount question was one of reproduction, which could be treated figuratively, and which brought in its train questions of nurturance, loyalty, gift, debt, fertility, and discord.[16] The authority of the sovereign is linked with the role of sovereign as provider. Central, in particular, to the courtly fictions of the later Middle Ages is the representation of magnificence—of the sovereign's power to create a splendid, indeed a paradisal, court; of the court's reflection of the splendor of its sovereign creator. Through the representation of magnificence,

15. See Leah Sinanoglou Marcus, "The Christ Child as Sacrifice: A Medieval Tradition and the Corpus Christi Plays," *Speculum* 48 (1973): 498.

16. Philippe Ariès, *Centuries of Childhood: A Social History of Family Life*, trans. Robert Baldick (New York: Vintage Books, 1962), 26: "The idea of childhood was bound up with the idea of dependence: the words 'sons', 'varlets' and 'boys' were also words in the vocabulary of feudal subordination. One could leave childhood only by leaving the state of dependence, or at least the lower degrees of dependence." See also Jean-Louis Flandrin, *Families in Former Times: Kinship, Household and Sexuality,* trans. Richard Southern (Cambridge, Eng.: Cambridge University Press, 1979), for the premodern use of the word "family" to refer to "an assemblage of co-residents who were not necessarily linked by ties of blood or marriage" (4), and on the dependence of servants and on the importance of "service" in the education of children (64). The structure of the medieval *maison*—the well-to-do household—made for particularly intense relations between nurturance and the discipline of violence. In the *maison*, the symbolic domination of the "gift" coexisted with overt violence; this was the matrix of the inseparability, for the aristocracy and those who lived within it, of familial, political, and economic dependence.

The elision of production as an ideological strategy has been explored by Raymond Williams in *The Country and the City* (New York: Oxford University Press, 1973); he stresses the significance of Christianity's elision of a "charity of production" in favor of a "community of consumption," so that the feast—rather than the labor that produces it— becomes the dominant symbol of Christian togetherness (30–31). In the medieval *maison*, consumption and production are merged in the banquet's function as expression of the lord's magnanimity and of the strength of his community.

the courtly text proclaims the paternity of the sovereign. And it seeks to locate, in the sovereign, maternal love as well as paternal power, each conceived, as Burke might put it, in the "register" of rule. The sovereign's rule is imagined as enabling the fertility of the land; maternity is seen to depend on the monarchical phallus; human production and reproduction are dependent on sovereign agency. The confluence of relations of domination and nurturance in the "family" of the princely or baronial household constitutes the place wherein problems of creation are experienced and imagined. The problem of the city, in turn, is imagined as the problem of its relation to the court.

In late fifteenth- and early sixteenth-century Scotland, Edinburgh became the imaginative site of apparently contradictory ideas of the city: on the one hand, a royal creature, dependent on crown patronage for its privileges and therefore its life, owing services to its lord in return; on the other, a possible source of disorder, a threat (though, ideally, not a lasting or true one) to the good life of its creator and its country. Insofar as the king "creates" the city by granting its privileges—by giving it life—he is its originator, and thus they share the kind of identity that links parent and child.[17] Yet the gift given to the city by the king is the gift of difference: the city is demarcated, contained, and inside it special activities are pursued. The creation of the city is thus a kind of divisiveness; it sets up different categories of things, a fall from Edenic simplicity into things equal and unequal.[18] As a dependent whose dependence is undependable, the city is imagined as a site of change, of passings-away, of a narrativity of limit and loss. Though contained within the aristocratic order, it seems at

---

17. That the interests of medieval monarchy and burgh had been particularly closely identified in Scotland is suggested by the sudden irruption of the burghs into documentary life towards the middle of the twelfth century, a time when David I (1124–53) was proceeding to remodel Scotland, insofar as circumstances permitted, on the basis of Anglo-Norman feudalism, a project which in turn seems to have involved the fostering or outright creation of urban settlements. But the significance of the burgh's sudden appearance has been debated. See note 1 and esp. Dicks, "The Scottish Medieval Town," 26–27.

18. See Burke, *The Rhetoric of Religion,* on the language of Genesis: "the possibility of a 'Fall' is implied in the idea of the Creation, insofar as the Creation was a kind of 'divisiveness,' since it set up different categories of things which could be variously at odds with one another and which accordingly lack the proto-Edenic simplicity of absolute unity" (174).

times—in Deleuze and Guattari's terms—to "haunt" that order as a "nightmare" and "anxious foreboding."[19] Included, it may be the "free maternal city" of plenitude, at once *sinus* and *aula;* repudiated, it may be the city of earth.

The following discussion tries to understand the city's figurative function for two different textual and historical situations. The first part of the discussion considers the poetry of James Foulis, a burgess of Edinburgh and a prominent advocate and courtier during the reign of James V of Scotland (1513–42). Thanks largely to the work of Dr. John Durkan, Foulis's poetry is now known to scholars of Scottish human-ism and has recently begun to receive serious textual and editorial treat-ment. This essay studies Foulis as a poet of the city, and in particular as a poet whose figurations of infantile and parental strands are worked out through his identification with Edinburgh. Foulis wrote at a time when Edinburgh, Scotland, and Scotland's kings had suffered much from calamity: from continuing economic depression, plague, disas-trous battles, the death of James IV, the disorders of the fragile minority of James V and his virtual imprisonment in Edinburgh. In Foulis's po-etry, the recovery—the re-membering—of childhood, city, and mon-archy are mutually implicit. The ensuing discussion also addresses a crisis of creatureliness and creativity: in 1482 James III of Scotland was imprisoned in Edinburgh Castle. Analysis of James III's charter of priv-ileges granted to Edinburgh in 1482 permits us to explore another kind of re-membering of relations between monarch and city: the king's at-tempt to repossess his creature through its devotional practices. I will discuss Foulis first, in contravention of chronology, because his poetry offers a rich context for a reading of James III's charter; for those un-familiar with the literary interpretation of such historical documents, the complexity and interest of the charter will be more accessible if presented by way of literary treatments of the city. I will begin with a brief survey of the material and discursive circumstances in which Fou-lis's poetry was produced.

19. Gilles Deleuze and Felix Guattari write that capitalism "haunts all societies . . . as the nightmare and anxious foreboding of what might result from the decoding of flows" (*Anti-Oedipus: Capitalism and Schizophrenia,* trans. Robert Hurley, Mark Seem, and Helen R. Lane [Minneapolis: University of Minnesota Press, 1983], 144).

I

Thomas Davidson, burgess and guild-brother of Edinburgh, seems to have become the favored royal printer during the reign of James V. Instances, at least, of Davidson's patronage by the crown date from the time of his greatest activity as printer of government documents and "croniclis."[20] Davidson printed "The hystory and crankliss of Scotland" (Bellenden's translation of Hector Boece's Latin work) and the "Actis" of Parliament of James V. Colophons in both the "Croniklis" and the "Actis" style Davidson as "Prenter to the Kingys nobill grace"; for the latter job he was apparently chosen by Sir James Foulis, Lord Clerk Register.[21] Davidson was also responsible for printing a Latin poem known as the *Strena* and addressed to James V "on taking up the king-ship of the country."[22] Since the poem alludes to James V's assumption of power in 1528, it is likely that the poem was printed in that year, perhaps commissioned for a royal welcome.[23] It is possible, too, that

20. *Roll of Edinburgh Burgesses and Guild-Brethren, 1406–1700,* ed. Charles B. Boog Watson (Edinburgh: Scottish Burgh Record Society, 1929), 144. In October 1541 the king appointed Davidson "searcher" of English merchants, ships, and goods arriving in Scotland without sufficient conduct; in 1542 Davidson was granted the tavern and booth that had formerly belonged to Walter Chepman, who, with Andro Myllar (and James IV), had begun Scottish printing in 1507. See R. Dickson and J. P. Edmund, *Annals of Scottish Printing: From the Introduction of the Art in 1507 to the Beginning of the Seventeenth Century* (Cambridge, Eng.: MacMillan and Bowes, 1890), 105.

21. The reverse of the title page of the "Actis" records "the copie of the kingis grace licence and privilege granted to [our lovit] Thomas Davidson, prentar, from Imprenting of his gracis actis of Parliament," and specifies that Davidson was chosen by the lord clerk register. Dickson and Edmund comment that "this evidently placed him in the position of king's printer"; Davidson also used a woodcut of the royal arms of Scotland, perhaps designed by Sir David Lindsay. See Dickson and Edmund, *Scottish Printing,* 123, 105, 109.

22. The title page reads "Ad Serenissimum Scotorum Regem Iacobum Quintum de suscepto Regni Regimine a diis feliciter ominato STRENA"; the colophon at the end of the print reads "Impressum Edinburgi apud Thomam Dauidson." The print is in the British Museum; a facsimile of it, with a translation (spirited but not very precise) by Archdeacon Wrangham, is printed in *The Miscellany of the Bannatyne Club,* vol. 2, ed. David Laing (Edinburgh: Bannatyne Club, 1836), 3–8; J. IJSewijn and D. F. S. Thomson have edited the poem in "The Latin Poems of Jacobus Follisius or James Foullis of Edinburgh," *Humanistica Lovaniensia* 24 (1975): 135–37. I would like to take this opportunity to thank Matthew Glendenning and Lori Berger for their work in preparing the translations of Foulis's poetry used in this essay.

23. Dickson and Edmund, *Scottish Printing,* 122; and see the *Miscellany of the Bannatyne Club* 2:3. John Durkan, in "The Beginnings of Humanism in Scotland," *Innes Review* IV (1953): 8 n. 16, suggests 1525. IJSewijn and Thomson, "Latin poems of James Foullis," accept 1528 (151). At a much later date Foulis "was chosen with Adam Otterburn and David Lyndsay to compose a French welcome to the new queen"; see Durkan, 8–9, and n. 18, and A. J. Mill, *Medieval Plays in Scotland* (Edinburgh: Wm. Blackwood & Sons, 1927), 180. Cf. *Extracts from the Records of the Burgh of Edinburgh, 1403–1520,* ed. Sir James

the poem represents an early collaboration of Sir James Foulis with the Davidson press; for though the *Strena* is anonymous, John Durkan has suggested that James Foulis is the most likely candidate for its authorship.[24] Foulis's connections with Edinburgh and with printing, his interest in Latin poetry, and the strong thematic and rhetorical resemblances between the *Strena* and his other poetry persuade me of the sense of this attribution.

James Foulis was a burgess of Edinburgh; his father may have been a member of the guild of Skinners, and his mother was the daughter of Sir James Henderson or Henryson of Fordell, an advocate to James IV.[25] Foulis himself became King's advocate in 1527; held the post of secretary to the king in 1529, one year after the probable publication of the *Strena;* served as Lord Clerk Register from 1532 to 1549; and was a member of the privy council in 1542.[26] He was also a neo-Latin poet. His *Calamitose pestis Elega deploratio* was published in Paris c. 1511, and dedicated to Alexander Stewart (the illegitimate son of James IV who became Archbishop of St. Andrews), to whom he wrote that "his object in publishing was to entice students at home to take up the study of polite letters."[27] Foulis seems to have worked at a pitch of nationalist, royalist, and belletristic fervor for most of his life. After his stay in Paris he studied at Orleans, famed for its instruction in law and host of

---

Marwick (Edinburgh: Scottish Burgh Records Society, 1869–92), 2:89–91, 17 July 1538, hereafter cited as *Edinburgh Burgh Recs.*

24. Durkan remarks that Foulis "may be the unknown author of the poem *Strena* published in Edinburgh on the occasion of James V's assumption of power" ("Beginnings of Humanism," 8).

25. *The Account Book of Sir John Foulis of Ravelston 1671–1707,* ed. Rev. A. W. Cornelius Hallen, Scottish Historical Society 16 (Edinburgh: at the University Press by T. and A. Constable, 1894), xiv–xv. (Sir John was a descendant of James Foulis.) Foulis's *Carmina* contains an epigram in honor of Sir James Henryson; see Durkan, "Beginnings of Humanism," 8.

26. *Dictionary of National Biography,* vol. 20, ed. Leslie Stephen (New York: MacMillan and Co.; London: Smith, Elder and Co., 1889), 70; John MacQueen, "Some Aspects of the Early Renaissance in Scotland," *Forum for Modern Language Studies* 3 (1967): 207.

27. The dating is John Durkan's; see "The Cultural Background in Sixteenth-Century Scotland," in *Essays on the Scottish Reformation 1513–1625,* ed. David McRoberts (Glasgow: Burns, 1962), 290, and "Beginnings of Humanism," 7–9. See also *Biographie Universelle: Ancienne et Moderne,* vol. 14 (Paris: Ch. Delagrave, 1854–1865), 500. A recent edition of the *Carmina* may be found in "Latin Poems of James Foullis," 106–22. IJSewijn and Thomson date the *Carmina* print as 1512 (103–4). And see John B. Dillon, "Some Passages in the *Carmina* of James Foullis of Edinburgh," *Studies in Scottish Literature* 14 (1979): 187–95. Thanks to John Durkan, a copy of the *Carmina* is now in the National Library of Scotland.

a vigorous Scottish "nation" for which Foulis was a "specially active and zealous" procurator.[28]

Foulis's *Calamitose* is a nightmarish vision of disasters that have befallen Edinburgh. In the letter to Stewart, Foulis explains that plague had driven many students from Paris to Orleans; and he recalls the terrible plague that had ravaged Scotland some years before. Written, then, "under the influence" of the later plague in Paris ("suppressa memor bissenos fata per annos / Horrende repeto tela cruenta necis," 45–46), the *Calamitose* memorializes the plague of the late 1490s, during which Foulis lost his entire family: the poem tells the story of how, while Foulis himself lay seriously ill with the plague, his small sister and brother died, and finally his parents. Personal loss and municipal and national catastrophe intertwine.

Nature is represented as demonic. Scotland is a white land clothed with Thracian snows and rivers formed of marble ice (11–12). Into this landscape Death rushes, a wolf, an archer, shooting arrows of plague whose poisoned iron crushes the innermost limbs, destroys bone marrow, and stiffens the body with ulcers (20–40). In the *Calamitose,* the human body is dismembered and decomposed; the body of the world, too, is dead or dying. The *Calamitose* is an attempt to give voice to the body in pain, to the tortured body of whose isolation, exposure, and voicelessness Elaine Scarry so movingly writes. According to Scarry, it is the destruction of community—the destruction both of the community's beliefs about itself and of the victim's capacity to experience community—that is at stake in acts of torture and of war; great pain is both "language-destroying" and "world-destroying."[29] Plague is, in the register of disease, the apocalyptic form of the world- and word-destroying power of pain: in the plague, says Girard, "all life, finally, is turned into death, which is the supreme undifferentiation"; plague "symbolizes desymbolization itself."[30] The destruction of the body and of the human world that has been made for and by the body is also linked, in the *Calamitose,* to the destruction of temporal community: time, too, is full of horrors. Foulis repeatedly alludes to previous catas-

28. See John Kirkpatrick, ed. "The Scottish Nation in the University of Orleans, 1336–1538," in the *Miscellany of the Scottish Historical Society,* vol. 2 (Edinburgh: at the University Press by T. and A. Constable, 1904), 55–56, 64. Kirkpatrick gives information on the Scottish nation at Orleans, and an edition of "The Book of the Scottish Nation" with translation appended.

29. *The Body in Pain,* 19, 29, and 45.

30. "The Plague in Literature and Myth," 834, 849.

trophes (Niobe, 65, or the fall of Troy, 350), creating a dynamic of re-membering in which the experience of loss serves perpetually to recall earlier losses. Memory is an instrument of self-extension, of struggle against the reduction of world and self to the painful body; it links Foulis's, and Scotland's, injuries to a history of catastrophe. But memory thereby becomes, at the same time, an instrument of further torture: the suffering memory finds in history no resting place. Losses are displaced only to reappear at every turn; continuities bespeak only the experience of discontinuity.

So much so that the narrator of the *Calamitose* chooses to end his complaint simply by appealing to the Muse to cease her lamentations; if one were to weep for the living—for creatures subject to decay—this would be a task for more tongues than there are stars in the sky and fish in the sea. Lamentation would be endless. The moment of the poem's most ambitious attempt to speak the unspeakable, to resymbol-ize that which has been desymbolized, is also the moment at which the human voice breaks down. Nearly all writers on mourning remind us of how grief impoverishes the subject's world; grief is that negation of desire, that disappearance of the object, which participates most closely in the world-destroying character of physical pain. The *Calamitose* treads the borderline moment at which language begins to break down from grief and pain, the moment at which the radical embodiment of death makes its appearance. Foulis's vision of the impoverishment of the human voice by mourning, of the need for an infinitude of voice in order to speak unendurable loss, thus gives way to an invocation of divinity; recognition of the limits of the human voice—recognition of creatureliness—paves the way for reparation of the relation to the Cre-ator.[31] The poem concludes: "Pone igitur questus gemebundi pectoris altos, / Et sit pacato purior aura Deo" (495–96).[32]

---

31. Scarry, *The Body in Pain*, argues that, in the Hebrew Scriptures, God—the Crea-tor—has voice; humans have bodies. To transgress this distribution—either by embody-ing the Creator or by giving voice to the human—is to undermine the structure of belief and bring on the readjustments of injurious punishment (181). Her analysis of torture contends that the reduction of self and world to body that is effected through pain is also accompanied by the destruction of the victim's voice; the goal of the torturer, the reason for his endless questions, is to be all voice, to be radically disembodied, free from the constraints—the mortality and vulnerability—of the human body.

32. The closing passage reads as follows: "Lumina iam sistant lachrymas; compese sonoros, / Musula, singultus; fletibus ora vacent. / Singula si fleres livente cadavera tabo, / Que misere extremum tacta obiere diem, / Pluribus esset opus, quam lucent sidera, lin-guis, / Quam ludat vitreo squammea turba mari, / Gramina quot gignit tellus, quot volvit

The *Calamitose,* then, is at once a protest against persecution and an acceptance of its terms and structure. Foulis describes the traumatic and ominous outbreak of fire in St. Giles (the parish kirk of Edinburgh) as the impiety responsible for the scourge of the plague (149). As in *The City of God,* terror is explicated as an effect of divine wrath and punishment. The obverse of healing miracle, plague instances the immateriality of the Creator in the form of arbitrary power, because it signifies God's transcendence of all conceivable limits on the extension and creative power of the human body. As a manifestation of that force which emanates unilaterally from God, plague contrasts with, bypasses, and indeed puts an end to the historical processes by which human production and reproduction make the world. It is a response to failure of belief or of worship; it is the demand that human materiality be sacrificed in resubstantiation of the immateriality of God, that human interiority be sacrificed to an exteriorized Creator.[33] Thus the failure of municipal vigilance and worship which leads to the outbreak of fire in St. Giles will be atoned for through a "shattering" of the city; the blankness within an interior that has forgotten what is due to the Creator— the blankness of carelessness—is, moreover, projected onto and temporarily reflected in the blankness of the Creator's gaze. Jupiter looks down, with no apparent concern for the future of the human race (435). The possibility of absolute ending is envisaged as an inability to see care (*cura,* 436) in the gaze of the Judge. In the place of an icon of

---

arenas / Pontus, habet vernas cedua silva comas; / Ora tibi valido si tot clamore sonarent / Pulsaretque tuam iusta querela lyram; / Nec satis efferres damnose incommoda pestis, / Nec pareret finem longa querela suum. / Turgida continuo maculares lumina fletu, / Lassarent vocem verbe canora tuam. / Pone igitur questus gemebundi pectoris altos, / Et sit pacato purior aura Deo" (The light already puts an end to tears; Muse, stifle your noisy sobs; the shores may be free from tears. If you weep for every livid, decaying corpse— for things that, once touched, move wretchedly on to the last day—this would be a task for many tongues: for more tongues than the stars that shine; than the scaly crowd that plays in the glassy sea; than the blades of grass that spring from the earth; than the grains of sand turned around in the sea; than the green grass of the forest. If, so many times, the shores resounded for you with a strong clamor, and a just complaint plucked your lyre, you could not spread widely enough [the truth of] the disasters of the plague's destruction; nor would a long complaint help to hasten its end. You may [only] defile eyes swollen with continual crying, and melodious words may [only] exhaust your voice. Put aside, therefore, profound complaints of the heart's lamenting, and may heaven be purer, with a peaceful God, 481–96).

33. Scarry, *The Body in Pain,* links the plague of Exodus 12 to this "shattering of the reluctant human surface and repossession of the interior": "The fragility of the human interior and the absolute surrender of that interior . . . *is itself belief*—the endowing of the most concrete and intimate parts of oneself with an objectified referent" (204).

belief, Foulis registers a moment of frightening emptiness. Forgetfulness unmakes the relation between creature and Creator, which is—since the Creator must be imagined by the creature—a relation of belief; pain re-members that relation through dismemberment.

In keeping with the spectacular qualities of this poem—in which the absolute Judge ("Tu, criminis ultor / Et iudex, nulli sceptra secunda tenes" [You, punisher of guilt, and judge, you hold a kingdom second to none, 439–40]) marks his power on the bodies of the guilty and the guilty city—Foulis's poem materializes figural narrative links, so that everything, however apparently insignificant, threatens to become a matter of life and death, of absolute proportions. Plague means that one death not only prefigures but causes another, provoking images of earlier devastation and apocalypse. Contagion turns particular losses into universal destruction. The impious breakdown of the boundary, hence of the relation, between Creator and creature, issues in universal breakdown—the dissolution of all boundaries, including, again, the boundary between life and death.[34] In other words, the remaking of belief through pain must be total, for there is no space—no interior—that can remain obdurate or careless. Edinburgh's impieties thus threaten the well-being of the entire nation. The power of the city's fortunes to affect those of the land depends upon the poem's sense—its fear—of the impossibility of inconsequence. Narrative inexorability—the horrifying significance of a nonevent, an absence of care or activity—narrows the space of human life to a pinpoint, overwhelms it with the revenge of the sacred.[35] Apparently local events lead rapidly to—indeed are—enormities. The city's absolute connectedness to the fortunes of the realm is a principle inculcated by the poem's demand for vigilance, for acceptance of responsibility. In Foulis's poem, the city finds its relation to its judge and to its country by locating itself as criminal. Its reinclusion in the community, indeed the reconstitution of the community of the realm, is predicated upon its temporary exclu-

---

34. Girard discusses contagion in "The Plague in Literature and Myth," 836.

35. Geoffrey Hartman, "The Voice of the Shuttle: Language from the Point of View of Literature," in *Beyond Formalism: Literary Essays 1958–1970* (New Haven: Yale University Press, 1970), argues that "human life, like a poetical figure, is an indeterminate middle between overspecified poles always threatening to collapse it. . . . In human history there are periods of condensation . . . where the religious spirit seems to push man up tight against the poles of existence. Middles become suspect; mediations almost impossible" (348). Hartman's essay does not adequately stress or investigate the extent to which these "overspecified poles" are themselves a product of the human imagination.

sion—an exclusion that, once again, mirrors the creature's own forget-
ful exclusion of the Creator.[36]

It is within this context that we can best understand the *Calamitose*'s
lamentation over the blindness of youth ("Sed ruit in cecas fragilis natura tenebras" [But fragile nature rushes into blind shadows, 55]),
which is understood as the capacity of youth for suppressing deadly
things ("Quid suppressa memor bissenos fata per annos, / Horrende
repeto tela cruenta necis" [What doom I remember, suppressed for
twelve years; horribly I remember the weapons of slaughter, 45–46]).
Foulis's lament links his own forgetfulness with the guilt of the community; at the same time it is a plea for the forgivability of youthful
error, for the possibility of inconsequence ("Omnia, ceu veniunt, stulta
iuventa facit. / Et licet expertis novit resipiscere damnis" [All things,
just as they come, youth makes foolish. And, losses having been endured, youth may learn to come to its senses, 58–59]). In the *Calamitose*, remembering what has been suppressed is thus figured as reparation for wrongs; it is a re-membering of the interior, a restoration of
past to present through a newly heightened consciousness and vigilance. Remembering thus seems, in the *Calamitose*, to offer recovery of
continuity with one's youth; and it expresses a wish for the chance to
grow up, to survive failures of vigilance. For growing up poses a threat
to the boundary between Creator and creature; having a life threatens
to push back the poles of the sacred, to reduce narrative inexorability.
It is for this threat that Foulis wishes to atone.

Linked to this form of reparation is the shift from the displayed,
carnal, marked, suffering body of the city to its obverse, the gaze of the
monarch. The poem turns from "Aspicis, augende non ulla propaginis
extat / Cura; timent homines conciliare pares" [You look down, but no
care for the increase of children is visible [in your face]; like people are
afraid to unite, 435–36])—where the uncaring gaze seems to neglect
not only a particular *iuventus* but the entire progeny of humankind—
to the assertion of belief in God's concern for men, a concern shown
through his stern instruction.

> Tu, criminis ultor
> Et iudex, nulli sceptra seconda tenes.

36. See Girard on the mythical guilt of the scapegoat, "The Plague in Literature and
Myth," 841.

Regia sit, quamvis rigida, pro lege voluntas
Et rata sunt verbo condita cuncta suo.
..................................................

Imperio calum et terram regis omnia lato,
Cunctaque iudicii sunt rata verba tui.
Tu gemitus miserare pios, per quinque precamur
Vulnera, sis nostris prompta medela malis!
Cura tibi sit quanta hominum, tua seva docet mors.

(You, punisher of guilt, and judge, you hold a kingdom second to none.
There will be royal will, however stern, according to the law; all things
have been established by your word. . . . You rule all things of land and
sky with vast power; your words have established courts of justice. You
pity pious groans; through wounds we pray that you may be a prompt
remedy for our evils! Your cruel death tells us how great, for you, is the
care of men.)

(439–51)

*Cura* has been recovered for the paternal gaze through the latter's very
harshness. The turn from absent to present *cura* is, moreover, mediated
through the creature's plea to the creator for guidance: "O genitor,
moderare manum" (O creator, guide my hand, 439); the acceptance of
creatureliness, once again, permits reparation of the parent and of his
relation to the child. The poem's belief in the reparation of the threatened progeny of the Creator—the reparation of the body of mankind,
and its relation to its Creator—depends upon the creature's ability to
decipher *cura* in the downwards glance of the *genitor. Potestas*—the absolute power of the Creator, symbolized by his "distance from the
body," his capacity to injure and not be injured—is similarly recovered
for the purposes of the kind of love that makes, and lets, creatures grow,
through the figure of Foulis's uncle James, who after the death of Foulis's family, supports the stricken orphan like a big tree (*magna arbore,*
273), and who is thanked in the *Calamitose* for thereby preserving the
fortunes of the Foulis family and its future progeny.[37]

Foulis's response to the primal scene of plague is, finally, a theo-
dicy—a registration of the agony produced by disruption in the creature's love for the Creator, and a reinvestment in the powerful love of
the Creator for his creature. Difference—the sense of particularity, autonomy, even isolation produced by the crisis of origins—is viewed by
Foulis either as illegitimate rupture or as reparable through reunions
that restore fullness of presence. The *Calamitose,* like Augustine's *City*

---

37. The phrase "distance from the body" is Scarry's, *The Body in Pain,* 57.

*of God,* is finally a sublimation of the terror of discovering one's own particularity and contingency, of the terror of being a creature the nature of whose relation to the Creator is radically in question. And again like the *City of God,* Foulis's poem thus becomes a reading of human history *against* the absolute, an inhabiting of exclusion (an acceptance of creatureliness) as the only means of reinclusion in the peace of god's heaven: "Pone igitur questus gemebundi pectoris altos, / Et sit pacato purior aura Deo" (Put aside, therefore, profound complaints of the heart's lamenting, and may heaven be purer, with a peaceful God, 495–96).

The Edinburgh of Foulis's youth was indeed ravaged by calamity. Grandgore—venereal disease—had arrived in 1497.[38] Plague came the following year: the burgh records for the period 1498–1500 contain a number of provisions for trying to contain "the daynger of perilous siknes of pestilence now rissin in the eist partis and lairgelie spred."[39] The crowded space of the burgh—Edinburgh was notorious for its constriction even among medieval burghs—meant rapid spread of infection. In Foulis's *Carmen elegum,* however—a poem written after the *Calamitose,* when Foulis was a student at Orleans—Edinburgh is young, happy, flourishing, an idyll of plenitude rather than a city of earth struck down by misfortune and chaos. The poem is a patriotic one: it opens with "Scotorum eterna nomen cum laude triumphet." Scotland is warlike but brief in wrath, loves truth and hates broken faith:

> Precipuus celi cultus, magnique Tonantis;
> Debita huic pietas, non simulata, placet.
> Duratura diu crescat sub sidere fausto
> Scotia, cristicolis terra beata viris,
> Augeat ut nostri longevos principis annos
> Juppiter, huic patri stemmata longa trahat
> Candida protelent fatales pensa Sorores,
> immemor officii sit soror aspra sui!
> O sua semper ames Jacobum Scotia quartum,
> Quo duce te celo fama secunda feret.
> Vivat Edinburgi felix, generosa iuventus,
> Gaudeat, et veris floreat aucta bonis.[40]

38. Ranald Nicholson, *Scotland: The Later Middle Ages* (Edinburgh: Oliver and Boyd, 1974), 564; and see *Edinburgh Burgh Recs.* 2:71 (22 September 1497), "Ane grandgore act."

39. *Edinburgh Burgh Recs.* 1:74 (17 November 1498); see also 76–77 (27 April 1499 and following), 84–85 (14 October 1500).

40. "Triumph, O name of Scots, with threefold praise! / Ennobled be thy race by noble deeds! / . . . She [Scotland] loves to serve heaven's mighty Thunderer, / And wor-

The conclusion of the *Carmen elegum* transforms Edinburgh from a scene of plague into the happy youth, blessed with every good, whom Foulis might have wished himself to be. The *Carmen elegum* is the idyll that displaces the trauma both of the city's and of the poet's loss; and its wishes for Scotland's triumph are inseparable from its wish for the longevity of the monarch and his scions—for the superreality of enduring dynasty. Thus the *Carmen elegum* reconstitutes the body and future history of a nation. The shift from the *Calamitose* to the *Carmen elegum* repeats, on an intertextual scale, the split within the *Calamitose* itself between the nothing of an abandonment so devastating that it cannot be adequately mourned, and the all of reunion with the Creator. The split thus makes possible Foulis's belated identification with the figure of the protected and flourishing child; it protects the ideality of the relation between Creator and creature. And it thereby enables the reappropriation, for Foulis's icons—Scotland, James IV, Jupiter—of what Scarry calls the "vibrancy," the "certainty," of pain.

The *Carmen elegum*'s revision of privation, disease, and death proceeds through images of vitality, images that recover life from death and thereby assert, for Foulis, the invulnerability of the borderline. Life, moreover, is made urgent and compelling through the use of imperatives. The jussive subjunctives *vivat, gaudeat, floreat* evoke the obverse of absolute unmaking, of plague: they command vitality.[41] In contrast to the belatedness of hope in the *Calamitose*—the despair, figured by contagion, over the powerlessness of human intervention—the jussive subjunctives of the *Carmen elegum* evoke the power to command desire into existence, to transcend the limitations of human making.[42] Narrative in the *Carmen elegum* is thus overwhelmed, not by the radical

---

ship him with piety unfeigned. / Long, under favouring stars, may Scotland thrive, / And long be blest with worshippers of Christ, / That Jupiter may then be pleased to grant / Our king long life and scions in long line! / Long may the Fates defer their righteous tasks, / Long may the cruel sister stay her hand! / Love James the Fourth, O Scotland, with whose aid / Auspicious fame will thee to heaven exalt! / Long live Edina's happy, generous youth, / Rejoice and flourish, dowered with every good." The translation of the *Carmen elegum* is taken from "Extracts from the Book of the Scottish Nation," in Kirkpatrick, "The Scottish Nation", which also contains a version of the Latin text; see 83 and 97. The text of the *Carmen elegum* used here is taken from IJSewijn and Thomson's edition (134–35).

41. "Jussive" has the sense of "ordering"; the jussive subjunctive is a more polite way of expressing a command than is an imperative proper. We could describe it rather loosely as a mediation of imperative and optative moods.

42. In "The Plague in Literature and Myth," Girard remarks that "in cases of massive contamination, the victims are helpless, not necessarily because they remain passive but because whatever they do proves ineffective or makes the situation worse" (836).

limits set by plague to human intervention, but by a kind of purposiveness of imagination. The coalescence of imperative and optative becomes, after the despair of the *Calamitose,* the primary "mood" of narrative in Foulis's poetry. Thus in the *Strena,* Foulis foresees (like Jupiter), prophesies, casts his glance backward on a history of calamity made tiny by the view; history is read as omen.

The subjunctives of the *Carmen elegum* are appropriate, moreover, to a poem suffused with reminiscences of the diction and motifs of Virgil's imperial *Aeneid* (*pietas, fama, fatales,* a Jupiter who directs the destiny of empire from on high, the fantasy of a protective fate in which narrative becomes not a contingent or open-ended process of change, but rather a spinning-out of sacral anteriority). These reminiscences of a poem that takes as its subject the struggle to undo catastrophic loss—the devastation of Troy, the cruelty of Juno, Aeneas's loss (and abandonment) of Creusa and Dido, his ultimate founding of an empire that was to be identified with the name of its great city, Rome—are in turn appropriate to the *Carmen elegum* in its culminating celebration of a city happy in its youth.[43] The threat posed to youth—to the chance to grow up—by jealous divinity is present, too, in the *Carmen elegum,* in Foulis's wish to defer the *soror aspra,* the cruel sister. As Edinburgh is imagined—a happy youth—through tropes of plenitude, death and loss are imagined as the disappearance of the maternal strand: woman appears in the *Carmen elegum* in her capacity not as giver of life but as destroyer, the overseer of the timing of men's lives—of human narrativity. And yet her cruel dictates may be overturned by a truly loving God. Fruitfulness—here in the form of the fullness of a life—is appropriated for, and dependent on, the intervention of the Creator.

The study of Latin poetry—and Foulis's surviving poetry is in Latin, not in what Gavin Douglas called "Scottis"—gave Foulis a language, a poetics, and a tradition whereby he could write and rewrite calamity, isolate fortune from misfortune, true *cura* from its mere appearance.[44] The *Carmen elegum* is Foulis's reinscription of himself and his city—both products of human making, refigured as wayward but repossessible creatures—into a scene of inclusion. Hence Foulis's fervor in pur-

43. The *Calamitose* is also crisscrossed with reference to the fall of Troy and to the *Aeneid:* see 59–82, 213–14, 376, in IJSewijn and Thomson for examples.

44. It is perhaps of interest in this connection that the title page of the *Strena* is the earliest instance of the use of Roman type in Scotland. See Dickson and Edmund, *Scottish Printing,* 122.

suing the well-being of the Scottish "nation," in exile at Orleans; hence his encouragement of students "at home" in the pursuit of letters. In the *Carmen elegum* poetry is, for Foulis, a means to innocence; the imperative mood and the tropes of Latin imperialism are a way of wishing calamity away. Foulis's humanism, his Latinity, his studies abroad, constitute an "imperial" way of including, at the periphery of Europe, all of Western culture and history—and thus a way of making one and making good the world, of struggling against exclusion from the world. The elision of Foulis's own pain—of the pains, too, of city and nation—serves, once again, a dream of "self-extension," of vastness, of the unlimited imagination.[45]

The wish expressed by Foulis at the end of the *Carmen elegum* for James IV's long life was not, however, to be fulfilled. James IV—along with James Henryson, Foulis's uncle and patron—met his death at Flodden in 1513, the year after Foulis entered the *Carmen elegum* into the "Book of the Scottish Nation."[46] James IV's death seems to have abandoned Scotland to a crisis of confidence in the capacity of *potestas* to protect its creatures, a crisis exacerbated by the fragile infancy of the new king.[47] James V was crowned at Stirling on 21 September 1513; he was seventeen months old. In the struggles for power that ensued, Edinburgh played a critical role; and we should, at this point, remind ourselves of Edinburgh's economic and political centrality in late fifteenth- and early sixteenth-century Scotland.

It was during the later fifteenth century that Edinburgh emerged as the effective capital of Scotland. Its claim was based partly on its wealth,

45. See Scarry, *The Body in Pain*, on the torturer's "swelling sense of territory" (36); "the torturer's growing sense of self is carried outward on the prisoner's swelling pain"; "it is not the pain but the regime that is incontestably real" (56). My purpose is to draw an analogy between, not to equate, Foulis's art with the art of the torturer.

46. Henryson's death is noted by IJSewijn and Thomson, "Latin Poems of James Foullis," 140.

47. The crisis is exemplified by Edinburgh's long travail in building the fortification known as the Flodden wall (see *An Inventory of the Ancient and Historical Monuments of the City of Edinburgh* [Edinburgh: His Majesty's Stationery Office, 1951, for the Royal Commission on the Ancient Monuments of Scotland], lxiv); by the persistence of reports, as late as the 1570s, that James was still alive and journeying in distant lands (see R. L. Mackie, *King James IV of Scotland: A Brief Survey of His Life and Times* [Edinburgh and London: Oliver and Boyd, 1958], 268, referring to John Lesley, *The History of Scotland from the Death of King James I in the Year 1436 to the Year 1561* [Edinburgh, 1830], and *De origine, moribus et rebus gestis Scotorum libri decum* [1675], 96 Sc [Scottish], 349L [Latin]); by the long years of civil strife that ensued after his death; and by the elegiac writing Flodden still prompts from Scotland's historians (see, for example, the closing passage of Nicholson's *Scotland: The Later Middle Ages*, which quotes from the *Carmen elegum*, 606).

partly on the pressure of monarchical centralization, which—though a more halting and experimental process by far than in England or France at the same time—had, by the early sixteenth century, located nearly every important judicial, administrative, and military machine in Edinburgh.[48] As Norman Macdougall has emphasized, the policies of James III (r. 1460–88) in particular appear to have been of crucial importance in assuring the preeminence of Edinburgh; unlike his predecessors, James III "ran his administration from Edinburgh," and while James IV and V took up once again the peripatetic administration of civil justice, there was really to be no turning back from the course set by James III.[49]

Gordon Donaldson's account of the troubles of James V's minority amply illustrates the importance of the role played by Edinburgh in national politics at this time. He notes that the Earl of Angus exploited, in his struggles with the Earl of Arran's government,

48. From the beginning of the fifteenth century through the reign of James IV, Edinburgh almost always contributed over half of the Great Customs. Its nearest rivals, Dundee, Perth, and Aberdeen usually lagged far behind. See Nicholson, *Scotland: The Later Middle Ages,* 391, 440, 565, and map C; and Gordon Donaldson, *Scotland: James V to James VII* (New York: Frederick A. Praeger, 1966), 11.

Jennifer Brown (Wormald) has argued that the kings of Scotland "could not, even if they had wanted, aim at anything like the degree of centralization of the government of England and France, nor begin to build up power at the centre at the expense of power in the localities" ("The exercise of power," in Jennifer Brown, ed. *Scottish Society in the Fifteenth Century* [New York: St. Martin's Press, 1977], 35). Her essay successfully challenges unexamined comparisons of the power of the Scottish crown with that of its neighbors, and demonstrates the fluidity of the crown's reliance on a wide variety of local and regional powers and interests in the work of governing. But the revisionist urgency of her essay has swung too far in the opposite direction. A number of the Scottish kings of the fifteenth and sixteenth centuries "wanted" some degree of centralization, however hapless in practice their efforts may often have been; and they tried to pursue it.

49. Under James III, all parliaments (with one exception) were held in Edinburgh, as were the sessions of the Lords of Council; and "from 1469 onwards . . . all traceable royal characters under the great seal—some 650—were granted at Edinburgh" (Norman Macdougall, *James III: A Political Study* [Edinburgh: John Donald, 1982], 303). The same story is told by the innumerable payments, recorded in the Treasurer's Accounts for 1473–74, to messengers summoning people to come to Edinburgh on crown business; see, for example, the entry for payment to David Rudman in *Compota Thesaurariorum Regum Scotorum: Accounts of the Lord High Treasurer of Scotland,* ed. Thomas Dickson (Edinburgh, 1877–), 1:50, hereafter cited as *LHTA.* Dr. Macdougall has kindly reminded me that all James IV's parliaments were held in Edinburgh (see also Macdougall, *James III,* 304). The exchequer was held most frequently in Edinburgh (*LHTA* 1:xvi); the king's treasure and the records of the royal administration were housed in Edinburgh Castle; the king's artillery was likewise made and stored there (*LHTA* 4:lxiii on "Artillery" and 1:48 [1474] and 54); James IV's naval ambitions, "typified in the *Great Saint Michael,*" were partly executed there (S. G. E. Lythe, "Economic Life," in *Scottish Society,* ed. Brown, 74); there, too, coins were minted (Adams, *The Making of Urban Scotland,* 41).

the popularity which he and his Douglas kinsmen enjoyed in Edinburgh. In July 1517 there had been 'ane inordinat motioun of the people' in that town; there was an 'actioun and debait betuix my lord of Arane and the toun' in November 1519; and in March 1520 Arran declared that 'he sould nocht cum within the toun quhill my Lord Chancellar [Beaton] maid ane finall concord betuix him and the nychbouris thairof.' . . . [In] April 1520 . . . the Hamiltons were driven out of Edinburgh by the Douglases.[50]

Scotland's and Edinburgh's fortunes continued to be hectic: twice James was "erected" to power by those who controlled him; in February 1525 Arran and Margaret Tudor, the Queen Mother, held Edinburgh Castle, while Angus held the town.[51] It was arranged in July of that year that the leading nobles should hold custody of the king in turn, but in November Angus declined to give up the king and kept him, in effect, a prisoner. Efforts were made to liberate him, but none succeeded until, between the 27th and the 30th of May, 1528, the King escaped from Edinburgh to Stirling Castle after reaching a "secret agreement with his mother"; he returned to Edinburgh to begin his rule of the country on July 6, Angus having fled the town.[52]

Clearly Edinburgh was both participant in and chief locus of a long, complex, and volatile struggle for national power. Those living in Edinburgh at the time could scarcely have failed to be affected in some way by the events of the day; and in 1528, the year of James's assumption of power, the question of burgess loyalty to the king would likely have been a critical one. This is the background to the *Strena*—a poem probably written by a burgess of Edinburgh and printed by a burgess of Edinburgh.[53] It is not possible, given the state of our present knowl-

50. Donaldson, *Scotland: James V to James VII*, 35; and see *Edinburgh Burgh Recs.* 1:192, 196, 201. James Hamilton, the first Earl of Arran, was next in line to the throne after John, Duke of Albany and heir presumptive, who had for a time governed Scotland, but then returned to France, leaving behind a commission of regency that included Arran and Angus. Archibald "Bell-the-Cat" Douglas, 5th Earl of Angus, has traditionally been held responsible for controlling James III in the crisis of 1482. Macdougall, in *James III*, describes him as a "chronic rebel" but minimizes his role in 1482 (166–67). Margaret Tudor, widow of James IV and Queen Mother, had been appointed tutrix to her sons and given, along with a council, powers of regency; these were withdrawn when she married Archibald Douglas, grandson of the Earl of Angus. She later became estranged from him, eventually cooperated with Arran, and finally arranged for the release of her son from the clutches of the Douglases. My discussion of the events of James V's minority is at all points heavily indebted to Donaldson's third chapter, "Albany, Arran and Angus," 31–42.

51. Donaldson, 39; *Edinburgh Burgh Recs.* 1:221.

52. Donaldson, 39–41.

53. The *Strena* may have been commissioned for a royal welcome; at a much later date (in 1538) Foulis "was chosen with Adam Otterburn and David Lyndsay to compose a French welcome to the new queen"; see Durkan, "Beginnings of Humanism in Scotland,"

edge, to say what part, if any, Foulis played during the time of the troubles, nor exactly where his loyalties lay. But since in James V's early years Edinburgh had been the scene of the king's imprisonment, and since the king's wardens had been popular in Edinburgh, we may be sure that any burgess of Edinburgh hoping to advance himself through future royal patronage—and certainly any burgess whose royalist identification was as powerful as that of James Foulis—would be happy to signify his loyalty to the king. It is clear, in any case, that the *Strena* is in thoroughgoing fashion a poem and a production of Edinburgh and its vicissitudes.

Both the title page and the opening lines of the poem declare its status as prophecy of happier days: "Tempora magnanimo que nunc felicia Regi / Sydera portendunt, dicere Musa cupit" (The stars foretell a fruitful time for the great-souled King, [a prophecy] which the Muse now longs to sing).[54] The stars themselves foretell the fruitful or fortunate time (*tempora felicia*) that is thus, from the inception of the *Strena*, linked to the destiny of James V. The beloved of the Muses, James V, is appealed to for guidance; then the narrative begins. Jupiter sends a message to Phebus lamenting Scotland's disorders and demanding that reformation be effected. The message bids Phebus shine brightly upon Scotland; he obeys without delay, and the fertility of the land is renewed. The poem ends with a vision of James V ruling justly over a tranquil land. In the *Strena*, foresight, fortune, and kingship are joined together in a wish for protection. If one can look into the future, one will see not a helpless child imprisoned in the toils of political plague—of, in Girard's terms, "sterile rivalries," reciprocal violence— but rather a great king (*magnanimo Regi*).[55] By bringing together anticipation and memory, hindsight and foresight, the *Strena* subjects the story of James's growing-up to a radical compression. It is a poem in flight from historical narration, from chronicling the oppressive changefulness of the preceding era.

---

8–9 and n. 18; and Mill, *Medieval Plays in Scotland*, 180; cf. *Edinburgh Burgh Recs.* 2:89–91, 17 July 1538. It is worth noting that Davidson's later printing of Gavin Douglas's "The palyce of honour"—Douglas had been active in pursuing the interests of the Douglases and was imprisoned during Albany's regency—may have been of factional significance, though it seems unlikely.

54. All citations are to IJ Sewijn's and Thomson's edition of the poem, in their edition of the *Carmina* (135–37).

55. Girard, "The Plague in Literature and Myth," 837, 839.

After invoking the muse's desire for a prophecy of fortunate times, the poet says that he will undertake this hazardous enterprise only if supported by James, dear to the Muses:

> Ausus ob hec nimium tenui cantare Camena,
> Incipiam auspiciis, rex Iacobe, tuis.
> Pieridum tu dulce decus, concede favorem
> Edere Iudicio metra legenda bono.
> Torpentes fracto repares cum pectine nervos,
> Et moveas docilem per tua fila manum.

(Therefore, having dared to sing with too-weak verse, by / your auspices, King James, I will begin. / You, the sweet honor of the Muses, grant me the support / to bring forth strains to be decorously sung. / May you repair the strings, listless, [the] plectrum broken, / and may you move my easily-led hand across your strings.)

(3–8)

The poet's earlier poems—perhaps he refers to the *Calamitose*—have been feeble (*tenui* has the sense of physical enfeeblement, and can be used of a sound too low to hear as well as of an inability to hold on or to hold course). The poet's voice is thus styled from the outset as the kind of voice appropriate to a creature: no rival to the voice of the Creator (whose voice signifies His transcendence of the limits of the human body), the voice of the poet is imagined simultaneously as physically weak and as *physical,* as barely emergent from the body.[56] The threat of ambition, presumption—of "any capacity for self-transformation into a separate verbal or material form"—is immediately defused: like the paradise that it will describe, the *Strena* is itself a gift, a favor, the effect rather than the cause of royal patronage.[57] It is

56. See Scarry, *The Body in Pain,* on the weakness of the human voice in the Old Testament: "God is their voice; they have none separate from him. Repeatedly, any capacity for self-transformation into a separate verbal or material form is shattered" (200).

57. As the logic of Marcel Mauss's *The Gift* would imply, the Creator—and, in the human realm, the king—must be the supreme giver, for giving is an act of power. To accept the gifts of the king is to eat his "food," his materialized honor; it is to be incorporated by him, hence to allow the surface of the body to be penetrated by him so that its interior can be ritually rededicated to him (*The Gift: Forms and Functions of Exchange in Archaic Societies,* trans. Ian Cunnison [Glencoe, Illinois: The Free Press, 1954]). Mauss stresses the strong association of the gift with nourishment (84 n. 10; 105 nn. 142 and 144). Mauss also finds in the cultures he studies a contrast between the gift as an aristocratic form of exchange (*kula* among the Trobrianders), conducted in the spirit of etiquette and generosity, and the "straightforward exchange of useful goods" (*gimwali* among the Trobrianders), conducted in the spirit of immediate gain and "distinguished by most tenacious bargaining on both sides, a procedure unworthy of the *kula*" (20, 34). By deferring the immediacy of exchange, or by obscuring the relation of equivalence and

the king himself, the "sweet honor" of the Muses, who grants the poet's strains, who moves the poet's docile hand over the strings. The poet's gift to the king—as the *Strena* was perhaps intended to be—is really the king's gift to the poet; the king's body is in him, moving the strings, the poet's hands. The poem marks its own paternity, its origin; the hazard of beginning—of the radical break—is wishfully made secure by the poem's affirmation of its creatureliness, of its status as the new creation of the Sovereign. The previous enfeeblement of the poet is thereby revivified, given "vibrancy." The possibility of new life thus depends upon the permeability of the human surface, its willingness to open itself to possession by the Sovereign. And by including greatness, Foulis becomes part of something greater: the repaired communion of servant and Sovereign.

Not only, then, is the language of the poem rescued from the enfeebled body; the possibility of "self-extension" into the world, of a community of language, is likewise restored through the elaborateness of communication that follows the invocation. Jupiter, considering all things in his lofty mind (*alta mente,* 11, a phrase that appears in royal charters of the later fifteenth century), immediately (*protinus,* 11) commands his winged servant to come before him; he gives his *nuncius* writings to bear to the shining god, Phebus; the messenger flies below and announces to Phebus that the immeasurably great ruler of Olympus has sent him a letter. Phebus quickly halts his horses, reads the subscript without delay (*nec mora,* 21), splits the seal, and reads, in golden letters (*auratis notis,* 22) the text I have described. Considering James V's need to smuggle secret messages out of Edinburgh in order to secure his release from the clutches of the Douglases, Foulis's vision of the rapidity of the messenger and the efficacy of the sovereign word is both especially pointed and poignant. The immediacy of textual transmission is an image of the royal word's ideal power of immediate penetration, and of the trust that can therefore be reposed in an obe-

---

obligation between one gift and the gift that returns the "favor," "aristocratic" exchange dreams of a nonreciprocity, an asymmetry, in giving; the asymmetry thus can be used to figure hierarchy and the relation between Creator and creature. The creature "must" make return gifts to the Creator (though, again, the obligation must be concealed), but his gifts can never hope to equal the Creator's gift of his own life to him. Should they do so, of course, presumption is in the air.

dient servant, for whom the royal word is the only word. Letters are golden; Foulis was a good choice for the secretariat.

The opening invocation is followed by an allusion to Janus *bifrons,* who has begun the year—"Principium bifrons anni Iam Ianus apertum / Fecerit" (9–10)—and to "phebus celsius," who shines loftier in the sky. Time begins, in the poem, with a figure of the year's capacity to look backward or forward; and with the introduction of Phebus we are plunged into forward motion. Here as in the invocation, the poem is occupied with the hope of *renovatio,* of making a new beginning; the break from the past will reveal its disorders to have been themselves but a momentary break, capable of reform, in the design of order. As Scarry writes of the chapters in *Genesis,* "there is a sense of erasing, . . . beginning again, starting over," which "re-enacts the idea of original world creation"; at the same time, a continuity is asserted, the interior sameness of history. The Creator's "power of alteration"—which is also the power to maintain and multiply his children in life—will work, in the *Strena,* on the human body and voice, on the body of the land, and on time.[58]

Accordingly, we move from Phebus and from time to the potent father himself, who contains all things in his deep and lofty mind ("Ipse potens rerum pater alta mente reponens / Omnia," 11–12) and who foresees all destined changes. As in the *Calamitose,* the ability to see all things from this lofty height is linked with the Creator's "power of alteration." In the *Strena,* though, there is no frightening blankness in the gaze of the Creator; the primal scene becomes a reunion. Jupiter is fully present, protective, propitiated, as is suggested by the opening lines of Jupiter's letter:

> Nos qui celestes positis digessimus orbes
> Legibus; et certis volvimus astra modis,
> Cura hominum nonnulla tenet: terrena potestas
> Summa nisi faveant numina, nulla foret.

(We who arranged the swift planets with fixed laws, and / maintained the stars in their sure boundaries, the many / cares of men occupy us: the greatest earthly power / would be nothing if the gods did not favor it.)

(25–26)

58. See Scarry, *The Body in Pain,* 189, 199.

Jupiter takes care of man—without his blessing, we would be nothing.

It is significant, then, that Jupiter himself chronicles Scotland's calamities, transforming the Douglases and their ilk into haughty Catilines and scheming Lycurguses; spoken by the voice of the Creator, historical narration records the ultimate powerlessness of human violence. Jupiter explains that James IV was struck down by the power of fortune—the personification of meaningless change—and the malignity of the stars:

> Ut regem aversata fuit Fortuna potentem,
> Dira sub infausto sydere fata tulit.
> Nam desperatis languet pessundata rebus
> Scotia, que miseros ducere visa dies.

(As Fortune rejected the powerful king, she bore / harsh fates beneath an ill-omened star. / For Scotland was weak and ruined by hopeless circumstances, [and] seemed to protract its wretched days.)

                                                                    (31–34)

Scotland is cast into a mourning which threatens, from the perspective of the creature, to be endless.

In Scotland's troubled times *pax, amor, sine cede manus* (hands without bloodshed), *Gloria, iustitie, concordia* are gone from the land (37). They leave in their place only *rupta fides, pax simulata, falsus amor* (35), bloodshed and rebellion. In grief-stricken Scotland, everything is broken, bloody, deceptive. Human violence—the wrongful appropriation of the Creator's (and the Sovereign's) power of injury—dismembers; yet it is strangely insubstantial. It is linked to dissimulation, to the idea of a nothingness behind appearances, to bodiless words and smiles—hence, to a failure of the relation between origin and end. Human violence becomes, in the *Strena*, a parody of the Creator's "power of alteration." Thus, without the Sovereign only rupture and betrayal are possible; the Sovereign is the true source of Peace, Faith, Loyalty, Honor, Love, and Justice, in contrast with his rivals, who only seem, but are not. Behind the seeming chaos of the troubles, the creature will be able, finally, to decipher *cura;* chronicle is thus the story of a superficiality. The internal violence that threatens to engulf the community is split off, at once demonized and derealized; the ideality of the Sovereign Creator's power of alteration is thereby protected.

Jupiter, immediately after his narration of Scotland's calamities, declares the need for reformation, lest anyone think that no Jupiter rules above ("Cogimur errores tandem componere tantos, / Ne quis regnantem non putat esse Iovem" [We must finally right such great wrongs, lest it seem that no Jove rules, 49–50]). Jupiter sends to Phebus a message written in golden letters, which contrasts the insubstantiality of unauthorized human violence with the Sovereign's power of injury. The letter foretells James V's valor and prowess in war, his strength to subdue the prideful and the perjured: Scotland will rejoice more in him than Troy would have rejoiced in the survival of Hector—who was for so long Troy's stay, Troy's wall, against utter destruction ("Hectore nec tantum sua Troia superstite gaudens", 61]); under James's rule falsehood itself will be expelled from the land. The power to uncreate has been recovered from irreality by superreality. It will be James V who restores the threatened symmetry of earthly and divine governance by reasserting the power of the Creator to intervene in the affairs of men through the agency of his Sovereign child. (At the end of the poem, James V is described as *puer Jovis*; here the likeness rather than the unlikeness of Creator and creature is affirmed: their link is sovereignty, a special form of difference from all other creatures.) The *Strena*'s recovery of Scotland from political plague proceeds through a recovery of the Sovereign Creator's total presence within the interiority of the world.

Jupiter's letter then moves on to order the remaking of the land. Phebus is sent to make Scotland feel the stroke of his heat ("stroke" is "*plaga*," the root, interestingly, of "plague," and hence a primal word in Foulis's poetry):[59]

> Nos quoque pro nostre prolis faciemus honore
> Quod bene susceptum, secula cuncta canent.

(For the honour of our progeny we also will produce / something which, supported well, all generations will sing of.)

(69–72)

*Honore* has the sense of public honor, office, preferment, as well as of honorary gift, boon, favor; *susceptum* has meanings of esteem and admiration, but can also have the sense of sustaining, supporting, bring-

---

59. In the sense developed by Freud in his essay on "The Antithetical Sense of Primal Words," *On Creativity and the Unconscious: Papers on the Psychology of Art, Literature, Love, Religion,* ed. Benjamin Nelson (New York: Harper Torchbooks, 1958) 55–62.

ing up a child as one's own. The *Strena* itself fulfills Jupiter's prediction that his descendants shall celebrate in song both the god's power to produce and his magnanimity in giving honor. The rejuvenation of Scotland is thus neither the result of natural processes nor of human production; it is a miracle—a gift from Jupiter to his children, his creatures. The restoration of paternity and genealogy—the acceptance of creatureliness—results in the gift of love, conceived as the fertility of the land. The Creator—and the Sovereign through him—is the only source of plenty. This having been established, the poet is allowed to narrate directly the revivification of the land, his voice now the voice of the Creator.

Phebus obeys Jupiter's behest, dispelling the clouds so that "natura suas varie et subtiliter artes / Perque astra exercet, viscera perque soli" (variously and finely, nature works her arts over / the stars, and through the very heart of the country, 79–80). There follow adverbs of expectancy, of an end to waiting (*mox*); the world is being recreated. There are images of fauns in the woods, of Priapus tending gardens, of Flora clothing the countryside with flowers, of murmuring streams and clear-sounding rivers: Scotland is alive, sentient. And labor is impotent compared to this magical fertility: "Seminibus paleata Ceres fecundat opimis / Iugera, que nullo culta labore forent" (With plentiful seeds Ceres fertilizes acreages mixed with / chaff, which will be cultivated with no labor, 95–96). Peasants need struggle no longer—rule is what ensures abundance. And the economic power of the city is nowhere to be seen. The guilty city—chief site of Scotland's troubles during the minority of James V—is displaced altogether by the scene of plenitude, which closes with: "Maiori redeunt spumantia mulctra colostro, / Et solito pecudes grandius uber habent" (The beasts give back foaming milkpails from a greater milking, / and have udders more swollen than is usual, 101–2). Foaming milkpails and heavy udders (*uber,* etymologically related to *ubertatis,* the word used by Augustine to describe the "realm of unremitting plenty" that he and his mother discovered during their shared mystical experience) are the final images in Foulis's catalogue of plenitude.[60] The gift appears again as the form of exchange appropriate to the rejuvenated world; but since the relation to the transcendent and unmade Creator has been recovered, the gift may now be perceived as immanent within the world (*redeunt* has the primary sense of "giving

60. See Burke, *The Rhetoric of Religion,* 61, 118–19.

back"). With the restoration and hypervaluation of the everyday world, of the domestic—as opposed to the calamitous—the maternal strand has been recomposed into the fertile and lactating body of the land; and the flow of milk is associated, in the lines that follow, with the notion of favor, with the clemency (*clementia*) of the gods (*divum*): "Res ita disposuit nostras clementia divum; / Propitios meminit quis magis ante Deos?" (thus the clemency of the gods has set our affairs in order; / who was mindful more than the propitious gods?, 103–4). And lest this recomposed maternity slip away from its relation to paternity, the notion of discrimination is invoked (*disposuit*). Moreover, the following and final lines of the *Strena* remind us that the son of Jupiter— James V—wields his scepter over the calmest of lands and gives good laws to his people:

> Interea Iovis ipse puer placidissima regni
> Sceptra gerens, populo dat bona Iura suo.

(Meanwhile the boy of Jove, bearing the most gentle sceptre / of the kingdom, gives virtuous laws to his people.)

(105–6)

The maternal strand (*placidissima*) is indeed well ruled in Foulis's poem. Thus the calamity of the creature is made good through a making one of the paternal and maternal strands in the principle of sovereignty; the losses of Scotland are re-membered. In Augustine's terms, *sinus* coincides with *aula*.

Let us speculate once again, then, that the *Strena* was designed to rehabilitate Edinburgh and its citizens in James's eyes by voiding a history of treason and putting in its place a narrative of *renovatio* and of the eternity of the Stewart dynasty. Let Flodden and the Douglases— Scotland's antimasque—be banished from discourse like the clouds and winds expelled from Scotland by Phebus's warmth. Then finally what this story of expulsion and reparation suggests is that relations between king and capital need to be represented very carefully indeed—if the capital has reached the point of being a prison for the king. The reparation of the strained relations obtaining between crown and capital in the early sixteenth century—a reparation imagined as a restoration of magical fertility, so that the king seems to reproduce the city rather than to have been produced by its power and strife—constitutes, finally, the ideological project of the *Strena*. The *Strena* is Foulis's most ambitious poetic attempt to repair the damage done to his belief in *potestas* by the "knowledge" of the primal scene—of the *human* production of super-reality.

II

Foulis's poetry tells us how a burgess of Edinburgh and servant of the crown might, in the early sixteenth century, have imagined—and refused to imagine—the city and its relation to the sovereign. But we also need to understand something of how the city was imagined, in turn, by the sovereign—in particular, by James III, who more than any other fifteenth-century monarch produced the city's preeminence and thereby its role in his own failures. We need, in short, to understand something about the crisis of 1482. In his study of James III, Macdougall remarks that "the seizure of James III at Lauder in July 1482 was an event without parallel in fifteenth century Scottish political history."[61] While trying to muster an army at Lauder to meet an English advance on Berwick, the king was seized by two of his uncles—the earls of Atholl and Buchan—and subsequently imprisoned in Edinburgh Castle. Some of the members of his household were hanged by the rebels at Lauder.

Two factors that helped bring about the king's seizure and imprisonment will interest us particularly in this discussion. The first is the "black money": in need of money for defense against the English (and unwilling to drain his growing treasure hoard for the purpose), James III seems to have "indulged in a drastic debasement of the coinage over a period from about 1480 until 1482, producing very base billion coins and a large quantity of copper ones."[62] The issue of the black money was, to put it very mildly, unpopular; it was held responsible for great hunger and dearth, and hit the merchants and the peasantry particularly hard. By the summer of 1482, the debased money had been in circulation long enough "for the king to have lost the support, not so much of the nobility, but rather of the merchant class and those lower in the social scale." This gave the nobles a "popular cause to make their own."[63]

61. Macdougall, *James III*, 158.
62. Macdougall, 161. He links James's hoarding together with his policies of currency devaluation as part of James's new policy of financial enrichment of the crown in the 1470s—a response to "acute financial embarrassment" (301–2).
63. Macdougall, 161–62.

The second factor is what Macdougall refers to as "the breakdown of normal relationships among the royal Stewart kin." The later part of 1479, or early 1480, saw the imprisonment, death, and forfeiture of the king's brother John, the Earl of Mar; the king's brother Alexander, Duke of Albany, was also summonsed for treason, and he fled to England.[64] Perhaps understandably within this context, a remission, issued in March of 1482, for seizure of Edinburgh Castle during the king's minority seems to have alarmed rather than appeased the king's uncles, the Earls of Buchan and Atholl.[65] In 1482 the possession of Edinburgh Castle was, as Macdougall explains, the "key factor in the Stewart half-uncles' bid for political power"; thus in the summer of 1482 they repeated their earlier treasons by again taking over custody of the castle and overreached themselves by imprisoning the king to boot. It would have been particularly galling to James that Buchan, in particular, owed his prominence largely to the king's previous patronage.[66] Meanwhile, Albany had signed a treaty with the English that would make him a vassal king of Edward IV in exchange for English military support in seizing the crown.[67] Shortly after the king was removed to Edinburgh Castle by Atholl and Buchan, then, Albany and the Duke of Gloucester arrived at the head of a large English army to find the king whom they had hoped to coerce in quite other hands. James's relations with his kin were disastrous; by the early 1480s the royal family lay almost in ruins, and James's reign looked likely to follow.

James's "high-flown view of royal authority" seems, then, to have meant that no rivals could be brooked.[68] Nearly everything that has been known or written about James III's style of rule (its rigidities, its deceptions, its avarice, its intolerance of disloyalty) suggests that James identified monarchy with omnipotence, and that his style was accordingly omnivorous: to be all things—to be the representative of the Sov-

---

64. Macdougall, 171, 129–30.

65. Sometime before 1476 the uncles were granted a remission for this crime, and in the parliament of March 1482 the remission was renewed. The king's remissions were not known for their permanence. See Macdougall, 151–52, and *The Acts of Parliament of Scotland, A.D. M.C.XXIV–A.D. M.DCC.VII* (Edinburgh: Printed by command . . . 1814–1844) 2:138, hereafter cited as *AP.*

66. Macdougall, 166, 83–84.

67. See Macdougall, 153, for the terms of the Treaty of Fotheringay.

68. This is Nicholson's way of phrasing James's grandiosity (*Scotland: The Later Middle Ages,* 483).

ereign Creator—meant for James to have all things. He feared replace-
ment and robbery equally. Treason—always a concern for the medieval
monarch—was nothing short of an obsession during his reign.[69] And
his obsession with treason was unsurprisingly the obverse of his own
designs on everything everybody else had.[70] What seems, above all, to
have provoked the crises of James's reign was specifically James's inability to give, his investment of *potestas* at the expense of plenitude. His
subjects came to view him as dangerous, not merely because he had
fantasies of imperial grandeur, but because the stringencies of his rule
threatened to undo the fiction of *cura,* to provoke ideological crisis by
making *potestas* appear as atrocity.

The king was thus unable to maintain cordial relations with anyone
not his "creature"—with anyone not willing to signify a creaturely,
rather than a rivalrous, identity and difference. He could not have "sim-
ilars"; this is, I think, why his "familiars" became such an important
theme in his legend and in his reign.[71] The king's relation to Edinburgh
itself—as simultaneously a center that he might fully occupy, a way of
feeling himself to fill all available space, and a docile creature, more
dependent, at least in fantasy, upon his patronage than any powerful
magnate could have been—is something like a relation to a familiar.
James liked to create things; but it was, to him, unthinkable that his

69. Nicholson puts it rather mildly and constructively by saying that James III "notably developed the concept of treason" (498).

70. In addition to the issue of the "black money," the king's attempt to appropriate
the revenues of Coldingham Priory for the Chapel Royal—a move that did as much as
anything else to bring about his ultimate downfall—is a good example of the king's
avarice, particularly since he may have been planning to move the chapel royal to Restalrig, near Edinburgh. See Macdougall, *James III,* 236–39, on the role played by Coldingham in the crisis of 1488; and 231 on the "coincidence" that the king's supplication to
make Restalrig into a collegiate church was registered "little over a week after the pope's
suppression of Coldingham and the reallocation of the priory's revenues to the chapel
royal." Scotland's monarchs, always in need of fresh revenues, had throughout the
fifteenth century used forfeiture and other "grasping" methods to improve crown finances; but James III seems to have had a special fondness for strategies of enrichment,
ones that brought ideological crisis in their train.

71. While the role of the familiars in the rebellion at Lauder has clearly been over-
emphasized in chronicle accounts of the event, the familiars were also a significant theme
in James III's reign. See Nicholson, *Scotland: The Later Middle Ages,* 502; Macdougall, 163
and 190 for the histories of some of the men thus favored by the king, including one
Thomas Preston, who "may have been a well-to-do Edinburgh burgess," and was hanged
at Lauder. Macdougall's essay, "The Sources: A Reappraisal of the Legend," in *Scottish
Society,* ed. Brown, 10–32, is an essential discussion of the ideological biases of the stories
that grew up around the question of James III's familiars.

creations should grow up.[72] However, because James created his capital by ruling almost exclusively from it, ironically—and perhaps inevitably—its castle became his prison.[73] By the later fifteenth century, control of Edinburgh was beginning to mean control of the nation—at least in the minds of some of Scotland's most powerful actors and perhaps in the minds of Edinburgh's own citizens. Not least among the striking features of the crisis of 1482 was that the burgesses of Edinburgh were partly responsible for liberating the king from the consequences of their city's preferment.

Soon after Albany and Gloucester arrived in Edinburgh, it became clear to them that the pursuit of their own designs was impossible under the circumstances of the king's imprisonment by the uncles. Gloucester settled for money. On 4 August 1482 the provost and community of Edinburgh bound and obliged themselves to repay Edward IV "certain and diuers gret sommes of money" that he had sent to Scotland for the dowry of his daughter Cecilia—should the monarch decide not to pursue further a projected marriage between Cecilia and Prince James.[74] The price of Gloucester's departure was considerable—eight thousand English marks; the bond was produced to Edinburgh by Garter King at Arms on October 27.[75] If the capture and imprisonment of the king was "an event without parallel" in fifteenth-century Scotland, the turning-back of the largest English army to invade Scotland in eighty years by the sole expedient of Edinburgh's money was perhaps almost as striking.

Albany, casting about for some way of regaining his inheritance, decided to make a show of loyalty to the king. Accordingly, at the end of September—the king had now been imprisoned for two months—Al-

---

72. James's clearly marked and, as it was to prove, fatal preference for his second son during the latter years of his reign, is a further instance. His eldest son, the adolescent Duke of Rothesay, was perhaps simply too much to bear. He was next in line to the throne; he was nearing the age of fifteen; therefore, he could not be trusted (Macdougall, *James III*, 235).

73. Macdougall comments that "the concern of both major factions to secure Edinburgh castle underlines its importance as the repository of the records and the hub of the king's administration" (*James III*, 174).

74. *Charters and Other Documents Relating to the City of Edinburgh, A.D. 1143–1540*, ed. Sir James D. Marwick (Edinburgh: Scottish Burgh Records Society), 51:146–47, hereafter cited as *Charters, Edinburgh*. Marwick's edition of the charters includes translations.

75. *Charters, Edinburgh* 52:148–54. There is, however, no record of payments being made to Edward.

bany laid siege to the castle, along with the officers and community of Edinburgh.[76] The king was released from the castle on September 29, and since the castle itself had not been provisioned, it was surrendered by mid-October. This in turn implies that the town may have been provisioning the castle all along, though not necessarily with enthusiasm.

Meanwhile, Edinburgh was coping with further financial demands. Andrew Stewart (another uncle), bishop-elect of Moray, in league with Buchan and Atholl in their imprisonment of the king, aspired to the Archbishopric of St. Andrews, and by November 8, the burgesses of Edinburgh had pledged six thousand gold ducats to further his promotion at the papal *curia* in exchange for a bond obliging the uncles to pay them back.[77] By this time the uncles were still largely in control of the government, and James was a long way from regaining power.

That Edinburgh played an active role in any of the various conspiracies against the king seems unlikely. It is true that Archibald Crawfurd, the Abbot of Holyrood (near Edinburgh), appears as treasurer of the uncles' regime, but this need not indicate disaffection or complicity on the part of Holyrood's neighboring town.[78] It may, however, indicate that Holyrood—perhaps for reasons pertaining to Crawfurd rather than to the Abbey itself—did not find James a congenial neighbor. Signs of strain in the burgh itself are evident in the fact that Edinburgh had three provosts in 1482. In the terms of an indenture drawn up at Edinburgh on 16 March 1483—signed three days later by Albany, now fled to Dunbar, as capitulation to the once-again powerful James—it is specified that Albany's supporter, the Master of Morton, was to surrender the sheriffship of Edinburgh.[79] Whether Morton had any popular support or had been thrust upon the burgh by Albany is impossible to say; by this time, Edinburgh had been granted the right to choose its own sheriff, and Morton may have been either the result of, the exploitation of, or an obstacle to the execution of this new privilege.

It is safe to say, however, that the tradition of factional exploitation of Edinburgh offices—evident in the troubles of James V's minority—had begun, to be continued in 1487 by the striking appearance of Pat-

76. Macdougall, *James III*, 171.
77. *Charters, Edinburgh* 53:154–56.
78. Macdougall, *James III*, 165.
79. Nicholson, *Scotland: The Later Middle Ages*, 512–13; *AP* 2:31–33.

rick Hepburn, Lord Hailes, as "Lord Provost" of Edinburgh.[80] The compiler of the list of Edinburgh's provosts notes that "the minute of the election of Lord Hailes is curious, as containing the first known application of the title of 'Lord Provost' [a title taken up again by Lord Home in 1514 and by Arran in 1518], and also as empowering him to elect deputies and presidents."[81] Hepburn's election was the year before the king's fall at Sauchieburn at the hands of rebels led, nominally at least, by Prince James. Hepburn was instrumental in that fall; he was to profit from the rise of James IV perhaps more completely than any other of the young king's supporters, and the list of offices he received shows clearly that Edinburgh was one of his chief interests.[82] Macdougall notes that Hepburn was "the man who had been forced to surrender Berwick Castle to the English in 1482, and who may have been mistrusted by James III as a result"; he was also a neighbor of the Humes, with whom James, by 1487, had been feuding for quite some time over Coldingham Priory.[83] James would likely have noticed Hepburn's move on Edinburgh; it is therefore possible that Hepburn had some popular support, for the move might have been risky otherwise. And Patrick's uncle, Alexander Hepburn, who served as provost in 1490, was also sheriff of Edinburgh in 1482 and for some years follow-

80. Donaldson, *Scotland: James V to James VII*, explains how Edinburgh's preeminence in the sixteenth century made its provostship vulnerable to the political factionalism between the Douglases and the Hamiltons; "the provost of Edinburgh was a Douglas in 1513, 1517, and 1519 and a Hamilton in 1515 and 1518" (11). But the displacement of local candidates for the provostship by members of powerful aristocratic families seems to have begun much earlier, and suggests, again, Edinburgh's growing importance to national politics.

81. *Edinburgh Burgh Recs.* 1:266; and see the entry for 8 August 1487: "The quhilk day a richt nobill michty Patrick Lord Hales my Lord Provost, chosen of this burgh for this yeir to cum . . . hes with the consent of the baillies and counsale and a pairt of the community of this burgh chosin James Creichtoun of Felde to be his depute and president vnder him indurand his will" (52).

82. Hailes was made Master of the Household and given charge of the shires of Kirkcudbright and Wigtown, as well as Lothian and Merse jointly with Alexander Home, another well-rewarded supporter ("instigator" is probably more accurate). In less than a year Hailes became constable of Edinburgh Castle and governor of the Duke of Ross, the king's brother; sheriff principal of Edinburgh, collector of the king's rents and casualties from the shires of Edinburgh, Haddington, Kirkcudbright, and Wigtown; steward of Kirkcudbright, keeper of the castles of Threave and Lochmaben, and warden of the West and Middle Marches. He became Great Admiral of the realm, and ultimately the Earl of Bothwell. Other Hepburns appeared as household officers—keeper of the Privy Seal, for example—and as clerk of Council and Register (William Hepburn). See *LHTA* 1:lxix and n. 1; see also Macdougall, *James III*, 243.

83. Macdougall, *James III*, 243.

ing, until Patrick Hepburn himself became sheriff "in fee and heritage" in 1488.[84] If by 1488 Hepburn and his allies had cause to fear the king's "growing interference in the southeast," perhaps Edinburgh—or at least some elements therein—was likewise wearying of the king's constant attentions.[85]

Perhaps most significant for Edinburgh's role in the crisis of 1482, however, is the following complaint from the Seal of Cause of Edinburgh's Hammermen, dated 2 May 1483:

> In the first thair complaint buir and specifyit that thay war rycht havely hurt and put to greit poverty throw the doun cumming of the blak money, walking [and] warding, and in the payment of yeldis and extentis quhilkis thay war compellit to do be vse, and to be compellit thairto be our Lordis authoritie mandimentis and chargis.[86]

There is evidence, then, that Edinburgh was hard hit by some of the King's policies. And its sense of economic outrage would have been exacerbated further by the bleak possibility of having to pay eight thousand marks to the English and six thousand ducats to the uncles—all this following hard upon the heels of a devastating currency devaluation and the expensive demands of warfare. It seems again unlikely that the town had sufficient grievances against the king actually to seek his overthrow. Its behavior during the crisis is that of a town beset by factional politics, doing its best to play both sides against the middle and thereby at least minimize the damage. It must be emphasized, however, that nothing like this had ever happened to Edinburgh before (nor, for that matter, to any other burgh in Scotland); never before had it been thrust into the center of a national crisis as complex as this one, and the town proved itself equal to the challenge. For Edinburgh did have sufficient grievance to exploit the king's weakness in order to gain greater independence from royal domination. Its role in liberating the king may have meant that the town could not afford to refuse to help him; it may have meant that the town had nothing to gain from the uncles; it may have meant a desire to rescue the king who had made it his capital. It is likely that all of these motives were in play at different times on the part of different actors. But in any case, two charters of James III dated 16 November 1482—one week after the bond of obli-

---

84. *Edinburgh Burgh Recs.* 1:298. On Alexander's relation to Patrick, see Sir James Balfour-Paul, ed. *The Scots Peerage,* II (Edinburgh: David Douglas, 1905), 141–52.
85. Macdougall, *James III,* 243.
86. *Edinburgh Burgh Recs.* 1:47–48.

gation by the uncles—grant Edinburgh a wealth of new privileges, and it is to these charters that we now need to turn our attention.

The two charters in question—one "granting the office of Sheriff-ship" to Edinburgh and authorizing it to hold "a Peremptory Court of twenty-one days when necessary; and to make ordinances for the good government of the Burgh"; the other granting to Edinburgh "the customs from the harbour and road of Leith"—carefully list the names of the burgh officers involved in the siege of Edinburgh Castle and give an equally careful and complete list of Albany's newly restored titles.[87] This gives the charter almost the flavor of an unofficial pardon. It records the efforts made by Albany and the burgh on the king's behalf, perhaps in order to clear the parties concerned from blame, certainly to try to establish their entitlement to reward.[88] That one of the privileges granted by the first charter should be a reconfirmation of the burgh's ancient right to legislate for its own welfare may further suggest that the citizens of Edinburgh were seeking to guard against future retaliation by the king should he have any suspicions about their actions. On the one hand, then, we have Edinburgh recording its assistance to Albany in liberating the king from the clutches of the uncles. On the other, we have the following list of witnesses:

> the reverend fathers in Christ, John Bishop of Glasgow, our chancellor, James bishop of Dunkeld; our beloved uncles, Andrew elect of Moray, keeper of our privy seal, John earl of Athol lord Baluany; . . . the venerable father in Christ, Archibald abbot of our monastery of Holy Rood of Edinburgh, our treasurer;

and so forth; in short (with the exception of Buchan, who seems not to have been present), the uncles and their principal supporters.[89] The spectacle of the uncles witnessing, in full detail and panoply, charters rewarding Edinburgh for acting with Albany to release the king from the prison they put him in is to be wondered at; it generously illustrates the byzantine nature of national and city politics at this time. The

---

87. *Charters, Edinburgh* 54:157; 55:165.

88. Walter Bertram, provost of Edinburgh during the time of the siege, was also granted an annual pension of forty pounds payable during the lifetime of himself and his wife. See Nicholson, *Scotland: The Later Middle Ages,* 509, and *Rotuli Scaccarii Regum Scotorum: The Exchequer Rolls of Scotland,* eds. John Stuart, George Burnett, and J. G. Mackay (Edinburgh: Her Majesty's Register House, 1878–1908), 9:219–20; hereafter cited as *ER.*

89. *Charters, Edinburgh* 54:164.

uncles were still largely in control of the royal government, which means that they kept its seals; for the king to have issued any sort of charter, therefore, he would likely have had to do so in the presence of at least some of the uncles' men. The uncles, then, must have approved of the charters; but the pomp and completeness of the witness list suggests something beyond the pragmatics of doing crown business at Edinburgh Castle in the autumn of 1482.

The charters follow by just over one week the bond whereby the uncles pledged repayment of the six thousand gold ducats for Alexander Stewart's promotion as Archbishop of St. Andrews. Macdougall is probably right, then, to propose that the charters were a further *quid pro quo* in the same business: "a benevolence to the uncles, in Albany's name, at the king's expense!"[90] The charters signify more, however, than just a matchless piece of convolution. They attest Edinburgh's willingness to deal with all of the parties concerned in the crisis—its willingness, that is, openly to pressure the king with support from the uncles, in order to make good their losses; and the uncles' willingness, in turn, to appease the town's financiers with more than a paper I.O.U. (The king—caught between a rock and a hard place—may have seemed to the burgesses an unlikely candidate for survival; the uncles would surely have wanted to avoid, so far as was possible, the town's hostility.) Moreover, to give away rights of shrieval jurisdiction to a town so mixed up in current events was a proposition the uncles might have slept on, even if Edinburgh's chances of exploiting the privilege to the uncles' detriment would have seemed slim. They might, too, have slept on the notion of making the privileges granted by the charter an apparent *quid pro quo* for liberating the king—even if their action as witnesses might have seemed to record their dissociation from the agents who imprisoned him. Charters do not customarily go into such detail about the history behind, and reasons for, their issuance. Edinburgh may indeed have made the charters a condition of their pledge of the six thousand gold ducats. And the idea for at least the substance of the charters must have come from Edinburgh. The privileges granted are substantial and specific to Edinburgh's situation and desires.

The charters, in essence, confer upon Edinburgh greater independence from the techniques and structures of royal domination. The officers and community of the burgh receive the "honor" of having the

90. Macdougall, *James III*, 172.

office of sheriff "within themselves" (*infra se*), meaning not only that the profits of feudal justice would now enrich the burgh, but also that the burgh would now exercise the lord's traditional rights over the body of the criminal. In a sense, then, the privilege of sheriffship embodies the burgh by empowering the relations among bodies within the burgh; it grants to the burgh the power of alteration, of injury. The charter thus provides for the elaboration and intensification of the autonomy and the innerness of the city, its sense of itself as a particular "world." The burgh was also granted the right to hold a peremptory court of twenty-one days, because the procedures of the Court of the Four Burghs had become so tedious and slow.[91] And by acquiring the customs of Leith, and the provost's right to be sheriff within its bounds, Edinburgh's "stranglehold over its unfortunate port" was guaranteed.[92]

Thus not only did the privileges reinforce, as burgh privileges had always done, the extent to which the burghs were set apart from the rest of the population; they also enhanced Edinburgh's special difference from the other burghs of Scotland (its exemption from the process of the Four Burghs court), and enabled expansionism (its designs on Leith) as well as autonomy. The "worldness" of the city—its separation from the authority of its creator—is produced in part by drawing an even thicker line around it. The "worldness" of the *capital* city is produced by allowing it to engulf the resources of other regions, which it accomplishes by way of an internalization of certain feudal forms of extraction of surplus value (justice, tolls). The extent to which the charters distinguish Edinburgh from other burghs and cater to its economic expansionism bespeaks and reproduces precisely the unique prominence that led to the granting of the charters in the first place.

But by internalizing lordship, the merchants and burgesses of the town do little to transform lordship; insofar as the town appropriates

---

91. The Court of the Four Burghs—which was succeeded by the Convention of Royal Burghs—decided questions involving the usages of burghs and the rights and privileges of burgesses, and legislated regarding such matters as the principles of moveable succession. See *Records of the Convention of the Royal Burghs of Scotland, with Extracts from Other Records Relating to the Affairs of the Burghs of Scotland, 1295–1597*, ed. Sir James D. Marwick (Edinburgh: William Paterson, 1866, for the Convention of Royal Burghs), hereafter cited as *Burgh Convention Records*, for a helpful introduction to the records; and see also Theodora Pagan, *The Convention of the Royal Burghs of Scotland* (Glasgow: The University Press for the Convention of Royal Burghs of Scotland, 1926).

92. Nicholson, *Scotland: The Later Middle Ages*, 452.

rather than changes the techniques of feudal power—by, for example, treating Leith as a "vassal" port, rather than combining with it or engaging in some kind of economic reciprocity with it—the town will seem, in its difference, to mirror the king rather than present him with a face unrecognizable as such. The creature will resemble its Creator. But through its growing preeminence—the special difference of the capital, which in its specialness resembles the special difference of the Sovereign—the city may seem to threaten a "capacity for self-transformation into a separate verbal or material form."[93] The charter's linking of Albany and town might suggest that the creature has become a rival.[94] And the rulers of the city—the merchants and burgesses—as well as their own ruler may be "haunted" by the difference capitalism makes to feudalism, by the "flow" (however reluctant) of Edinburgh's credit and by the power (however fledgling and repressed) of the crafts. Finance and artisanal production were two severely codified aspects of burghal economic life whose access to privileged representation was, when not precluded altogether, carefully controlled. The repression of the "knowledge" that the world is produced by human creativity, labor, and desire, is frequently at stake not only in aristocratic representations of the late medieval burgh, but in the practices of power within the burgh itself—to the extent, at least, that those practices reveal an identification with aristocratic forms of power.

James III's charters assert the resemblance between town and crown by presenting bourgeois difference as a repetition of the feudal "same." The narrative in James III's charter treats Edinburgh not as a disaffected financier or a town full of angry craftspeople, but as—like Albany—a feudal vassal.[95] A story is told that describes the

> faith, loyalty, love, benevolence and cordial service which our beloved and the faithful the present office-bearers of our Burgh of Edinburgh, underwritten . . . with our dearest brother Alexander Duke of Albany

---

93. Scarry, *The Body in Pain,* 200.

94. On imitative desire, and the complex relations between rival and model which it sets in train, see Girard, "The Plague in Literature and Myth": "The divinity this desire is trying to capture never fails, sooner or later, to appear as the divinity of someone else, as the exclusive privilege of a model after whom the hero must pattern not only his behavior but his very desires, insofar as these are directed toward objects. . . . To imitate the desires of someone else is to turn this someone else into a rival as well as a model" (836–37).

95. Aside from the detailing of the privileges themselves, the language of both charters is substantially the same. For ease of reference I will cite Charter 54.

Earl of March and of Mar and Garviauch, lord of Annandale and Man, have already providently rendered to us in liberating our person from imprisonment in our Castle of Edinburgh, in which against the pleasure of our will we were held captive, exposing their persons to great peril of life, while besieging the said Castle with our said brother, in consequence of which our person now rejoices in liberty.[96]

The charter does not choose to tell a story of the English king's extortion of a promise of eight thousand marks out of the Scottish king's own subjects; nor does it tell a story of the merchants' ability (at least in theory) to buy the security of their country—a story that would feature the power of alteration of merchant capital rather than of aristocratic war, and might work as a tale of the merchants' good deeds in parting with their goods. Nor does it tell the kind of story we have told earlier in this chapter—the story of political plague: of factional rivalry, payoffs, intrigue, and manipulation. These stories are encoded in various ways in the charter—by its very existence, by its lists of witnesses and donees—but we do not have, for our story's heroes, either generous or canny merchants; we do not have, for our story's plot, the loss and reparation of capital.

Instead of economic loss and reparation we have risk and triumph: the romance story of the rescue and liberation of an imprisoned king. The romancing of James's imprisonment projects a closure in which he will be present, at the end, to distribute rewards to the faithful, to those willing to fulfill the feudal obligations of warfare and the demands of honor. Between James III and his subjects there has been no *pax simulata*, no *rupta fides*, no *falsus amor*, but the real thing—what the charter refers to as "fidem, legalitatem, amor, et beneuolenciam cordialeque seruicium." This is the idyll that conceals the trauma of loss, that repairs the damage done by the primal scene of betrayal and greed. The charter's conferral of aristocratic virtues on the merchants and burgesses of Edinburgh—nothing quite like this language is to be found in earlier burgh charters—is the remaking, as against betrayal, of the community

96. *Charters, Edinburgh* 54:157–58: "fidem legalitatem amorem et beneuolenciam cordialeque seruicium que dilecti et fideles nostri officiarii moderni Burgi nostri de Edinburghe subscripti . . . jam nobis prouide prestiterunt cum carissimo fratre nostro Alexandro duce Albanie comite Marchie ac de Mar et Garviauche domino Vallis Anandie at Mannie, et nostram de carceribus ex Castro nostro de Edinburghe liberando personam in quo contra nostre voluntatis libitum fuimus detenti, suas personas grauibus vite opponendo periculis dictum castrum cum dicto fratre nostro obsidendo, ex quo insultu nostra jam persona Regia libertate gaudet."

of honor, which is a community founded on fidelity. Treason threatens to dissolve the difference between sovereign and servant on which the very idea of sovereignty is founded; but like Foulis's *Strena*, James's charter repairs the communion of sovereign with servant, and in doing so reconstitutes both. The charter accomplishes this not only through the story it tells, but also through the very fact of its being a charter—an instance of royal patronage.

The language of the charter may be "deceptive"—it may have been extorted from an unwilling king, whose favorite emotion was not gratitude. But the language of the charter is also a restoration of voice, and hence a symbolic act: a way of making one and making good. Because it is split off from the sphere of Machiavellian politics, it allows the king—threatened with the loss of his kingship—to recreate himself as king, by symbolizing his own magnanimity and his capacity to produce community through the *fides* of his servants (who act, not independently, but dependently, through the dedication of the servant to the sovereign). The charter narrates a liberation; it is also, in the sense I have just outlined, the scope of the king's own freedom from dependence. The charter is presented as the effect not of the contrivances of servants but of the patronage of the sovereign. Thus his voice is not to be represented as bound by physical constraint; the charter enacts the transformation of imprisonment—a threatening form of embodiment, insofar as it limits the King's power to the space of his own body and hence radically limits his capacity for "self-extension"—into a powerful form of the royal word. Nor is the King to be seen as bound by the terms of pay-off or bargain; the charter, again, is a gift. The clauses that introduce the narrative read as follows:

> Since no act of duty between man and man is recognized as more necessarily belonging to the obligation of benevolence than that we should bestow most on those by whom we are most beloved: Hence it is that we, considering with thoughtful mind [*alta mente*] the faith, loyalty, love . . . [97]

And it is specified that the "labours" of the town were "free" ("et pro suis gratuitis laboribus et seruiciis nobis impensis et exhibitis").[98] Ser-

---

97. *Charters, Edinburgh* 54:157: "Cum ad benuolencie officium spectare dinoscitur vt hijs plurimum tribuamus a quibus plurimum diligimur nullus humanitatis actus magis necessarius: hinc est quod nos alta mente considerantes fidem legalitatem amorem . . ."
98. *Charters, Edinburgh* 54:158.

vices are rendered freely (and rewarded freely) because of a relation of loyalty and love. As Pierre Bourdieu might put it, *credit* is replaced, in this charter, by *trust*—like fidelity, a special form of belief.[99] The services and rewards thus exchanged are not ends in themselves—not the purpose of exchange—but, again, phenomenalizations and productions of community.

At the moment that the charter takes up the question of the nature of this exchange—and it is very clearly concerned to do so—the power of alteration conferred upon the giver by the gift makes its presence felt. The presence of this power is marked in part by the use of the phrase *alta mente:* from his lofty station, the king "considers" the services of those who love him, as though, like Foulis's Jupiter, he had been watching history take place below. The place of the king in the architecture of *potestas*—which, ironically, had become his prison—is thus recuperated: his verticality, his transcendence, is reasserted against his circumscription, through his possession of the high mind of Jove. One aspect of the gift—an aspect exploited in the charter for the purpose of asserting James's own freedom from coercion—is its apparent gratuitousness, its suggestion of the possibility of unearned love and endless plenty. The sovereign, as we have noted, must identify himself as the source of this endless plenty. But the sovereign's gift nonetheless is coercive, because it (re)makes the person to whom it is given; in the remaking of the person, the repossession of the servant's interior, the gift is returned by way of loyalty, which is the aristocratic form of religious belief. The gift is thus double: it duplicates within itself the doubleness of the power of alteration, which is both the power to unmake and the power to make. In James's charter, no less than in the works of Augustine and James Foulis, this doubleness is frequently experienced as a difference, often as a division: *sinus* and *aula,* the maternal and paternal strands, love and aggression, peace and war, paradise and plague. And yet this contradictoriness is somehow made one and made good, in the person of the sovereign or the Creator: the pain of being altered is reappropriated for the intensity and certainty of belief. It is the very fictiveness of the superreal—its requirement that a "construct" be re-presented as the Constructor—that demands, in the fig-

---

99. See Pierre Bourdieu, *Outline of a Theory of Practice,* on the effects of urbanization, which results, he argues, "in the collapse of the collectively maintained collective fiction of the religion of honour. *Trust* is replaced by *credit*" (239 n. 62).

ure of the Creator, the copresence of unmaking with making. Thus if it is the remaking of the Creator Himself that is really at stake in the *Calamitose*, in James III's charter it is the remaking of the sovereign, through the reconstitution of fidelity and loyalty, that is at stake.

The problem of loyalty pressures the shape of James's charter enough to produce the words *tenebuntur tamen*—nevertheless, says the charter, the officers and community of the burgh *shall be bound*

> to cause to be celebrated yearly for ever a funeral Mass of Requiem Placebo Dirige with chanting, in the Collegiate Church of St. Giles of the said Burgh on the third and fourth days of the month of August, for the weal of the soul of our late progenitor, and of our soul, and of the souls of our own ancestors and successors with suffrages of prayers for our prosperity [*pro nostro prospero statu*].[100]

*Status* has meanings of "condition" or "state," but also of "position" or "standing posture" (in English, too, one can have *a* status of any sort, but to have *status* means to be high up). *Prosper* has meanings of "fortunate," "favorable," "lucky," as well as "prosperous." The phrasing, in short, brings together once again *sinus* and *aula*—appropriate to a stipulation that asserts both the power of the *gift*, and the *power* of the gift. For it is not only that the power of the king's gift of privileges to the burgh has produced the rupture of the *tenebuntur tamen* in the otherwise unrelieved stylistic benevolence of this charter; it is also that the city, through its communal prayers, will dedicate itself to the eternal prosperity of the Stewart dynasty. The king has reminded the citizens of the earthly city of the ambiguity of the gift and the power of obligation to reproduce itself; the king's gift to the city will be returned in the form of the city's efforts on behalf of the king's eternal enjoyment of "a realm of unremitting plenty."

And this by way of a perpetual mourning. Whereas the *Strena* puts plenitude in the place of loss, James III will turn loss into plenitude by way of purgatorial mortification. The diminishment of the king's wealth and power through the privileges granted in the charters is here replenished by the demand that the king be forever memorialized, forever encrypted; that he and his gift live on in the devotional practices of his favorite city and the parish church that James himself had patron-

---

100. *Charters, Edinburgh* 54:161.

ized.[101] Thus, once again, the interior of the servant is penetrated and remade for fidelity. The gift turns into a perpetual possession, in both senses of the word; this gift truly bears with it the spirit of its giver and its homeland.[102] Such was James's response to the designs of his creature upon his person: he would be re-membered. In James III's charter the restoration of the sovereign's possession of the community will be enacted through memorialization. The damage done to sovereignty by the primal scene of trouble in the city will be repaired by the willingness of the servant perpetually to remake the sovereign in his memory. The transformation of human imagining into remembering is one of the most fundamental operations of power.

James might have wished the story of his relations with his preeminent city to have ended with its dedication to the worship of the ancestral blood, and the dynastic future, of the Stewarts. His own story ended not with his possession of a community, but with the fragmentation and loss of community. The year 1488, as we have indicated, brought another rebellion, caused, in part, by his designs on Coldingham Priory, and the subsequent alienation of Humes, Hepburns, and many more; in part by his preferential treatment of his second son, whose marriage he had been pursuing with greater assiduity than that of his first son, and whom he raised to the dignity of the Duke of Ross on 29 January 1488.[103] Evidence of his first son's disaffection may be found in Rothesay's apparent willingness to fall into the hands of the rebel party. And the Aberdeen Articles—a pact drawn up between the rebels and the loyalists, "casually" broken by the king—reveal the prince's dissatisfaction with the household and living permitted him by the king.[104] The creature had finally become a monster.

Whether James III's other creature—Edinburgh—had become a monster is less clear. James's preference for Edinburgh was so marked that we can only assume it must have been a serious crisis indeed to induce him to leave. Hepburn's role as Lord Provost of Edinburgh in 1487, Alexander Hepburn's control of the sheriffship from 1482 onwards, the attempt in 1487 to move the Court of the Four Burghs to

101. See *Charters, Edinburgh*, 42–45: 120–33; and I. A. Cameron's calendar of papal supplications to Rome (the relevant entries have not yet been published but may be consulted at the University of Glasgow) for 22 February and 12 March 1468, and 30 April 1470, for record of James III's support of St. Giles's erection to collegiate status.
102. See Mauss, *The Gift*, 9.
103. Macdougall, *James III*, 237.
104. Macdougall, *James III*, 249.

Inverkeithing, the disappearance of the burgh customs from the period of March to May 1488, remain troubling and enigmatic.[105] But the castle was held for the king; he returned to visit the "royal jewel house" once again, to make elaborate dispositions for his treasure, and to try to rally support before leaving to meet his death at Sauchieburn in a battle described thus by Pitscottie:

> The civill weir, the batell intestine,
> Nou that the sone with baner bred displayit
> Aganis the fader in battell come arreyit.[106]

Pitscottie was right to tell—in effect—the story of Laius. For it was, in large part, James's inability to make a space for his creatures that led him to his defeat at Sauchieburn; and everything he did to repress rivalry—his refusal, in particular, to empower his son—seems only to have brought him closer to his end.

The primal scene can help us to conceptualize the field of historical possibility in which the burgh and its citizens existed during late fifteenth- and early sixteenth-century Scotland; for the primal scene brings out not only the doubleness inevitable to all beginnings—the choice, presented by Foulis's image of Janus *bifrons,* of looking backward or forward—but also the openness of defining and theorizing anew both "origin" and "break," "creator" and "creature" in historical rather than theological terms. The primal scene makes clear how the fear of starting over on one's own can produce regressive positions, like that of Foulis, whose "backwardness" might conceal the strength of the challenge that produced them; it makes clear how, in the case of James III, the desire to create and the fear of having one's creatures start over on their own can produce a kind of tragedy of innovation. The primal scene also makes clear how the wish to start over on one's own might

---

105. For the Court of the Four Burghs, see Marwick, ed., *Burgh Convention Recs.,* vi; on the burgh customs, see Macdougall, *James III,* 245; *ER* 10:57.

106. Robert Lindesay of Pitscottie, *The Historie and Croniclis of Scotland From the Slauchter of King James the First to the Ane thousand fyve hundreith thrie scoir fyftein zeir,* ed. J. G. Mackay (Edinburgh: William Blackwood & Sons for the Scottish Text Society, 1899), lines 166–67, 1:212. The verses are taken from Sir David Lindsay's *The Testament of the Papyngo.* On the king's movements between Edinburgh and the north, and his concern for his worldly goods, see Macdougall, *James III,* 241, 254; Nicholson, *Scotland: The Later Middle Ages,* 527–29.

produce the historical concept of a multiple and decentered creativity that has itself been created. In the fifteenth and early sixteenth centuries, Edinburgh experienced something like a primal scene: a revisionist reading of its own status as creature. The texts that present this experience pose, in turn, sharp challenges to historical narration: to what extent was Edinburgh's charter "progressive," to what extent "regressive"? Does Foulis's poetry encode, in however infantile a fashion, the loss of one sense of beginning and the desperate need to formulate another? The difficulties of these questions insist upon the changeful character of the late medieval Scottish city. They insist, too, upon the danger of mobilizing secularizations of the "prime mover" or categorical ingenuities like Merrington's "internal externality" against the contingency and irreducibility of event. Thus they suggest, finally, the importance of embracing a decentered historical practice that gives to the project of beginning both the horror and the futurity of ending.

# Notes on Contributors

*Theresa Coletti*, Department of English, University of Maryland, is the author of *Naming the Rose: Eco, Medieval Signs, and Modern Theory* (1988) and of essays on Chaucer and medieval drama. She is currently writing a book on gender, society, and religion in medieval English drama.

*Louise Fradenburg*, associate professor of English at Dartmouth College, has published essays on Chaucer and on medieval Scottish poetry. Her book on late medieval Scotland is forthcoming.

*Anne Middleton* teaches in the Department of English of the University of California at Berkeley. She has published essays on Chaucer and Langland and the social climate of literary production in the later fourteenth century. The essay in this volume represents some of the concerns of a book nearing completion, *Life Work: The Historical Subject of "Piers Plowman."*

*Lee Patterson*, Department of English, Duke University, is the author of *Negotiating the Past: The Historical Understanding of Medieval Literature* (1987), of *Chaucer and the Subject of History* (1990), and of essays on medieval and historicist topics. He is currently writing on the politics of Middle English literature and of medieval studies.

*Larry Scanlon*, Department of English, University of Wisconsin-Madison, has written on Chaucer and politics. He is currently completing a book on the exemplum in Middle English literature.

*Paul Strohm*, Department of English, Indiana University, has recently published *Social Chaucer* (1989). He has written on generic terminology and fourteenth-century reading publics. He is now engaged in writing a series of essays on the ideological and textual "environments" within which fourteenth-century poems were composed and received.

*David Wallace* teaches at the University of Texas at Austin. He is currently writing a short book on Boccaccio and a longer one on poetics and political forms in Dante, Boccaccio, Petrarch, and Chaucer, and he is editing a collection of essays commemorating the nine hundredth anniversary of the death of Beatrice (8 June 1290).

# Index

| | |
|---|---|
| Compositor: | Graphic Composition, Inc. |
| Text: | 10/13 Galliard |
| Display: | Galliard |
| Printer: | Thomson-Shore, Inc. |
| Binder: | John H. Dekker & Sons |